STAGESTRUCK FILMMAKER

STAGESTRUCK FILMMAKER

D.W. GRIFFITH & THE AMERICAN THEATRE

David Mayer

UNIVERSITY OF IOWA PRESS   IOWA CITY

University of Iowa Press, Iowa City 52242
www.uiowapress.org
Printed in the United States of America
Design by Richard Hendel

Some of the material published here previously appeared
in abridged and altered form in The Griffith Project volumes,
Film History, Living Pictures, and Nineteenth-Century Theatre.

The University of Iowa Press is a member of Green Press
Initiative and is committed to preserving natural resources.

Printed on acid-free paper

Library of Congress Cataloging-in-Publication Data
Mayer, David.
    Stagestruck filmmaker: D. W. Griffith and the American
theatre / by David Mayer.
        p.   cm.—(Studies in theatre history and culture)
    Includes bibliographical references and index.
    ISBN-13: 978-1-58729-790-8 (cloth)
    ISBN-10: 1-58729-790-6 (cloth)
    1. Griffith, D. W. (David Wark), 1875–1948—Criticism and
interpretation.   2. Motion pictures and theater.   I. Title.
    PN1998.3.G76M39 2009   2008041453
    791.4302′33092—dc22

FRONTISPIECE
Poster, ca. 1900, for 'Way Down East depicting Anna Moore's
arrival at Bartlett Farm and the principal characters, less
Lennox Sanderson, gathered in the farmyard setting. Anna
is central to the image, and in all depictions of her first
entrance is isolated, an alien in an uncertain and initially
unwelcoming place. The image is probably derived from
the Joseph Byron photograph of Phoebe Davies as Anna
Moore, in chapter 7.

For

Helen, Cassie, Lise, Catherine,

and Isaac with much love

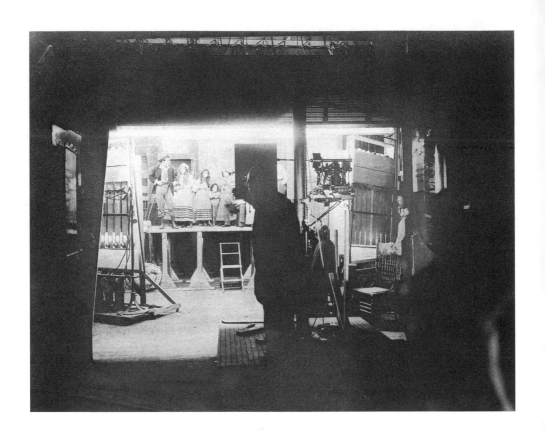

Contents

Acknowledgments

Some people don't realize that they're on a journey until a destination of sorts comes into view. I'm one of those people: traveling and enjoying the scenery but with no sense of moving from back there to right here to somewhere farther in the distance. But I was lucky, and this list of colleagues and friends who helped and sometimes accompanied me on my journey is an admission that I didn't travel alone and that I was constantly aided and befriended en route.

Above all, I traveled, from start to finish, with my wife, Helen Day-Mayer. A fine theatre historian in her own right, Helen saw every Griffith film with me, often more than once, read, advised, suggested emendations, and repeatedly drew upon her outstanding skills at describing and analyzing actors' performances and the effects of Griffith's directorial instructions. In all truth, Helen should be credited as joint author, and it is only her genuine and self-effacing modesty which keeps her name from the title page. I acknowledge her innumerable contributions with pride, gratitude, and love.

Additionally and importantly, Christine Gledhill drew Helen and me into silent film and thence to the Pordenone Silent Film Festival just as the Griffith Project was getting under way. Patrick Loughney directed my attention to the Library of Congress's Paper Print Collection and brought us directly into the Griffith Project's orbit, where Paolo Cherchi-Usai, Russell Merritt (who, years before me, had recognized and identified Griffith's early links to theatre), J. B. Kaufman, Scott Simmon, Yuri Tsivian, Eileen Bowser, Tom Gunning, Linda Williams, Joyce Jesionowski, Paul Spehr, Steven Higgins, Charles Musser, Lea Jacobs, Ben Brewster, and Cindi Rowell quietly and judiciously allowed me to discover Griffith's numerous theatrical connections while making certain that I continued to write about film. Their fellowship, multiple kindnesses, intellectual generosity, and their total lack of selfishness with Griffith information and artifacts sped my task. I had only to ask, and they supplied answers and essential interpretations. Helen and I have enjoyed the same measure of cordiality and assistance from Richard Abel, Rick Altman, and the many members of Domitor, who welcomed two theatre historians into their tight circle of film scholarship. They have been immensely supportive throughout, and I thank them individually and collectively. I was especially fortunate that my friend and Griffith Project colleague J. B. Kaufman read draft chapters and firmly led me from the quicksands of error into which I periodically strayed. Not a member of the Project, per se, Arthur Lennig was similarly generous with information and guidance. Arthur's salty views of Griffith's character enabled me to keep Griffith worship at a safe distance. Musicians Phil Carli, John Sweeney, Günter Buchwald, Donald Sosin, Antonio Coppola, Maud Nelissen, Gabriel Thibaudeau, and Neil Brand persuaded me to listen to, as well as to see, Griffith's films. Their sensitive and perceptive musical touch brought out nuances in text and performance which otherwise would have eluded me. David Robinson, who, more than many, already knows connections between the Victorian stage and early film, quietly encouraged me and welcomed my investigations. Laurence Senelick gave me access to his unequaled private collection of American theatrical ephemera.

Later, it was my colleague Mike Hammond who suggested that I turn my decade of Griffith Project work into a book. I am deeply beholden to him. Even before I contemplated this book, I received essential responses to the theatricality of Griffith's films from my University of Manchester colleagues George Taylor and Michael Holt, and, while I was still havering about whether to proceed, further advice, encouragement, and assistance came from Madeline Matz, Rosemarie Bank, Brooks McNamara, Richard Koszarski, Thomas Riis, Laurence Senelick, Mimi Levitt, Bryony Dixon, Laraine Porter, Luke McKernan, Claudette Williams, Leslie Midkiff DeBauche, and from my "post-Vardac" colleagues: Matthew Solomon, Joseph Sokalski, Stephen Johnson, Gwendolyn Waltz, Frank Scheide, and Victoria Duckett. Mollie Heron led me to Cincinnati's superb National Underground Railroad and Freedom Center, enabling a clearer perception of the issues surrounding Reconstruction that so bedeviled Griffith. Elizabeth Buchanek generously opened her home to Helen and me during our Washington stays.

My colleague and friend Tom Postlewait quietly and impartially assessed my proposal to the University of Iowa Press. Subsequently he stood at my elbow, judging my drafts with rigor and, drawing on his own knowledge of American theatre and film, nudged emendations, and helped me to say exactly what I intended. Any failures to do so are entirely my fault. Tom and Holly Carver, Press editor, guided the shape of this book and, with Helen, assisted with the labor of selecting illustrations. Mary-Lou Pilkinton made innumerable suggestions which materially improved the text. Madeline Matz provided the index and advised on the shape and contents of both playlist and filmography. I am deeply grateful for all that they have done for the finished book and for their help and generosity in realizing it.

Librarians and research specialists also guided my hand and frequently drew resources to my attention. I thank, in particular, Annette Fern, Betty Falsey, Geraldine Duclow, Cindy Murrell, Madeline Matz, Marcus Risdell, Mike Mashon, Steven Higgins, Gayle Harris, Elena Millie, Frederic Wilson, the libraries and collections of Harvard University, the Museum of Modern Art, the Billy Rose Collection, Ellis Island Museum, George Eastman House, the Garrick Club, the British Film Institute, and the British Library. Derek Trillo, Leonard Burns, Chris Eyles, and Catherine Mayer helped to overcome photographic and digital obstacles.

I am also grateful to the Theatre Historiography Working Group of the International Federation for Theatre Research—especially to Tom Postlewait, Kate Newey, and Rosemarie Bank—and to Le Giornate del Cinema Muto for allowing me occasions to test some of my conclusions about the fluid relationships between the nineteenth- and early-twentieth-century stage and early film. I have directly benefited from an extended Emeritus Fellowship from the Leverhulme Trust and have been the fortunate recipient of a Harvard University Library Fellowship, a Mellon Fellowship from Yale's Center for British Art, and a Research Fellowship from the Harry Ransom Humanities Research Center. None of these awards was granted with the intention that I should undertake this book, but each generously funded research opportunity led me along the path to its inception. I spent a long time gathering provisions and—from my superb colleagues—a reliable compass before my actual journey began.

STAGESTRUCK FILMMAKER

Introduction

In 1916, D. W. Griffith was recognized as the dominant creative figure of American motion pictures, widely acknowledged as a creator of remarkable screen spectacles, if not dramas of the human heart. Both *Judith of Bethulia* (1912–1913) and *The Birth of a Nation* (1915) had received national acclaim, but *Intolerance* opened in 1916 to reviews mixed in their praise and condemnation. Demoralized by the antagonism and anger directed at the perceived racism of *The Birth of a Nation* and, further, dismayed by lukewarm responses to his newly released *Intolerance*, Griffith gave a seven-part interview to a national film journal in which he proposed forever turning his back on motion pictures and "returning" to the live theatre. Film, he insisted, was a disappointing medium. Griffith condemned motion pictures for their cheap shoddiness and their expensive excesses. He insisted, "Of necessity, the stage must tell the truth more freely than any other method of expression. It is the only means existing today of even attempting to portray the truth. . . . I now contemplate turning to the stage in making an attempt to find freedom of expression."[1]

What is implied in Griffith's threat? To what theatre, truthful or otherwise, would he turn—or, to be more precise, return? He had largely failed in the professional theatre. Working as an actor between 1896 and 1907, he began in local Louisville semiprofessional profit-share companies, moving on to achieve small roles in provincial repertory companies in the Midwest, on the East Coast, and in California, and occasionally held leading roles in touring companies. Although he ever after declined to admit it—because he would be obliged to acknowledge working as a strikebreaker—he had also appeared as an actor in vaudeville sketches. He spent as much time working at menial, nontheatrical jobs as he acted. In 1908, unable to get regular or substantial roles as an actor but still concerned not to jeopardize his professional standing among theatrical colleagues, he turned, out of desperation, to the anonymous work of the film actor. At that date film actors were uncredited, their names never given on the screen or in the meager promotional material for the films in which they appeared. Griffith entered motion pictures working as a jobbing day-actor at the Edison and Biograph studios.

He was only marginally more successful as a playwright. He had written a brief dramatic sketch in which he toured and performed on the vaudeville stage. In 1906 and 1907 he wrote two plays, only one of which, *A Fool and a Girl*, had been produced commercially. In 1907 it was performed to small and diminishing audiences for scarcely more than a week. At Biograph his success in devising film scenarios and in directing films had followed from what he had hoped would be, at best, a brief career detour. He nourished expectations of being recalled to theatrical work, but, eight years later, Griffith, although successful and famous, was still a filmmaker. There was, in short, little of a conventional theatrical career that he could resume. On the surface, Griffith's boast, with its implication of returning in triumph to the live stage, seems hollow, far-fetched, grandiose, and perhaps self-deceiving.

Despite these early setbacks, David Wark Griffith's relationship to the theatre was intricate, complex, and enduring. He had entered film production knowing only theatre, and, in order to go forward, he was obliged to retreat, recalling, grasping at, emulating theatrical practices which he had acquired and absorbed in eleven years of stage work. Once he had found his first foothold as a director, and with that post had realized a small semblance of authority, his instinct was to configure Biograph's gaggle of established performers and day-actors into an effective repertory company[2] with acknowledged leads, supporting actors, ingenues, and comics. A more established director by 1909, and with increasing powers granted by the Biograph management, Griffith was encouraged to enter New York's theatrical haunts to recruit actors with stage experience. Later, in Hollywood, and still later, back on the East Coast, he again formed stable repertory companies of actors confident to work under his direction and prepared to perform together. Like other contemporary actor-managers, such as David Belasco and Herbert Beerbohm Tree, Griffith assumed total dominance over his company, at times imperious and paternalistic, at times inaccessibly remote, but at all times the alpha male with actresses jockeying for his attention.

An ineffectual actor himself, he nonetheless became a guide to other actors, showing, rather than describing, what he wanted from them, even to the point of enacting gestures and facial expressions,[3] but he also encouraged his company to find original and personal means of representing their screen characters. He was especially adept at persuading actors to find and use hand properties which spoke to their character's inner life and moral stature. A doll, a partly finished shoe, a single glove, an empty canteen became, under Griffith's guidance, a character's signature or metaphors for larger events or emotions beyond the reach of gestures or words. He used live animals—kittens and doves—as metonyms for the characters themselves.[4] Installed behind the camera, Griffith used theatrical techniques—means of arranging sets and deploying his actors—to defeat the cramped sets that primitive camera lenses required to keep actors in continual focus. Actors had to adjust to such conditions. Thus, Griffith's impact on screen acting and staging will necessarily arise throughout this study.

Although not the first director to have served an apprenticeship in the theatre, Griffith brought into films a keen awareness of prevailing dramatic structures and a memory for effective theatrical tropes. He frequently took advantage of the freedom allowed to "combination company" melodrama to mingle serious scenes with variety turns, and he brought from his experience of spectatorship at "ten-twent-thirt" melodramas a taste for thrilling last-minute rescues, for heroines disguising themselves in men's uniforms to effect daring rescues or escapes or for pursuits involving races between speeding automobiles and trains. His experience as a writer and performer in the vaudeville dramatic sketch had taught him to be brief and to compact entire plots into a few minutes of intense action. What he hadn't already learned from the theatre, Griffith later acquired by close study of the theatrical practices. His twelve Biograph films on the subject of the American Civil War and Reconstruction period, made between 1908 and 1911, reveal a growing sureness in appropriating and applying the conventions of the corresponding theatrical genre of Civil War plays. In using these conventions and becoming comfortable in deploying them, Griffith's films became more fluent and infinitely more nuanced.

Griffith's brief theatrical career had also exposed him to much melodrama and to some comedy. Melodrama was to become Griffith's favored genre, partly because, within the brevity demanded by early film, ethical and moral positions had to be unambiguously clear. Justice had to be served. It was easy for him to depict villainy or innocence and to devise strong situations in which wrongs were created and then overcome. But melodrama also accorded with Griffith's own Protestant and late-Victorian rearing in which justice (or the wish for justice and peace) sometimes mingled with a lugubrious piety and flatulent spirituality. With comedy, Griffith was less sure-handed. His efforts at farce were mechanical, his comic characters, unless they were performed by actors capable of rising above his sometimes leaden direction, often fail to amuse. Only occasionally, in such masterpieces as *Broken Blossoms* (1919), was Griffith able to step beyond melodrama into astonishing tragedy.

As well as grasping established theatrical forms, Griffith was also among the early workers in the performing arts who recognized the impact and growing presence of modern dance as a theatrical dimension and an emergent art in its own right. Although he never theorized—or even explained—his use of dance nor attempted to justify dance as a movement art akin to performance in silent film, Griffith consciously acknowledged current dance developments, engaging such artists as Ruth St. Denis and Ted Shawn, and pragmatically employed choreographed dance episodes as both allegorical and diegetic narrative elements in his films. Dance training became an essential part of his female actors' training, and, in making *Judith of Bethulia* (1913), his male actors were coached in the gestures and poses of the *ballets russes*. Dance episodes figured prominently in his live prologues—multimedia events concocted by Griffith and his associates—which, performed on sidewalks and small stages, were used to draw crowds outside theatres where his films played. More significantly, dances functioned in the screenings themselves, again as prologues and as live expansions between filmed episodes. Thus, his engagement with dance was a critical component of his film work.

Griffith had also brought with him into film an awareness of theatre as a commercial enterprise. Actors had to eat. Plays had to return the money and labor invested in them. The same applied to films. Moreover, the business of theatre was becoming more complex. Financial panics had changed the ways in which theatrical promoters and their suppliers organized and conducted their commercial activities. Motion pictures, which had begun as a cottage craft practiced by immigrant entrepreneurs and accomplished inventors and technicians, was rapidly transforming into a major international industry and would soon move from America's East Coast to Hollywood. Griffith understood this much and was among the first to shift filmmaking to California, but he rarely understood enough to avoid frequent financial crises. He had survived, albeit with discomfort and embarrassment, occasions when his theatre company was stranded far from home. He had seen his own play fail and lose money for its investors. Yet his ventures as an independent filmmaker revealed his inability to budget or to stay within estimated production costs. He made and lost fortunes. His personal tastes were austere. He indulged in the occasional luxury of tailored suits and expensive touring cars but otherwise eschewed the trappings of the Hollywood moguls. Despite employing business managers and financial advisers, much of his professional life was spent scrabbling for investors or desperately gambling, pledging his entire property to secure crippling last-minute loans.

Above all, and throughout his twenty-six-year career as a filmmaker, Griffith's outstanding skill lay in adapting theatrical works into motion pictures. At first, these were compacted versions of plays, abridged, on the pattern of the vaudeville dramatic sketch, to fit the brief running times—fifteen to twenty minutes—of one- and two-reel motion pictures. By 1912, Griffith was among the first American directors, perhaps the very first, to realize that films exceeding an hour's duration were the way forward and that the transformation of theatre into film offered, immediately to hand, materials that an adapter might reshape for the screen. At the time he left the Biograph company in 1913, Griffith had directed, acted in, or written the scenarios for approximately 490 films. More than forty of these films were direct adaptations, often unacknowledged, of identifiable stage plays. Once free of Biograph and at liberty to make multireel "feature length" films, his reliance on theatrical subjects grew. Nearly half of his most admired films are adaptations of stage dramas and are heavily reliant on theatrical practices for their effectiveness.

In his search for dramas which might be turned into films, he ransacked the American theatrical repertoire. The plays he admired and avidly pursued for screen rights, as well as those he subsequently transformed and reinvigorated as films, were not the magisterial "drama as it is known to dramatists" that Griffith imaginatively described to his interviewer. Nor was Griffith referring to the "New Drama" of Europe which he knew but chose to leave to other directors. Rather, Griffith's greatest motion picture successes were based on adaptations of pieces from the American commercial theatre, his choices of plays often drawn from the late nineteenth- and early twentieth-century stage. These popular works were well known, proven, theatrical successes before Griffith reworked them into films. Consequently, this study looks at the American theatrical repertoire as Griffith encountered it and as he reshaped it, breathing new life into a few established classics and many lesser pieces. It echoes and reinforces Lawrence Reamer's exultant headline to his review of *Orphans of the Storm* (1922): "Famous Old Plays Reanimated as Screen Dramas."[5] Although Griffith came increasingly to think of motion pictures as the essential art of the twentieth century, his film work derived many of its features from the contemporary—or earlier—theatre.

While he professed respect for the theatre and its ability to address issues of substance, Griffith rarely ventured into the modern theatrical repertoire—and only then in a supervisory role rather than as a director. Perhaps because these dramatists called for verbal exchange rather than the clash of ideas expressed through physical actions, or, more likely, because the New Drama of Europe rarely chimed with Griffith's inherent sentimentality—a sentimentality that sometimes bordered on mawkishness—he left such plays to other film directors. Rather, he sought his material among popular American stage classics—melodramas, comedies, musical pieces—turning these dramas into vivid metaphors which addressed contemporary life.

Transferred to film, these stories were often updated to a contemporary world, and thus their contexts and meanings shifted, creating fresh resonances and understandings. These new resonances are notably evident in his *Way Down East* (1920), where a modest-but-powerful domestic 1890s melodrama was made to address issues of female suffrage and social equality. For two decades 'Way Down East (1898) toured theatres as a bucolic drama in which an abused heroine puts behind her a tragic past to find love and redemption in the country. Griffith's film enthusiastically endorses the values—innocence, unsophistication, independence, and self-reliance—of a benign, traditional rural life but, unlike the stage version, also confronts these values with the hedonistic mores and superficial values of urban modernity. Griffith therefore adds the spectacle of amoral sybarites attempting and failing to corrupt innocent country people, his country characters shaming the smug city folk and spurning their frivolous luxuries. *Orphans of the Storm* (1922) offers a further example of reshaped metaphor. Griffith's film, which grafts onto the established theatre classic *Two Orphans* (1874) episodes from the French Revolution, turns a melodrama of loss and recovery into both an examination of modern fanaticism and a condemnation of "bolshevism."

Despite such decanting of old wine into new bottles, the core narratives of these plays-turned-into-films remain intact. The same narratives, as simple and as basic as folktales, are freighted with deep psychological truths, and the pleasures and emotional experiences they give their audiences, if not intensified, are as before. Thus, Griffith recognized the metaphoric value of drama: how plays disguised, made palatable, and opened to discussion various issues, political and social, which caused anxiety. He intuited that within its own historic context each play had life and meanings for its audiences. Although supposedly old, hoary, and distinctly unfashionable, these dramas nevertheless spoke to long-standing personal and domestic matters of human struggle which, revisualized on film and made graphic, invoked fresh pressures and concerns. In these and in other films, Griffith was a visual artist who reformulated American dramas, reinvigorating the theatrical repertoire and redeploying it in films. His narrative films explore social and cultural depths, alive in the moment of their cinematic re-creation while concurrently reinvoking the circumstances of their origins as stage pieces.

At the same time, the pathways of Griffith's adaptations are not as straightforward as they sometimes appear. Although he may cite a single theatrical source for a film, it is sometimes apparent that he has used multiple sources without acknowledging this fact. His films offer evidence that Griffith, as a part of a lengthy preparatory process, often read numerous variant versions of playscripts and related materials. Such multiplicity of theatrical sources may be less an instance of unacknowledged plagiarism than it is evidence of his broad knowledge of the American repertoire, acquired initially as an actor and thereafter as an enthusiastic playgoer and play reader. It indicates, perhaps further, his recourse to this repertoire for materials to enhance and resolve complicated plots. Further, Griffith rarely, if ever, paraphrased a play, reproducing it in miniature. He might have elaborated or abridged, cutting the original drama to a point well before the play has ended, but always to serve an artistic or polemical purpose.

It is therefore possible to recognize Griffith, throughout much of his professional career, as a scenarist-director who worked within a continuing performance tradition. He sought to convert stage dramas which aroused American audiences with their turbulence into even more powerful top-grade films. So varied were Griffith's skills and so pervasive his energy that there is no theatrical or film term adequate to describe his unique versatility. The term *auteur* doesn't answer because it implies that the subject matter originates with the creator, but Griffith's most artistically and commercially successful works originated as stage plays and, to a lesser degree, novels and short stories and narrative poems. These works were well tested before they came into Griffith's hands and were subsequently transformed into films. The European term *regisseur* partly meets the requirement of describing Griffith's breadth as an adapter and dramaturg, director, supervisor, recruiter, teacher and controller of actors, financier and fund-raiser, gambler, scene designer, and browbeater of conductors and composers, but it still falls far short in describing his armory of skills and the power of his imagination. His constant resort to theatrical praxis and his appropriation of America's theatrical repertoire characterize much of his film career.

My study thus provides a cultural, social, and theatrical account of the American stage in the final years of the nineteenth century and the first three decades of the twentieth. I investigate how and why this popular stage, fueled by homegrown materials and touring imports, offered Griffith such an eclectic selection of dramatic material and stage techniques to bring to the screen. Additionally, I offer stage histories of the plays that Griffith, often to the astonishment and dismay of his colleagues, chose to adapt, usually, but not invariably, to fresh success. It is therefore a study to be read as an erratic and irregular and entirely nonchronological history of the nineteenth-century American stage, and it is, equally, to be read as an account of Griffith's complex relationship to the theatre: pillaging, adapting, reshaping, revitalizing, preserving, and extolling. As well as nonchronological, my account is not, in any sense, a biography, but solely a sequential account of the dramatic materials chosen by Griffith, their places in the then-contemporary American culture, and the processes of gathering and adaptation that followed. For some of the latter plays there is specific evidence; for others there are dates and collateral information. The reader will be invited, variously, to read from play to play, play to film, and film to film.

Any critical study on almost any aspect of D. W. Griffith's work must address allegations of Griffith's racism as well as his fascination with ethnic and national cultures present in early twentieth-century America. These cultures were, severally, the result of native origin, the products of immigration, abduction, slavery and liberation, economic migration, foreign famines and pogroms and—no less important—the result of females attaining skills and entering the workplace. Those who became subjects of his plays and films were African Americans, Native Americans, Chinese laborers, Jews, Gypsies, Italians, indigenous West Coast Hispanics and Mexican migrants, and emancipated—working—females. Griffith is fascinated—and in one notable instance repelled—by the presence of diverse otherness within American society and continually, between 1906 and 1922, depicts the "other" in his stage plays and films.

These cultural and gender issues would not overshadow Griffith's reputation were it not for the dominance and lingering stigma of a single film—only one out of more than 570 motion pictures and two stage plays which Griffith made in his lifetime. Griffith is judged—and to some degree misjudged—in terms of The Birth of a Nation (1915). Because of this one film, and because of the failure of subsequent generations to understand America's racial climate in the first decades of the twentieth century, Griffith lost future audiences and impaired his standing as an American filmmaker. The Birth of a Nation, celebrated and defended by some of its first audiences, was also recognized from the outset by other audiences as deeply offensive, humiliating to some of its spectators, and racist. The Birth of a Nation is certainly racist by late twentieth- and twenty-first-century standards, and, accordingly, Griffith's reputation has been compromised by this notorious film that is openly anti-Negro. Griffith does not hesitate in ascribing ignorance, sloth, drunkenness, criminality, and savagery to the recently freed African American. Griffith's calamity and Griffith's success are, both and equally, products of the remarkable quality and impact of The Birth of a Nation, a film which, by its very grasp of subject matter, storytelling, and innovative cinematic language, drew national attention and outraged responses to Griffith's polemic. Inevitably, Griffith's film was measured against its sources, Thomas Dixon Jr.'s novel and play The Clansman (1905). Griffith's acceptance and elaboration of Dixon's racist assumptions are profoundly disturbing and prompted the American poet Vachel Lindsay to observe,

> On the films [sic], as in the audience, it turns the crowd into a mob that is either for or against the Reverend Thomas Dixon's poisonous hatred of the negro . . . Griffith is a chameleon in interpreting his authors. Wherever the scenario shows traces of The Clansman, by Thomas Dixon, the original book [or play], it is bad. Wherever it is unadulterated Griffith, which is half the time, it is good. The Reverend Thomas Dixon is a rather stagy Simon Legree in his avowed views, a deal like the gentleman with the spiritual hydrophobia at the latter end of Uncle Tom's Cabin. Unconsciously, Mr. Dixon has done his best to prove that Legree was not a fictitious character.[6]

Griffith further damaged his reputation by denying racism and insisting that he was merely recounting historical events. His assertion that The Birth of a Nation is historically accurate is both problematic and complex in its truthfulness and in its distortions of characters and events. He remained blind to the biased nature of his sources and to his own prejudices. Whatever Griffith may have felt about the numerous and vociferous adverse responses to the racism of The Birth of a Nation and whatever shame or remorse he may have experienced as a result, and although his subsequent African American characters were no longer lurking rapists and upstart domineering politicians, he continued, as late as A Romance of Happy Valley (1919), One Exciting Night (1922), and The White Rose (1923), to create condescending portraits of African Americans, depicting them through the comic actor Porter Strong as fearful, eye-rolling, craps-shooting, uneducated rascals and, in Lucille La Verne, as overly flirtatious and motherly. These were stage types inviting audience derision. In consequence, Griffith's racism has, in large measure, impaired study of his other work by encouraging dismissal of his oeuvre as the ravings and slanders of an unreconstructed bigot.

The Birth of a Nation and many other of Griffith's works should be placed in the context of the profound developments which happened to and within American life within the first fifty years of Griffith's own life. His lessons in racism came early. He was born in 1875 into a beaten and hugely demoralized South which had experienced eight years of the vicissitudes of postwar Reconstruction and which would experience a further two years of what his elders would describe as a vendetta enforced by the U.S. Congress. Ahead lay many more decades of festering resentment and hostility toward the conquering North.

Griffith's adverse position on race and African Americans was not exceptional for persons of his age reared in the Civil War's aftermath. His views on the

Reconstruction era had been shaped, not merely by the tale telling and gossip of his elders and by the activities of the Southern Historical Society, founded in 1869, whose speakers lectured in theatres and libraries throughout the former Confederacy, but also by Southern historians of the "Dunning School."[7] Above all, apparently reinforcing Griffith's racist stance, stood the preeminent historian of Griffith's own generation, Woodrow Wilson, who intentionally shaded the achievements of black leadership gained in that period.[8] These various historians distorted and impugned the motives of both blacks and whites who attempted, on the wreckage of the Confederacy, to rebuild conquered state and local governments, to foster black participation in political processes, and to seek fair and just solutions to property and labor disputes. Wilson's history of Reconstruction justifies the Ku Klux Klan and minimizes the harm done by this vigilante organization. Further, Griffith's knowledge of African Americans had been influenced by American political science, as developed by John W. Burgess, characterizing Negroes as incapable of self-government or of achieving any semblance of civilization. Burgess's studies had characterized blacks of being either childlike or base primitives, licentious and savage.

This cabal of Southern scholars was not entirely to blame. Northern historians[9] are still inclined to recast the Civil War as a struggle "to preserve the Union" and to bring errant states back into the national fold. Alternately, these writers chronicle battles and campaigns, focusing on military and strategic goals rather than on the lives of those whose destinies and liberty depended on the outcome of this conflict. These historians (and significantly, "Northern" professional dramatists) promulgated—from the late 1870s—a popular narrative of discord, fracture, and postwar healing of animosities among white families. Issues of slavery, black emancipation, and integration of African Americans into the larger national community were pushed aside in favor of a narrative of national (i.e., white) reconciliation. If Southerners constructed mythologies of lost causes and brutal Yankee occupiers, carpetbaggers and scalawags, and "uppity" blacks in accordance with their vision of Reconstruction, so Northerners built their own mythic histories of the late war and installed them as the "national epic." Griffith was to inherit and to employ both legacies in twelve Biograph films and finally, in The Birth of a Nation, to exploit and build on these myths.

To be sure, the decisions of the branches of the federal government in implementing Reconstruction between 1865 and 1877 were often ambiguous, contradictory, promulgated and abruptly rescinded, and open to claims and misunderstandings by all parties, especially where rights to suffrage and former plantation property were involved. Local, state, and federal courts, intent on restoring a patina of normalcy and incapable of eradicating long-held opinion about the character and worth of African Americans, largely upheld the rights of former land- and slaveholders and looked away when formers slaves, pursuing constitutional rights, were frustrated and brutalized. Emancipated African Americans, their rights recognized by the Thirteenth, Fourteenth, and Fifteenth Amendments to the U.S. Constitution, were nevertheless dispossessed, disenfranchised, and held in poverty. Woodrow Wilson—who fired all African American government employees when he assumed the Presidency—disingenuously justified these steps. Griffith never acknowledges this history and, perhaps unknowingly or perhaps disingenuously, claims a falsehood as a true account.

Moreover, and this factor must be taken into account, Americans in all parts of the continental United States and in newly acquired overseas territories were asking numerous questions about what constituted an American identity. Which people within a growing and unstable national population might legitimately call themselves *American* and thus enjoy the full privileges of citizenship allied with American identity? Americans of many stripes and conditions were no less racist than Griffith, and many were verbally outspoken and overtly abusive in their dislike and hostility toward several manifestations of the "other" within their national society. What further chapters of my book will establish is the presence of a prevailing climate of racism, much of it given utterance in stage plays and films because the American stage, no less than the popular press, gave rise to ethnic and racial typologies which played out a comic or threatening otherness before national audiences between 1825 and 1925. Minstrelsy and comedy promulgated the stage Negro. Comedy and vaudeville also created the stock Irish, "Dutch" (i.e., German), Chinese, and "Hebrew" characters. Melodrama exploited these types and added the stage "redskin." All of these roles stood in opposition to the American Yankee, the frontiersman (such as Davy Crockett and Buffalo Bill), and many variations of the assimilated white American.

My book will also establish—conversely—a nascent awareness that tolerance and assimilation were desirable national and sectional goals. As representations of race, ethnicity, and otherness recurrently appear in Griffith's films and sources, I intend, as my book unfolds, to address these matters. It is not my purpose to exonerate or exculpate Griffith, his sources, and his associates from charges of racism. Neither do I apologize for Griffith, his colleagues, and his contemporary sources. We Americans have a politically and socially flawed history. Rather, I attempt to understand, historicize, and explicate acts and utterances which today, with our twenty-first-century history of civil rights legislation and our dismay at "ethnic cleansing," dividing walls, and religious intolerance, appear offensively biased, disturbingly cruel, counterproductive, and dangerously divisive. I attempt to place Griffith within an overall template of American life in the closing decades of the nineteenth century and the early decades of the twentieth.

In addressing racist conditions and historical factors, it is also possible to establish a context for local, sectional, and national reception of Griffith's films. This turn-of-the-century period is notable for what were perceived as major crises: extensive labor unrest as unions challenged decades of autocratic rule and a massive rise in immigration in the United States' population. This period is also notable for the anxieties and curiosity and occasional near-euphoria—not to mention rage—that these events engendered.[10] What will partly distinguish Griffith from other American dramatic artists is his consuming curiosity with otherness. Repeatedly in his works, he depicts the unique strangeness of minority people. Yet what most distinguishes Griffith and determines his political and racist miscalculations is his self-confidence, bordering on hubris, that he knows and understands the American "other." He never questions his ability to depict accurately these numerous subpopulations.

Even before Griffith had set foot in a motion picture studio, he was making claims for his unique ability to depict the exotic "other" and to render it with complete accuracy. In a draft script of his only professionally produced play, *A Fool and a Girl* (1906)—its stage directions and production notes addressed to the actor-producer James K. Hackett—Griffith described the characters and mise-en-scène for two acts set in the hops fields along California's Russian River where California "digger Indians" and Hispanic braceros labor alongside city-born white hops-pickers. Detailing the music and dancing, Griffith boasted, "All music used in the action of the play is in our possession, the Mexican folk songs . . . being selected from over three hundred unwritten songs of Old Spain and Mexico by kindness of a Mexican family of musicians."[11] In point of fact, Griffith's transcriptions of the authentic unwritten songs are in garbled Spanish—inaccurate phonetic transliterations of Spanish lyrics. It is immediately clear that Griffith understands neither Spanish nor the meanings of the lyrics he offers. His melodies, traditional in Mexico and California, had already found their way into musical anthologies, the lyrics rendered in Spanish and translated into English. However, it is equally apparent that Griffith is captivated by the proximity of these ethnic groups. He was aware of the theatrical potential and immediate appeal of characters whose identities hadn't previously been shown on the stage. In this sense, he quickly recognized and responded to the visible—and to many people—disturbing changes in the American population.

Between 1896 and 1914, the number of immigrants entering America reached an all-time peak. Many of these fourteen million migrants were from eastern and southern Europe. Unlike their light-skinned, often blue-eyed, fair-haired western European predecessors, the newcomers were of sallow complexion, brown-eyed, and brown- or black- or red-haired. Many immigrants were Christian but, rather than the predominately Protestant migrants who had emigrated from Britain, Scandinavia, and Germany, these newcomers—from Portugal, Italy, Greece, and the Balkans—were Roman Catholic or members of Eastern Orthodox sects. In addition, large numbers of Jews entered from Poland and Russia. In 1898 the United States had the questionable fortune to win its war with Spain, a victory which automatically bestowed citizenship upon Hispanics and Philippine Roman Catholics. Within the same two decades, large waves of Mexican migrants arrived in California to work on railroads and farms. These new citizens were added to a national population which, thirty years earlier, had experienced the liberation of hundreds of thousands of African American slaves[12] and had notionally, if not in practice, invested these freed people with citizens' rights. Chinese migrants had arrived at West Coast ports to work on the railroads and in mines and, from the 1880s, found their rights challenged by repressive legislation. A still-large number of Native Americans—"Indians"—although assigned and sometimes confined to "reservations," moved and worked among the general population.

The sense of swelling numbers and of both local and national overcrowding was exacerbated in 1890 by the U.S. Census Bureau's declaration that the western frontier had "closed." Three years later, speaking to a convention of scholars in Chicago, the historian Frederick Jackson Turner described the frontier in terms of an imaginary line running from the Canadian border to the Rio Grande. It had been the obligation of the American pioneer, claimed Turner, to push that frontier, "the meeting point between savagery and civilization," ever westward to be rewarded with free land. However, that liminal frontier line was already at the Pacific's edge. There no longer was any free—unowned or unoccupied—land. There was nowhere to go.

Cities were increasingly crowded. In the perception of assimilated Americans, their fears fed by the "yellow press," immigrant people were entering America in record numbers—the taps admitting foreigners were still wide open, and the land was filling up like a vast urn, hitherto only partly filled, but its contents now lapping at the rim. When, in 1904, Russian forces were defeated by the Japanese navy at Port Arthur, it seemed possible that once-dominant white colonizers might soon be colonized by "colored" peoples. From this perspective, there would soon be few places where the alien, the stranger, would not be visibly present, and there seemed small likelihood that these newcomers would be assimilated.

In keeping with this possibility, the subordinate comic characters of the 1890s "Western" frontier stage play were likely to include a Negro, an Indian, a Chinese cook or laundryman, an East Coast "dude," and a spinster.[13] Thus, a roster of alien diversity was present, but none of these "others" was wholly accommodated within the dramatic narrative nor made welcome or essential to the dramatic action. Similar—and more numerous—alien roles appeared on the variety stage. Griffith and other early filmmakers, reared in the shadow of the legitimate and variety theatre or former theatre workers themselves, were fully aware of these stage typologies and introduced them, as their current film demanded, for comic or sinister effect.

By 1900, the United States had become a visibly racist nation, acutely aware of what mainstream journals openly referred to as "the black and white problem." Griffith, a populist and a nationalist even more than he was a racist, fits within the national profile. Issues of race and ethnicity were closely allied with those of national and—in an immigrant-conscious society—personal identity. Maintaining the so-called integrity and purity of the white race became a national preoccupation. A favored solution was to keep the "other" at a safe, manageable distance. Some people resisted absorption of racial and ethnic difference by exclusion: separating the races in the former Confederate states, zoning housing and neighborhoods in American cities,[14] placing restrictions on Asian immigration,[15] forming all-white, all-Christian lodges, brotherhoods, trade unions,[16] Klans.[17] In 1896, the year in which Griffith passed his twenty-first birthday, the U.S. Supreme Court, in the case of *Plessy v. Ferguson*, upheld that racial segregation was legal, provided that equal public amenities were made available to all races. With this decision, the phrase "separate but equal" entered the American language.[18]

American professional sports were rigorously segregated: African Americans, who had previously dominated horse racing, were, in 1894, denied licenses by the new all-white Jockey Club, ostensibly founded to further thoroughbred racing but which established hegemonic domination over most aspects of American horse racing. Baseball was divided into separate leagues for black and white players; even professional cycling restricted participation to white cyclists. Virulent antiblack feelings and a correspondingly virulently antiblack national press, quite prepared to attack with epithets of "nigger," "buck," and "gloating coon," inveighed against the black boxer Jack Johnson for over a decade in attempts to forestall the contender Johnson's bouts with white champions. When, in 1907, Johnson won the World Heavyweight Championship, the same journals and white sporting figures campaigned relentlessly for a "White Hope" to wrest the championship back to a "member of the White Race."[19] Nevertheless, some people, sometimes the same who resisted close associations with the new "other," their curiosity whetted, purposefully attended world's fairs and expositions, artfully displayed "native villages," and midways and museums where other cultures and their artifacts were on display.[20]

Thus, immigrant and native-born differences brought elements of interest and exoticism and potential danger. In respect to the latter element, there is a political dimension to immigration, sometimes viewed as a peril, sometimes, in Griffith's films before 1920, a source of strife: the presence of the foreign workman whose alleged links to bolshevism, anarchism, and general labor unrest threaten misunderstandings, faction, and poverty. But the laboring man sufficiently interested Griffith to the point that industrial tensions figured prominently in his work, although only occasionally so in films adapted from stage plays. By contrast, Griffith's female characters are rarely employed in factories or undertake physical labor other than agricultural field work. We see in Griffith an awareness of class and social difference, a fascination with "colorful" people who can be tolerated and scrutinized as long as barriers to casual social integration remain in place. What we shall come to understand is that Griffith was both aware of boundaries and, equally, of the drama explicit in transgression. His films establish frontiers—the exotic "other" or the *different* on one side, the more traditional on the opposite, with liminal zones between— then put in motion dramas which enact or threaten transgression.

To these visibly different ethnic and religious "others" was added a further element of strangeness: the "working girl" or, simply, the "girl." There were the typewriter girls, the telephone girls, the shop girls, the matinee girls, the young females who, standing apart from their families, were suddenly conspicuous by their numbers and by their presence in a hitherto male urban world. Females claimed and sought financial and social independence. Sexual liberation and sexual choice were dramatized options. As Griffith developed his one- and two-reel Biograph films, he reached out to include as subject matter the adventurous, resourceful "girl." These girls, invading what was previously male work space, demonstrate learned commercial skills and work at responsible jobs. They confront criminals who invade their homes or the homes of respectable people, they deal with difficult situations and dangers until male help arrives. Sometimes these girls work in circuses or in the lower strata of theatre where their claim to respectability is potentially suspect because the work itself is deemed to be transgressive or morally uncertain, but they usually rise above such circumstances to win admiration and approval. These heroic "girls," reflecting the introduction of similar roles in late-Victorian theatre,[21] were a kind of novelty, variations on the interloper, but they were also a step forward in acknowledging the complexity of the early twentieth century, and depicting American diversity.

Intrigued by, and aware of, the possibilities the active female character held for drama, Griffith developed within his several repertory companies a small cluster of leading female performers: Florence Lawrence, Mary Pickford, Lillian and Dorothy Gish, Mae Marsh, Dorothy West, Blanche Sweet, Dorothy Bernard—and, later, Carol Dempster—who were repeatedly cast in roles requiring displays of initiative, acumen, strength, physical skills, and the conquering of girlish fears. Yet despite these films in which assertive women so prominently figured, Richard Schickel is one of several Griffith scholars who, with some justice, claim that Griffith could not depict females with sympathy or insight.[22] To a degree, these abridged female characters are merely theatrical stereotypes whom Griffith recalled from stage melodramas and farces; to a degree, these characters reflect the brevity of the one- and two-reel Biograph films which demanded that they be easily read by audiences and eschewed nuances that might be unreadable in adverse conditions of projection. His early works—plays and films—depict women either as infantilized ingénues, skipping and fluttering, sexually naive, saintly and nurturing, or sexually predatory, or criminal. There are few shaded female characters.

However, there is also evidence that Griffith's psychological profile impeded the realization of multidimensional female characters. Schickel, noting Griffith's collections of actresses, describes him as if he were a patriarchal manipulative Svengali to their compliant, competing Trilbys, and recognizes in Griffith's rotating list of female leads the exercise of directorial authority a taste for power and, perhaps, an unrealized wish for droit de seigneur. Away from the studios, Griffith's experience of women appears to have been limited. He was said to have been socially gauche and formal and domineering. He often lived and dined alone. He worked long hours in solitude. Schickel makes much of Griffith's patronizing of brothels and his restricted contact, apart from actresses, with females within his own environment.[23] As a director, he often found it difficult, in Kim Marra's words, to "construct their femininity . . . and display their sexuality for public consumption,"[24] and his heroines and villainesses and supporting female characters consequently tend to reflect his narrow concepts of womanhood.

However, there were occasions—and it will be one of the strands of this study to identify such occasions—when Griffith sufficiently trusted and encouraged his repertory actresses, notably Lillian Gish, Blanche Sweet, and Mae Marsh, to create dramatic characters and to enrich their roles by drawing on their own intellects and emotional resources. These occasions are conspicuous in films which Griffith adapted from novels and stage plays and where female characters had been developed and fleshed out by earlier, not necessarily male, authors. On such occasions these actresses bring depth to characters whom Griffith had merely sketched but not formed as fully rounded roles.

Apart from his representations of blacks and females, most of Griffith's depictions of diversity in America are benign, and at their worst patronizing and naive. Griffith frequently depicted Native Americans and West Coast Hispanics and, somewhat less often, "Orientals." Although Griffith admired and, in general, romanticized Native Americans, he nonetheless worked from theatrical and penny-dreadful clichés of the "redman." His "Indians," much like those in Edward Milton Royle's stage play *The Squaw Man* (1905), are either buckskin-and-feather-wearing forest dwellers who travel in canoes and live in wigwams, as in *The Squaw's Love*, or, alternatively, as in *The Broken Doll* or *The Battle at Elderbush Gulch*, savages who drink excessive quantities of alcohol, attempt to steal family pets for their cooking pots, and attack and burn white settlements. If they are "civilized," it is, as in *Ramona*, to serve as farm laborers. There is scant middle ground and little sense of observation or study.

Similarly clichéd, his Hispanics, as in *The Greaser's Gauntlet* or again in *Ramona*, wear sombreros, flared trousers studded with silver conchos, serapes or huipils, multitiered skirts, hair combs and full black wigs. But their stories, filmed against the backdrops of California missions, are rarely more than simple narratives of love, jealous rivalries, thwarted honor, and parental feuds. Again, there is a deliberate invoking of alien exoticism, a decorative strangeness, but there is no evidence that Griffith has brought an anthropologist's curiosity or insight to the dramas he enacts.

Griffith's Biograph portraits of the Chinese and Japanese are few, and those who figure as leading characters in a number of his films are portrayed with respect and admired for the antiquity and wisdom of their civilization. Elsewhere (most notably in theatrical renderings of the California gold camp Chinese by Bret Harte and Mark Twain and interpreted by the Caucasian actor Charles T. Parsloe) the Chinese are figures of amusement and derision. Nonetheless, neither the authors nor the actor, who went on to create other comic Chinese characters and whose characterizations gave rise to numerous imitators, were stigmatized for racist depictions.[25] On one occasion only, in Griffith's rendering of Charley Lee, a California gold camp laundryman, the central character and hero of *That Chink at Golden Gulch* (Biograph, 1909), is there an attempt to develop a multidimensioned character whose nobility and generosity exceed those of his white acquaintances. *That Chink* is a Griffith version of a popular gold camp melodrama, *The Golden Gulch* (1889). And, whereas the stage play is set wholly within the miners' shantytown and makes no mention of Charley's Chinese background, Griffith, in contrast, went out of his way to orientalize Charley, creating a prologue located in China where the sacredness of Charley's queue—later a device for capturing and securing the drama's villain—and his relationship to his deceased ancestors are emphasized. Thus, in at least some cases, if Griffith's racism is obvious to his audiences, it is a passive sort, more neocolonial and patronizing than actively denigrating his subjects.

In all of the above, Griffith's Chinese, African Americans, Mexicans, Native Americans, as well as his urban others, Jews and Italians, were performed by Griffith's company of white actors. Apart from lesser roles and supernumeraries in *The Birth of a Nation* and a single Native American adviser-actor who appeared in Griffith's Biograph films, his white repertory performers appeared on-screen "blacked-and-wigged-up" and costumed, as considered appropriate, to the locale and the manner in which these same roles were concurrently depicted on the American stage. In this respect, Griffith was merely following a well-established theatrical precedent. While African American and other dark-skinned character roles were written for the theatre, they were performed by white actors. The usual justification for such casting was that there were no people of color sufficiently skilled to interpret the role. Caught in the dialectic between tradition and innovation, black actors were denied roles in "white" plays until the 1920s.

It is with particular reference to representations of African Americans that Griffith stands apart. In 1915, a mere twelve years from the peak year of alien immigration into the United States and fifty years from the ending of America's cataclysmic Civil War, Griffith's motion picture, *The Birth of a Nation*, was released to wide acclaim and substantial consternation. Based on two novels (1902 and 1905) and a widely viewed stage play (1905) by a former preacher, the Reverend Thomas Dixon Jr., the film depicts the machinations of white Northern abolitionists in fomenting the Civil War. The film vividly—and unquestionably—shows the intense personal hardships of the war and memorably and graphically restages some of its conflicts. Griffith's film introduces President Abraham Lincoln, characterizing him as humane and compassionate and, significantly, as one with sympathy for the South and Southerners, if not for the Confederacy. Having introduced Lincoln, Griffith shows, in some detail, his— for the Confederacy as well as the Union—disastrous assassination. The final half of the film depicts alleged atrocities of the Reconstruction period, atrocities committed by former African American slaves with the connivance of the same Northern abolitionists, which, both Dixon and Griffith insisted, would never have happened had Lincoln lived. Some of the subsequent allegations, those relating to the war's causes, are partly true. Some, the humiliations visited on the postbellum South, are exaggerations. And some, the conspiratorial plotting and sexual promiscuity of the abolitionists as well as the racial identity of the South's new governors, are total fictions. Moreover, Griffith's citing of historical sources in the film's intertitles, are deliberate misquotations.

Dixon's play and Griffith's film argue that racial tensions were exploited by Northerners and that Southern blacks were encouraged in their crimes against white females by a covert Northern society promulgating intermarriage between blacks and whites. Both play and film depict African Americans attempting to dispossess white townsfolk from their comfortable residences, an armed, ill-disciplined militia of Negro men, a state legislature packed with incompetent African American delegates, an African American man pursuing a Southern white, adolescent girl to the point where she commits suicide rather than submit to rape, and, finally, a mulatto lieutenant governor threatening a Northern woman with rape and forced marriage (or death) until her timely rescue by the Ku Klux Klan.

The Birth of a Nation is a substantial improvement upon its disturbing source, Thomas Dixon's *The Clansman* (1905), a drama effective in its own terms. Despite contemporary critical opinion to the contrary which accused Dixon of pandering to low prejudices, Dixon and W. T. Price, his unacknowledged collaborator,[26] used the techniques of melodrama to remarkable effect, notably the ability to employ suspense, to effect rescues of an endangered heroine and restore justice, and to force the audience to judge the characters, villainous and virtuous, in terms of Southern ethics, morality, and family values. Their plotting is strong, their characters well delineated, their sensational moments appropriate to the novel's lurid narrative. Griffith builds on Dixon's evident skills, successfully making the offensive and the disturbing and the historically unsound into a compelling drama where, as spectators caught up and immersed in the convincing cinematic control of the dramatic action, we are made to empathize wholly against our better judgment. Instead, we find ourselves taking sides with white victims, white landowners and helpless white legislators, lynch mobs, and the Klan. Against our wishes, we are implicated in racist crimes. Dixon's narrative skills, apart from his unsavory theme, are sophisticated.

Griffith's depiction of African Americans in *The Birth of a Nation* is altogether of a different order from his other foreign exotic characters: drawing directly on sources which are hostile to any rapprochement between whites and blacks. There is neither novelty nor exoticism in his South Carolina Negroes, who are portrayed as people of low intelligence, yet cunning and devious. Morally, they are shown to be dangerously lascivious and corruptible. His mulatto lieutenant governor is "proof" of the dangers of racial interbreeding; his Negro sergeant-turned-would-be-rapist provides "evidence" that bestowing authority on former slaves and permitting them to hover on the perimeter of the white world is to encourage criminal traits. Apart from a few servants loyal to their white masters, blacks are, unambiguously, the enemy.

Because this film and Thomas Dixon's two novels and play are the subjects of my fifth chapter, and because understanding the particular racial circumstances is essential, I discuss these matters at length at that point. I demonstrate the degree to which Griffith was influenced by the prevailing climate of national, especially Southern, opinion and, as he undertook research, by Dunning-led historians. These historians, in the years following the war, wrote their racist justifications and distorting interpretations of the Civil War and the Reconstruction era. Their accounts are significantly biased against the Union North in that they assert that had Lincoln remained alive and in office, he would have shown clemency toward the South. They also assert that Lincoln's former cabinet officers, President Andrew Johnson, and the Republican Congress acted with deliberate malice. These persons, the historians claim, instigated a policy of cruel, vindictive reprisal. While there is some grain of truth in these assertions, there is also speculation, wishful thinking, hostility, and bias.

The author of Griffith's principal source was, successively, president of Princeton University, governor of New Jersey, and, for two successive terms, president of the United States: Woodrow Wilson. Wilson's five-volume *A History of the American People* is still in print. Even if he had wished to—and, of course, he showed no desire to—Griffith was in no position to argue history with Wilson. Although the conduct of the Civil War and its military, political, and civilian participants are the subjects of numerous histories and a multiprogram television series, many Americans remain unaware of the Reconstruction period, ca. 1867 to 1877, in particular of the punitive policies that the conquering Union Congress and their Southern deputies and hangers-on imposed upon the vanquished South and the resentments which arose from these policies. Such unawareness occasionally includes late twentieth-century theatre and film historians who, dismayed by Dixon's and Griffith's evident racism, neglect to step back into the Reconstruction era and grasp the complexity of circumstances and the lingering, if exaggerated, animosities passed like family heirlooms into the present. Few of us—Americans, Griffith, Dixon, even the Southern historian, Woodrow Wilson—can be let off the hook.

In a chapter that directly precedes discussion of Dixon and Griffith, I argue that Griffith's evident skill in devising *The Birth of a Nation* had its theatrical origins in the ways in which Civil War veterans' organizations and the American professional stage dramatized the Civil War from the 1870s through the 1920s. That chapter, my fourth, will explain how professional dramatists, developing a "Northern melodrama," attempted to depict the Reconstruction period as an era of healing and reconciliation. I further describe and elaborate on Griffith's strategy, which is to bring together the structure, conventions, and audience expectations of the "Northern" melodrama and, using the Lincoln assassination episode as the adhesive, laminate the reassuring Northern drama to Dixon's hellish vision of a South subjugated by African American overlords and Yankee interlopers. Brought together by Griffith, the conventions of the Northern play and the audience's familiarity with characters already presented as deserving sympathy held the power to make *The Birth of a Nation*'s spectators receptive to a succession of fresh experiences in a broken South. So conditioned, audiences were thus rendered susceptible to Dixon's and Griffith's misuse of their historical sources and to Dixon's and Griffith's views of a fractured-but-rebellious populace.

Every performance of the four-act *The Clansman* was broken by three intervals, each intermission disrupting audience concentration, and each successive act would have had to reengage the audience's attention. In contrast, to Griffith's advantage and in creating a format for receptivity, *The Birth of a Nation* never allows its audience respite and distance from the action on-screen until Lincoln's assassination is followed by a brief intermission. *The Birth of a Nation* spectator, consequently more closely engaged with the action on-screen and largely convinced of the historical veracity of the film's first half, has little space in which to reflect on the plausibility of Dixon's polemical views or to question Griffith's rewriting of history. Griffith, having been engaged to tour through the border and Southern states as an actor in Dixon's *The One Woman* (1907), had to be aware of numerous negative responses to *The Clansman* and to Dixon's reputation for stirring up angry controversy. Yet, in retitling Dixon's *The Clansman* as *The Birth of a Nation*, Griffith chose not only to restate, and perhaps amplify, Dixon's racial attacks on African Americans but also to present himself as a writer of American history and his film as a means of telling a national—not merely a partisan sectional—history.

In short, in surrendering to his own prejudices, using tainted historical sources, and selecting *The Clansman* as the model on which to build his vision of the war and its aftermath—in which there is neither peace nor reconciliation— *The Birth of a Nation* challenges our willingness to confront and also to enjoy and appreciate further Griffith films. Even—or especially—if we admit to being manipulated into siding with Griffith's racist heroes, an act of faith is required to step beyond *The Birth of a Nation*. Only after experiencing *Intolerance* (1916), either as a multilayered, braided narrative or in five discrete segments ("The Babylonian Story," "The Huguenot Story," "The Judean Story," "The Modern Story," and "The Eternal Story") or viewing his less ambitious full-length films *Broken Blossoms, 'Way Down East, Orphans of the Storm,* and *Sally of the Sawdust* (1925), we acknowledge Griffith's remarkable ability to tell a story visually and with great impact. Awe and admiration may wait until then. But it is a journey we must undertake to comprehend how Griffith, using the raw materials of theatre and the newer visual codes of motion pictures, became the first acknowledged artist of America film.

Beyond the matters of racism and American social history in the Reconstruction era and in Griffith's films, there is a further issue with which this book must engage: the emergence of screen acting and a response to the argument—often an unmediated assumption—that "bad" melodramatic performance was required by the limits of early silent film. Supposedly, it took many years before screen actors learned to practice contained, almost gesture-free, acting. Actors, the myth runs, began to use the face and posture, rather than what some modern critics have perceived as windmilling arms to express thought and emotion. Two historical narratives exist side by side, with little recognition by scholars that they contradict one another. There exists among some historians of silent film the conviction that Victorian and Edwardian stage performances were "melodramatic" (*melodrama* here used as a pejorative term to describe drama that was overblown in its emotions and ideas, but, in particular, in acting that was excessively gestural, emotionally exaggerated, and, in a word, "stagy").

In a serious but flawed study of silent-screen acting, Roberta Pearson labels gestural acting as "histrionic."[27] Ben Brewster and Lea Jacobs, with lesser grasp of stage practice, belittle melodramatic performance as a series of poses and frozen gestures.[28] Pearson, Brewster, and Jacobs criticize late-Victorian stage acting as overlarge and unrealistic. They have no idea why acting was gestural, how actors gestured and used their bodies, and how incidental music worked with gestural performance. For these historians, screen acting, as it approached naturalism or an acceptable form of pictorial realism, finally matured. Such film historians will argue that film, with its use of the close-up, saved acting from excess and that, finally, stage actors learned how to control themselves, thanks to the new medium of film. Similarly, these same critics stigmatize melodrama, seeing it only as an antithesis to naturalism. Because many of Griffith's dramas are melodramas and because melodrama remains an essential expressive mode on stage and screen, it is essential to reclaim this genre.

This assumption of excess and melodramatic performance is supported by the experiences of many newcomers to silent film. Current spectators are often confounded and dismayed by—or, frequently, view with condescending amusement—what they read as the pantomimed exaggerations of the actors. Television producers further—and all too frequently—compound problems of audience condescension and derision by exhibiting films deliberately scored with "comic" music which undermines and trivializes on-screen actions. Some film scholars attempt to explain away these apparent excesses with reassurances to the effect that, "Never mind. It will get better" and with promises that, by 1910, Griffith will have reformed acting styles to the point that screen performances are "realistic," "natural," and "unaffected." These arguments lead to a single teleological destination: the "verisimilar." Those performances which fail to conform to the verisimilar are denigrated, their theatrical excesses said to derive from "cheap melodrama."

A further tenet of this argument is that gestures become "eloquent," i.e., more likely to convey meaning, as actors, guided by a new film aesthetic, gradually reduce their gesticulations, and that such self-restraint is visible in Griffith's films after 1910. Film scholars and Griffith's biographers, claiming for him this role in the transformation of American acting, cite, on the one hand, a species of semaphoric gestural acting allegedly endemic to the stage and, on the other hand, a more restrained realistic or naturalistic screen performance which can—sometimes—be observed in the work of some performers in some films. Almost invariably, such accounts inflate the claim of a progressive change and exaggerate Griffith's role in furthering subdued gesture and expression. I subscribe neither to this thesis nor to this date.[29]

Theatre historians tell a different story of "natural" effects in the nineteenth-century theatre. This second narrative charts the ways that a natural or restrained acting style, from at least the 1840s forward, emerges in domestic melodrama, in social comedy, in the work of major Shakespearean actors, in response to electric stage lighting, in historical antiquarianism. Theatre historians have no need to invoke Ibsen or Zola to demonstrate the spread of restrained acting. By the 1880s, the period of Griffith's youth, a thousand approaches to acting, relating to more restrained performances, can be traced and woven together. For example, the English actor E[dward] S[mith] Willard, touring America in the 1880s, specialized in a newer, quieter style. The American actors Minnie Maddern Fiske and James K. Hackett, later to produce Griffith's play *A Fool and a Girl*, both toured in romantic, commercial pieces, but brought what was recognized as a casual, quiet realism to their roles. Initially a robust performer, Edwin Booth gradually mutated into a quieter reserved style which gave an intellectual depth to his Shakespearean roles. The dramas of Augustus Thomas, James A. Herne, and David Belasco, while neither naturalistic in depicting character as a direct function of environment nor altogether "realistic" in acting style and mise-en-scène, were recognized as less declamatory than some of the dramas of their contemporaries.

The question remains, which of the two narratives, the film historians' narrative of an excessively "melodramatic" stage tamed by the motion pictures or the theatre historians' narrative of progressive changes in performance style, is to be believed? My book will be siding with the theatre historians and offering evidence of a bewildering range of histrionic diversity which, rather than taming screen acting, allowed and encouraged oversized performance in films well past the moment when it was claimed to have disappeared.

What is often overlooked in both the stage and film actor's performance was the presence and use of accompanying incidental music. Orchestral music was an essential element of Victorian stage performance, the music enabling and partly interpreting extended and sustained gestures. Music, moreover, enabled spectators to read each emotional moment and to assess the moral register of characters and episodes. Victorian acting was not dance, but some of the physical qualities of dance—with music providing vital support and propulsion for gesture, setting or underlining tempo, and serving as a medium of resistance to gesture which the actor had to heed—were present in Victorian and Edwardian theatrical performance. It was a change of some significance when the stage, gradually responding to theatrical naturalism, slowly discarded music from the pit and relied wholly on diegetic music.[30] Likewise, music was, for many of the same narrative reasons, an invariably essential element of film exhibition, a piano or other instruments always accompanying screenings. Equally, music was a necessary ingredient of the filming process. Musicians were employed on the film set to set tempo for the actors and to establish appropriate emotional moods. Griffith is frequently reported as dancing to the on-set piano between takes,[31] and it is unclear when he finally banished the piano.[32] In 1927, Lillian Gish gave an extended interview to Liberty Magazine in which she insisted that she personally objected to the use of music to accompany her scenes, but the interviewer noted, as he and Gish walked across the Metro-Goldwyn-Mayer back lot where Gish was filming The Wind (1927) with Victor Sjöstrom, on each stage the presence of chairs and music stands for the obligatory standby quartet.[33] The continuing presence of musical accompaniment right up to the beginning of sound film, in itself makes a statement about the long alliance between actors' gestures and music and to some degree suggests why practices which contained and restricted gesture were slow to arrive.

In the face of such practices, Griffith's alleged reforms are largely mythic. My third chapter will examine acting practices as Griffith encountered them at the

Biograph studio, his attempts to recruit experienced stage actors betwee 1908 and 1910, and his stated views on stage versus screen performances. What the reader will find—both in reading this book and in viewing films made through the 1920s—is that both stage and film acting were, at best, inconsistent in style and irregular in application. *Orphans of the Storm* (1922), a film which draws heavily on the American and English stages for its sources, offers a mélange of performance styles which Griffith tolerated and encouraged.

It is possible to trace a pattern of restraint in acting technique as the vocabulary of filmmaking, notably mobile camera work, the close-up and the medium shot, and crosscut editing, enabled the spectator to see more of the actors' faces and to read in those faces inner emotions and thoughts. The framed screen, tighter and more constricting than a theatre's proscenium, drew attention to broad gestures and gradually exerted its own discipline on actors' performances. Consequently, although he periodically claimed credit for these changes, Griffith's overall role in reforming acting is questionable. This book, as a part of its examination of the correspondences and divergences between stage and screen, will consider the historical developments and the degree to which Griffith's preferences translated into national practice. My own studies of stage and screen acting[34] reveal an inconsistent and often contradictory development, both in Griffith's personal work with his actors and in screen acting as a whole. Various styles existed side by side—in the same company, in the same film, even in the same performer. It is rare to find a harmony of actors' performances in Griffith's films much before 1918, but, as we move from play to play and play to film, some overall developments are apparent and a new aesthetic is gradually expressed.[35]

There remains the further thorny question of motion picture audiences and their responses to Griffith's films. This is a frustrating topic because, for numerous reasons, the identities and opinions of film audiences in the twenty-six-year span (between 1908 and 1934) in which Griffith was involved with filmmaking remain elusive and obscure. Active and regular reviewing of motion pictures in the daily and weekly press didn't begin until around 1910 and didn't become a function to be taken seriously until 1913—about the time that films began to appeal to middle-class spectators and to increase in length from one or two reels to what might be described as "feature length," that is, anywhere from five to fifteen reels. Correspondingly, small storefront picture houses and "nickelodeons"[36] gave way to purpose-built film theatres, and, with this evolution, changes in the distribution of films and the technologies of exhibition. Before 1913, films were sold individually, often by the linear foot, and it remained the perquisite of the exhibitor to determine how to edit and display his purchases. Gradually, a system of film-exchange developed, and, after 1913 and the advent of the studio system of film production, a means of regional distribution and rental, similar to the modern system, was in place. As important, films were increasingly sold, and acquired popularity by the skill, appeal, and on-screen personalities of the performers who, if identified at all, featured in these early movies. Stars attracted audiences and sold films, not directors.[37]

Griffith's earliest films to have gained critical acclaim and a popular following are those which followed his departure from Biograph in 1913, but their success was measured in box office earnings, not in testimonials. It was only after the release in 1915 and the attendant controversy surrounding The Birth of a Nation that Griffith's audiences became visible and, albeit briefly, somewhat identifiable: those who held him to be a great narrator and dramatizer of American history and a superb artist-craftsman and those who found his work inflammatorily racist, biased, cruel, humiliating, and factually—historically—wrong. Both parties expressed their views in polemics, protests and counterprotests.[38] Griffith's films never again polarized audiences to such an extent, and there is a consequent dearth of reaction and comment. No one criticized or defended his depiction of other ethnic groups or challenged his portrayals of females. What is significant is that, from around 1915, Griffith was one of the advocates of "the two-dollar movie," a strategy by filmmakers and exhibitors to increase the price of moviegoing to first-run films from ten cents to twenty-five cents to a hefty two dollars. As the two-dollar admission price took hold in large metropolitan centers, attendance, which in the earlier, smaller nickelodeons had been composed of lower middle-class, working-class, and immigrant audiences, increasingly reflected the more affluent middle class spectators who could afford the cost. But movie admission prices fluctuated, so it is misjudged to characterize Griffith's audiences as middle-class. What is known, and probably the only reliable test of audience appeal, although not at all an indication of the identities of audiences— age, gender, class, race, nationality, and political profile—is that some of Griffith's films made money and that others failed to do so. Overall, measuring in commercial terms, Griffith achieved more successes than failures.

As this book unfolds, it will be occasionally necessary to reach beyond Griffith to consider the work of the young film industry—other filmmakers and film production companies, some American, some foreign, who became similarly aware of the potential of developing motion pictures derived from theatrical subjects. It must be understood that Griffith was not the only motion picture director-producer to be attracted to the stage and to translate dramas into films. He may have been a propelling force in creating commercially viable films from popular stage materials, but there were notable rivals in Guazzioni and Ambrosio (Italian), Pathé Films d'Art (French), and Famous Players-Lasky, the Shubert Organization's Paragon, Klaw and Erlanger, Thanhauser, and Imp (American), which all put feature-length theatrical films onto the screen. Dennis Gifford identifies 861 authors who had their works adapted to film.[39] Some writers, such as Alexandre Dumas, père, had over a dozen works adapted. Between 1898 and 1915, sixty-two films appeared based on the works of Charles Dickens. For Shakespeare the number was seventy-four. What partly distinguished Griffith from his rivals is the sheer longevity of his career, surviving and continuing when his competitors had long faltered, but also the individuality of his work. Griffith's rivals were corporate, less frequently individuals. Significant directors, with the backing of corporations, briefly appeared and made important adaptations of stage pieces, but they and their companies disappeared. Griffith endured as a powerful filmmaker from 1908 to 1934.

It is essential that I explain the historiographic thinking which underpins this book. Since the early 1950s, the field of film studies has been strongly influenced by a single work, A. Nicholas Vardac's *Stage to Screen: Theatrical Method from Garrick to Griffith*,[40] which purports to explain the relationship between the late-Victorian stage and early motion pictures. Vardac offers a narrative of separation: of one medium, the stage, failing and being supplanted by a newer, more technically adept medium, cinema, which could achieve the effects and illusions and maintain an environmental "realism" which allegedly was believed to elude the paint-and-canvas scenery which the theatre offered.

Vardac's scholarship, at the time he wrote, was neither better nor worse than other studies of the nineteenth-century English-language stage. In 1949, the only twentieth-century scholars to have written on the Victorian stage were Ernest Reynolds, Allardyce Nicoll, and Ernest Bradlee Watson.[41] Vardac also drew on a clutch of amateur scholar-historians—journalists and fans—who wrote lurid, occasionally perceptive, but largely inaccurate accounts of the stage. George Rowell would publish the first acceptable history of the Victorian theatre seven years later, but it is not a history to which Vardac would subscribe.[42] What characterized Reynolds, Nicoll, and Watson is the view propagated by the adherents of naturalism and advocates of the New Drama (chiefly William Archer) that the Victorian stage represented a terrible lapse in the "literary" and cultural standards of British drama. America, these historians decided, had yet to develop its drama, and what emerged in the United States was a debased imitation of the British stage.[43]

One of the serious faults that Vardac acquired from his sources is a crippled understanding of the nineteenth and early twentieth centuries, and therefore he treats this period of time as a vast solidified and undifferentiated lump. Vardac,

the sources he has consulted, and his adherents are largely unable to see subtleties, nuances, developments (not necessarily "progress") and changes in the
Victorian stage: to them it was all coarse, crude, pandering to low common
denominators, noisy, performed by unsubtle actors roaring their tirades and
gesturing extravagantly. In other words, much of the criticism they level against
the stage is of the sort which "modern" film critics level against much silent
film. When these scholars do detect change, their historiography is strongly
teleological, that is, it moves from the alleged crudities of Edward Fitzball, John
Baldwin Buckstone, T. P. Taylor, and Dion Boucicault to the quiet harmonies of
Tom Robertson's cup-and-saucer romantic comedies or from H. J. Byron to
Pinero and Barker. There is no attempt to place dramatists and theatres and
actors and audiences in any sort of historical context beyond a most general and
derogatory one. Few modern theatre historians with today's knowledge of the
Victorian stage would accept Vardac's description.

Vardac's overriding assumption is that the Victorian stage ran out of steam
for two reasons. First, it aspired to a pictorial realism (distinct from naturalism,
which Vardac simply fails to understand) unattainable on the stage and that this
visual realism was only attainable when dramas were made on motion picture
film. He cites numerous plays and stage productions by both Dion Boucicault
and David Belasco which, even in "sensation" scenes, strained for the authenticity of photographic verisimilitude but which were compromised by being
staged in paint-and-canvas scenery. His second reason is that the stage aspired
to illusion, spectacle, and fantasy, and that these attempts were similarly limited
by the scenic deficiencies of the Victorian stage. Here, Vardac cites Augustus
Harris's spectacular Drury Lane pantomimes which, in his view, could not
approximate, in quality or imagination, the surreal fantasies, tricks, and juxta-
positions found in Georges Méliès's magical illusions. Early film, Vardac spec-
ulates, soon convinced dramatists and theatre audiences that the stage had
fallen behind the new film technologies. Here, Vardac is wrong on several
counts. While William Archer argued that stage realism was the culmination of
evolutionary development,[44] the stage had already found and was employing
major alternatives to illusionism in the theoretical writings and practical work
of Appia and Craig. Moreover, both Ibsen and Strindberg, from the 1880s, had
moved beyond naturalism into symbolic staging. The avant-garde theatre was
already moving in a direction tangential to pictorial realism. It was not until
after 1915 that there was some sense among theatre people that the stage failed
to match the scenic possibilities of film.

Vardac further assumes (and categorically states) that, as the stage ran out of
steam, it surrendered to film. What he does not recognize is the extent to which

there was a long period of exchange of technology and effects between the stage and film, stage plays incorporating film sequences, film intercutting with live moments. There were no fixed boundaries but, rather, a continual series of fluid interchanges.

Vardac assumes that the principal source of narrative material was the full-length play. He is altogether unaware of the effect or influences of other narrative theatrical sources such as the dramatic sketch which could be found in music halls, vaudeville theatres, and other variety houses from the 1890s through the 1940s. The form, brevity, and quasi-legally enforced silence (or limited dialogue) of the sketch had a marked influence on the development of early silent narrative film. The nature and impact of the dramatic sketch will therefore be examined in subsequent chapters.

Finally, Vardac attempts to capture all of the above in a single all-embracing paradigm: that of a necessary handover of tradition and mission from stage to screen. It is a wonderfully simple idea which has appealed to theatre historians and film historians for better than sixty years. It has appealed even when the paradigm began to become tattered and unworkable, when whole sections—especially Vardac's understanding of the Victorian stage—were seen to be imprecise and unable to stand up to scrutiny and later scholarship. But obsolescence hasn't led to the abandonment of the Vardac paradigm, especially by film scholars, who often appreciate a formula to describe the relationships between theatre and film. Therefore, as a consequence of the continuing presence of this obsolete Vardac model, I state that my approach from this point forward will be to ignore Vardac and posit, rather, the relationship between the late-Victorian and Edwardian stage and early film as a fluid period of explorations and experimentations, developments, borrowings, and mutual rip-offs.

Should we even chase after a new paradigm? Isn't the search for a single historical model part of the problem? In my view, it is misguided to replace the Vardac paradigm with yet another simplified and reductive paradigm. An overarching paradigm may prove to be inappropriate, and, because the relationships that have governed the creation of each Griffith or rival film are so unsteady and changeable, it is necessary to deal, instead, in individual cases. The historical relationship between stage and screen is far more complex—and far more interesting—than we have granted. Surely, after a century of false and unreliable narratives, we can begin to do justice to the shared history of theatre and film.

As I have previously indicated, the book's chronology derives from the order in which Griffith selected his materials. However, there are some alterations to this chronology and some compressions, most notably apparent in my decision to introduce dance and multimedia works in film production and presentation as early as 1912, although both dance and multimedia were more prominent after 1915–1916. Griffith introduced his first modern dance episode in Oil and Water (1912), and it is with Judith of Bethulia (1913) that dance became a recurrent and serious element, perhaps influenced by Blanche Sweet's association with the dancer Gertrude Hoffman and the continuing presence in the Griffith company of Gertrude Bambrick. Between Judith of Bethulia and Intolerance (1916) and the Intolerance spin-off, The Fall of Babylon (1919), Griffith was experimenting with live multimedia (stage and film) production. I have likewise devoted two chapters to The Birth of a Nation, one to outline the professional theatre and cinema's long engagement with the American Civil War and a second chapter to focus on Dixon's and Griffith's treatment of the Civil War and Reconstruction. I devote a further chapter to Griffith's adaptation of the stage classic 'Way Down East. In Way Down East, Griffith reached the apogee of his powers to produce a film drama with notable characterization and emotional depth. To be sure, Way Down East lacks large-scale, crowd-filled episodes that helped to define The Birth of a Nation and Intolerance and would again be deployed in Orphans of the Storm and America. Way Down East, however, achieves personal intimacy in a drama which I regard as the most subtle and appealing of Griffith's 570-odd works. The final chapter describes Griffith in the final decade of his film career, beset by mounting financial crises, his personal life in turmoil, and drinking to excess. Despite this falling away of power and failing to adapt to changes in the film industry, Griffith continued to make movies, seven of these derived from theatrical sources. One was the powerful, if overwrought and overlong, The Two Orphans, filmed by Griffith as Orphans of the Storm, another, Poppy, filmed as Sally of the Sawdust. I also partly invent a circular trajectory for these years, as Griffith returned to earlier subject matter to fashion America (1924) from his earlier unsuccessful stage play, War (1907) and his vaudeville sketch In Washington's Time (1901). His final film, The Struggle (1932), was Griffith's reprise of the temperance melodrama, ironic in the light of his unsuccessful battle with alcohol. Long retired, but, in 1945, three years before his death, still contemplating a comeback, Griffith wrote a screenplay based on his experiences as a touring actor. My study, I reiterate, is not a biography. It remains concerned with examining the lifelong relationship between Griffith and live performance—theatre, circus, minstrelsy, dance—and examines how Griffith, known for denigrating the theatre, but sometimes threatening or promising to return to it, was regularly inspired to use the very material he sometimes pretended to despise.

The Mobile Theatre

The birth of narrative film—and, indeed, Griffith's film career—did not begin in a camera or with the technological innovations of such pioneers of filmmaking as Thomas Edison, Edwin Porter, Sigmund Lubin, or even D. W. Griffith himself. Instead, it began for Griffith, as it did for other pioneer filmmakers, in the 1890s. Film began in live performances attended by spectators who had no expectations that any other means of entertainment would ever displace stage attractions. These audiences beheld theatrical productions which, for the most part, had originated elsewhere. They were written or devised elsewhere, their subject matter, dramatic structures, casting, and management policies and practices had all been determined elsewhere. Productions arrived and departed by rail, rarely lingering anywhere for more than a week or two. Thus, the beginnings of American dramatic film can be located on the vaudeville and music hall stages, in the comedies and melodramatic plays that captivated popular audiences in the touring shows of the growing cities and small communities throughout America.[1] Touring "combination" companies, carrying both actors who enacted dramatic narratives and variety artists who performed specialty acts, provided one developmental line of this early history of film, just as the popular dramatic sketches of the variety stage offered another line. Although film historians prefer to celebrate the individuals, auteurs, who invite us to tell a story of genius triumphant, the actual history of narrative film before 1925 is a gradual and fitful attempt to replicate the products and strategies of the commercial stage.

Griffith's choice of film subjects, his staging techniques, the structures of his films, the organization of his acting companies, and his promotional and management strategies are all legacies of his experiences in the theatre. To understand Griffith as a filmmaker, we consequently require an overview of the American theatre at the turn of the century. We must recognize a pivoting economic balance between the metro-politan centers and the more rural hinterlands and the theatrical forms which arose in response to these fluctuations. Above all, we must recognize a mobile theatre.

The necessary mobility of most theatrical companies affected the roles of large cities, chiefly New York, in determining entertainments for the road. For much of the twentieth century, New York City and Broadway have lain at the eco-nomic core of the American theatre industry. Sizeable revenue or outright fail-ure has been largely contingent on a play's reception by Manhattan critics and audiences. However, this pattern did not prevail a century or more ago. New York, in 1900, served equally as a tryout place for traveling companies and a des-tination for shows after lengthy road trials. Annually, some twenty dramas and musical comedies were designated as successes, but there was no priority accorded to New York, no obligation that a drama be stamped with the New York imprimatur for it to achieve financial success. An actor might make his or her reputation on the New York stage, but many leading performers drew audi-ences based on their reputations in the provinces. Of course, New York was the "nerve center"[2] of the theatre industry for numerous producing organizations, booking offices, and theatrical agents that had their principal offices there. Many plays intended for the road gathered their operating capital from New York and East Coast investors. Nevertheless, because of the transportation network of railroad companies, the principal theatrical economy was widely dispersed, away from New York and, to some degree, from East Coast metrop-olises. The overall reception and consequent earnings of a drama—and, indeed, the physical conformation of many popular pieces—were strongly determined by considerations of the road.

The Great Train Robbery (1893–1897), first a stage play and, seven years later, a seminal film, offers such an example of the American theatre on the move. Scott Marble's stage melodrama opened at the Bowery's Star Theatre in October 1896. A month later, by way of New Haven, Hartford, and Providence, The Great Train Robbery company moved northward to Boston's Columbia Theatre before travel-ling westward along the Pennsylvania rail network to Philadelphia, Cleveland, and into the Ohio Circuit, dipping southward to Cincinnati and, following the Louisville and Nashville spur line, further south to Louisville's Avenue Theatre.[3]

Although the play was first noticed by New York critics, the immediate and continuing success of The Great Train Robbery was not contingent on the approval of metropolitan critics and audiences. Rather, devised and organized for travel, it earned the dramatic company and its producers their livelihood in provincial America, where it played to appreciative, if not necessarily discriminating,

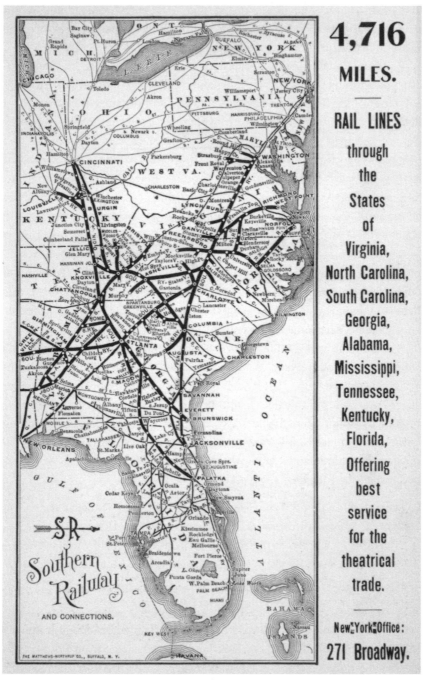

Railway map, 1896, advertising the Southern Railway line to theatrical patrons and depicting connections through Griffith's hometown of Louisville.

audiences. The play remained immensely popular in provincial playhouses and a remunerative theatrical property through 1904, when, after the release of the Edison-Porter film, it repeated its earlier tour.

Davis and Keogh, the play's proprietors, owned outright *The Great Train Robbery*'s performing rights and held joint copyright with its author. These theatrical entrepreneurs had intentionally mounted and organized *The Great Train Robbery* as a "combination" company, which, designed for mobility and economy, carried on its tour a permanent cast of actors and a second, more fluid, cast of specialty variety performers. Davis and Keogh worked closely with the author to shape the play's narrative structure. They determined the duration of the tour and the principal stops along its circuitous route, cast both the company of actors and the specialty variety performers so essential to the second act, and changed these variety components periodically as the play toured. The company moved between agreed play dates along established railroad routes—its movements and engagements controlled through offices both in New York and in Ohio, as well as by a tour manager who traveled with the company. It was this hands-on tour manager who, sensing fresh audiences or aborting unprofitable engagements, determined intermediate stops at lesser venues.

As a dramatic work, *The Great Train Robbery* is in no way singular. Its subject is similar to numerous railroad-crime melodramas which circulated along provincial circuits through the 1890s. Such plays, built upon robbery of the mail or special shipments of valuable freight, featured derailings, wrecks, and timely rescues. Its author, Scott Marble (1845–1919), although proficient in generating numerous commercially successful melodramas, comedies, and occasional musical drama, remained unknown and unheralded. At best, his work was occasionally listed in the trade press:

> Scott Marble is the author of *Black Diamonds*, *The Colonel*, *The Cotton Spinner*, *The Diamond Breaker*, *Exiles of Siberia*, *The Free Quaker*, *Furnished Rooms*, *[The] Gold Key*, *[The] Great Train Robbery*, *[The] House with Green Blinds*, *The Investigator*, *The Linwood Case*, *Man and His Idol*, *Mugg's Landing*, *My Wife's Husband*, *Over the Garden Wall*, *Miss Plaster of Paris*, *Rexina*, *The Royal Pass*, *[The] Sidewalks of New York*, *Tennessee's Pardner*, and various other plays.[4]

Yet Marble's was never a name to draw investors or audiences. Adept at contriving visual sensations for the stage, Marble switched in 1910 from writing plays to devising motion picture scenarios. Not surprisingly, *The Great Train Robbery*, strong on physical action, barely reliant on dialogue, and with a love narrative which could be cut without impairing action or meaning, lent itself to adaptation as a film.

The Great Train Robbery, if not altogether typical of the stage fare of the 1890s, may nonetheless be read as an analogue of the theatrical world the young D. W. Griffith was to enter, first as a spectator, later as an actor, and—eventually—as a filmmaker and film promoter, organizing and dispatching numerous productions to support his films. Griffith was to draw on this world of peripatetic actors, mobile theatre companies, and entertainments which frequently and successfully blurred or ignored traditional distinctions between genres for the duration of his professional career. Indeed, Griffith's choice of film subjects, his staging techniques, the structures of his films, the organization of his acting companies, and his promotional and management strategies were all legacies of his experiences in the theatre. To understand Griffith as a filmmaker, we consequently require an overview of this theatrical milieu. The Great Train Robbery, because it was a successful stage drama soon translated into a landmark film, is our first step into this theatrical environment.

In 1897, the year in which The Great Train Robbery reached Louisville, Griffith was twenty-two years old. He had witnessed theatrical performances in most, if not all, of Louisville's theatres and, impressed by what he had observed and enjoyed, had determined on an acting career. Sometime in 1895, Griffith left his job as clerk in a local bookshop to take his first steps as an apprentice actor, progressing from amateur theatricals to a local profit-share company and to small roles with professional companies. For the first time since 1890, when the Griffith family had migrated from Shelby County to Louisville, Griffith left home, traveling beyond Kentucky to Ohio, Indiana, Michigan, Minnesota, and North Dakota, experiencing America—as so many other Americans were doing—by rail. The Griffiths had brought their furniture and personal possessions by spring wagon, traveling at a mule team's pace. Now, although the rail journeys between small-town theatres were short, Griffith was encountering rapid motion and, through the coach windows, sensing speed and observing a linear progression of framed flashing images. These early experiences of the railroads—and of motion, speed, sequential linked images, and mobility—seem never to have left him and repeatedly appear in his films. Many of these— for Biograph and for his own film companies—feature what became a Griffith cliché: last-minute or final-reel rides-to-the-rescue, first on horseback, and, later, in frantic attempts by the occupants of a hastily commandeered automobile to overtake and halt a speeding express train. His experience of being stranded in Minneapolis and traveling home "grabbing the blinds"—clinging to the rods beneath railroad boxcars—furnished material for a comic sequence for W. C. Fields and Carol Dempster in Sally of the Sawdust. Even when he depicted natural landscapes, Griffith turned stillness into motion and speed.

Dissatisfied with the snow-covered, hard-frozen lake onto which Anna Moore flees in the theatrical version of 'Way Down East, Griffith changed the motionless lake into a racing river with a pack of broken ice floes slowly gathering momentum in the spring current and accelerating downstream toward a crushing waterfall. Using the river's speed to set the tempo of the sequence, Griffith made the spectacle of her lover, David, perilously leaping from floe to unstable floe to rescue the unconscious Anna before she is swept away, a superb on-screen race between man and relentless natural forces.

Griffith also would have encountered motion as seen through the cine-camera. Periodically, in Louisville between engagements and unable to find theatrical work, Griffith took in the cheap entertainments, including vaudeville and minstrel shows, touring melodramas, and the new penny-in-the-slot mutoscope. Thus, his first views of moving pictures may have been through the eye-piece of a "what-the-butler-saw" machine, with its cranked handle and positive photos rotated before the viewer. And, most probably, he also looked through the viewing lens of another optical device, the kinetoscope, with short loops of film presented to the single spectator, in a Louisville amusement arcade or kinetoscope parlor. Projected film soon followed. In September 1896, Macauley's Theatre offered Louisville's theatre-goers the "Veriscope portraying the contest between James J. Corbett and Robert Fitzsimmons at Carson City, Nevada, March 17."[5] Again, in January 1897, attending a program of Shakespearean tragedies (Othello, Julius Caesar, and Romeo and Juliet) at Louisville's Grand Opera House, Griffith would have witnessed its highly promoted afterpiece "The American Biograph," a succession of films billed as: McKinley at Canton, Niagara Falls, Herald Square Fire Department, Joseph Jefferson's Rip Van Winkle, Trilby and Little Billee, Beach at Atlantic City, Stable on Fire, Niagara Upper Rapids, New York Boulevard, and the Empire State Express. Some of these projected films—falling water, speeding fire apparatus, and passing locomotives—emphasized power, speed, and mobility. Two further films in this group, Rip Van Winkle, and Trilby and Little Billee, hinted at the numerous, still unexploited links between the stage and motion pictures.

Griffith's experience of theatre was directly affected by another major development which began in 1873, two years before his birth. At that date, theatre companies were largely linked to single playhouses. Theatres employed, season by season rather than play by play, a permanent company of actors, each engaged to play roles predictable by the actors' ages, appearance, growing and practiced skills, years and experience in the profession, and favor with the local audience.[6] However, because of a severe national market crash in 1873, these "stock" companies were immediately affected with loss of revenue as local economies collapsed. For similar reasons, variety theatres also found that their patrons could no longer afford to attend, and these theatres also faced bankruptcy. In the face of these grim developments, the railway companies, themselves affected by the depression and seeking fresh business, offered theatrical entrepreneurs a lifeline: an extension of the "combination" system with favorable rates and appealing schedules for traveling theatre companies. The theatre industry was quick to recognize the worth of this proposal. As early as June 1873, as managements prepared for the 1874 season, the *New York Clipper* recognized in an editorial the gravity of the problem and with remarkable prescience forecast its solution:

> [Business]is trifling . . . theatres are closing altogether, or venturing a brief season with light or inexpensive entertainments. New York is now the objective point of managers and performers . . . and it is here that all meet to compare notes and fix upon some plan of action for the future . . . A number of companies have been partially formed, fair salaries meeting with ready acceptance, performers clutching a sure thing rather than hold out for better terms which may never be offered. The country will [be] pretty well travelled by combinations next season, this sort of business paying much better than a permanency in the stock of some city theatre, where the chances of a rise are not so good as in a Wall-street stock. . . . What is called "legitimate" does not meet with the proper encouragement. . . . People don't take to it; they prefer something sensational, spicy, emotional, spectacular, etc. The variety element is in good demand, and clever specialists command salaries which, in the olden time, would have been considered big terms by first-class stars.[7]

As local repertory or stock companies vanished, touring combinations increased. In 1876–1877, there were one hundred such companies on the road; by 1880, there were three hundred; by 1900, as many as five hundred combination companies were touring.[8]

The combination system merits our attention not only because of its centrality to the American theatre in the latter decades of the nineteenth century and the first two decades of the twentieth. Its configurations, although largely unrecognized, are strongly embedded in American narrative films from their earliest days. Not surprisingly, Griffith encountered combinations frequently in the dramas he witnessed in his adolescence, and later, as an actor, toured with a combination company. Given their ubiquity, he was acutely aware of the combination as a dramatic structure and as an established theatrical convention to be met in production. His two plays, *A Fool and the Girl* (1906) and *War* (1907), severally recognize the combination convention by creating framing spaces for variety acts which Griffith goes to some pains to specify—Mexican musicians, singers, and dancers, and British Christmas revelers—and which are in harmony with the milieux he depicts. Combinations also directly influenced his films—and other Hollywood films well into the 1930s. Griffith still acknowledged the combination structure in such major films as *A Romance of Happy Valley*, *Way Down East*, and *Orphans of the Storm* even as combinations, no longer necessary to draw audiences or financially viable, had largely fallen from favor.

Combination, as a mutable theatrical term, had been in circulation from 1872 or earlier[9] and was understood, initially, to refer to a dramatic or musical or variety entertainment which toured with its own cast of performers and full complement of scenery. The term also described a business arrangement but not a theatrical result, in effect a temporary partnership and capitalization as two managements pooled their resources for a joint theatrical enterprise. Combination further described a touring theatrical program which brought together numerous stars or headliners on a single bill. Such a program was usually a sequence of variety and short dramatic pieces with the dramatic content being supplied by one-act plays or sketches. All combinations were distinct from their theatrical predecessors in that each production had been capitalized as an individual venture. Loss on a combination's production and its tour almost invariably meant that loss was contained and could not affect other ventures.

After 1873 the understanding of a combination expanded to include a theatrical and commercial response—a compromise and innovation—in the face of trying economic circumstances. This kind of combination, again a touring vehicle, was characterized, first, by two casts, a dramatic cast (actors) and a variety cast (variety, musical, dance, and novelty artists). These two casts, chosen for altogether different performance skills, were brought together in scenes or episodes which provided a framing for musical and variety acts or which integrated musical and/or variety acts into the action. This mixing of genres was not new to melodrama or to comedy. It was the degree to which drama and variety were deliberately combined as an established theatrical practice and the sheer volume of variety traffic within a dramatic piece which admitted the combination (or combined) label.

Although the structure and the contents of the drama—the framing device for the variety, music, and dance elements—were stable and largely unchanging during the life of the production, the composition of the variety element might change frequently as the drama toured. Performers might be added because they were novel (without in any sense being apposite to the drama) or because they were appealing, or simply because they were available. Variety performers were dropped from the combination because their appeal was perceived to wane, because they were expensive to carry on the tour, or because they could be readily replaced, locally or from other sources. After 1874 the predominance of any one of these varieties of combination did not mean that others had disappeared. Rather, all varieties of combination were on tour until about 1915, when they slowly diminished in number and had altogether disappeared by 1939.

Early 1900s film audiences, many or most of them theatre-goers as well, still expected their drama to be leavened with variety turns, even after combinations had declined in favor. The first two films to present the full plots of stage melodramas in abridged form, Edwin S. Porter's The Great Train Robbery and Uncle Tom's Cabin (both 1903), make it clear that Porter entirely understood the appeal of combination plays, as both filmed dramas are alike in that each interrupts the serious incidents of the narrative to inject variety turns. In both films these interruptions are nondiegetic dance entertainments which do not forward the narrative but which nonetheless contribute to the dramas' overall ambiance.

Edison-Porter's The Great Train Robbery bears only a notional resemblance to Scott Marble's 1896 melodrama from which the film takes its title. What film and stage drama share in the way of plot is a conspiracy to rob a gold shipment carried in a railway mail car. Both play and film depict the robbers dynamiting the gold chest, an explosion of small consequence in the film, but which, onstage, wrecks the mail car and precipitates a final gun battle between outlaws and pursuers. Stage play and film draw closer to each other in the manner in which both dramas use the convention of a frontier cabaret to incorporate variety turns.

In Marble's play, this device is clear enough to require little explication. We observe Marble creating spaces for musical and variety numbers which could be changed at short notice during their westward tour from Boston into the Ohio Circuit with the Davis and Keogh combination company. Reviews from the play's 1896 opening tour and its subsequent 1904 revival are alike in referring derisively to The Great Train Robbery's convoluted plot and extensive gunplay, but the same reviews are invariably enthusiastic about the variety acts on offer.

Toward the end of the second act, set in The Never Shut Saloon of an unnamed frontier settlement, Marble's script introduces Broncho Joe, improbably both a U.S. Marshal and a saloon proprietor. These overlapping identities will enable Broncho Joe to apprehend the gold thieves and train dynamiters, but, more immediately, to act as master of ceremonies to a sequence of variety specialties in an impromptu cabaret, the acts cast from a pool of artists in any given section of the tour.[10] As supernumeraries, dancers, and the principal characters come on stage, Broncho Joe greets them and calls for attention: "Boys and Gals, we're going to have an entertainment tonight. The first man that pounds on the table with a beer glass or shoots out the lights will have to answer to me. Got that?"

This cabaret format gives Broncho Joe's character a free hand in controlling variety turns. He may introduce, as numerous reviews and a surviving Davis and Keogh playbill with penciled-in emendations suggest, whip acts, knife throwers, trick shooters, rope spinners, acrobats, and Miss Wolfe, an artist who simultaneously played the harp and danced.[11] When these turns finish, Broncho Joe demands a song, "Frank's Specialty," performed by a female member of the melodrama company who wears male attire as a disguise enabling her to accompany her brother into western territory. A further variety turn, introduced as "Sergeant Flynn of the U.S. Cavalry," brings on a bear which wrestles first with its trainer and then, comically, with the character Joshua Glue—who has previously boasted of his no-holds-barred wrestling prowess.[12] As the bear act concludes, Broncho Joe commands the company:

> Take your partners for a dance. (Music cue. No.11)
> Music. (All rise, put tables and chairs aside. Clear stage for dance)

As the dancers begin their reels and squares, a drunken "bad man from Dead Man's Gulch" enters demanding a fight and is quickly disarmed and ejected from the saloon. With the dancing continuing, Crazy Dog, an Indian hostile to Broncho Joe, enters and attempts to knife him, but is caught and restrained by supernumeraries costumed as cowboys. Still, without interrupting the dances, the violent bad man reappears, attempts to abduct the heroine, and the act finally concludes in a tableau in which local cowboys, with pistols drawn, face armed bandits and Indians, while the dancers freeze in poses of terror.

A similar episode in Porter's film, with its mixture of gunplay and hoedown, echoes Marble's melodrama: Porter's cabaret, an episode with dancing as the form of variety which will effectively translate to the screen, begins after the mail train has been robbed and its guard killed in a shoot-out with the bandits. The train's fireman has also been killed, his body thrown from the moving train, and a fleeing passenger has also been shot dead. A small girl, bringing her father, a telegrapher, his lunch at the railroad depot, finds him tied up and thrown to the floor. She frees him, and he rises up to give the alarm. Pursuit might begin immediately at this point, but, instead, and perhaps to a modern audience's frustration, the film cuts first to an intertitle, "A lively quadrille,"[13] and then to a frontier dance hall where four couples enjoy a square dance. Their dance is interrupted as a city dude is pushed center stage and, to the accompaniment of gunfire, executes a nimble step dance. The cowboy and cowgirl

Poster for *The Great Train Robbery*, ca. 1897, drawing attention to one of the play's variety features: a cowboy wrestling a bear. Library of Congress.

dancers then re-form for a reel. Only when this third dance, with its complicated figures, is nearing its conclusion does the newly freed telegrapher burst
into the dance hall to report the crime and to recruit an instant posse from the
dancers. This deliberate break in narrative to enjoy variety turns is the visible
legacy of combination melodrama.

In Porter's other 1903 feature, *Uncle Tom's Cabin*, filmed with the performers
and scenic drops[14] from an unidentified "Tom combination" passing through
New Jersey,[15] the combination structure becomes even more apparent. Here,
two discrete companies of performers—a troupe of white actors, some of them
"blacked-up" for Negro roles within the melodrama, and a second troupe of
African American dancers—have been introduced into a single drama: the
white actors advance the drama's plot and necessary incidents; the African
American dancers appear among the white actors in three different scenes. The
black dancers contribute first, an energetic dockside shuffle as a Mississippi
steamboat ties up. They return in a later scene to enliven a quite evening with an
exuberant cakewalk as Tom and Eva sit placidly in a plantation garden. Finally,
they perform an inappropriately lively dance, quite out of keeping with their role
as disposable chattels soon to be auctioned to white bidders.

In both live performance and the filmed drama, interruptions in narrative
for the sake of these variety turns did not unduly frustrate audiences anxious for
the plot to move forward. Rather, spectators appeared to enjoy such digressive
moments and were capable of picking up plot threads as the dramatic action
again moved forward. With the arrival of sound films, variety turns again
appeared as nightclub scenes in screen melodramas and film noir. Placed in
comedies, variety entertainments were more promiscuously scattered, although
in many instances a single entertainment, rather than a sequence of turns, was
on offer.[16]

All combination companies were obliged to travel. All needed to meet local
conditions, proclaim their arrival, and draw audiences. All had to house and
feed their performers, then depart for their next destinations as efficiently as
they arrived. *Julius Cahn's Official Theatrical Guide*[17] underscores the strategies for
mobility and on-the-road efficiency necessary to theatrical survival. Cahn's
Guide also functions as an infallible index to the state of the American theatre
during the fifteen-year period which spans Griffith's introduction, as a spectator, to the theatres of Louisville and, later, his actor's apprenticeship, and, still
later, his success as a scenarist, actor, and director at Biograph. Sold for a dollar and published annually between 1896 and 1913, Cahn's *Guide* is, first and
foremost, an exhaustive listing of every theatre in North America served by
professional theatre companies during the years when many hundreds of pro-

Poster for Al W. Martin's combination company touring of *Uncle Tom's Cabin*, 1898. Rather than stressing the drama's narrative of slavery and abuse, Martin promoted the company's variety acts and, in this instance, its cakewalk dance performed by its second cast of African American specialty acts. Martin advertised that his company numbered fifty white and African American performers.

fessional theatre companies toured the continent, thanks in great measure to the network of railroads linking over 3,500 theatre buildings in cities, towns, and villages. Each of these communities, the *Guide* demonstrates, was dependent on the regular and efficient deployment of such entertainments as comedies and melodramas, Shakespearean plays and pieces from the modern classical repertoire, burlesques, musical comedies, circus, and vaudeville.

Addressing tour managers and entrepreneurs who would, of necessity, require the vast and remarkably intricate national railway network to plan their touring schedules and carry scenery appropriate to the venues in which they performed, Cahn supplied the horizontal and vertical dimensions of each stage, enumerating traps, bridges, electrical supply, and other technical features (but not film projection equipment), the seating capacity of every auditorium, admission prices, the identities of the local house management and musical director, details of services for the transfer of baggage and scenery from the railroad depot, the titles and frequency of local newspapers, the names and price ranges of hotels catering to theatrical people, and the names of local poster and program printers and bill posters.

Further portions of this producer's and manager's vademecum separately listed the theatrical facilities of the nation's principal cities. New York, for example, had forty-eight "legitimate" theatres in 1900, venues which featured the spoken or musical drama where, annually, approximately 170 new plays appeared between September and May.[18] Cahn listed thirty-one variety houses or "illegitimate" theatres where vaudeville and burlesques were on offer. Louisville, with a population of 210,000 during the period of Griffith's adolescence and early manhood, had, by contrast, some seven to nine commercial theatres which offered drama, variety, minstrelsy, burlesque, and pyrodramas (firework spectacles). The number of theatres in operation fluctuated as theatres changed owners, went dark, or were replaced by new or refurbished playhouses. Four daily newspaper reported Louisville's news and theatrical events. Significantly, its theatres were served by ten railroads, making it one of the more accessible theatre venues in the nation.

Further segments of Cahn's *Guide* listed theatres, state by state and town by town. Tent theatres and other itinerant show places were not included. It listed, separately, theatrical production agencies, actors' agents, and those theatres controlled by the Theatrical Syndicate (also known as the Theatrical Trust). Further lists identified those theatres, about 200 in number, which were stock companies—theatres with more or less permanent companies offering a seasonal repertoire of plays and other entertainments. Of even greater importance to the theatrical economy and in determining the configuration and content of numerous stage plays, Cahn identified traveling companies and their managers. Thus, in any year there were approximately 850 traveling drama companies, more than half of which were combinations. The remainder were companies built around actor-managers who appeared in a limited repertoire of Shakespearean and modern classic plays, companies in which stars—actors and athletes—recreated their metropolitan successes, and musical variety troupes.

Also, separately cited by Cahn, were approximately a dozen traveling circuses, ninety burlesque companies, and twenty minstrel troupes. Cahn irregularly listed touring African American musical and dramatic companies which began to appear on circuits, mainly after 1890,[19] but he did not identify the theatres under black management which booked these companies or list hotels or other amenities which accommodated black performers on the road. Although a smaller parallel theatrical world for African American performers was emerging, with distinct circuits and venues for black performers and audiences (who would later protest at The Clansman and The Birth of a Nation), these developments went unnoticed by Cahn's Guide.

Serving the primary need for company mobility, Cahn's Guide identified the names of railroad booking agents and the railroads they served. The Guide reveals the sheer scale of the late nineteenth-century continental railway system—the distances covered and the cities and hamlets which lay along their routes. Detailed railway maps, the routes of major and lesser routes, appeared throughout, often in immediate proximity to listings of theatres served by these routes. The annual publication of Julius Cahn's Official Theatrical Guide emphatically demonstrated that the theatrical economy of America, closely leagued with the railway industry, was located in the hinterlands as much as in the metropolitan centers.

The importance of the railways to theatrical touring is apparent in the career of Julia Marlowe, whose performance, most likely as Parthenia in Ingomar, was recalled by Griffith as his introduction to theatre.[20] Marlowe appeared in New York in 1887, but, failing to win critical approval, defiantly and resolutely toured her repertoire of Shakespearean pieces (Romeo and Juliet, Twelfth Night, As You Like It, Henry IV) and modern repertory classics (Ingomar the Barbarian, The Hunchback, Pygmalion and Galatea) throughout the South and the midwestern and border states from 1890 until 1897. Traveling by rail, she appeared semiannually, or even at quarterly intervals in Louisville at Macauley's Theatre with her then-husband Robert Taber. Marlowe's company traveled exclusively—and almost continually—until 1897, when New York audiences became more receptive to her performances. She could then undertake long engagements in that city and enjoy the luxury of shorter hauls to other eastern cities. Separating from Taber in 1899 and marrying Edward Sothern in 1900, Marlowe continued national and regional touring well into the twentieth century. In 1912 she was recognized as an actress whose evident wealth was earned almost entirely through touring.[21]

Whatever financial inducements combination companies held for theatrical entrepreneurs, life on the road for the actors in the company was arduous, uncomfortable, and exhausting. However, with time, theatrical touring, directly dependent on the railways, was to some degree responsible for bringing comfort to railway travel. Railroads upgraded the standard of their accommodations and, in advertisements aimed directly at theatrical managers and producers, proclaimed the efficiency of their operations and the ease of connection to towns and cities along their routes. An advertisement for the Pennsylvania Line, found in Cahn's *Guide*, depicts a man in an easy chair, feet up, smoking a cigar and declaring, "Ah! This is something like it! Really pays Managers to route their Companies over the Pennsylvania. The trip is a pleasure; keeps everybody in good spirits; they work better." Another advertisement for the same line depicts a couple in a private compartment, he sitting, she standing at a full-length mirror. Their dialogue reads, "Dear, don't you think long jumps are delightful when they are over the Pennsylvania?"—"Indeed I do! Any trip over 'The Standard Railroad of America' is a pleasure."

Griffith was to grow familiar with theatrical circuits, formerly routes for "star" actors making their journeys between stock companies, but latterly railroad routes and endless successions of small-town and modest city "opera houses" to which companies traveled until paying audiences dried up. In the 1880s, as theatrical companies established and cemented their alliance with the railway system, these previously rudimentary circuits were vastly elaborated and consolidated. Railway maps provide some indication of the regional configurations of some circuits, but, as these were published by discrete rail companies, they fail to suggest linkages to other rail lines and means of expanding tours. Many circuits were geographic: the Montana Circuit (extending from Spokane through Anaconda, Missoula, Butte, reaching into Idaho and eastward to Minnesota and south to Milwaukee), the Ohio Circuit (dipping into the border states and Indiana). Other circuits were known by the communities served: the Petroleum Circuit (Pennsylvania) and the Silver Circuit (Colorado's mining communities). Still other circuits became known by the names of theatre owners and lease holders who determined bookings in their region: McVickers-Miner Circuit (theatres eastward from Chicago), Jacobs and Procter Circuit (Midwest).

Theatres and theatrical facilities, although supposedly standardized for touring, might vary substantially. In Leadville, Colorado, where coal was mined as well as metallic ores, the Tabor Grand Opera House (later the Elks' Opera House) was illuminated by coal gas from its opening in 1879 until 1908. Just across the Continental Divide in Aspen (formerly Silver City), where the Roaring Fork's rushing current had provided hydroelectric lighting and power for the mines from the 1870s, the Wheeler Opera House, erected in 1889, was lit with electric bulbs. The Tabor's stage house was built with its gridiron far enough above stage level to permit flown scenery, whereas the Wheeler stage, like the Tabor's, located on the top floor of a three-story building, was constructed with an "underhung" gridiron which was suitable for rolled canvas backcloths but permitted no large scenic pieces to be flown.

A further consequence of the theatre's increasing link to the railways is visible in the emergence of the theatrical agent. It was the area of theatre management which Griffith best understood. Beyond this comparatively low function, his business acumen disintegrated. The agent functioned as the intermediary between financial investors and theatrical companies. Agents booked companies, sought major theatres to receive the companies, and negotiated percentages of takings to be allocated to the touring company at each venue played. Such centralized bookings enabled predetermined circuits for each tour. Agents thus managed to control companies and the circuits themselves without the necessity of either owning or leasing theatres. Agents accordingly chose the major destinations for each tour and allowed company managers discretionary responsibility for fitting in intermediate stops and lesser venues. By the early 1880s agents began to acquire performance rights and outright ownership to new and profitable scripts and to obtain dramatic copyright in their own names. This degree of managerial control, dominating the playwright, and continually encroaching on the authority of the actor-manager and company manager, immediately foreshadowed the advent of the Theatrical Syndicate which soon became notorious for supporting popular performers and easily enjoyed—and commercially successful—dramatic pieces while suppressing the New Drama and barring more challenging young performers[22] from its circuits.

The Theatrical Syndicate, or "Syndicate," as it came to be known, was a further shaping element in Griffith's introduction to the theatre. As an actor, a touring vaudevillian appearing in his own sketch, a dramatic author, and—eventually—a film director, his work thrust him into contacts and contracts with the Syndicate and other trustlike business structures for the first twenty years of his professional life. The Syndicate was organized by Marc Klaw, Abraham Erlanger, who controlled theatres in the southern states, and Charles and Daniel Frohman, owners of theatres in New York, Baltimore, Philadelphia, and in the western states.[23] The Syndicate, undeniably, was an ambiguous presence, a monopolistic dictatorship—or a dictatorial monopoly—which, through its coast-to-coast ownership and control of more than 700 theatres, brought a ruthless efficiency to parts of the theatrical world. For example, the Syndicate meticulously organized the seven-month tour for Henry Irving's 1899–1900 American visit. Every theatre on Irving's route was a Syndicate-owned and -controlled theatre. Sir Henry was a prize package. He was treated with consideration and accorded comforts wherever possible, but the schedule was unremitting; the logistics of maintaining that schedule are astonishing. Other tours may have been similarly efficient and some even more rigorous, but lesser acting companies and individuals would have expected fewer comforts and experienced lesser considerations. Whether comfortable or rigorous and austere, such tours could not be duplicated today.

The same protective mantle of the Syndicate shielded the several tours of Thomas Dixon Jr.'s The Clansman between 1905 and 1907. Its tour dates organized by Klaw and Erlanger, performing exclusively in Syndicate-owned or -controlled theatres, and bolstered by Klaw and Erlanger–retained lawyers, The Clansman survived hostile receptions from African Americans and other parties who sought the play's closure.

However efficient the Syndicate may have been, it also destroyed actors' and managerial careers and fomented—or replicated—labor strife comparable to the strikes, blacklistings, and lockouts experienced in other professions and crafts during this period. Depending on one's view of the Syndicate, it was a successful business operation to create a theatrical monopoly or a deliberate strangling of the theatrical trade—keeping shows from touring and actors from appearing in theatres of their choice. In fact, it was both. The Syndicate was formed in August 1896, and remained active until 1912, although its restrictive practices lasted somewhat longer and impacted the American motion picture business well into the 1920s. Klaw, Erlanger, and the Frohmans, together with a small group of other regional—Southern, Midwestern, and Eastern—theatre owners, devised a system which assured that leading theatrical companies and individual artists were booked with them and thereafter routed by them. Once contracted by the Syndicate, appearances in non-Syndicate theatres were forbidden, appearances and deviations punished with blacklisting and financial ruin. Sarah Bernhardt held out against the Syndicate and toured America, appearing, as a consequence, in a circus tent, hired for the occasion from Barnum & Bailey, and public skating rinks.[24] It is certain that the Syndicate inspired the innocently named Motion Picture Patents Company (MPPC) which, for a limited and difficult time, held motion picture companies and creative workers in a stranglehold.

The Motion Picture Patents Company was originally formed to extract royalty payments from users of the Edison camera and projection equipment and to bind these users into an exclusive contract to prevent patent infringement. However, because the cameras of Griffith's employer, Biograph, and other film producers worked effectively without Edison devices and because it was possible to obtain Edison cameras and to use these cameras in remote locales out of sight of the MPPC's agents, film production companies became adept at circumventing the MPPC. One of the principal reasons behind Griffith's 1910 wintertime expedition to California and the dusty village of Hollywood was that the West Coast lay beyond the range of the MPPC's spies. Nevertheless, the MPPC, in attempting to maintain control, resorted to blacklisting actors and producers who chose to work for the "independents" and attempted to control distributors and exhibitors by denying MPPC films to those which exhibited independent-made films. The MPPC's power was challenged under antitrust legislation, and, by 1912, it was declared illegal.

It is characteristic of Griffith that, with respect to the Theatrical Syndicate and, to a lesser degree, the MPPC, he worked both with the monopolizers and, more evasively and less openly, against them. His own sketch, In Washington's Time, was toured along American vaudeville circuits as a strikebreaking act at a time when the vaudeville artists' union, the "White Rats," was boycotting the Keith-Albee partnership for having attempted to extend Syndicate-like control over variety performers. Yet business monopolies and trusts and restrictive clauses figure in his films as unfair practices harmful to working people and, ultimately, to the American economy. Films, none of them derived from stage plays, in which Griffith ventures into the workplace owe their settings and their subject matter to the troubled history of the American labor movement: the founding in the late 1880s of the radical International Workers of the World and thereafter the fruitful agitations and polemics of various "Wobblies," free thinkers, democrats and others who, influenced by European socialism, authored the allegedly seditious manifestos, led the strikes, and theorized political actions which resulted in the modern labor movement. Griffith's entry into the acting and motion picture professions coincides with a succession of miners' strikes, worker uprisings, assassinations, and armed railway seizures counterbalanced and opposed by covert presidential and congressional maneuvering, political kidnappings, arbitrary imprisonments, massive infiltration of nascent unions by private detectives and agents provocateurs, conspiracy trials, and the shooting of factory workers by private agents and the U.S. National Guard, which preoccupied the American people from 1902 through 1914. Griffith's responses to these events are varied, inconsistent, but always immediate and visceral.

Both the Edison-Porter *Uncle Tom's Cabin* and *The Great Train Robbery* are notable for their brevity, and that brevity extends to other films derived from stage plays. Entire dramatic plots—a four- or even six-act play—are crammed into films rarely exceeding a fifteen-minutes projection time. In the first years of motion pictures and up to the year 1913, the point at which the middle classes began to patronize films and when longer films accordingly became desirable and financially viable, all films were necessarily brief. Porter's audiences experienced a complete melodrama compressed into a twelve-minute span. In the single instance of *The Great Train Robbery*, the incidents and narrative are self-explanatory and are not compromised by the film's brevity. Other contemporary and near-contemporary films adapted from stage melodramas posed severe problems of clarity and, given the need to compress or abridge their numerous incidents, tended to be episodic and disjointed. The addition of intertitles informing of locations and containing scraps of dialogue further lengthened a film and added to its cost.

By the early twentieth century, American audiences and readers had become familiar with the plots and major incidents of long-established plays and novels. Professional dramatizations of *Uncle Tom's Cabin* were known to American audiences in several popular adaptations from the mid-1850s.[25] Dion Boucicault's version of Washington Irving's novel *Rip Van Winkle* was toured by Joseph Jefferson from 1870 and was pirated and emulated in rival versions well into the twentieth century. Henry Herman's and Henry Arthur Jones's *The Silver King* was being performed on American circuits beginning in 1883, only a year after the play had opened in London. Nagged and cajoled by Abraham Erlanger and Marc Klaw of the Theatrical Syndicate, Lew Wallace, the novelist, eventually permitted William Young to dramatize *Ben-Hur* (1880), the most popular novel ever, for a spectacular production which appeared in 1899 and toured into the 1920s. The Edison-Porter film version of *Uncle Tom's Cabin* (1903), Kalem's *Ben-Hur* (1907)—illicitly adapted from William Young's six-act drama and compressed into six "tableaux,"[26] Sigmund Lubin's *The Silver King* (1908), and the several adaptations of Joseph Jefferson's *Rip Van Winkle* (1896, 1897, and 1902),[27] all took advantage of their audiences' prior familiarity with the dramas and the capacity to fill in lacunae within the narrative. Without that prior knowledge of the plot points, many of these filmed adaptations are unintelligible. Such films consequently offer substantial evidence that audience members who could afford to do so habitually attended both live theatre performances and exhibiting films.

The brevity of early narrative films further suggests that, rather than full-scale theatrical melodramas and comedies, there is likely to have been a more appropriately compact model for brief dramatic films. Undeniably, there were strong and continual influences from the major theatrical genres, but there was another live theatrical influence closer to hand. Apart from early attempts to introduce motion pictures to American audiences, cinema was not viewed in legitimate theatres but—invariably—in variety houses, chiefly in a revived vaudeville which included a selection of films—the biograph or bioscope—as a part of its standard program of live entertainments. Programs across a range of national variety styles—British music hall, French café-concert and vaudeville, American vaudeville—reveal two species of live variety performance which might have influenced narrative film: the dramatic sketch and the narrative ballet. Both were brief, dramatic, and narrative; both prepared variety audiences for short narrative dramas on film. Griffith was exposed to both, but was immediately influenced by the sketch.

The dramatic sketch was more prevalent than narrative ballet across Europe and America because it used fewer performers. It did not oblige touring with a musical director and ballet master; it required less in the way of mise-en-scène, and, overall, was cheaper to tour. Narrative ballet was popular and common in the metropolitan centers but far rarer in the provinces and small circuits. Therefore, the vaudeville or music hall dramatic sketch often served as the convenient model for early narrative film. Unsurprisingly, many of these first narrative films incorporate actual sketches or were devised by persons who had direct experience with the vaudeville sketch. Skill in sketch writing entailed dramatizing a complete narrative, devising characters who were recognizable and individually distinct, while assuring that plot situations and subtle hints to characters' intellectual and emotional states were made unambiguously evident through visible physical action. Dialogue might be employed, but its virtue lay in sparseness. The sketch actor was obliged to show rather than explain, to do rather than speak. A sketch might be marginally longer than a two-reel narrative, but the requirements for each métier, sketch, and one- and two-reel films remained similar. Griffith, experienced as an actor in sketches and an author of a successful sketch, brought his ability to compress narrative into this compact form to his productive years with Biograph.

As a theatrical form, the dramatic sketch entered American vaudeville as a foreign import, initially characterized as a complete drama, its playing time rarely exceeding eighteen minutes' duration, performed by no more than six actors, with its dialogue restricted to short lines and the explanatory narrative needed to clarify the action either printed in the program or, more often, sung by an actor at the side of the stage. Dance, usually in the form of a narrative ballet, might be a further feature, but such additions did not enable the sketch to exceed the agreed playing time. This compact and terse form of drama was the invention of the English music hall and arose, and rapidly took hold, in the early 1890s.

Performers in sketches and the sketches themselves became a part of the transatlantic traffic between Britain and America. Sketches appeared in American vaudeville as early as 1895, a year before the first motion pictures were exhibited in American vaudeville theatres. Initially, the constraints of British rules and practices regulating the duration and extent of speech employed in the sketch together served to keep dialogue sparse. In America, however, there were fewer constraints. As the popularity of the vaudeville sketch expanded and as more American authors and performers developed their own sketches, the quantity of dialogue increased, and the sketch's duration lengthened above twenty minutes. It was not uncommon to find longer stage dramas, both comedies and melodramas, severely abridged for vaudeville or to find major stars playing pared-down versions of their vehicles to vaudeville audiences. Sarah Bernhardt, for example, contrived to make a vaudeville sketch from a medley of roles in which she had formerly toured American legitimate houses.[28] To appear in vaudeville was not a descent from the lofty heights of the legitimate stage to the degradation of the itinerant variety artist which some film and theatre historians might imagine. Rather, stepping into vaudeville was, in the closing years of the nineteenth century and the early decades of the twentieth, a conventional tactic for prolonging the life of a stage play whose popularity was marginal or visibly waning. It was a favored way of earning a theatrical livelihood when the national economy, and with it, the legitimate stage, experienced fallow periods. Actors of stature—the entire Drew and Barrymore clans, Gertrude Lamson ("Nance O'Neil") in whose company Griffith worked in 1904, and Griffith's mentor, friend, and employer McKee Rankin—moved their dramas onto variety circuits when business slackened, then returned to the theatre when conditions improved or new roles beckoned.

Three sketch performers, Denman Thompson, Will Cressy, and his wife Blanche Dayne, deserve recognition because, through the agency of vaudeville, they contributed to a regional stereotype which Griffith and other filmmakers were later to draw upon: the "rube," a sagacious, crafty, slow-speaking, warmhearted New England farmer. Thompson (1833–1911) moved between the legitimate stage in America, Canada, and England, turning to American vaudeville at the end of the Civil War. At some point in the 1870s he created a sketch character, "Uncle Josh Whitcomb," a rural New Englander searching for his errant son in New York City and beseeching New Yorkers for assistance and advice. With his Uncle Josh at the center of his sketch, Thompson was able to introduce a brief medley of New York characters, comic and serious and, frequently, eth-

Orpheum Circuit poster, ca. 1900, advertising a b'gosh comedy
vaudeville sketch by Will M. Cressy and Blanche Dayne.

nic—and replaceable as the sketch toured—who helped him reunite with the
missing boy. In 1885, Thompson rewrote his sketch as a four-act combination
drama, *The Old Homestead*, and thereafter toured legitimate circuits to critical
acclaim and considerable profit. *The Old Homestead* substantially repeats the plot
of Thompson's original sketch but also enabled the introduction of further
characters from rural New Hampshire and New York who would entertain with
their own comic shtick. To this degree *The Old Homestead* follows the pattern set
by Leonard Grover's combination light comedy, *Our Boarding House* (1876),
which mixes narrative drama with eccentric boarders, the roles usually taken by
variety performers and character actors, who break up the narrative with comic
turns. Other comedies used the setting of a Pullman parlor car or a pawnbroker's establishment as a means of introducing variety acts. Thompson's Uncle
Josh, meanwhile, became an autonomous character, taken up by other vaude-
villians and memorably made the central character in an Edison film, *Uncle Josh
at the Moving-Picture Show* (1902), who, patronizing a nickelodeon, runs from a
projected image of a locomotive rushing toward the camera.

Will Cressy's rube character was developed on Martin Beck's Orpheum
vaudeville circuit. Unlike Thompson's Uncle Josh, Cressy's characters, apparently naive and unacquainted with city ways, showed themselves smarter than

the sophisticated worldy urban intruder, usually played by Blanche Dayne, who enters their lives.[29] In his sketch, *Grasping an Opportunity* (1900), Cressy outwits a female photographer searching for local color. The settings for Cressy's sketches were variants on the standard New England farm set with a layout used both by Thompson for *The Old Homestead* and by Brady when staging *'Way Down East*.

Despite the numerous variants of the vaudeville sketch, each sketch nonetheless conformed to the structural needs of the vaudeville bill. Performers were engaged and their acts spaced through the program in accordance with the effect each "turn" was expected to create. Normally, there were two slots on the bill for sketches or "playlets," but drama increasingly encroached on territory formerly filled by singers, dancers, jugglers, and comics. In 1915—in Brett Page's *Writing for Vaudeville*—the rationale for the bill's structure was published to guide aspirant sketch writers. Page explained:

> There is no keener psychologist than a vaudeville manager. Not only does he present the best of everything that can be shown upon a stage, but he so arranges the heterogeneous elements that they combine to form a unified whole.

Page then enumerates the preferred sequence of a nine-act program: a "dumb act"—dancers or animals—to open the show, a "typical vaudeville act"—"man and woman singing"—to settle the audience, then, crucially,

> With number three position we count on waking up the audience. The show has been properly started and from now on it must build right up to the finish. So we offer a comedy dramatic sketch—a playlet that . . . holds the audience every minute with a cumulative effect that comes to its laughter-climax at the 'curtain.'

The sketch is followed, Page explains, by a headliner and this act is then followed by another major turn, "a big dancing act—one of those delightful novelties vaudeville likes so well . . . so we select one of the best acts on the bill to crown the first half of the show." The conclusion of this fifth turn brings an intermission.

The program's second half begins, Page specifies, with "an act that is not stronger than the acts that are to follow . . . [preferably] a strong vaudeville specialty, with comedy well to the fore." A further sketch then follows:

> The second act after intermission—number seven—must be stronger than the first. It is usually a full-stage act . . . very likely it is a big playlet. . . . It may

be a comedy playlet or even a serious dramatic playlet, if the star is a fine actor or actress and the name is well known.

This second sketch is followed by "the comedy hit of the show, one of the acts for which the audience has been waiting . . . one of the famous 'single' man or 'single' woman acts that vaudeville has made such favorites." Finally, in ninth position, is "the act that closes the show. We count on the fact that some of the audience will be going out."[30] That "act which closes the show" was increasingly, from 1900, the bioscope or vitascope, a program of mixed films—some narrative, some actuality footage.

The dramatic sketch became an accidental model for one- and two-reel narrative films partly through its close proximity on the variety bill to the bioscope portion of the vaudeville or music hall program and partly because of the conditions which accompanied performance and film projection. In the early 1880s, theatres and music halls began turning down or eliminating the gas lighting in their auditoriums to better accommodate the new electric stage lighting which could be focused and add color to costumes and settings. When, some fifteen years later, vaudeville theatres and music halls began to exhibit films, low levels of auditorium lighting became essential. Audiences, seated in the dark, viewed a film program, usually of some twenty-five minutes' duration, in which approximately ten films were projected. By custom, the bioscope became one of the final events on the variety program, often immediately following the dramatic sketch, a drama between eighteen and twenty-five minutes long, frequently the penultimate turn on the variety program. Both of these entertainments were accompanied by incidental music which interpreted situations, actions, and characters. Variety house audiences, thus exposed, were conditioned by the condensed narratives of the dramatic sketch to expect—and to understand—film narratives of comparable duration.

Henry Jenkins and Robert C. Allen severally argue the existence of a distinct vaudeville aesthetic which differentiated vaudeville from the legitimate theatre and which subsequently transferred from vaudeville into film. Jenkins, describing the relationship between the spectator and the individual turn, cites the immediacy of vaudeville. The performer was obliged to engage immediately with the spectator, and the spectator required immediate gratification. Unlike the legitimate theatre, there was no pretense of a "fourth wall" separating the performer from the audience.[31] Neither was there expectation of a narrative coherence to the overall program. Allen adds that the spectator never needed to question the relationship of one turn to another, and the narrative content of the sketch, which audiences were capable of understanding and enjoying, was contained wholly within it.[32] The bioscope segment of the vaudeville program was similarly made up of discrete films, few, if any, of which had any connection with other films shown on the program. Each film was selected for its immediate appeal or discarded when it failed to amuse. Brief narrative films, as they arrived, were treated with the same concentration as the dramatic sketch.

The theatre which Griffith was to encounter, first as a spectator, and, later, as an apprentice actor, and, still later, as a dramatist, was in flux between 1890 and 1908. Collapse of independent stock companies, large-scale movement of dramatic productions by the nation's revived and expanded rail system, capitalizing of individual productions designed to tour, merging and uniting of drama and variety into combinations, standardizing scenery, systematizing touring practice, attempts to impose monopolistic business practices on a dispersed theatre, and the advent and proliferation of the dramatic sketch, all, jointly and severally, point to a major realignment of theatre commerce. This flux was not occasioned by a collision between—as sometimes imagined—an established comfortable commodity theatre and a bumptious avant-garde. Rather such instability was the result of the American theatre changing from a cottage craft to a burgeoning industrial economy bringing faster and more efficient transportation and factory disciplines imposed on reluctant and non-comprehending workers. Combinations, organized variety, trusts, and strikes tested and shaped the industry. Narrative motion pictures, copying the vaudeville sketch, transferred the stage onto celluloid. What no one could yet foresee was the way in which these images on film, mechanically and cheaply copied and widely distributed so that actors could be viewed performing in more than one venue at a time, would further industrialize the American entertainment business. Motion pictures were to be even more ruthlessly industrialized than the stage, the camera, projector, industry-standard 35 mm film, would-be monopolies and blacklists, and efficient distribution systems: the tools which enabled eventual change. These developments, like Griffith's entry into theatre, lay beyond the horizon.

2 Actor and Playwright

A publicity photo taken for the *Miss Petticoats* tour between mid-September and mid-October 1903, shows the actor, "Lawrence Griffith," standing right of center stage, his legs apart, knees locked, weight awkwardly and uncomfortably back on his heels, Anchored thus, there is no actor's energy to carry him forward to his next moment. Nor is there energy in his shoulders. His arms hang by his sides. His idle hands convey no gesture. His head is upright. There is no expression of alarm or dismay or dumbfounded innocence on his unperturbed face. And yet, in his role of the caddish serial philanderer Guy Hamilton in this adaptation of Dwight Tilton's 1902 novel *Miss Petticoats*, he faces an alarming situation. The woman he has pursued, insulted, and compromised, Agatha Renier, "Miss Petticoats," here portrayed by the leading actress Kathryn Osterman, is sheltered within the protecting arm of his Aunt Sarah Copeland (Agnes Worden). Aunt Sarah, with an imperious, commanding gesture and with words to match, demands that Guy leave at once: "I tell you, Guy, nephew of mine though you are, that I would rather see Agatha dead at my feet than your wife. Now go; my house can be your house no longer." If, as the cliché runs, "acting is reacting," Griffith fails to return the ball. He is not acting.

If this publicity photo had been taken in 1896, or even 1897, when a young Griffith was still very much in his actor's apprenticeship, his physical disengagement and facial blankness might be excused as the responses of an actor who had much to learn. But, because this photo was made in 1903, and as he had at least six years' stage experience, this photograph depicts Griffith, a man of deplorably finite acting prowess, in a dead-end job.

In 1896, Griffith was preparing to enter the theatre as an actor. He had witnessed theatrical performances for at least three years as a

Agnes Worden (Aunt Sarah) reproves the philanderer Guy Hamilton
("Laurence" Griffith) for his caddish behavior to Agatha Reiner
(Kathryn Osterman), *Miss Petticoats*, 1903. Private Collection.

spectator in most, if not all, of Louisville's eight playhouses, and, for two years,
he had studied voice and elocution with a local teacher. This much is known
about his earliest years. Much else is, of necessity, speculation. In 1890, thirteen
years before Griffith appeared in his first and only known theatrical photographs, the Griffith family had moved to Louisville, and a nineteen-year-old
David Griffith made his first theatre visits. There is no exact record of what he
saw and what he enjoyed. Griffith's own recollections of his Louisville theatre-
going are few and do not stand up to close examination. But it is possible to
suggest what Griffith may have seen—what was there to be seen—and remembered.

Griffith's practical theatrical education emerged from the roles which he
undertook from 1896 and from other productions which he may have encountered on the road. It was not uncommon for touring actors to see the final acts
of plays and to attend matinees and benefits at adjacent and nearby theatres,
entering the foyers, encountering ushers or doorkeepers, and, once recognized
as professionals, "getting in on their [make-up streaked] collars."[1] Some of
these plays and dramatic sketches witnessed on the road may have appealed to

A second photograph of "Laurence" Griffith onstage as Guy Hamilton, here attempting to justify a failed attempt at seduction. *Miss Petticoats*, 1903. Private Collection.

him as an aspirant playwright. From this limited and sometimes conjectural information it is possible to describe the theatrical environment, and the profession of the actor, especially the minor actor, as Griffith experienced it.

Griffith's years as an actor and the arc of that brief career have been documented by the film historian Russell Merritt.[2] Merritt views the theatre as an unhealthy environment from which Griffith required "rescue." Further, Merritt describes Griffith's entry into motion pictures as a fortuitous "escape." Richard Schickel, without demurring, echoes this view. Merritt and Schickel briefly described the theatrical environment itself, but they are understandably reluctant to valorize or even explore this environment. Theatre is mere prelude to be passed over quickly, an obligation, rather than an opportunity for the biographer.

In the 1890s Griffith could not have aspired to a career option that did not exist—that he could not have imagined. He drew upon what he knew in order to create his motion picture career. Theatre is what mattered, to Griffith and to a large majority of early film innovators. It was what they knew. It was their environment and their aspired profession. Moreover, it remained one of the primary viewing contexts for their audiences well after 1912, the point at which purpose-built movie theatres began to be constructed. Consequently, the historian, wherever possible, must reconstruct the theatrical environment as Griffith explored it, to comment on circumstances of employment, company organization, and venues in which these companies performed. Equally important, the historian needs to note the gaps between acting jobs, almost invariably times of stress and privation, because these breaks are always a part of an actor's life and invariably affect immediate choices and longer-term actions. Indeed, these very privations drove Griffith at the end of 1907 or the earliest days of 1908, to take the step of seeking work as a motion picture actor. Acting in films was a move he regarded as desperate and shameful. His true identity was disguised by pseudonyms, lest he be recognized and discovered, damaging his stage career. It was never Griffith's intention to remain a film actor.

Griffith's occasional turns to playwriting, devising both vaudeville sketches and full-length plays, signals a further manifestation of the irregularities and privations of the actor's life. His vaudeville sketch (1901), known only through reviews, and his two full-length plays (1906 and 1907) surviving only in the form of early typescripts, offer scant evidence of how his one produced play, an artistic and financial failure, was reshaped in trials and rehearsals. This material confirms that Griffith possessed a strong sense of the dramatic and the ability to visualize complex action on stages crowded with actors and supernumeraries. His two plays provide immediate evidence that he had a bad ear for dialogue and was strongly inclined to the mawkish and sententious. What can also be inferred from this aspect of Griffith's career is that his experience of the dramatic vaudeville sketch, in which action had to be compressed, and thought and decision making expressed through activity and mimed emotion, directly prepared him for both devising film scenarios and directing one- and two-reel films with running times that rarely exceeded twenty minutes. Further, Griffith's plays offer evidence of his capacity to recycle early material. Moments and segments of plots, "strong situations," and arresting characters from his plays make reappearances in his films, even to the final years of his directorial career.

Arriving in Louisville in 1890, Griffith first found work, dusting and stacking books, in the Flexner family's bookshop. At some point in 1893, hoping to soften his rural Kentucky accent and to improve his singing voice, he began to study elocution and singing with Annie Boustead. What drew him to acting is uncertain, but commercial entertainment in Louisville was a microcosm of the national scene, with active and varied theatrical traffic. Most players arrived and departed within a week. Some companies played only "split weeks"—two or three nights in Louisville—before going north to Cincinnati or east to Lexington or Frankfort. The adolescent Griffith had to be quick to catch these performances, and he needed coins in his pocket to enter theatre balconies. In his incomplete autobiography, Griffith hints at frequenting Louisville theatres and states that his first theatrical experience "was *America's National Game* starring Pete Baker at Macauley's Theatre."[3] In a 1916 interview, Griffith elaborated:

> I determined to become a dramatist. . . . I received emphasis for that inspiration on seeing my first theatrical performance; it was Pete Baker [performing, as always, in blackface] who sang "America's National Game." Then I saw Julia Marlowe and Robert Taber in *Romola*.[4]

The dates for this sequence of events are not specified, but Baker appeared in Louisville on three occasions when Griffith may have been in the audience: once at Harris's Theatre in January 1894, when Baker starred in his own musical review, *Chris and Lena*, and twice at Macauley's Theatre, once in September 1894, as a member of Al G. Field Minstrels, and again in September 1896, when Baker had joined Primrose and West's Minstrels. Griffith would have been nineteen or twenty-one years old.

Julia Marlowe and her then-husband, Robert Taber, played periodic engagements at Macauley's Theatre from 1890, on each occasion offering a repertoire of at least four plays, some Shakespearean, some from the nineteenth-century popular repertoire. If Griffith's theatre-going began soon after his arrival in Louisville, it is also possible that Griffith saw Marlowe as Parthenia in Maria Lovell's *Ingomar the Barbarian*, one of the first plays Griffith was to abridge and adapt early in his tenure at Biograph.

Griffith assumes a man-of-the world swagger when describing Louisville attractions, but he is nonetheless evasive (or forgetful) in describing what he actually saw. He does appear to have become familiar with the principal playhouses. In his memoirs he observes, "Louisville at the time was quite a place. There was Macauley's Theatre where all the best dramatic and light opera companies played." While he attended performances at Macauley's, visited by first-run tours and major repertory companies playing both full- and split-week engagements, his heart may have been captured by the attractions of Louisville's more robust theatres:

> There was the Fourth Avenue Theatre[5] of the "ten-twent-thirt" melodramas. In the latter all the villains in the course of one season would spill veritable rivers of blood, spiced with multitudinous shootings and sword play. The producers of these plays dared anybody to sleep during performances . . .[6] for just as you would be about to commit such a heinous crime, out would come

Jack the Ripper, a cigarette in his mouth, a pistol in each hand, and all three smoking as he diligently and everlastingly pursued Little Nell. Just as he was about to seize her, entered Handsome Jack the Hero, and then the fun began. . . . As for the various Nells who played the heroines, it was a waste of words for the other characters to tell how virtuous and beautiful they were. You knew that they were both the minute they came on stage and you glimpsed their blonde wigs.[7]

Although Griffith recalls only one melodrama house—probably conflating in his memory Harris's Theatre, later The Avenue, on Fourth Avenue with the nearby Bijou—both theatres offered patrons dramas with remarkable and frequently noisy smoke-filled effects. In January 1893, Harris's staged a week of safe-blowing exhibitions, following lessons in safecracking with "the Great Railroad drama," The Fast Mail, in which a safe carried by fast freight was attacked by bandits and exploded. This melodrama, not dissimilar to The Great Train Robbery, which would appear at Harris's at the year's end, was followed by the Civil War melodrama, A Fair Rebel, and that play in turn was succeeded by The Midnight Alarm, which featured onstage fire engines and horses racing to fight blazes. In the same winter months, the Bijou, which billed itself as "Louisville's Family Theatre," offered a cluster of urban melodramas which included New York Day by Day, an Americanized version of George R. Sims's London Day by Day, and a nautical play, The Stowaways. Neither of these theatres was, in Griffith's terminology, a "ten-twent-thirt" melodrama house with seats priced at ten cents, twenty cents, and thirty cents. The lowest price for admission to the gallery was twenty-five cents. Admission to the main floor was fifty cents.

The Masonic Temple Theatre escaped the label of a melodrama house because it offered more varied fare. As in the melodrama houses, railroading and railroad plays pleased Louisville audiences. Henry C. DeMille's rail melodrama, The Danger Signal, was followed by The Great Monster Iron Locomotive Show, in which a railroad snow plow, freight train, and the Cannonball Express were seen to cross the stage billowing steam and smoke. Variety acts such as Mrs. Tom Thumb and the Lilliputians and The Arctic Alaska Eskimos—so successful an attraction that their three-day booking was extended for a month—forced a delayed appearance of Creston Clark in his repertoire Richelieu, Hamlet, and The Fool's Revenge.[8]

Professional athletes were known to exploit their skills on the dramatic and variety stages during the off season and between matches. Among the better known of made-to-measure sporting melodramas starred the boxer John L. Sullivan, who, from 1890, toured in Duncan Harrison's Honest Hearts and Willing *Hands*, and who, in 1897, performed at Louisville's Grand Opera House with Eugene O'Rourke in *The Wicklow Postman*. Sullivan's presence in Louisville and his known drinking habits—benders and consequent absenteeism—prompted advertisements in the Louisville *Courier-Journal* promising that "in conjunction with this great production John L. Sullivan and [his sparring partner] Paddy Ryan will positively appear at every performance." Even more successful were James J. Corbett's appearances in *Gentleman Jack*, in which he appeared at Macauley's in April, 1895, and in *The Naval Cadet* (1897), both tailored by Charles Vincent under the eye of William A. Brady.[9] Brady promoted sporting events and theatrical productions with flair and acute judgment of the public's taste. In *The Naval Cadet*, briefly at the Buckingham burlesque house, Brady encouraged a drama which allowed Corbett to demonstrate the fine points of boxing and, also, to use these skills in a choreographed fight-to-the-death in which an unarmed Corbett fought an armed and murderous adversary. *The Naval Cadet* was directed by McKee Rankin. Griffith would be in Rankin's employ by 1904, and he would negotiate with Brady in 1919 over the rights to '*Way Down East*.

What makes Griffith's actual theatre-going so difficult to trace lies in two related matters: although he appears to have enjoyed attending performances in the full range of Louisville theatres, these are mostly undated and updateable, and his theatre-going appears to follow from, rather than precede, his appearances as an actor—and how many people have determined to be actors without ever witnessing professional performances? Griffith's self-mythologizing (he never let truth impede a good story) has created a period undefined by a precise chronology. Griffith conflated experiences and misremembered names. His early years—and indeed many of the episodes of Griffith's life and career—are problematic in that few events happened as Griffith described. He was a consummate storyteller, burnishing his past successes, eliding his false steps and gaffes, inventing relationships which, in all probability, didn't exist. It is easy to describe and dismiss Griffith as a chronic liar or, at best, a fantasist. However, to do so is to shade his ability to construct—or to reconstruct—pleasing and disturbing, and ultimately, compelling narratives. Griffith, the fantasist and liar, shares an identity with Griffith, the master storyteller. It is only after Griffith attempted to become a professional actor that his trail may be followed with any degree of certainty.

Nevertheless, it is possible to deduce Griffith's Louisville theatre-going based on dramas he later adapted or from which he lifted key moments or, more generally, which may have furnished ideas: settings, characters, and social themes. In all likelihood, he witnessed at Macauley's Theatre *Two Orphans*, '*Way*

Down East, and *Ingomar the Barbarian*. He also saw *The Middleman* (with the English actor E. S. Willard) and *The Ironmaster*. Both plays lie behind Griffith's films which challenge and castigate industrial capitalism. Given the content of his future films, Griffith is likely to have witnessed performances of *The Old Homestead*, *The Only Way* (with Edward Morgan, John Martin-Harvey not yet touring this vehicle in North America), *The Lady of Lyons* (with Otis Skinner in the role of Claude Melnotte), *Blue Jeans*, *Under the Red Robe*, *Rip Van Winkle*, *Sam'l of Posen*, and *Claudian*.

A prominent theatre in a "border state," Macauley's frequently booked touring productions which refought the Civil War or dramatized issues arising in the postbellum South. These dramas included *Shenandoah*, *A Kentucky Colonel* (with McKee Rankin, who for a time became Griffith's mentor and adviser), *The New South* (with Phoebe Davies and Joseph R. Grismer, both of whom took leading acting roles in major tours of *'Way Down East*), *Forbidden Fruit*, *A Southern Romance*, *A Southern Gentleman*, *Alabama*, *In Mizzoura*, and *The Carpetbagger*. Such plays would have given Griffith the form and conventions of Civil War drama that he so fully exploited in his films for Biograph and to which he returned in *The Birth of a Nation*. Griffith also may have attended lectures at Macauley's on themes related to the Civil War and Reconstruction: Colonel John Walker speaking on "The South Before the War," Bob and Alf Taylor discussing "Yankee Doodle and Dixie," and the Reverend D. T. Stanton lecturing on "The American Citizen," the latter's lecture querying the right, as expressed in the Fourteenth and Fifteenth Amendments to the U.S. Constitution, to citizenship irrespective of race.

Macauley's Theatre also rented its house for amateur theatricals, chiefly favoring drama societies from nearby universities. A frequent offering from these groups was John Banim's and Richard Lalor Sheil's 1821 verse play *Damon and Pythias*. The attraction of this by-then-obsolete melodrama is understandable. Formerly a vehicle for Edwin Forrest, *Damon and Pythias* is crammed with sententious verse (or, as the prologue expresses it, "pure and lofty sentiment"), easily turned into bombast, on themes of loyalty, friendship, and patriotism. Both the rhetoric and opportunities for declamatory acting proved irresistible. Further, to Southern audiences and to Southern collegiate amateur actors, *Damon and Pythias* offered a covert text of resistance to what was perceived as an illegal abusive tyranny. Unlike some of the states of the Deep South, the border state of Kentucky was only briefly occupied by Federal troops and—unlike Piedmont, South Carolina, the predominant setting of *The Birth of a Nation*—never experienced the presence of local militias of armed black soldiers. Further, many holders of small farms were supportive of the Union, but the rhetoric of

Northern abuse and mistreatment of the defeated South still permeated Kentucky thought. Griffith was susceptible to such rhetoric, and this susceptibility is apparent in his Civil War films.

Damon and Pythias, set in Grecian Syracuse, begins as war veterans, led by Dionysius, plot to seize the city. When Damon, a senator, protests this successful and distasteful military coup, he is arrested and sentenced to death by Dionysius, now tyrant head of state. Damon's friend Pythias, however, offers himself as a temporary substitute so that Damon might say farewell to his wife and child who, on Damon's instructions, fled Syracuse before the coup. Damon's long absence jeopardizes Pythias's life, but Damon's timely return impresses Dionysius who grants reprieves to both Damon and Pythias.

Damon and Pythias would be of small interest were it not for the fact that Griffith undertook one of his first professional roles as the tyrannical Dionysius when, on May 8, 1896, Robert Haight's company presented the play at the Opera House in New Albany, Indiana. Thereafter, Griffith seems to have been more comfortable in villain's roles than in those of hero. Moreover, discovering in a popular play the subtext of subversion and resistance to an abusive occupying tyranny may have contributed to Griffith's subsequent filmic treatments of a beleaguered postbellum South.

Griffith's career began as an actor in 1895, when he was twenty years old. That career ended in 1908 when he was thirty-three. In this thirteen-year period, he found irregular employment with a mixture of traveling companies and, less frequently, with small, resident stock companies. Griffith managed to be in paid theatre-related employment for fewer than seventy months out of a total of 156 months. His longest period of unemployment of eleven months occurred between 1902 and 1903.

During his first years in the profession, Griffith largely worked with local companies made up of aspirant actors. Although these profit-share companies traveled as far from Louisville to as far away as southern Indiana, and although Griffith was briefly to find acting roles with the Twilight Revellers[10]—who played small theatres in Indiana and Ohio—most of his and his group's activities were based in Louisville's smallest and least prepossessing theatre, the [Masonic] Temple Theatre, a two-story frame and brick building with businesses on the ground floor. From September 1897 through May 1898, Griffith appeared periodically at the Temple Theatre as a member of the Meffert Stock Company, its name taken from the theatre's manager, W. H. Meffert.

Actors with day jobs who joined the Meffert company on a profit-sharing basis regularly hired the Temple Theatre. The Temple could be described as a base for the Meffert company only to the extent that it was their sole Louisville venue. This playhouse began its life as a speculative venture by the Masonic order who then leased the theatre, seating approximately 1,300 spectators, to visiting companies, or otherwise used the hall for their private rites. Whereas other Louisville playhouses had their auditorium on the ground floor, the Temple Theatre's was located on the second floor. The stage had four traps. Scenery was a combination of old-style wing-and-groove flats and backcloths flown and rolled down from an underhung gridiron. There was no workshop or scenery dock. Other Louisville houses were illuminated by electric light. The Temple used both gas and electric lighting.[11]

Touring attractions came and went at the Temple, but the Meffert stock players performed one evening per week. Oscar W. Eagle, later a Broadway director, served as the Meffert's stage director. Eagle would, in 1899, take some of the company's actors on a tour of Kentucky and Ohio venues. Meanwhile, Griffith, under the name of "Lawrence Griffith," appeared in Joseph Clifton's comedy *Myrtle Ferns*, and in an adaptation of the Ouida (pseudonym of Maria Louise Ramé) novel, *Moths*, then, changing his name to "Thomas Griffith," undertook roles in *Trilby*, David Belasco's *The Wife*, Wilde's *Lady Windermere's Fan*, and Henry Arthur Jones's *The Silver King*. He also appeared in Frances Hodgson Burnett's *Little Lord Fauntleroy*, Sir Charles Young's *Jim the Penman*, and William Gillette's *All the Comforts of Home*. It was with the Meffert company that he had his first professional encounter with D'Ennery's *The Two Orphans* (which he would adapt in 1921 as *Orphans of the Storm*), and George R. Sims's *The Lights o' London*. Griffith was part of a tableau in which applicants for beds in the local workhouse queued for places, the actors and supers freezing in position to "realize" Sir Luke Fildes's famous painting, *Applicants to a Casual Ward*. He was later to parody this picture in his 1909 Biograph film *A Corner in Wheat*, employing the same grouping, but the "applicants," the poor and starving, now queuing to buy bread in a bakery as they desperately seek food.

Griffith's contractual arrangements with the Meffert Stock Company and the Mefferts' own tenuous purchase on the Louisville theatrical scene were both loose enough for him to undertake brief—and largely unsuccessful—engagements with traveling companies playing venues in the border states and Midwest. On the road he played small parts—probably multiple roles—in an adaptation of *Faust*[12] and in *Richard III*. He appeared in Sidney Grundy's farce *The Arabian Nights* and undertook the villain Sir Francis Levison in *East Lynne* and the role of Leucippi in W. S. Gilbert's *Pygmalion and Galatea*.

In the spring of 1898, Griffith left the Meffert company to find work away from the Kentucky circuit. He secured a brief engagement in Chicago with the James Neil Stock Company, remaining long enough to portray Abraham Lincoln in William Haworth's *The Ensign*, to appear in William C. DeMille's *The Lost Paradise*, and to again take a role in *The Two Orphans*. In September he joined the Walker Whiteside Company, traveling through Indiana, Ohio, Minnesota, and Iowa, playing in repertory *The Red Cockade*, a melodrama of the French Revolution, and an adaptation of *Eugene Aram*, in all likelihood different from that performed by Henry Irving on his North American tours. By spring he was back in Louisville once again performing with the Meffert players and remained with them through the summer of 1899.

In late August, Griffith again left the Meffert players and headed east to find work. By February 1900 he had found a berth in a combination company touring Martyn Field's and Arthur Shirley's *How London Lives* (alternately titled *London Life*). It was Griffith's longest experience of the road and his first experience of a play on its first run. Moreover, he was cast as one of the male leads, that of "Happy Jack" Ferrers, who, falsely accused of murder, must prove his own innocence. Beginning in February, the company played consecutive engagements in Ontario, New York, Ohio, Michigan, Indiana, Illinois, Tennessee, Georgia, Alabama, Mississippi, Texas, Arkansas, and Wisconsin. In Minnesota, though, his luck ran out. The company foundered in St. Paul, and Griffith, cold and hungry, was forced to return to Louisville riding as a hobo in railway freight cars.

Again looking for theatrical work and taking anything that came his way, Griffith, in October 1900, took a not-wished-for and unexpected detour from acting on the legitimate stage. It was a side trip he was never to acknowledge, but it was a change not so much of direction as of focus. In terms of his subsequent career as a filmmaker, it was to prove his most useful and productive period until necessity brought him to the Biograph studio: Griffith entered vaudeville.

There are notable elisions in Griffith's rudimentary and incomplete autobiography.[13] Some of its elisions are accidental or the result of an inaccurate memory, but there are omissions which are intentional. Griffith took care to conceal embarrassing truths. One of these occluded periods, 1900–1903, involved his employment as a vaudeville actor. References to vaudeville are wholly elided from Griffith's autobiography and similarly omitted from various reminiscing interviews given from 1916 onward. In one of his few references to his short-lived career as an actor, Griffith admitted to appearing in the J. E. Dodson company's production of *Richelieu's Stratagem*. Speaking as if the production had toured "legitimate" circuits (i.e., playhouses, as opposed to variety theatres), he boasted to *Photoplay Magazine* of his role and the critical response it generated. Significantly, he mentioned neither vaudeville houses nor the name of the sketch in which he toured:

> It isn't all so long ago, yet I played one season with Helen Ware before she was discovered, and then with J. E. Dodson as de Maupret to his Richelieu, and was given a good notice by Alan Dale,[14] which confirmed my suspicion that I was quite a good actor. It secured me as well an increase in salary.[15]

Indeed, were it not for Russell Merritt's meticulous account of Griffith's stage career, 1895–1906, we would not even possess an outline of this critical decade in the development of a scenarist and director whose theatrical skills, such as they were, transferred directly into film. Despite Griffith's determined reticence, Merritt describes Griffith's activities throughout this period. While grasping the relationship and significance of the vaudeville sketch to early narrative film, Merritt concentrates on other aspects of these prophetically productive years. He acknowledges that

> the vaudeville stage gave Griffith important training as an actor and future screen writer. . . . There was a considerable vogue for one-act versions of famous plays and literary works. . . . Later, such sketches became Griffith's principal source for his Biograph literary adaptations, the vital crib sheets that enabled him to film all those Great Works—the leviathan novels, Victorian poems, and short stories—without actually having to read them.[16]

Merritt and Schickel alike, aware of Griffith's obvious deficiencies as a performer, agree that acting was not for Griffith. He was never destined to attain the sort of recognition he desired or to acquire the aplomb, relaxed concentration, poise, and freedom from self-consciousness which would liberate his imagination and enable him to respond to other actors. Griffith, they acknowledge, was in a dead-end career from which he required "rescue" and "escape."

Briefly summarized, this three-year span of variety-house touring between 1900 and 1903 began when Griffith joined J. E. Dodson's company to play the juvenile lead role of Talleyrand in *Richelieu's Stratagem*, Dodson's abridged adaptation of *Under the Red Robe*. It was Griffith's longest paid acting job. Griffith, continuing as Talleyrand, stayed with Dodson until January 1901. This engagement was followed by a year of touring and appearing in his own vaudeville sketch, *In Washington's Time*. Finally, Griffith joined the actress Kathryn Osterman's company to take the villain's role in George Tilton Richardson's dramatization of Dwight Tilton's novel *Miss Petticoats*.[17] The intended East Coast and Midwest tours ended prematurely when Osterman was injured and the company consequently obliged to disband. Griffith thereafter returned to the legitimate stage for a further three futile years, on one single occasion reviving his vaudeville sketch. Then, in 1906–1907, he attempted playwriting, a craft for which he had little talent. Finally, in desperation and acute financial need, he turned to Edison and Biograph to work in motion pictures. There, Griffith was quickly successful as a film scenarist and director. His experience of writing and performing in the vaudeville sketch had prepared him to meet similar requirements—compact storytelling and direct, unambiguous acting—from narrative film.

Griffith concealed his time in vaudeville but not because he believed that variety carried less cachet than legitimate theatre. There was a darker, more embarrassing secret that obliged lifelong silence and which sharply contradicted his reiterated posture as a man sympathetic to the concerns of the working man. It is now apparent that the creator of A Corner in Wheat and The Mother and the Law and earlier Biograph one- and two-reelers in which workers resist tyrannical managements and exhibit bravery and defiant independence, entered vaudeville as a strikebreaker.[18] To have acknowledged vaudeville experience between 1900 and 1903 would have been to admit to "scabbing."

The events which placed Griffith in the position of an opportunist who used the situation of a prolonged labor dispute to obtain an acting role in a vaudeville sketch resemble those preceding the founding of the Theatrical Syndicate and the Motion Picture Patents Company. All were created with the intent to introduce and to operate monopolistic practices in the entertainment business. Beginning in 1896, B. F. Keith and Edward Albee, owners of the Keith-Albee Circuit, and the Orpheum Circuit's Morris Meyerfeld and Martin Beck contrived a means to control major chains of vaudeville theatres. At the time of Griffith's joining J. E. Dodson's company, legitimate and variety actors, although represented by the Actors' National Protective Union (ANPU), lacked bargaining leverage, since the ANPU substantially failed to address the concerns of variety performers. In 1900, vaudeville actors organized their own union to oppose Albee and Beck. The new union's determined strike action and a consequent shortage of dramatic sketch acts available to the Albee Circuit created the vacuum into which Dodson—and Griffith—stepped.

J. E. Dodson had appeared in Manhattan from 1896 in Edward Rose's Under the Red Robe, a romantic melodrama newly imported from England by the impresario Charles Frohman. Success with this drama of conspiracies, duels, and political intrigue led to a national tour which lasted until 1900. By this date, rights to the play had been sold to various theatrical entrepreneurs, and Dodson's unique hold on the role of Richelieu had ended. Dodson then enlisted the sketch writer, John Stapleton, to condense Rose's four-act play—with an approximate running time of three hours—to a brief twenty-five-minute performance, to retitle it *Richelieu's Stratagem*, to reduce the cast size from thirteen actors, plus supernumeraries, to a mere six, and to book his diminished drama as a Keith-Albee Circuit sketch. Dodson's sketch offered plotting, which although compressed and abridged, still remained tortuously intricate.

The *Dramatic Mirror*'s unnamed reviewer described Dodson's sketch:

> The scene is laid in a chateau near Rochelle during the siege of that town. To Henri de Talleyrand, a Huguenot spy, has been allocated the task of securing an audience with the Cardinal for the purpose of securing his signature to a decree granting the Huguenots perfect freedom to practice their religion without interference. If he fails in his mission, he is to slay Richelieu.

Henri—Griffith—encounters his fiancée Blanche Michelle. A series of schemes and counterplots follows, with the cardinal remaining several steps ahead of the lovers. Eventually, the lovers, separated by the cardinal, "are reunited and the curtain falls on a pretty tableau."

The reviewer, commending Dodson's performance, added a further paragraph:

> Mr. Dodson has chosen his supporting company with great care. Lawrence Griffith was dignified and effective as Henri, the Huguenot spy, and Gertrude Perry was thoroughly charming as Blanche. W.T. Clark as Joseph, and Mr. Neville as the captain played small parts capitally.[19]

That difference between a play running for approximately three hours and an abbreviated version lasting between twenty minutes and a half-hour partly explains the nature of the dramatic sketch. Griffith was to participate in and to have a hand in creating three versions of this form of compacted drama: Dodson's pared-down melodrama, his own twenty-five-minute Revolutionary War drama, and a comedy-melodrama starring Kathryn Osterman. This latter piece, depending on the type of theatre, legitimate or vaudeville house, in which it was to play, could either be performed as a full-length drama or shrunk to a twenty-five-minute précis. Although Griffith was unaware of it at the time, it was his brief period of apprenticeship as a screenwriter.

Only three weeks passed between the end of *Richelieu's Stratagem* and Griffith's reappearance in a new sketch—his own. It is thus likely that he was writing it and seeking means to mount it even as the Dodson tour was running out of steam. Without the financial resources to mount his sketch, *In Washington's Time*, Griffith leased the rights to Mary Scott's company, newcomers to vaudeville, for a tour playing East Coast vaudeville houses from February to July 1901.

No script for this sketch is known to exist. Reviewed in the New York *Dramatic Mirror*, it is apparent that Griffith managed to persuade Mary Scott to assign him the lead role of Paul Lawrence and that the sketch was the opening number[20] on the bill at Keith's Union Square, to be followed by fourteen additional turns. Griffith's acting came in for unfavorable comment.

> The plot is melodramatic and full of action. Paul Lawrence, a soldier in the American army, bearing important dispatches to General Washington, stops on the way at the house of his sweetheart, Molly Seawell, and is there overtaken by Corporal Blake of the English Army, and a guard. . . . Lawrence conceals himself in a tall clock, while Molly conceals the dispatches in her luxuriant black hair. The British search the house without finding their man, but the Corporal, not convinced . . . shortly after surprises Paul and Molly together and learns the whereabouts of the dispatches. At the point of a musket he is compelling the delivery of the dispatches, when Lawrence . . . seizing a revolver [sic] . . . turns the tables on their captor and makes him a prisoner. . . . The climax is an effective one, and the dialogue throughout is spirited, though sometimes conventional. . . . Mr. Griffith, the author, was a fervid and somewhat stagey hero. . . . The play held the interest of the audience and was well received.

The theatrical climate in which this sketch appeared is best indicated by the other turns on Keith's bill: a comedy sketch, a comedy pianist, trick cyclists, an acrobatic team, a pair of Yiddish comedians, a monologuist, and six unspecified acts, with the program concluding with "a change of views on the Biograph."[21]

When Griffith's engagement with Mary Scott's company ended, he experienced a full six months without an acting role, then found three months' work in a touring melodrama company. When that stint finished, Griffith was obliged to endure almost twelve months—from April 1902, until April 1903—of unemployment, but then was engaged by another melodrama company. This engagement lasted approximately three weeks. He again found temporary employment in a road company, but was then idle from July into September. It was in that month, toward the end of 1903, that Griffith was engaged for the society villain's role to menace Kathryn Osterman's[22] heroine in Richardson's *Miss Petticoats*, the third sketch company he was to know.

A mawkish, but famously popular novel of an orphaned young woman coming into her just inheritance and threatening to avenge herself against those who besmirched her reputation, *Miss Petticoat*'s plot covers a span of five years and moves rapidly from incident to incident. It easily furnished material for a five-act play. It can, however, be compressed into a few scenes, notably Agatha's adolescence (which featured a scene of a New England clambake), the circumstances in which Agatha (Osterman) is compromised by Guy (Griffith) who is exposed as a predatory villain, and the episode in which Agatha begins to exact revenge but is brought under the influence of a clergyman who loves and guides her. Richardson adapted his novel for a cast of twenty actors, but some of the roles were excised for vaudeville performances. Regrettably, no script of the sketch is known to survive. The sketch opened at the Hyperion Theatre in New Haven, Connecticut, on September 11 to an audience estimated at two thousand, but the Hyperion, once a legitimate playhouse, had deteriorated and was by that date a venue for burlesque and vaudeville. From New Haven, the company traveled to Boston, other Massachusetts cities, Providence, Rhode Island, and Hartford, Connecticut, where Osterman was injured. Again unemployed, Griffith had a three-month gap which he filled in with manual labor jobs before landing a stage role in January 1904. Apart from a four-day revival of In Washington's Time in San Francisco in November 1904, performances in which Linda Arvidson and Griffith played opposite each other, Griffith's vaudeville years had ended.

The conclusion is inescapable. Griffith—although thereafter reluctant to admit to crossing union picket lines, a reason too controversial for a now-respected film director to mention—learned, from observing and performing in the vaudeville sketch, how to condense a narrative into a brief span and how to make it intelligible through the agency of mimed actions and without recourse to more than the occasional word or sentence. Writing and acting in vaudeville sketches served as an unintended training ground and apprenticeship for Griffith's Biograph years. There, obliged by the constraints of the one- and two-reel film, he became a master of concise storytelling.

The abrupt collapse of the Miss Petticoats company marked Griffith's departure from vaudeville and brought him back to legitimate stage. In January 1904, he joined Edward McWade's touring production of Winchester, the title a reference to the Civil War battle site in Virginia. Griffith was cast as a Confederate officer in charge of a firing squad. Unaware of the direction in which he was traveling, Griffith was again moving toward motion pictures by appearing in a play whose audiences alternately watched live actors on a stage and filmed action on a screen. As described by the New York Dramatic Mirror,

> the scene is laid in and around Winchester during the days of the Civil War. The heroine . . . is in love with a Union army officer . . . who . . . taught her telegraphy. . . . Later she makes use of her knowledge, taps a wire that runs directly across the roof of her house . . . thereby sending to her brother, a Captain in the southern army, all the movements of the northern troops. She

Kathryn Osterman imagined as Miss Petticoats, a promotional souvenir photograph made for the 1903 vaudeville and theatre tour. The image, a composite, was made by superimposing Osterman's facial portrait upon Charles H. Stephens's frontispiece for the 1902 Dwight Tilton novel, *Miss Petticoats*.

is finally discovered to be the spy, but the men who know the secret do not use it against her because they want evidence to dishonor and, if possible, hang her lover. . . . He is therefore sentenced to be shot at sunrise. Under cover of the night, the heroine rides to Kernstown . . . confesses to the General commanding, and obtains a reprieve. After an encounter on the road, during which she shoots the villain from his horse, she arrives in time to prevent the execution.[23]

In the initial run of this melodrama in 1897, Virginia Randolph's ride-to-the-rescue was staged utilizing a treadmill apparatus and moving backcloth. In December, 1902, it was reported that "the racing machine used in the last act has been cast aside and a vitascope [made by Edison] is now used to heighten the effect of Virginia's ride to Winchester. . . . A horse is also introduced, and with the combined use of the [film] machinery and horse, the audience is treated to something out of the ordinary in attempts at stage realism."[24] McWade was not the first dramatist to combine live stage action with projected film,[25] but he was a playwright-actor-producer who, in Winchester, realized the narrative possibilities of a filmed sequence combined and alternated with live stage action. The motion picture segment took the spectator outside the theatre and also provided the resultant ability to say "meanwhile" and show, counterpointed against stage activity, a second action occurring elsewhere beyond the theatre's walls—before filmed action and live performance converged in the final moments of the act.

When Griffith's engagement with Winchester ended, he struck out for the West Coast, seeking roles in San Francisco. No reason was ever offered for this decision, but Griffith must have been aware that touring circuits in California, Oregon, Washington, and Nevada had developed incrementally and that there was a reassuring likelihood of regular stage work for experienced, if not necessarily well-known and popular, actors. In his account of this phase of his life, Griffith replayed his West Coast experiences as a rollicking adventure in which he found irregular theatrical work, in effect using this picaresque narrative of his last years as an actor to disguise a falling trajectory.[26] Joining the Melbourne MacDowell Company based in San Francisco's Grand Opera House, Griffith played supporting roles in a season of plays by Victorien Sardou. The principal plays in the MacDowell repertoire, Fedora, La Tosca, Theodora, Gismonda, and Cleopatra, had been written for Sarah Bernhardt to perform in France but had been translated into English under license and performed throughout America by Fanny Davenport, MacDowell's wife. For years Griffith dined out on stories of having worked as a supernumerary in Bernhardt's company and having witnessed her backstage tantrums and repentant generosity, but it is more likely that he observed Ethel Fuller, Davenport's successor, and improved his tale by substituting a more famous protagonist.

It was while on tour with the MacDowell company that Griffith met Linda Arvidson and began a relationship that would continue in marriage in 1906. Arvidson was performing the role of a boy servant in Fedora; Griffith played the role of the police inspector Gretch in the same play. Griffith's path also crossed that of Claire MacDowell (stage and screen name Claire McDowell), daughter of Melbourne MacDowell and Fanny Davenport. Claire McDowell and her husband, Charles Hill Mailes, later toured in one of Thomas Dixon's The Clansman companies and were among the first stage-trained actors Griffith recruited to Biograph in 1909. Both subsequently experienced long motion picture careers.

Fired by MacDowell for undisclosed reasons,[27] Griffith found a week's engagement in a lurid San Francisco passion play, The Holy City, less concerned with sanctity than romance between Mary Magdalene and Barabas. Nevertheless, Griffith's John the Baptist was noticed and commended by local critics. Then, according to his memoirs, beginning in February 1905, he collaborated with the actor-dramatist Virginia Calhoun to adapt Helen Hunt Jackson's novel Ramona for the stage.[28] This claim is patently untrue. Ramona was, in fact, the joint work of Johnstone Jones and Virginia Calhoun, and copyright had been granted in their names a full eight months before Griffith joined the Ramona company. His claim to have been a collaborator and the florid pedigree he gave himself in the company's publicity blurbs[29] testify to the virulence of Griffith's capacity for myth-making. Griffith was cast by the company's director, Mr. Farrell, in the leading role of the Indian, Alessandro, who, defying implacable racial taboos, falls in love with Ramona and fathers the Mexican woman's child.

As with his John the Baptist, Griffith's playing was praised. The Los Angeles Times said of him:

> Mr. Farrell . . . assembled the company [in San Francisco] from the best New York had to offer. He secured Lawrence Griffith for the part of Alessandro, and anyone who sees him in the death scene of this play will acknowledge with tears and delight his right in this heroic Indian character. He looks the part to perfection. He is tall, straight as an arrow, spare, swarthy, and handsome with the classic mould of feature necessary to this role.[30]

Apparently believing that only the judgments of New York critics were to be taken seriously, Griffith appears to have discounted his West Coast critics and later made no mention of this or other encomiums.

Ramona is noteworthy because it shows Griffith succeeding in a leading role and sustaining that role for the two months that the play toured California venues and also because he later recalled the power of this drama and recognized its suitability for adaptation as film. In 1910, Griffith persuaded Biograph to purchase the screen rights to *Ramona* for one hundred dollars. Remembering Calhoun's stage version as well as returning to Helen Hunt Jackson's novel, he adapted *Ramona* for the screen and shot it as a one-reel drama with Mary Pickford as Ramona and Henry Walthall as Alessandro.

At the end of the *Ramona* engagement, Griffith joined Barney Bernard's West Coast company for a six-week tour through the Northwest, Nevada, and Colorado. Their vehicle was a farce by a California dramatist, Harry D. Cottrell, whose works invariably failed when taken east of the Rockies. In this drama, Griffith played the role of a detective who was obliged to disguise himself as a drunkard, a grizzly bear, and a society matron. Then, again at liberty in November, he and Linda Arvidson reentered vaudeville where "Lawrence Griffith and Company" restaged *In Washington's Time* at a San Francisco vaudeville house.

On December 10, 1905, Griffith began what was to be his penultimate theatrical tour as a member of Nance O'Neil's (Gertrude Lamson) company. Griffith's named roles were Sir Francis Drake in Paolo Giacometti's *Elizabeth, Queen of England*, and Father Ignacius in McKee Rankin's version of *The Jewess*. O'Neil's repertoire included dramas by Sudermann, Ibsen, and Shakespeare, and, although there are no cast lists which reveal Griffith's name, there were numerous small parts which, as a member of a repertory company, he may have performed "as cast." In 1904, O'Neil and Rankin, her acting partner and business manager, had added Giacometti's *Judith* to the company repertoire and soon after induced the Boston novelist and poet Thomas Bailey Aldrich to rewrite Giacometti's piece as *Judith of Bethulia*. Griffith's name again is missing from surviving programs, but here too, it is likely that he assumed small roles as required and without demurring. In any event, he appears to have been familiar with both the Giacometti version and the Aldrich version and relied on both for his own *Judith of Bethulia* (1913–1914).

Griffith, meanwhile, understudied Rankin, and in February 1906, when Rankin's heavy drinking and disputes with O'Neil caused him to miss performances, Griffith appeared as Judge Brack in *Hedda Gabler*, Banquo in *Macbeth*, Ulrik Brendel in *Rosmersholm*, Borso in Maeterlinck's *Monna Vanna*, Pastor Heffterding in Sudermann's *Magda*, and Pastor Haffke in Sudermann's *Fires of St. John*.[31] In spite of this fraught association, Rankin and Griffith became friends. Griffith was to seek advice from Rankin, and Rankin, in turn, would, in 1910, bring his son-in-law, Lionel Barrymore, to Griffith's notice and secure

Photograph of Nance O'Neil as Judith in *Judith of Bethulia*, 1904. Her oriental dress emphasizes her otherness and alienated status as well as her distinctiveness.

him acting work at Biograph. O'Neil's company gradually moved eastward, returning in May to her home base of Boston, where, on May 14, Linda Arvidson and Griffith were married at Boston's historic Old North Church.

Griffith briefly stayed with the company to perform in O'Neil's version of *Oliver Twist*, then he and Linda Arvidson left to make their base in New York. Unable to find immediate stage work and desperately short of money, Griffith returned to writing. He and Arvidson, meanwhile, were cast as the leads in a touring production of Thomas Dixon's *The One Woman*, but were informed that rehearsals would not begin until the fall. He sold an essay on southern cooking to the *New York World* and was further heartened when a poem he had written, "The Wild Duck," was published by *Leslie's Weekly*, bringing a check for six dollars. He later sold a story to *Cosmopolitan* which brought in seventy-five dollars. Buoyed by these slight successes, he set to work on a four-act play, drawing on his experiences of San Francisco, hops picking with Arvidson, and his glimpses of the seamy sides of urban American life. By August, the first draft of his play, *A Fool and a Girl*,[32] was complete, and—audaciously—he sent it to James K. Hackett. Hackett in 1907 was a leading actor of romantic melodrama. He had made his first success in 1896 playing Prince Rudolph in Anthony Hope's *The Prisoner of Zenda*, and the income from that production had enabled Hackett to support other ventures in which he played the lead. Linked by business to Marc Klaw and Abraham Erlanger, he had managed to break free of the Syndicate. Now a successful producer, he invested in various theatrical enterprises which he tested on the road before bringing them into his own West Forty-second Street playhouse, formerly Wallack's Theatre.

Griffith's and Arvidson's accounts of what happened next vary. According to Griffith, Hackett read the script and then sent Griffith a check for one thousand dollars with a promise to produce the *A Fool and a Girl*.[33] Linda Arvidson states that the couple began their engagement in Dixon's *The One Woman* but were replaced after two months by actors whose weekly salaries came to half the amount she and Griffith had earned.[34] She then paints a bleak Christmas Eve dinner of hamburger and baked potatoes enlivened when she found beneath her plate a check from Hackett, payable to Griffith, for $700. Either way, *A Fool and a Girl* had found its producer.

A Fool and a Girl, as it survives in Griffith's manuscript, enacts an encounter between a worldly young woman and a naive Kentuckian. The woman, Effie, is being used as bait by her co-conspirators to trick the moderately rich young man, Albert Holly, into circumstances where he can be bilked of his fortune. Albert, charmed but also captivated by the California climate, insists that the group accompany him to the hops fields on the Russian River where they will pick hops and enjoy a taste of country life. Reluctantly, because they will be away from their city habitat, the conspirators agree. In the second act, the romance between Effie and Albert develops, stimulated by romantic singing of Mexican hops pickers. A third act moves the action forward by a week, when the romance is threatened by the conspirators' drunken behavior. Albert proposes marriage but then insists that Effie's mother be present at the wedding ceremony.

Whereas the previous acts had sustained a serious and romantic tone, the fourth act played as farce until the final moments when, once again, bleak seriousness returned. The conspiracy has been successful. Albert and the conspirators are in a San Francisco hotel preparing for the imminent wedding. The latter have made various unsuccessful attempts to find a woman who might be bribed to impersonate Effie's mother. A drink-befuddled prostitute is interviewed for the task. Albert is adamant that the wedding be postponed until her "mother" arrives. Meanwhile, the conspirators, greedy for Albert's money, demand that Effie supply them with cash. As a further unlooked-for complication, Effie, who has become increasingly respectful of Albert's honesty, generosity, and gentleness, has begun to fall in love with him. In the final moments of the act, Effie confesses that she has been a party to the conspiracy to dupe Albert but acknowledges that she now loves him. Albert, horrified and revolted, expresses rage and dismay at his own gullibility. In the fifth and final act, fifteen years have elapsed, and Effie, poor, respectable, and worn with toil, lives in a San Francisco tenement inhabited by various women and children whom she has befriended. The tenement's new landlord arrives. It is Albert, who has used his wealth to buy up and renovate slum properties, turning them into comfortable dwellings. Albert has regretted abandoning Effie, and now, as the two meet, he confesses his loneliness and enduring love for her. He again asks Effie to marry him, and she, also still in love with Albert, agrees.

A Fool and a Girl is Griffith's only commercially staged play. The performing rights to *A Fool and a Girl* were purchased from Griffith by Hackett and jointly produced by Hackett and the Klaw and Erlanger management (Klaw and Erlanger expressing their approval by allowing Fanny Ward, then a thirty-five-year-old leading actress, to play the role of Effie). The play was rehearsed in Washington, D.C., in September 1907, Griffith frequently revising the script under instructions from Klaw and Erlanger's stage director, Mr. Duane. It was first performed at Washington's Columbia Theatre on September 30, where it ran for a week receiving reviews both indifferent and hostile. A second week's tryout engagement followed in Baltimore, and the play and company of players, presumably en route to Toledo, then disbanded. *A Fool and a Girl* never reached the Broadway destination Griffith envisioned.

Attempts to establish a wholly accurate account of the play's journey from Griffith's imagination and experience to its final performances are thwarted by the dense mythology surrounding this period of Griffith's life, much of the myth-making provided by Griffith himself who was adept at embellishing personal and creative events which might otherwise seem prosaic. A Fool and a Girl is autobiographical to the extent that Griffith depicts himself as the provincial, priggish, partly—and self-consciously—educated Kentuckian, Albert Holly,[35] and offers in Effie Smith a rouged-up, coarsened rendering of Linda Arvidson, who said of San Francisco girls, herself one of these, that they were notably "piquant,"[36] i.e., sharp-tongued and worldly. His romance with the more urbane Arvidson opened his eyes to an aggressive, complex, multilayered environment and to its underworld infestation of predatory city slickers.

There is only a meager record of the rehearsal and rewriting processes, but it is apparent that Duane and Hackett saw the necessity of reducing Griffith's cast. In the only draft script to survive, more than forty-one speaking characters are specified, many of these small roles which cannot be doubled effectively, as well as two onstage orchestras and somewhat above twenty supernumeraries. The cast list for the Washington premiere calls for no more than twenty speaking roles, some Mexican singers, two Mexican dancers, and a small handful of supers. Additionally, Duane, supervising Griffith's rewrites, compelled the shortening of the play from five acts to four. In all likelihood, this step involved fusing the second and third acts into a single act set on "the edge of [the] Hop[s]-Pickers' camp on [the] Russian River," enabling the action of the play to go forward, but also providing—and perhaps elaborating—an effective setting for the various dance and musical numbers which Griffith builds into both acts in the extant draft: the heritage of the combination company. The Mexican singers and dancers were not merely present to add local color. Their presence in A Fool and a Girl was virtually obligatory in meeting the expectations of American audiences long accustomed to melodramas mixing dramatic action and musical interludes.

Such abridgments to his text as Duane wrought distressed Griffith. Banished by Duane to the alley at the back of the Columbia Theatre, he encountered Hackett, who had arrived from New York for the final dress rehearsal, and complained. Hackett responded, "Well, Griffith, they have certainly done a lot of spoiling of the play I bought—but it's too late now to do anything about it."[37] Griffith reported that Hackett attempted to make changes to the cast before A Fool and a Girl embarked on its tryout tour, but that Klaw and Erlanger refused to permit further alterations. Moreover, neither Hackett nor Klaw and Erlanger sought to share Griffith's copyright. At this date it was not at all unusual for producers, sensing the imminent success of a production, to apply for a joint share of the copyright alongside the author's original right, but, in the instance of A Fool and a Girl, neither management found this drama a commercially viable proposition, and the copyright, assigned August 5, 1906, remained Griffith's alone.

Despite the play's failure, A Fool and a Girl reveals underdeveloped dramatic situations to which Griffith would later return and enlarge in his Biograph films: episodes of marriage and separation, plots of estrangement and reconciliation, dramas of mute loneliness, evidence of his recurring fascination with otherness, especially the Mexican and Native American "other," bolstered by his conceit that he understood and could interpret these marginal cultures. It is therefore inevitable that we view this play retrospectively through the lens of his film successes.

Whatever its few virtues and its bearing on future Griffith works, A Fool and a Girl is clumsy, unoriginal in plot and situations, cloyingly sentimental, with many of its characters—as reviews testified, offensively coarse to early 1900s audiences—constricted by dialogue which, while deliberately slangy, is never easy or natural. In style and approach, the play is conspicuously derivative. The works of other, more successful, American near contemporaries, most conspicuously the West Coast plays of David Belasco and the regional melodramas of Augustus Thomas, loomed in Griffith's mind, and there are hints that he was experimenting with theatrical naturalism but lacked the knowledge, dexterity, temperament, and courage to push his material very far in that direction. Like Belasco, but with demonstrably less of Belasco's dramatic skill, Griffith instead opted for a kind of "romantic realism." Above all, A Fool and a Girl is overly ambitious in that, again emulating both Belasco and Thomas in mise-en-scène and addiction to exotic environments and local color, it required an expensive production and a large cast, far in excess of what Klaw and Erlanger would make available to novice dramatists.

One of the problems which Duane and Hackett failed to address was the play's language. Griffith, in overloading the dialogue with current slang, is attempting to re-create a natural division between the slow, hesitant Kentucky-bred speech of Albert Holly and the racy modernity of the plotters' hard-boiled city talk. This kind of dialogue was finding its way into American drama, but was largely found in comedies as a kind of character signature. In serious melodrama, such as Griffith's play, it was still alien. Moreover, Griffith (or Duane) added dialogue which is not found in this draft and clearly shocked audiences. According to Griffith's autobiography:

The next scene (the new third act) finds the prostitute (Evangeline) indignantly bellowing out over the footlights, "Say, there ain't a single goddam blue-eyed mother in all San Francisco. Belasco has a pretty good one working for him over at his theatre, but she's got coal-black lamps. I got some tramp tied up downstairs, but what a ham! She'll blow our lines in the first act."[38]

Griffith elaborates. This was the first "dam-dam American drama," (i.e., the first in which "goddamn" was spoken from the stage). The effect, according to Griffith, was instantaneous: "Ninety patrons walked out, leaving eleven practically alone. One critic wrote, 'If this be art, it is the art of Zola, and Washington wants none of it.'" Griffith adds, "Of course, such advertising packed the house for the rest of the week."[39] The New York *Dramatic Mirror* accorded the play scant space, merely observing that "first-class audiences will not accept it in its present form. Business at the Columbia theatre with a new production was far below par."[40]

War (1906–1907) is Griffith's second surviving play.[41] Griffith recounts that the money he received for performing rights to *A Fool and a Girl* provoked a fever of writing activity during which he attempted several plays. Linda Arvidson recalled that Griffith had written *In Washington's Time*, but, despite the similarity in subject matter, there is no direct evidence to connect his vaudeville piece with *War*. She also recalled joint intensive research into the American Revolution at the New York Public Library but does not indicate dates when the pair collaborated. Griffith appears to have completed this draft of *War* in early spring 1907 and applied for dramatic copyright soon thereafter. Copyright was granted on May 17, 1907. There is no indication that the manuscript was sent to agents or theatrical producers, nor are there later versions of the script which suggest that Griffith was revising his play for eventual production. As a consequence of this solitary script unrealized in production, any understandings of *War* must be based on readings of the script, on what can be surmised to have been Griffith's understanding of contemporary playmaking and theatre practice, and on the few biographical facts and contemporary events which help to establish a climate in which the drama was composed. It is tempting to read *War* as a matrix from which he would extract future films, especially his late film *America*. However, it is as helpful to regard *War* as Griffith's attempt to write a large-scale epic drama and, equally, a drama which, in critical detail, bears a close resemblance to his more domestic *A Fool and a Girl*.

Whereas Griffith dramatized elements of his own experience in *A Fool and a Girl*, he turned in *War* to popular melodrama played out in the period of the

American Revolution. *War* is set in the American colonies, specifically Massa-chusetts, New Jersey, and Pennsylvania, in the years between 1775 and 1781. The play follows the trajectory of Jackson White, a bond laborer who has exchanged his liberty for five years in order to clear debts and to pay for passage from Eng-land to colonial Massachusetts. Against the background of reaction to the "Boston Tea Party" and the imminent arrival of British troops to forestall rebel-lion, White meets Virginians who will be prominent in the Revolution and, with them, accompanying her aristocratic father, Jennie Randolph Graves. White joins the rebellion and with other "minutemen," marches toward Concord. The second act finds White in New Jersey, encamped with George Washington on the Delaware River and suffering extreme privation from wintry cold and hunger. The Americans realize that a sudden assault on Trenton will catch the British and Hessian mercenaries unaware. White is ordered to slip into Trenton and spy out the locations of enemy units and then report his findings to Wash-ington. The secret march on Trenton begins.

The third act, divided into three scenes, two of these set in the British mili-tary garrison in Trenton, poses the conflict between personal considerations and a higher duty to the American Revolution which will hereafter affect White's and Jennie's relationship. As White slips into the enemy camp, orgiastic Christ-mas revels are at their height in the quarters of the English forces. Jennie is brought a captive into the room. Justifying his power and the license that war allegedly gives to rapine and savage cruelty, the commander attempts to seduce Jennie, who resists and expresses contempt and dismay. At this point White, disguised as a Quaker, enters. White grasps the situation and the danger in which Jennie has been placed. He is confronted with the choice: either effect a rescue of Jennie and compromise his mission to bring intelligence of the British and Hessian troops back to Washington or to complete his mission and so abandon Jennie to rape by the British officer. White, with Jennie's knowledge of the nature of his secret mission and insistence that she be sacrificed to assure its success, departs. A second scene, on the bank of the Delaware River, is the setting for the American advance. American scouts stalk and kill British sen-tries. Signaling with lanterns back across to the American side, the Americans give the all clear to the Continental Army. Washington and his troops, ferrying men and cannons by raft, are seen crossing the icy Delaware. After this brief mimed action, the play returns to the British Trenton quarters where, amid the detritus of the Christmas celebrations, officers awaken from drunken sleep to the havoc of Washington's surprise attack. White bursts in to receive from Jen-nie acknowledgment that he has arrived too late to save her from rape. White defeats the British commander in a duel as Jennie is led away under her uncle's care. Later, White has been seriously wounded in the action at Yorktown, Virginia. Lying in a hospital bed, he is visited by Jennie, who has traveled from Boston to see him, and by a comrade who brings a citation from Washington which adds to his battle honors a grant of Virginia land and freedom from his former bond. He asks Jennie to marry him and, after some hesitation, at first arguing that she is condemned to a solitary life, she agrees.

Griffith's decision to set his drama against the conflicts of the American Revolution was misjudged. Examination of the New York theatrical successes in the decade prior to the composition of *War* reveals that the American Revolution figures minimally. There was little money to be earned with this topic. Only three previous plays approach this subject, and only Clyde Fitch's *Nathan Hale* (1899) enjoyed a substantial run. *Nathan Hale* does, however, offer a pattern found in Griffith's drama: a well-bred American heroine oppressed by a loutish British officer but championed and defended by an American patriot. As in *War*, Fitch's melodrama offers a cruel choice: betray the Revolution or the heroine, do one's public duty or meet private responsibilities. This configuration of heroine, American patriot, and enemy villain paired with the moral and social choice between the lesser of evils—between the greater public good and the private individual—can be found in any number of contemporary plays. It is not particular to Fitch or Griffith. Nevertheless, far more popular than dramas of the American Revolution are plays set in the American Civil War, only thirty-odd years in the past, and—even more popular—plays set during the recent Spanish-American War. Griffith chose not to follow the well-beaten and more remunerative path.

What was therefore likely as an inspiration, if not a source, for *War*'s subject matter and actual staging was less a drama than a pair of paintings. In 1897 New York's Metropolitan Museum of Art had accepted the gift of Emanuel Gottlieb Leutze's 1851 *Washington Crossing the Delaware*. This iconic American history painting depicts General George Washington standing upright in a skiff as he and his Continental Army cross the frozen Delaware River to surprise the unwary British at the Battle of Trenton, December 26, 1776. In the brief second scene of the third act, which ends with the tableau of Washington and his forces crossing the Delaware by raft, Griffith partly "realizes" Leutze's iconography, clearly referencing, but perhaps not explicitly duplicating, the painting. Griffith, using the parades which end the first act as well as the first scene of the fourth act—twice realizes another American iconic painting, Archibald Williams's *The Spirit of 1776* (1876), in which a trio of ragged American patriots are depicted marching resolutely with an anachronistic "Betsy Ross" flag, a drum, and a fife. Thus, clumsy as *War* is, it reveals Griffith's theatrical sense: an ability to grasp the importance of the end-of-act tableau, a capacity to visualize a stage full of moving and grouped actors, and an understanding of how to move between large-scale action demanding a full stage and brief-but-significant scenes which are staged "in-one," that is, downstage above the act curtain and below the first or second set of tabs.

What linked *War* to *A Fool and a Girl* were two overriding characteristics. As with Griffith's earlier play, his imagined cast size is again vast, calling as it does for more than forty speaking roles and allowing little opportunity for actors to double in multiple roles. Additionally, Griffith specifies numerous supernumeraries, many of whom can be doubled, but whose costuming and hand properties would nevertheless make extravagant demands on any theatrical wardrobe or armory. In concept and in this draft, *War* requires a conspicuously expensive production. Were *War* to have been commercially produced, Griffith would have been set the task of simplifying his cast. He would have been obliged to reduce the first and second acts, both stuffed with research but neither act offering much dramatic incident—only the arrival of messengers.

Even more significant as a link between *A Fool and a Girl* and *War* are Griffith's characterizations of his hero and, more so, his heroine. Both dramas enact encounters between idealistic men and the principled women whom they love—women physically as well as mentally and emotionally abused and damaged by privation, war, rape or prostitution, and penury. In Griffith's lexicon, they must be degraded, and only then redeemed, before consummation is possible. The hero, too, is chastened and suffers, undergoing his own anguished self-recognition and verbal abasement. Nevertheless, it is Griffith's heroine who is subjected to excessive pain and degradation and—again in Griffith's eyes—sanctified by her suffering and purged of sexual contamination before the couple can reconcile their differences and end their painful estrangement.

We can follow this recurrent motif in Griffith's work. An arc of degradation, guilt, expiation, and recovery—or a similar arc of maltreatment, damage, rejection or exile (self-imposed or wrought by the community), and eventual forgiveness and reintegration—enter Griffith's films[42] as early as 1910 in the character of Bella in *The Dancing Girl of Butte*, resurfacing in the rejected, but heroic, Jennie Baker in Biograph's *Swords and Hearts* (1911), and again in Blanche Sweet's nameless "woman of the camp" who selflessly mothers an orphaned baby in *The God Within* (1912). Sweet's Judith in *Judith of Bethulia* (1913) would face risk from the enemy and excoriating invective from her city before being received as a heroine, a victor, and savior, but her heroism would cost her the loss of love and sexual fulfillment. However, it was through the lengthy collaboration between Lillian Gish and Griffith that the abused or damaged or seemingly transgressive heroine—always a victim who somehow managed to rise above her oppression—was most regularly realized: Lucy Burrows in *Broken Blossoms* (1919), Susie Mae Trueheart in *True Heart Susie* (1919), Anna Moore in *Way Down East* (1920), and Henriette in *Orphans of the Storm*. When Gish left Griffith's stock company after 1922, these roles fell to Carol Dempster, whom he cast in such films as *The White Rose* (1922) and *America* (1924) where again heroines unduly suffer.

War completed and set aside, Arvidson and Griffith traveled to Jamestown, Virginia, for roles in a centennial pageant where Griffith briefly appeared as a Native American, reprising his role in *Ramona*. Back in New York, acting work dried up. No roles were on offer. In desperation, first Linda, and then Griffith, turned to New York's film studios.

Griffith at Biograph

In December 1907, Griffith walked into American Mutoscope and Biograph Company's studio. He found himself in a strange and unfamiliar world, a performance space without the familiar accoutrements of performing and enacted storytelling. Nothing he saw at Biograph suggested a theatre space or setting. There was no stage of the kind with which actors and audiences were familiar. There were no heavy velour "legs" to mask wings or overhead pleated "teasers" to conceal battens and border lights. There certainly was no space for spectators to watch.

Studio lighting was unlike theatrical lighting. There were no footlights and no spots or limelights. Rather than the various hanging and stand-mounted lamps found in Victorian and early-twentieth-century theatres, film studios were illuminated from overhead by banks of three-foot-long glass tubes—mercury vapor lights—which gave off intense glare. Stage actors trained to "find their light" in a spotlight or Fresnel lens would not see a glowing central filament to guide their positioning. Looking directly into these lamps was known to be damaging to the eyes. Because these lamps and strategically placed reflectors and linen diffusers provided the source of all illumination and because illumination was general rather than intended to duplicate natural light, this multidirectional broad lighting drove shadows to the floor or dispersed them altogether.

The very materials of filmmaking conspired against those who arrived with theatrical experience and who expected to work as before. Film stock was coated in emulsions which reacted slowly to light and required careful exposure. Because of the intense lighting and because film responded erratically, actors, used to makeup for stage roles, were instructed to use cosmetics sparingly. Without careful exposure, developing, and fixing, early film read cosmetics and scene paint strangely and unpredictably. Reds were often unreadable or became black and appeared improbably opaque.[1] To avoid errant readings of color, painted scenery was rendered in gradations of gray. Not until orthochromatic film came into general use around 1906 was there a predictable link between stage and film makeup. Orthochromatic film, while rendering black-and-white images, recognized color and reproduced subtle gradations in hues and tints.

Camera lenses had to be kept "open" to admit sufficient light, and this very openness restricted the depth of field in which actors were held in sharp focus. That lack of visual depth—the shallowness of a focused zone—is the principal reason why early films most often show actors in lateral motion, moving across the picture plane. Actors rarely and ineffectually moved from an upstage position toward the camera—unless that camera was filming an outdoor episode. Then, with the action illuminated by daylight and reflectors, the actors might appear from great distances, move toward the camera, and finish their movements behind the camera. Griffith would have noted a piano, the only object to connect the Biograph studio with a theatre.[2] Live "takes" were often accompanied with music to assist the actors in finding the emotional tone and gestural vocabulary of the scene being filmed.

Unlike some of the larger film companies, Biograph did not occupy a purpose-built structure, such as the Edison studio in the Bronx, a building not unlike an airplane hangar. Rather, Biograph rented premises—studio, office space, processing rooms, property storage, and wardrobe—in a dilapidated brownstone mansion at 11 East Fourteenth Street. Its former ballroom was all the indoor space available for shooting films.

The actual space for indoor filming—Griffith's "stage"—was cramped. A photograph, taken in Biograph's Fourteenth Street studio in 1908, shows a studio cameraman standing with his camera on a raised dais. At a distance of about ten feet from his camera is a small stage, no more than twelve feet across and no more than five feet deep, raised approximately four feet above the floor and supported on wooden trestles, on which seven actors are crowded together.[3] There is little space for movement of any kind. Griffith's actors were similarly confined to assure that their expressions, gestures, and actions remained in focus throughout the shot:

a [studio] "scene" was set back center, just allowing passage room.[4] . . . Johnny Mahr [the assistant cameraman] with his five-foot board would get the focus and mark little chalk crosses on the floor, usually four, two for the foreground and two for the background. Then Johnny would hammer a nail in each cross and with his ball of twine, tying it from nail to nail, enclose the set.[5]

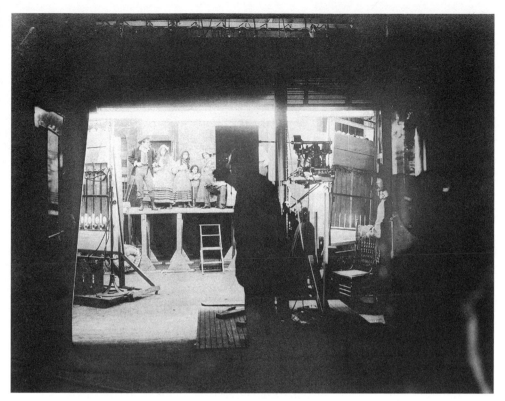

A crew filming Griffith's *The Cord of Life* at the Biograph studio,
1908. The actors, crowded on a narrow platform stage, hold the
action in focus. Museum of Modern Art Film Stills Archive.

From 1910 onward, improved lenses and "faster" film allowed actors and directors greater latitude in their movements, but, for the moment, Griffith, first an
actor, then a director, was restricted in his use of space.

In such conditions, Griffith began as a jobbing actor. His early films for Biograph and Edison show him assuming roles in which he is distinctly stiff and
visibly uncomfortable and which cast further light on the limits of his stage
aspirations. His height and rigidity drew attention to his awkwardness as an
actor. In his first Biograph film, *Professional Jealousy*, a theatrical drama, Griffith
appeared briefly in the role of an actor performing in a scene from H. Grattan
Donnelly's *Darkest Russia*. At the Edison studio, he was cast as a hunter in *Rescued
from the Eagle's Nest*, attempting to rescue a child stolen by an eagle and in his
rescue attempt forced to do battle with a stuffed eagle (Griffith seems equally a
victim of indifferent taxidermy). Again at Biograph, in *Ostler Joe*, which he also

adapted and directed in May 1908, Griffith assumed the role of an English squire who seduces a married woman. None of these roles or other early parts suggests that the theatre had lost an actor of significance. His cameraman Billy Bitzer confirms just how inept and unsuited to film performance Griffith's acting could be:

> [Griffith]. . . seemed to have three or four arms instead of the usual two. He acted with so many gestures because . . . that has been his stage style in costume dramas with Nance O'Neil and other stars of the theater. The second time I encountered him, he overacted the part of a bartender. . . . I asked him if he was trying to get me fired, or wasn't he aware his mugging was taking the action away from the lead? He confided that a friend had told him that was the way to act in pictures, but now that I had brought it to his attention, he wouldn't do it again. He told me he was a writer, accepting movie jobs for money. He asked my advice about directing. I advised him against it, for I couldn't see how a man who wasn't a passable actor could direct a flock of geese. I also told him if he tried for director and didn't make good, his acting career in our studio would be over.[6]

He was obliged to adjust rapidly to this alien environment or lose his one certain source of income. Arvidson, who followed Griffith to Biograph, apparently only days later, was faced with the same Darwinian option: adapt or perish.

Griffith, meanwhile, settled in as an actor, working under the instructions of Wallace McCutcheon Sr. Although, according to Arvidson's account, Griffith had been encouraged to supplement his three dollars' acting wage by submitting scenarios for films, each to earn fifteen dollars, he appeared as an actor in McCutcheon-directed Biograph films and one Edison film before his first scenario, *Old Isaacs the Pawnbroker*, was accepted and shot in March 1908. He then appeared in a further fourteen films, still clinging to his actor's job and the certain wage that this work earned, and meanwhile submitting six successful scripts to McCutcheon. Griffith began directing films in June 1908, but there are quiet hints that he began his directorial apprenticeship by filming "smokers"— semi-pornographic dramas for use in mutoscopes. These "off-color" films were traditionally shot on Biograph sets after hours, once regular actors and staff had left for the night.[7]

What his films tell of this process of adjustment is that he worked from what he knew best, fashioning a simulacrum of the theatre and a theatrical organization, abridging plays for the screen, building a repertory company of actors from the corps of Biograph players who worked on a guarantee of so many days' employment each week,[8] and gradually, from 1908 onward, recruiting more actors with professional stage experience. Motion pictures made different demands on him, requiring him to devise scenarios and, only weeks later, to realize his own scenarios—and those of others—on film. In responding to these new demands, Griffith, incompetent actor and unsuccessful dramatist, had inadvertently reached the threshold of a new environment. But, in order to go forward, he had to step backward into a craft and milieu, the theatre, with which he was already familiar.

Despite Biograph's constricted space, Griffith employed theatre tricks to create the illusion of greater space even when there was none available. Tables and shop counters which, in earlier Biograph directors' shots, had been placed parallel to the focal plane, were turned at angles to suggest a room's depth. A favored device (used sparingly) was to place actors "downstage" with their backs to the camera and to station the principal actor "upstage" and off-center facing these actors. The upstage actor appeared farther away than he actually was, and the overall effect was to suggest a larger room with space between the upstage and downstage actors.

When Griffith was first permitted and, later, encouraged to direct, he had several examples of successful directors to choose from before developing his own methods. David Belasco was said to have been his lifelong idol,[9] and he aspired to work for Charles Frohman,[10] but initially, he would have known these men only from afar, as a member of an audience attending plays which they had directed or underwritten. He would have known of Belasco's directorial techniques and staging methods only by hearsay or by watching productions well past the rehearsal stage and with awkward moments long resolved. But he was a close observer. He saw, and presumably, remembered and learned.

Gradually, Griffith's orbit and Belasco's overlapped. Griffith had appeared briefly in San Francisco's Central Theatre, then under the management of Fred Belasco, David's brother.[11] Mary Pickford was to come to Biograph in 1910 directly from David Belasco's stage production of The Warrens of Virginia, but Griffith was to lose Pickford entirely and Lillian Gish briefly when, in 1911, they accepted offers from Belasco to appear in The Good Little Devil. Griffith used the occasion of the play's pre-Broadway openings in Philadelphia and Baltimore to attend the first-night performances and go backstage, ostensibly to congratulate his two actresses, but more likely to meet Belasco.[12] Earlier, in 1909, when Griffith's California westerns were beginning to reach screens, he was said to be hugely flattered when a trade journal critic described him as "the Belasco of motion pictures."[13] Like Belasco, a womanizer, Griffith tended to surround himself with women and, like Belasco, he expected to dominate them as evidence of the director's power and unchallenged authority. As motion pictures rivaled and then outstripped the theatre in popularity, Griffith, unlike some of his filmmaking colleagues, held back from criticizing or ridiculing the faltering, aging Belasco—who had become an easy target for anti-theatre satire.[14]

In all probability, his mentors were closer to home. Oscar Eagle, in whose company Griffith had toured Ohio River Valley towns in 1899, was now directing in New York, and Griffith's immediate teachers were the two Wallace McCutcheons, father and son. The McCutcheons emphasized the physicality of film performance. What mattered was action conducted at a speed that would register in the camera and which would be legible when the film was later projected upon the often wrinkled and non-light-reflecting screen of a storefront nickelodeon. Lillian Gish, who had had occasion to work with both Griffith and Belasco, contrasted the difference in their approach: with Belasco, she said, "much time was spent on words rather than action."[15]

Set dressing and actors' costumes created further problems. Biograph's store of properties and furnishings was meager, and the same familiar chairs, curtains, vases, pictures, crucifixes, dolls, and cooking utensils reappeared with a mesmerizing frequency. With the company's growing prosperity, that store increased, but Biograph relied on the short memories of their customers to overlook familiar items shared between the homes of various characters. Wardrobes presented a similar problem of reappearing garments. The same dresses appeared in numerous films, their appearances altered with new tassels or buttons or different collars or sashes. Arvidson recalled:

> Any one with "clothes" had a wonderful open sesame. A young chap whom we dubbed "the shoe clerk"—who never played a thing but "atmosphere"—got many a pay-check on the strength of his neat tan covert cloth spring overcoat—(An actor could get along in the spring with his winter suit and no overcoat!). . . . Clothes soon became a desperate matter, so Biograph consented to spend fifty dollars for wearing apparel for the women. . . . We needed negligees, dinner dresses, ball gowns, and semi-tailored effects. The clothes were to be bought in sizes to fit, as well as could be, the three principal women.[16]. . . How those garments worked! I have forgotten many, but one—a brown silk and velvet affair—I can never forget. It was the first to be grabbed off the hook. . . . Arrayed in the brown silk and velvet, there could be no doubt as to one's moral status—the maiden lady it made obviously poor, the faithful mother, self-sacrificing. . . . Deciding, impromptu, to elaborate on a social affair, Mr. Griffith would call out: "I can use you, Miss Bierman, if you can find a dress to fit you." . . . Spotting a new piece of millinery in the studio, our director would thus approach the wearer: "I have

no part for you, Miss Hart, but I can use your hat for this picture. I'll give you five dollars if you will let Miss Pickford wear your hat for this picture."[17]

Griffith's first scenario, Old Isaacs the Pawnbroker, came with a lengthy theatrical pedigree. It was, in many ways, to be typical of his adaptations of theatrical pieces: using characters known to theatre audiences and taking situations and elements of plots but abridging them so that the shorter film elided emotional nuances found in the longer work which led to solutions different from those reached in the stage play. Griffith's screenplay about a widowed Jewish pawnbroker who, moved by a child's poverty, intervenes to assist her destitute mother with food, money, and medical treatment, drew most immediately upon Charles E. Blaney's Old Isaacs from the Bowery (1906), which had moved into the American touring repertoire. Old Isaacs from the Bowery was itself a rip-off of several plays which depicted Jews disposed to Christian charity, most notably The Auctioneer (1901), the joint work of Lee Arthur, Charles Klein, and, covertly, David Belasco, and an older play, J. H. Jessop's Sam'l of Posen (1881), which Griffith may have seen at Macauley's Theatre in Louisville. What apparently linked these plays in Griffith's mind was the pawnbroker's shop as a setting for an impromptu charitable act, a moment when the hard-hearted businessman astonishes himself by succumbing to his own generous impulses.

As directed by Wallace McCutcheon, Old Isaacs the Pawnbroker is overtly and continually sentimental. When Griffith, directing and frequently devising his own scenarios, returned to the subject of a Jewish pawnbroker in The Romance of a Jewess, written and shot just six months later in September 1908, the pawnbroker's counter (now angled away from the picture plane) becomes a site for comic action as a succession of improbable clients—an Irishwoman, a drunk, and an actor—attempt to pawn their trifles and snatch articles of clothing from their bodies. Griffith, drawing especially on Sam'l of Posen and the pathos of an Irishwoman seeking to pawn the shawl that wraps her baby, plays against the film's dominant sentimentality. He took his camera into Rivington Street to catch the fervid commercial activity of the New York ghetto and, with his pawnshop interior and its parade of Lower East Side character types, added to the film's comedy and also to the sense of lives touched by need and exigencies.

Ostler Joe, which Griffith next adapted for McCutcheon, and in which he performed in May 1908, was taken from a narrative ballad by the English melodramatist George R. Sims. It was Sims's melodrama The Lights o' London (1881) in which Griffith had appeared while on tour. Griffith's decision to adapt Sims's ballad for the screen reveals that he was already aware how this film would be exhibited: accompanied both by music and by live recitation of the full ballad.

Accordingly, the Biograph Bulletin, which was sent to exhibitors to induce them to buy this film, published the full text of Sims's ballad, putting into their hands a text from which a narrator or bonimenteur might read.[18] No other words of explanation were necessary.

Griffith's Ostler Joe is a film which, in its use of narrative material, refers back to the Victorian showmen and their dissolving-view slides, and which, in its brief mimed drama, refers to the music hall dramatic sketch. "Ostler Joe" had been first published in a weekly London sporting journal, The Referee, in 1879, and the next year in an anthology of Sims's poems, The Dagonet Reader. The ballad then moved thereafter by turns into the recitation repertoire, into photographic slide sets, and into film. By 1885, the American reciter-actress, Mrs. James Brown Potter, was insisting that Sims had composed "Ostler Joe" for her exclusive use. In Britain, Madge Kendal made a similar claim on the poem, and a bemused and exasperated Sims, who had earned no royalties from the numerous American recitations, denied an intentional connection with any performer. Not at all surprisingly, "Ostler Joe" was ripped off—first, by manufacturers of photographic slide sets such as Banfords of Holmfirth, Yorkshire.

A ballad, which requires approximately twelve minutes to recite, established the duration of a film which required approximately twelve minutes to project. Ostler Joe's overall structure is tailored to the lumpy episodic structure of Sims's ballad, with each episode of the cinema narrative elongated or abridged to coincide with the text. The result is a lumpy episodic film, but equally a film which, yoked to a supporting ballad declaimed as the film is projected, is nonetheless entertaining and moving.

Griffith's former familiarity with the comic routines of Louisville's Buckingham burlesque theatre, as well as the likelihood that he was generating similar burlesque-related material for Biograph's off-color mutoscopes, emerge in his Monday Morning in a Coney Island Police Court, shot on a single day in August 1908. Habitués of America's burlesque theatres would have recognized in this film one of the standard plotless sketches enacted in such establishments. Griffith provided a parade of petty malefactors—a drunken tramp, a snake charmer from a Coney Island sideshow booth who has been arrested for stealing a hot dog, a prostitute, and two brawlers—as well as two rival lawyers, an indolent and inattentive policeman (played by Mack Sennett, who would leave Biograph in 1912 to create the Keystone Kops), and a sleepy court page. Each petty malefactor appears before a rowdy gavel-wielding judge, whose sentencing is either uncompromisingly harsh or excessively lenient. The sausage thief is given the choice of life imprisonment or death; the streetwalker, who captivates the judge, has the charges against her dismissed. The film shares with Griffith's previous pawnshop-counter scenes a determination to give each actor space in which to develop his or her comic schtick and then move on. Beyond this loose sequence of sight gags, there is little structure or anecdotal shaping.

In his early months at Biograph, Griffith, failing to find a convincingly strong climax to a film he had directed, was drawn back to the vaudeville dramatic sketch. In August 1908, he had directed *For Love of Gold*, adapted from a Jack London short story of two prospectors falling out over the division of their accumulated takings and killing each other in their greed. In December, he turned again to greed, division, and murder in *Money Mad*, a drama in which two thieves rob a miser, then dispute their shares of loot and battle to their deaths. To end this second film, Griffith turned to the climactic episode of John Lawson's 1897 sketch *Humanity*, a drama which remained popular on American and English variety circuits until 1913, when Lawson, succumbing to the enticements of British filmmakers, turned his sketch into a three-reel film. Lawson had based his original sketch upon an actual crime in which two robbers fought in a burning London tenement, wrecking the apartment they had shared and setting fire to the stairs, down which they tumbled, still fighting, both expiring at the bottom. Griffith appropriated Lawson's fiery ending, omitting the stairs, but adding an old woman who intended to steal the robbers' loot but was frustrated when all the miser's hoard, jewels and money, were consumed in the fire.

Also in September 1908, adapting the Victorian stage classic *Ingomar the Barbarian* as his vehicle, Griffith made his first film confronting questions of race and nationality. The drama, an 1851 adaptation by Maria Lovell from Friedrich Halm's *Son of the Wilderness* (*Der Sohn der Wildnis*), had remained in the American repertoire into the twentieth century, and it is likely that Griffith had seen the play in Louisville theatres, as the roles of Ingomar and Parthenia were favorites with touring stars, and three separate productions had reached Louisville between 1894 and 1896. Written by Halm in 1842 for Viennese audiences, this five-act play had always been associated with issues of foreignness, assimilation, and national loyalties. Set in Massilia (now Marseille) in the fourth century at a time when the Roman occupation was threatened by invasions of Visigoths, the drama enacts conflicts between these cultures. In Halm's original play and in Lovell's English language adaptation, Myron, a Massilian armorer traveling between communities, is abducted and held for ransom by Goths, led by the barbarian chief, Ingomar. When penny-pinching Massilians plead unwillingness to assist with the ransom, Myron's daughter Parthenia goes to the barbarian camp to plead for his release and, when her pleas fail, to offer herself as a hostage until Myron can earn his freedom. She is given a dagger to protect herself. Alone with the barbarians, she is threatened with being sold to slavers and with gang rape, but, although she defends herself, she requires rescue from both threats by Ingomar, who has fallen in love with her and escorts her back to Massilia. There the two marry. Later, settled and farming near Massilia, Ingomar is spurned and derided as an ignorant foreigner, an alien, an interloper. When barbarians subsequently attack the city, Igomar's loyalties are put to the test, and when he sides with the Massilians and drives off the barbarian invaders, he is recognized as belonging to the community, and his former detractors are shamed.

Griffith, obviously influenced by contemporary American thought on national identity and by jingoist rhetoric, departs from this plot and the conclusions which may be drawn from it. Between Lovell's play and Griffith's 1908 filmic adaptation, an intense tide of nationalist polemic had arisen, characterized by attempts to define and reinforce "Americanism." The principal voice in this call for explicit American values and instant assimilation of foreigners was that of the nation's twenty-sixth president, Theodore Roosevelt (1901–1909). Between 1894 and 1915, in a series of books, pamphlets, and speeches,[19] Roosevelt inveighed against "hyphenated-Americans" who resolutely clung to Old World ways while concurrently benefiting from American life. Initially, his rhetoric was directed against Chinese and Japanese immigrants on the West Coast and their distinctive otherness, but as Americans became increasingly aware of immigration from southern and eastern Europe, Roosevelt's demands for assimilation became more inclusive. In his second term in office, Roosevelt supported a congressional inquiry and subsequent legislation relating to "new immigrants" from the Balkans, Russia, and southern Europe. Curiously, his dismay at aliens who remained apart did not extend to African Americans, perhaps because he viewed them as inherently distinct and beyond the possibilities of assimilation into white culture. His rhetoric thus stood apart from much of the current antiblack polemic, although it ran in parallel lines and doubtless fueled the overall climate of racism to which Griffith would contribute.

Griffith's The Barbarian Ingomar is more than a reversal of the title. He shares Halm's and Lovell's contempt for the Massilian bourgeoisie, but he altogether avoids issues of national rivalries and cultural difference which characterize the earlier stage plays. Rather, by entirely eliminating the last two acts of the drama and concluding his film with Parthenia's rescue by Ingomar, Griffith draws a different inference. Concentrating on two final episodes, the first in which Ingomar, having driven off the rape-determined barbarians and holding Parthenia in his power, relinquishes his barbarian ways to court Parthenia with gentleness and civility, and a second, in which he brings Parthenia back to her Massilian family and appears to acknowledge their Roman customs and to promise to forgo his barbarian life, Griffith underscores Roosevelt's demand: in accepting civilization (read Americanism), and in rejecting the characteristics which stamp Ingomar as dangerously alien, Ingomar is made welcome—as immigrants will be made welcome when they agree to assimilate. Then, and only then, will they truly be welcomed into American homes. Only then will foreign-born and native-born intermarry.

As is evident by *The Barbarian Ingomar* and by *A Fool's Revenge*, which Griffith shot in February 1909, much of Biograph's narrative output consisted of costume dramas. The source for this latter film was Tom Taylor's 1859 adaptation of Victor Hugo's *Le Roi s'amuse*, better known to modern audiences through Giuseppe Verdi's opera *Rigoletto*. Although many of Biograph's costume films show little regard for period accuracy and tend to resemble masquerades where any costume will do, Griffith's adaptation was praised for its resemblance— in mise-en-scène, texture, and fine acting—to Pathé Films d'Art. The American trade press praised Owen Moore's self-indulgent Duke, unscrupulous in his abduction of attractive females, Charles Inslee's nameless fool, who caters to his patron's whims until his daughter becomes a victim, and Marion Leonard's rendering of his abused and self-sacrificing daughter.[20]

Now recognized by Biograph studio heads as a director whose films were popular with exhibitors, Griffith was increasingly given a free hand in planning and casting his films. He sought performers who knew their craft and who would be responsive to his instructions. To this end, he began trawling New York theatres, cafés, and theatrical clubs where actors congregated. Contrary to much of the prevailing mythology which stresses the theatrical inexperience of Griffith's performers and Griffith's alleged preference for unskilled actors who could be molded to his requirements, Griffith, from the moment of his arrival at Biograph, was already working with actors who had some personal experience of live theatrical performance. Those actors in Griffith's first stock company included John R. Cumpson, Charles Inslee, Arthur Johnson, Michael Sinnott (later taking the name of Mack Sennett), and Harry Solter. Marion Leonard, Florence Lawrence (who had been a dancer), and Linda Arvidson were Biograph's leading actresses. None of these performers was named in Biograph's advertisements or promotional literature, but Florence Lawrence was already beginning to receive fan mail addressed to the "Biograph Girl." Gradually, Griffith built his second stock company while losing Arthur Johnson to alcoholism and Florence Lawrence and Harry Solter to a rival film company. His recruiting through 1912 brought in Henry Walthall, Gladys Smith (later renamed Mary Pickford), Adolph Lestina (with whom Griffith had acted in Nance O'Neil's West Coast company), W. Christie Miller, Lillian and Dorothy

Gish, Dorothy Bernard, Claire McDowell and her husband, Charles Mailes Hill (both of whom had acted in a 1905 road company of Thomas Dixon Jr.'s *The Clansman*), James Kirkwood, Lionel Barrymore, and Herbert Yost. He also recruited two dancers from the Gertrude Hoffman company, Gertrude Bambrick, who was to dance and choreograph for Griffith's films, and Blanche Sweet, who became one of Griffith's principal actresses.

It was in the course of building this second company of actors that Griffith entered the Lambs' Club. Although there is no evidence of their meeting, nor even of casual conversation between the two men, Griffith would have observed the noted English actor, Charles Warner. Warner was to become, albeit inadvertently, an important influence on Griffith's next film. In June 1897, Warner had appeared in the part of Coupeau in Charles Reade's *Drink*, an anglicized adaptation of Busnach's and Gastineau's theatrical adaptation of Emile Zola's novel *L'Assommoir*. The effect of this play and Warner's performance as Coupeau, a role in which he moved from tender gentleness to the heights of delirium tremens, was startling, a revelation of anguish and psychological trauma. For a full thirty years, Warner was identified with this role. Coupeau was his golden goose, but it also was a prize Warner could not discard, nor could he successfully persuade booking agents and foreign tour managers that there were other strings to his theatrical bow.

Emile Zola's 1878 novel *L'Assommoir* is one of a series of narratives describing the interlocking lives and desperate struggle of two families, the Rougons and Macquarts, to survive in both rural and urban France. Gervaise, a simple country girl from one of these families, arrives in the Paris suburbs, is seduced and betrayed. Virginie, her rival, the one who leads her partner astray, is a fellow employee in a laundry. Finding a new partner whom she can respect for his industry, the sober and respectable roofer, Coupeau, Gervaise starts a new life and appears headed for happiness. A child, Nana, is born to the pair. Unfortunately, Coupeau is then injured in a workplace fall, made idle, and takes heavily to drink. So excessive is Coupeau's alcoholism that eventually he dies experiencing horrendous delirium tremens. Gervaise, introduced to drink, becomes more and more slatternly and promiscuous, and she, too, dies in squalor. Nana grows into an opportunistic tart. The novel shocked readers with its detailed account of wretched slum life, of alcoholic degradation, of a Darwinian display of the unfit and unadaptable perishing in a hostile and predator-filled environment. There is no evidence that Griffith had read Zola's novel, but there is little doubt that he knew one or more variants of Reade's stage version, which in 1909 became the source for his own *A Drunkard's Reformation*.

The English stage actor Charles Warner, ca. 1880.

Charles Reade's Drink, simplified from the novel and made more palatable to English audiences—who were not prepared to see a woman succumb to alcoholism and blowsy promiscuity—enacts the downward trajectory of Coupeau alone and concentrates on his battle with the bottle. Any promise of recovery is shattered because the drama's villainess, the "adventuress" Virginie (who has openly flirted with Coupeau and is visibly jealous of Gervaise), sneaks into Coupeau's household and places before the feeble Coupeau strong brandy decanted into a Bordeaux bottle. Coupeau drinks from the gift bottle. It immediately produces an alcoholic frenzy, the sight of approaching demons, delirium, and sudden death. Although Warner's playing throughout Drink was consistently strong, this scene of temptation, sudden inebriation, and careening delirium was Warner's signature moment. The London Daily News described the scene as Griffith was later to restage it:

> Coupeau is left alone with the supposed bottle of claret which the treacherous Virginie has sent in. Shall he have half a glass just to warm him? . . . with trembling hands he . . . takes out the cork. . . . Then a spasm of horrible delight thrills him as he makes the discovery that it is brandy. He recoils from it and crouches at the other end of the room, putting all the space possible between table and wall between him and the tempter. . . . He will just taste it. With horrible gleaming eyes and convulsive fingers he approaches the table, seizes the bottle, and drinks. At first the spirit revives and strengthens him, and with new vigour he rushes out of the room, carrying the bottle with him. When he comes back his wife has returned, and finds him a raving maniac with the empty bottle. So he dies on the stage . . . the most terrible scene ever presented on the English Stage.[21]

Warner had undertaken three conspicuously remunerative American tours of his London stage success.[22] Warner's tours did not take him to Louisville, and while it is possible that Griffith saw a full performance of Drink during his years as an itinerant actor, it is more likely that their paths briefly intersected in vaudeville. Sometimes, to meet the requirements of the Keith-Albee Circuit, Warner had toured a pared-down version of this play, and Griffith would have noted the play's critical scenes and observed Warner's performance. In 1908, Warner again sailed to New York to see his son "Harry"[23] on Broadway and, with misplaced optimism, intended to persuade American managements to underwrite a tour of material other than Drink.

On the morning of Friday, February 12, 1909, Griffith would have read the headlines and lead story in the New York Times: "C. J. WARNER, ACTOR COMMITS SUICIDE. Man who became World-Famous In "Drink" Hangs Himself in

Fig. 14. Mr. Charles Warner.
(*Showing Outline of Features.*)

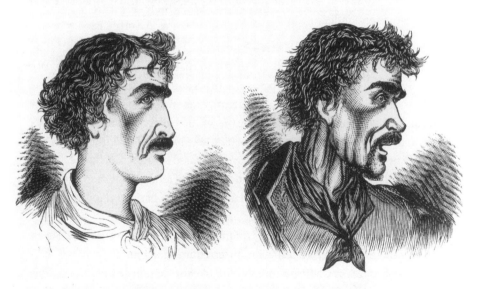

Fig. 15. Mr. Chas. Warner as Coupeau,
in "Drink."
(*Showing Unfinished Make-up.*)

Fig. 16. Mr. Chas. Warner as Coupeau,
in "Drink."
(*Showing Finished Make-up.*)

Charles Warner's makeup for his role as Coupeau in Charles Reade's *Drink*, as depicted
in Charles Harrison's *Theatricals and Tableaux Vivants for Amateurs*, ca. 1885.

His Room in the Seymour." For a full column of this broadsheet, the unnamed reporter describes how Warner was found hanged in his Manhattan hotel suite. Sent by transatlantic cable to London, the report of Warner's death was repeated with even greater dismay in the British press a day later. News of Warner continued through February 14, the day of his funeral at the Church of the Transfiguration ("the little church around the corner").

If Griffith felt pity or sympathy for Warner, those feelings never compromised his next project. There is no indication that he had been planning any sort of temperance piece or if, with Warner's suicide, the final element—the inner drama, a visit of a drunkard father and an earnest, frightened child to a performance of Drink—suggested itself. What survives as evidence of Biograph and Griffith exploiting this calamity is the final film, A Drunkard's Reformation, its intertitles missing[24] and the Biograph Bulletin's explanation of what may be either or both Biograph's marketing strategy and Griffith's aesthetic approach:

> The whole construction of the picture is most novel, showing as it does, a play within a play. It is a sort of triangular [sic] in motive, that is to say, the play depicts to the leading actor in the picture the calamitous result of drink, while the whole presents to the spectator the most powerful temperance lesson ever propounded.[25]

The everyday domestic problems—a husband, father, and breadwinner sliding into chronic inebriation and the threat to marriage, family, and security which intemperance implies—serve as Griffith's outer framing device and principal narrative. Within is a secondary narrative, an obvious parallel with a conspicuously similar family under the same threat and failing to survive, which acts as the spur to reformation. This image of parallel plots and "triangular" viewing may have been Griffith's starting point as he prepared his scenario, but he treated without cynicism the idea of the redemptive power of temperance drama, specifically, the prospect of an alcoholic husband restored sober and reformed to his family after witnessing Charles Warner's performance in Drink.[26]

Griffith began filming A Drunkard's Reformation on February 25, a mere eleven days after Charles Warner's burial. Filming continued for another two days, February 27 and March 1. Griffith's intent to invoke the memory of Warner's Coupeau and to celebrate the redeeming, wholesome power of the temperance stage were unambiguous. For the play-within-a-play, which so moves the errant Arthur Johnson that he immediately forswears drink, Griffith cast David Miles as Warner and contrived that Miles was made-up in replica of Warner's own appearance in the role.[27] Miles's costuming echoed, but did not altogether duplicate, Warner's wardrobe. Like Warner, he appeared successively in countryman's

The Biograph actor David Miles made up to resemble stage actor Charles Warner's Coupeau. Frame enlargement from Griffith's *A Drunkard's Reformation*, Biograph, 1909.

clothing and a workman's smock, but whereas Warner in his final scene wore a ragged corduroy jacket over his smock, Miles, collarless, wore only the same smock, now disheveled, unbelted, and filthy. Florence Lawrence (Gervaise), Marion Leonard (Virginie), and Gladys Egan, who played Nana, were costumed much as their stage counterparts. The settings, some of them familiar pieces from Biograph's modest scenic and property inventories, had been chosen to meet the needs of the outer narrative and the stipulations of *Drink*. In re-creating the memorable sixth-act episode, Miles had been coached in Warner's mannerisms and moves—exactly as described in the London *Daily News*.

It is difficult to assess—or to underestimate—the influence of temperance melodrama upon Griffith. The only temperance piece to appear with any frequency at Louisville's upmarket Macauley's Theatre during Griffith's youth had been Denman Thompson's *The Old Homestead*, a drama which mixed "b'gosh" rube comedy[28] with a parade of urban comic and serious stereotypes encountered as the melodrama's hero, "Uncle Josh" Whitcomb, searches for his errant, alcoholic son in New York, eventually finding the youth and restoring him to the healthy countryside and family life. Griffith may have seen this play while at home, or he may have seen Thompson in abridged versions of The Old Homestead on the vaudeville circuit. Perhaps because Warner's death had stimulated fresh interest in Drink, Griffith chose not to follow this specific earlier pattern, but the message of temperance melodrama: that characters, trapped in addictions and excesses which threaten their own welfare, the tranquility of their family, and their livelihoods, may be led to repent and to expiate their misdemeanors and, eventually, to be restored to full, useful, and pleasurable domestic lives, recurs as a motif in Griffith films for two or more further decades. Given the speed at which Griffith was turning out Biograph films, it was almost inevitable that some of those works for which he devised the scenario and subsequently directed would be failures. He was snatching at ideas without always thinking through the mechanics of plot or how a lengthy narrative could be encapsulated into a few reels. The Slave, shot in June 1908, is one of these rushed failures, aptly described by Russell Merritt as "chloroform in a toga." Although his capacity to make an effective film from this material was limited, Griffith had not erred in choosing a subject with its action set in the ancient Roman empire. "Toga plays," melodramas brought to American audiences by the English actor-manager Wilson Barrett, had proved conspicuously remunerative. In successive North American tours mounted in 1885, 1886, 1889, 1893, 1894, and 1896, Barrett successively introduced Claudian, Clito, The Sign of the Cross, and The Daughters of Babylon, each set in the ancient world, each dealing with damaging precipitant actions which compelled the drama's leading character—Barrett's role—to pause and reflect and, inevitably, to experience guilt, remorse, and thereafter to endure a painful interlude of repentance. Claudian, by W. G. Wills and Henry Herman, enacted the prolonged anguish and frustration experienced by a wealthy, powerful Roman, who, in an act of headstrong folly, abducts a sculptor's young wife. Admonished by a seer-priest, Claudian impetuously slays him, but is subject to a terrible and unforgiving curse by the dying man who demands that Claudian live, striving, but invariably failing, to do good, "until the vaulted rocks be split." The abducted young woman, whom Claudian would restore to her husband, then dies. Claudian's cursed life lasts for centuries. He cannot die until, finally, for the sake of a woman he loves, he sacrifices himself in an earthquake.

Griffith could not directly adapt Claudian, well known and protected by Barrett's copyright, but he appears to have to have taken material from the dramatic prologue to fashion in The Slave a one-reel film about a woman, pursued by a Roman aristocrat but married to a sculptor, who, in a failing attempt to save her child's life and to feed her family, sells herself into slavery and allows the patrician to buy her. The patrician, touched by her suffering, restores her to her husband.

By the early months of 1909, Griffith was producing an average of 2.7 films per week. Some weeks, working six days, he shot five films.[29] The speed at which he worked had two consequences. First, some of the Biograph actors complained that Griffith denied actors time in which to establish mood and atmospheric detail in their scenes and insisted, instead, upon immediate action once they stepped before the camera. Already aware of their professional standing and contrasting Griffith's films with French films—Pathé Films d'Art—they insisted that his method worked against the interests of their craft.[30] The second constant of such haste was the need for new scenarios which would sell Biograph films to exhibitors. To achieve this objective, film companies had to avoid copyright infringement. The young film industry had learned a hard lesson in 1907 when Kalem's unauthorized motion picture adaptation of Ben-Hur had been challenged not only by Klaw and Erlanger, who held the stage rights and whose stage adaptation by William Young was still on tour, but also by lawyers acting for the author, Lew Wallace. Brought before the New York Federal District Court and charged with creating a work which lacked the artistic excellence of either play or novel, Kalem was fined $25,000, and the prints and negatives of the film were ordered to be seized and destroyed.[31]

Klaw and Erlanger's legal action had only a limited effect in suppressing plagiarism. As late as 1911, William Brady, having assumed the presidency of the National Association of Theatrical Producing Managers (NATPM), spoke to the *New York Evening World* expressing his indignation at the manner in which filmmakers were plagiarizing theatrical properties and indicating the intent of the NATPM to halt piracy:

> It's the simplest thing in the world. A film company sends its chief stage director and a number of its actors to see a play. They watch it with an eye to the scenes and the "business," caring nothing, of course, for the dialogue. They absorb the story and carry away the action of the play in their minds. The rest is easy. The name of the play is changed, but the principal scenes are reproduced, and the result is a money-making success. We have already suppressed films amounting to the value of over $20,000.[32]

Griffith's recourse was to seek dramas known to be in the public domain—or those on which he held copyright.

Pressed for fresh subject matter, Griffith turned to his earlier vaudeville sketch *In Washington's Time* and to his unsuccessful play *War*. He would again return to these dramas toward the end of his career, but he first sought to recycle moments from them in *1776; or, The Hessian Renegades* which he shot in July and August 1909. In 1776, an American patriot carrying an important confidential dispatch, hides from pursuing Hessian mercenary troops in his parents' home. Recalling the clock hiding place in *In Washington's Time*, Griffith at first conceals the young patriot in a chimney and later in a wooden clothes basket, but he varies this ploy by having a suspicious Hessian captain fire a shot into the hamper which kills the youth. Meanwhile, remembering *War* and its heroine menaced by a British officer, Griffith has the youth's sister intimidated by another of the mercenaries and using her wiles to distract and overpower him. Civilian patriots then rout the Hessians and avenge the young American's death.

A few months later, in January 1910, as the Biograph company spent its first winter in California filming chiefly in open-air locations, Griffith reworked *Ramona*, the drama in which he had appeared as an actor in 1905 and for which he subsequently claimed joint authorship. Helen Hunt Jackson's novel and Griffith's film depict the romance, crossing racial boundaries, between Ramona, stepdaughter of a California rancher, and Alessandro, a Native American farmhand. Ramona rejects marriage with her stepbrother Felipe and elopes with Alessandro. The two live as exiles but face continual encroachment from white settlers. Eventually Alessandro is killed by one of the whites, and Ramona, now with a small child, returns to the ranch and Felipe's protection. Because the stage version by Johnstone Jones and Virginia Calhoun, in which Griffith took the role of Alessandro, no longer survives, it is uncertain how much of that play found its way into the film. Biograph publicized the "absolute authenticity"[33] of the adaptation in following Helen Hunt Jackson's novel, and it is known that Biograph, previously unwilling to pay novelists and publishers for screen rights to their properties, paid Little, Brown and Company one hundred dollars to secure permission to dramatize *Ramona*.[34] Biograph's publicity claimed that settings were based on drawings found in the early editions of Helen Hunt Jackson's novel and on sites in Camulos, Ventura County, associated with the *Ramona* narrative. However, as the film scholar Yuri Tsivian argues, it seems unlikely that Griffith bothered to reread the novel. For example, the synopsis provided in Biograph's publicity fails to correspond to the film's content.[35] It is therefore likely that the film draws on three sources: a synopsis of the novel, Griffith's recollection of the earlier *Ramona* stage play, and on Griffith's ability to improvise as he worked. *Ramona*—with the single exception of *Judith of Bethulia*, which Griffith was to film three years later—was the last subject to be taken directly from his earlier experiences as an actor. Henceforward, he would rely on his instinct and acumen as a director in determining stage pieces suitable for the screen.

When Griffith next chose a theatrical subject to develop, he worked from a melodrama popular with amateurs and professionals alike. To craft *That Chink at Golden Gulch* (1910) he abridged a full-length play, reducing the number of characters and eliminating digressions and subplots to fit a four-act drama into a single reel. He nevertheless managed to retain much of its original plot. His film also elaborated upon one of the drama's lesser characters, a Chinese laundryman, and moved him into the central role. The immediate source for *That Chink at Golden Gulch* was Charles Townsend's 1889 melodrama *The Golden Gulch*.[36] This play, set in the California hamlet of Golden Gulch, enacts the efforts of its villain "Gentleman George" Dixon (in the *Biograph Bulletin* "Gentleman Jack")[37] to frame Frank Evarts, a government scout, for crimes which Dixon has committed: the robbery of express-mail riders and stagecoaches and the apparent murder of a Jewish peddler. Dixon also attempts to corrupt the affections of Evarts's fiancée, Jess Horton. Eventually Dixon's villainy is unmasked, but only because the peddler, whom "the dandy" Dixon has failed to kill, makes a timely last-act appearance to avert Evarts's conviction before a frontier court. *The Golden Gulch*'s Chinaman, One Lung, is but one of a number of ethnic, class, and gender comic roles—Jew, Irish, Negro, Native American, New York "dude," fastidious spinster—who pad out Townsend's slender plot.

Griffith, aided by his scenarist Emmett Campbell Hall,[38] focused on his Chinese hero with a prologue set in China where, before leaving for America, the young Charlie Lee promises that he will never dishonor his family by cutting his queue. Later, a laundryman in a Californian mining town, Charlie is tormented by local men until befriended by a young woman and her cowboy sweetheart. One of Charlie's tormentors is a well-dressed idler and, secretly, a bandit who robs the mail. The cowboy and bandit become rivals for the girl's affections. Suspicious of the bandit, Charlie follows him, observes him robbing a mail carrier, and contrives to capture him, cutting off his queue to bind the bandit. Rewarded for the bandit's capture, but disgraced in his own eyes for dishonoring his family, Charlie gives the cash reward to the young couple and surreptitiously leaves Golden Gulch. The film's treatment of Charlie Lee reveals the extent to which Griffith remained fascinated with racial otherness and the tantalizing ambivalence which this status generated. *Broken Blossoms*, Griffith's most ambitious treatment of an oriental character, lay almost a decade in the future, but a seed of passive exotic orientalism had been unconsciously sown.

To a twenty-first-century viewer, Griffith's leading character, Charlie Lee, would appear an unlikely hero. He is vulnerable, grateful, hugely self-sacrificing, and brave, but also meant to be viewed as faintly ludicrous. Generous and civilized and the product of an ancient civilization—in contrast to the barbarism of the California gold fields, Charlie's limited command of written and spoken English, his peculiar gait—walking with toes turned in—and posture—standing with knees slightly bent, his hands concealed in opposite sleeves—his habitual subservience, and his nonsexual adoration of the young heroine invited the spectator to condescend to him and to find him unthreatening. Griffith's film thus modified a popular stage character, the gold camp Chinaman, who had become a staple of American literature and drama from the mid-1870s. He shortened and reshaped a stage piece, this time with the effect of partially humanizing and making intelligible and sympathetic what was previously—and merely—an overworked comedy stereotype.

Griffith and his audience would have been familiar with the stage "Chinaman." This stock character, in speaking or writing, replaced the letter r with l and promiscuously appended *ee* to many words ("House empty. No bollee in! Bellee bad—leave a bottlee—no corkee. Me no let him go to wastee . . ."[39]). He walked with bent knees turned outward and with hands tucked into opposite sleeves and exhibited an unhealthy fondness for strong liquor and Caucasian females. The "Chinaman" was the joint creation of the author [Francis] Bret Harte and the actor Charles T. Parsloe as they collaborated in 1876 to adapt as a comic melodrama Bret Harte's short story "Two Men of Sandy Bar." "Hop Sing," the first of many such comedy oriental characters,[40] was a literary-theatrical response to the thousands of Chinese who had been persuaded to emigrate to North America in the 1850s to work on the expanding rail network and in the western gold fields. So numerous were the Chinese and so willing to work long hours for small wages that by the late 1870s their presence in California and Nevada was met with hostility and occasional violence.

By 1882, the U.S. Congress had enacted the Chinese Exclusion Act deliberately restricting further Chinese immigration. Parsloe's and Harte's character reflects some of this accumulated hostility and misgivings which the Chinese occasioned, and Hop Sing and Harte's subsequent Chinese character Ah Sin depict the Chinaman with derision. Parsloe thereafter repeated this comedy role, first as Washee-Washee, "a helpless little Heathen" in Joaquin Miller's The Danites in the Sierras (1877), then as Ah Sin in Mark Twain's and Bret Harte's Ah Sin (1877), and subsequently as Wing Lee in Bartley Campbell's My Partner (1879), and finally in the role of Very Tart, a Chinese character belatedly added to James McCloskey's already-successful Across the Continent (1870). Moreover, the popularity of the comic stage Chinaman induced other dramatists and actors to copy Charles Parsloe's success and to take "Chink" roles into the twentieth century. Griffith in 1910 was inheriting from Parsloe a theatrical convention which he was destined to subvert and change. But also at that date, immigration from the Far East was a lesser source of friction, and American attention had refocused on new aliens from eastern and southern Europe.

Townsend's *The Golden Gulch*, first performed more than a decade after the last of Parsloe's roles, softened the harsh mockery aimed at the Chinese character and, in introductory instructions specifying the costume of One Lung as the "... usual Chinese suit—loose blouse, baggy trousers," added the restraining caveat about "... the customary stage Chinaman": "... In playing this character do not overdo it. The Chinese are not jumping-jacks, remember; therefore play the part rather quietly." Griffith heeded Townsend's injunction. Subordinating conflicts between Miss Dean, Bud Miller, and Gentleman Jack while foregrounding Charlie Lee, Griffith made him the decisive hero motivated by honorable and altogether laudatory motives. Further, by eliminating all other ethnic, class, and gender stereotypes common to melodrama, Griffith raised the comic stage Chinaman to a new prominence. Although Anthony O'Sullivan displays some of the "jumping-jack" movements of the American stage Chinaman, he had comparatively few of the excessive disfiguring mannerisms specified for the Chinaman in earlier stage scripts. The use of Charlie Lee's queue as a means of capturing and binding Gentleman Jack was original to Griffith. Also original to Griffith, but of greater significance, was the depiction of an Oriental character who, albeit misunderstood and proscribed by an Act of Congress, a menial (a laundryman who cleans what others soil), is recognizably a good, deserving, and deeply civilized citizen of Golden Gulch. Gentleman Jack's cruelty to Charlie and Charlie's rescue by Miss Dean and Bud Miller are important in signaling vice and virtue and in helping the spectator to identify Charlie as the film's protagonist, not as a peripheral comedy role.

Although Griffith was initially unaware that his tenure at Biograph was drawing to a close, three overlapping incidents in 1913 coincided to provoke his angry departure. Despite Griffith's productivity during this period, there were obvious signs of strain between Griffith and Biograph's president, Jeremiah Kennedy, and the company's vice-president, H. N. Marvin. Both chafed at Griffith's independence and presumed autonomy. In retrospect, it is apparent that these executives were blind to major developments in the motion picture industry, in particular to the sudden preference for longer films, especially films that were derived from stage plays.

In 1912, Adolph Zukor had entered partnership with the theatrical entrepreneurs Charles and Daniel Frohman to create the Famous Players Film Company, promising in their advertising slogan, "Famous Players in Famous Plays." Their first production featured Sarah Bernhardt and Jean Mounet-Sully in Paolo Giacometti's *Elizabeth, Queen of England.* Between 1912 and 1919, when the company (later Famous Players-Lasky) was absorbed into Paramount, Famous Players produced 140 films. Theatrical managements increasingly saw the value of turning their stage properties into motion pictures. Although the initial capital outlay of a film might exceed the initial cost of a stage play, a film, once made and simultaneously distributed in multiple prints to different cities, soon recouped the money invested in it. Theatrical entrepreneurs accordingly realized the potential profit in maintaining film divisions or in establishing commerical connections with existing film producers.

It is clear from his actions that Griffith was attempting to make longer films, and it is equally apparent that Biograph was resisting—or at least delaying—these attempts. Although he bccn successfully directing Biograph films for five years, Griffith had not established a public reputation as an artist or storyteller which he might use in bargaining with obdurate executives. Apart from withholding his labor or going elsewhere, he was powerless, and his options for employment were limited. Outside the motion picture business, where Griffith's work was increasingly recognized and admired, he was still unknown. Also, apart from being able to offer employment to stage-trained actors, he held no credibility in theatrical circles. Film studios were only just beginning to identify their leading players. Biograph, in particular, withheld the identities of its actors and directors. In cosequence, Griffith remained anonymous, receiving no screen credits. The young film industry was still dominated by the Motion Picture Patents Company, and Biograph was a leading member of this trust. He could not expect to find work in any MPPC studio. The "independent" studios were fewer in number and had less capital to invest in film projects. Griffith, happiest when working at a distance from Biograph's management, was spending more time in California and had ordered the construction of a frontier village which he soon used in The Battle at Elderbush Gulch. This film, a two-reel western, showed a growing maturity in Griffith's capacity to develop intricate, multiple-strand narratives on film. It was further distinguished from other westerns by displaying even-handed sympathy to the besieged homesteaders and the attacking Native Americans and by depicting a wide-ranging battle with numerous participants.

Despite the The Battle at Elderbush Gulch's merits, rising construction costs and salaries for larger numbers of actors alarmed studio executives back in Manhattan. J. C. Manning, Biograph's accountant, was dispatched from New York to query Griffith's expenditures. Manning remained in California monitoring production costs and reporting back to Biograph's New York headquarters. Uneasy about the film's four-reel length and cautious about its eventual reception—but perhaps as a chastisement to Griffith—the Biograph executives postponed the film's release until 1914, by which time Griffith had quit Biograph and was working elsewhere. *The Battle at Elderbush Gulch* eventually made money for Biograph and received favorable press attention, but it was too late for Griffith to derive anything but hollow satisfaction from its success.

In 1913, Biograph was commissioned by the theatrical management Klaw and Erlanger to turn nine of their successful stage plays into motion pictures. Each film was to be released in lengths up to five reels, more than double the length of any previous Biograph motion picture. In conversations with Kennedy and Marvin, Griffith, whose films had never exceeded two reels, was assigned overall supervision of these films but was denied the opportunity to direct any. Each film was to be assigned to junior directors whom Griffith had trained.[41] Two of these plays, in particular William C. DeMille's 1904 *Strongheart*, a drama about racial friction and American identity arising when a Native American attends a white university, and Henry Mawson's 1891 Civil War melodrama *A Fair Rebel*, dealt with subjects which Griffith had proven his ability to handle.[42]

When contractual negotiations with Klaw and Erlanger were conducted in Griffith's absence from New York, Griffith's exact role was not specified and, if considered at all, was left to the discretion of Biograph's managers. Griffith's biographer Richard Schickel regards this event as an attempt to rein in Griffith and to remind him of the authority of his studio paymasters. It was a powerful insult and understood by Griffith as such. He was, however, permitted to continue work on what, in the event, was to be his final Biograph film, *Judith of Bethulia*. *Judith* was already in production in California. Biograph's conservative management had been persuaded by Griffith that the film drew upon a biblical subject—a buffer against some moralists' complaints that motion pictures were indecent—and that it had a respectable literary pedigree. These elements apparently satisfied Kennedy and Marvin.[43] Allowed to return to California, Griffith was pressed to reduce his expenditures.

Whatever Kennedy and Marvin's intentions had been, the contract with Klaw and Erlanger and Griffith's exclusion from directing these films proved disastrous for Biograph. The completed films, shot between 1913–1915, were held back and not released because Biograph remained uneasy about feature-length motion pictures and, further, lacked a distribution system which would have enabled the release and marketing of multiple-reel films.[44] Meanwhile, other American studios released sixty-nine longer films. Biograph released its first Klaw and Erlanger film in February 1914. Concurrently, Griffith's Biograph acting "company," dismayed at his departure, gradually abandoned Biograph to join Griffith in California. By 1916 Biograph had ceased to make new films.

A further event added to Griffith's frustration. Concurrently, the Italian director-producer Enrico Guazzoni released a twelve-reel adaptation of Henryk

Sienkiewicz's 1896 novel *Quo Vadis? A Narrative in the Time of Nero*. American audiences had previously known *Quo Vadis?* in two separate stage adaptations, each five acts in length, far longer in playing time than any film. At that date few American films ran for as long as an hour. Guazzoni's "toga film," imported by the American showman George Kleine and reduced to eight reels, ran for three hours. Although charging an admission price of $1.50, approximately thirty times the standard admission to most American films, *Quo Vadis?* played to full houses for a twenty-two-week run in New York and moved on to a remunerative national tour. Griffith was in California when *Quo Vadis?* was premiered, and it is believed that he saw it only after his return to New York. He was already well advanced with plans for *Judith of Bethulia*, but these plans were being impeded by Biograph's executives. Witnessing Guazzoni's film determined Griffith to press ahead, regardless of expense, with his feature-length *Judith of Bethulia*.[45] Renting space on the Chatsworth Estate south of Los Angeles, he ordered the construction of the ramparts of Bethulia. All exteriors were to be shot in California. Interiors were later filmed in Biograph's new studio in the Bronx.

The theatrical source for *Judith of Bethulia* was Thomas Bailey Aldrich's *Judith of Bethulia*, a four-act verse drama premiered in Boston in October 1904. This play was closely associated with the thirty-year-old actress Nance O'Neil (1874–1965) in whose theatrical company the young Griffith had briefly acted in 1905.[46] However, there was a further influential person from Griffith's theatrical past, the Canadian-born actor-manager McKee Rankin (1844–1914), a major figure in the late-Victorian American theatre. Rankin brought O'Neil into his company in 1894, and their fifteen-year partnership was largely responsible for developing the theatricalized *Judith* narrative which Griffith began adapting sometime in 1912. A serious quarrel between O'Neil and Rankin in 1909 fractured their professional and private relationship and had the further effect of erasing Rankin's name from later accounts of O'Neil's career. Griffith acknowledges Aldrich (1856–1907) in the title credits to his film but, simplifying his sources, omits any mention of Rankin and O'Neil as codevelopers of *Judith of Bethulia*.

However, the *Judith of Bethulia* which Griffith draws upon is not Aldrich's play alone. Aldrich's drama is itself a commissioned reworking of an earlier play, an Italian drama which had been known to American audiences since 1866 when it was introduced by the Italian actress Adelaide Ristori (1822–1906). Griffith, initially undecided how guide Blanche Sweet in her realization of Judith's character, made numerous experiments based on performances, nearly forty years apart, by the two actresses, the Italian Ristori and the American O'Neil. These experiments were captured on a reel of outtakes and described by the film scholar J. B. Kaufman.[47] Thus Griffith's acknowledged source, the stage *Judith of Bethulia*, is a fusion of two dramas, Ristori's touring piece and Aldrich's subsequent poetic revision, both further developed under the direction of Rankin and O'Neil. Griffith, as he again was to do with *Way Down East*, went back to the earlier, as well as the later, dramatic texts, choosing scenes and characters and bits of theatrical "business" which suited his purposes. The Griffith screen version was equally indebted to both plays, to both actresses, and to Rankin as much as it was to Griffith's singular vision and dramatic skill.

Although the subject of Judith—the Jewish patriot who leaves the seclusion of her celibate widowhood to captivate, seduce, stupefy, and decapitate the Assyrian general Holofernes and so end the invaders' siege to the city of Bethulia—gave rise to more than a handful of plays and operas in the second half of the nineteenth century and the opening decades of the twentieth, the chief theatrical source for Aldrich and an unacknowledged source for Griffith was the Italian dramatist Paolo Giacometti's *Giuditta*. Giacometti (1816–1882) is chiefly remembered as the author of romantic dramas for Tommaso Salvini (1829–1916), but he contributed two plays, *Elizabeth, Queen of England* and *Judith*, to Ristori's touring Compagnia Drammatica in the late 1850s. Both dramas, *Judith* especially, appealed to the patriotic fervor and intense Italian nationalism which accompanied the Risorgimento. When Ristori toured Britain and the United States in 1866, the American Civil War had ended. Giacometti's drama of an embattled nation almost reduced to capitulation—with his Jewish characters advocating steadfastness, unity, and uncompromising fidelity to a prophesied national destiny—evoked demonstrations from Italian spectators and, more remarkably, from English speakers, who followed the action with the aid of a literal interlinear translation, which was sold in the theatre as a program-playbill. This verbose text,[48] intended only as a guide to the play, survived as the only English-language script of *Judith*. Other late-Victorian actresses who undertook the role of Judith were obliged to use this text.

Eventually, late in 1903, Nance O'Neil and her producer-director-manager, McKee Rankin, sought a play which would enable O'Neil, at the time much criticized for her strident, unflattering portraits of socially questionable transgressive women,[49] to find a more appealing and plausibly virtuous role. O'Neil, playing the Giacometti *Judith*, introduced the play to Boston audiences in March 1904.

Both Ristori and O'Neil were described by contemporary critics as *emotional* actresses. Applied to Ristori in the 1860s and 1870s, the term signified the ability to reach and project a range of emotions arising from dramatically intense situations. The term included gentleness, quiet pathos, and debilitating sorrow as much as it covered calculating, revenge-focused jealousy, rage, pain, and acute bereavement. Ristori's gestures were large and forceful, but they were disciplined and, by mid-nineteenth-century standards of acting, capable of control. Nance O'Neil was well aware of Ristori's performance of Judith and collected Ristori's stage jewelry and properties[50] for the inspiration they offered. However, O'Neil was attempting to re-create, or to emulate, a theatrical style which had largely passed from fashion two decades earlier. Reapplied by turn-of-the-century critics to Nance O'Neil, the word *emotional* acquired a somewhat derogatory coded meaning, the term covertly referring to the rawness of O'Neil's performing. A largely self-taught actress, at least in her early years before she was brought into McKee Rankin's company, O'Neil was thought to be at her best when performing strongly declamatory, emotionally fraught scenes where expansive, semaphorical gesturing and a voice knowingly—and sometimes excessively—modulated might be found appropriate to the text. O'Neil's development along the touring circuits curbed some of this theatricalized emotionalism, but emotionally intense parts also colored her choice of roles. Griffith had, of course, seen O'Neil's performances in such roles.[51] Giacometti's Judith retained and justified strong scenes, but it also called for emotional subtlety. Griffith sought emotional subtlety which could be reached through less overt theatricalism by using gestural techniques, still very much a part of the actor's expressive means, more sparingly and more tellingly.

Griffith's *Judith of Bethulia* offers points of familiarity, if not exact similarity, with Giacometti's five-act Judith, which is less compressed than Aldrich's four-act drama and which offers scenes set in locales other than the besieged city of Bethulia and Holofernes's tent. Giacometti's influence is apparent in Griffith's early scenes outside the city walls, an episode in which Bobby Harron and Mae Marsh make a futile attempt to draw water from the well held by the Assyrians. His debt to Giacometti is also apparent in the several appearances of Lillian Gish holding her baby who is dying of thirst, and like Giacometti, Griffith uses the baby as a symbol of the city's plight and an implied reproach to Judith for her own barren marriage to Manasseh. In Giacometti's version, Judith finds a well and distributes water, only to find that the source has been poisoned and a child inadvertently killed through her premature assumption that she had outwitted her city's besiegers. It is partly in atonement for this shortsighted hubris that Judith goes to Holofernes's camp.

Unlike Aldrich's subsequent version, Giacometti's script makes much of the license and sexual debauchery of the camp and the brutal danger of Holofernes, "the Bull of Assur." Judith is warned that, "He kills with his sword, and poisons with his eye. He has endless orgies in his camp and perfumed harems. His cup is a horrible mixture of blood and wine." She is not to underestimate his effect nor presume that she can enslave him sexually and thus alter the war's course: "It is thou rather who would fall in the dust at his feet, slave for a day, destined for his bed. He will coil around thee as a serpent, but he will leave and go far away, thou remaining alone, dishonoured, and powerless to avenge thyself." Griffith, as he reworked the Judith myth for the screen, translated this sexually charged atmosphere and physical danger into four sensuous dances, performed by Holofernes's concubines, and the crucifixion of a rebellious captain. These acts precede Judith's own sexual awakening from her widowhood. Griffith further underlined the sensuality and abusive power of Holofernes's court by imaginatively "realizing" a well-known painting, Ernest Normand's 1895 Royal Academy entry Bondage,[52] which depicts a "Middle Eastern" tyrant, lounging on a divan as Holofernes does, viewing a cluster of naked female slaves. This image became widely popular throughout Britain and America when inexpensive engravings were struck.

The closest points of comparison are the stupefaction of Holofernes at one of his feared orgies and his subsequent murder. Giacometti and Griffith both depicted Holofernes succumbing to an excess of wine, collapsing on a divan, which has always threatened Judith's celibacy, and both author and director showed Judith, Holofernes's heavy sword in hand, initially torn between striking at the supine tyrant and yielding to the recently aroused sexual feelings which now restrain her arm.

Few outtakes survive from Griffith's films, but fragmentary outtakes from Judith of Bethulia reveal Blanche Sweet and Griffith rehearsing—and mutually negotiating—Judith's approach to the comatose Holofernes and her delayed decision to proceed with his murder.[53] Griffith suggests gestures, facial expressions, and movements. Sweet listens but, finding her own means of communicating pity, sexual arousal, revulsion, and, crucially, recalling Bethulia's plight (which Griffith augmented with shots of parched, starving, and dying citizens) and patriotic necessity, finally strikes at Holofernes's neck. Giacometti's Judith thereafter displayed her reddened hands as she held aloft Holofernes's severed head, an effect which repeatedly thrilled audiences. Griffith, however, cut away—on Judith's downward stroke of the sword—to a scene outside the tent, where sentries are startled by sounds of the murder, then cut back to the tent's interior as Sweet and Kate Bruce bundle the unseen head into a shawl, carrying it back to Bethulia. Only when Judith is back within the city walls is the head impaled upon a Bethulian sword and brandished before a jubilant crowd as the Jewish army routs the leaderless invaders. Griffith, concerned with the effect of Holofernes's death on Judith, who has, in effect, been widowed for a second time, is not concerned to show the bloody carnage but Sweet's stunned shock and bereavement.

In both the Giacometti and Aldrich versions, Judith is found in the enemy camp by people of her own side and is confronted by someone she knows and who knows her. Her conduct is thus suspect to the Assyrians and to her own townspeople. In the Giacometti version it is Eliakim, the Hebrew high priest captured by the Assyrians; in the Aldrich text it is Achior, an Ammonite, who, chastely devoted to the widow Judith and unable to win her love, follows her to the Assyrian camp to offer protection he cannot give. Griffith eliminated this role entirely to focus wholly upon Blanche Sweet's Judith. Her maid, a fixture in both plays, was given less voice by Griffith and is elderly rather than young—a typical Kate Bruce role. The concubine Arzaele, replaced by Bagoas, survives in the Aldrich version as the leader of the troupe of dancers from Holofernes's harem. She is visible in Griffith's film in the person of Gertrude Bambrick.[54]

Aldrich's *Judith of Bethulia* was received with mixed responses, the critics praising the poetic language of the play and the absence of extended rhetorical passages but uniformly critical of the reduction in "melodramatic situations." They disparaged the killing of Holofernes, now hidden behind the draperies of an inner alcove where he lay drunk. They complained that Aldrich had shrunk the play, removing the scene in which Judith and other Bethulians, Eliakim, the high priest, included, scour the mountains for water. They regretted the omission of a scene in which Eliakim, taken captive, is brought to Holofernes's tent where he unexpectedly confronts Judith. Compromised by Holofernes, who embraces her passionately and states, "This woman is the spouse and lover of Holofernes," Judith is condemned by Eliakim as a traitor to her city and "a wanton." Secretly, she convinces the priest of her mission, her patriotism, and her virtue, acknowledging that she has tolerated Holofernes's advances and compromised her reputation for the good of the city. This confrontation is one of the episodes which underlines the differences between the earlier Judith of Giacometti and Aldrich's reworking: Giacometti's Judith is a galvanizing patriot dedicated to her mission and is not averse to chaste seduction as a tool; Aldrich's Judith is a seer who cannot immediately grasp the import and shape of her mission and who continually relies on divine inspiration. The audience witnesses Judith receiving such a vision, a "white mailéd hand," visible only to her, pointing toward the town gate leading to the Assyrian encampment. Blanche Sweet also experiences such a private vision, but the nature of the vision is not clarified for the viewer. Both stage Judiths use their sexuality to entice, Giacometti's Judith more knowingly (she goes to Holofernes "as beautiful as the bride in Solomon's song") and more compromised, both by leading Bethulians to a poisoned spring and by apparent complicity with Holofernes.

Yet, for some critics, the more overt sexuality of Giacometti's Judith was unsettling. Edward Crosby, writing in the Boston *Globe*, breathlessly commended O'Neil's treatment of the Aldrich Judith for its restrained eroticism:

> The Boston stage has not in many days witnessed anything so sensuous, so seductive, and yet at the same time, so free from coarseness. She practiced the wiles of a Cleopatra, a Circe, or a Lorelei, and through it all there was not the slightest detail to which the most fastidious might take exception. It was as though some beautiful Grecian tradition was being enacted in the twentieth century.[55]

Crosby's observation underlines how, in the early years of the twentieth century, critics for the popular press and a majority of theatre and filmgoers insisted that American entertainment was to conform to conventional ideas of behavior and morality. At the same time there is an unexpressed fear that enacting a narrative of Judith might erupt into something less decorous or more offensive to "the most fastidious" spectator. Whereas both Giacometti's *Judith* and Aldrich's *Judith of Bethulia* offer heroines who, despite being attracted to Holofernes, abstain from sex, paintings, frequently with nude or partly clothed Judiths, have implied that his murder is postcoital. Griffith, restrained by Biograph and fearful of censorship from dramatizing greater intimacy between Judith and Holofernes, chose to depict through Sweet's performance a reluctantly celibate Judith who is caught between her desire and her patriotic and spiritual mission. Her options—welcoming Holofernes's overtures and condoning the slaughter of her people or resisting and slaying Holofernes—are entirely incompatible and all the more powerful because they cannot be reconciled, a point not lost on Griffith.

It is in this fin de siècle climate that we must consider the Judiths of Giacometti, Aldrich, and Griffith. All Judiths and Judith performances walked a fine line between overt sexuality and cautious restraint. That instability was a part of their appeal to audiences, and it was a challenge to the actor to be both sexually alluring and pure. (This duality is undeniably one of Griffith's preoccupations, and it is difficult to name one of his post-Biograph films where the disturbing combination of sexiness and chaste virtue are not present and conflicted in the same actress.) But the fine line was also a factor which constrained and challenged the abilities of the actors who took on this role. Ristori's, O'Neil's, and Sweet's Judiths were severally caught between contemporary views of acceptable morality, biblical (or apocryphal) text, and theatrical and artistic representations of sexual conduct. Add to this critical balance the ingredients of religiosity, sanctity, austerity, and American puritanism and their antitheses—secularism, corruption, luxury, and carnality—and a volatile mixture resulted. The decades from 1880 through the years in which Griffith's *Judith of Bethulia* was made and exhibited and reissued form a period in which a favored dramatic subject was the compromised woman. There is a substantial legacy of dance and theatrical works from this period which have incurred censorious comment, if not outright censorship, for their portrayal of females forced by extreme circumstances into having sex with an oppressor or whose unrequited sexual desire turns murderous or who display independence in determining their sexual choices. A handful of examples may suffice: Alfred Tennyson's *The Cup* (1881) shocked with its portrayal of a woman's revenge upon her husband's slayer; the American dancer Maud Allan (born Ulah Maud Durrant, 1873–1956) was excoriated by the press for lascivious dancing when she appeared in Paris in Marcel Remy's *The Vision of Salomé* (1907) and was the continual subject of controversy when she danced in London in 1911; the American dramatists Paul Potter, Clyde Fitch, and David Belasco were fiercely criticized and sometimes—belatedly—applauded for their dramas *Trilby* (1895), *Sapho*, (1900), and *Adrea* (1905), which showed women by turns active and helpless in negotiating their sexual roles. Sweet's Judith, by turns devout, independent, knowing, seductive, tenderhearted, furtive, devious, brutal, and ultimately remorseful and bereft was partly the result, not merely of two plays and two actresses, but also of this ongoing turbulence—a jostling for priority and control—between religious conservatism, a stage in transition between older traditions and newer methods, the New Woman, literary innovation, and theatrical exoticism. And this state of flux, instead of compromising dramatic options, liberated, creating further possibilities, and materially assisting Griffith in generating a compelling film drama.

Between 1908 and 1912 and reaching a peak of productivity in the years 1910 and 1911, Griffith devised and directed a dozen Biograph films which variously dealt with the subject of the American Civil War and its troubled aftermath. All twelve of these films were directly influenced by a large body of theatrical melodramas of which Griffith was doubtless aware. These numerous dramas, written by a diverse group of American dramatists, held the stage from 1875, the tenth anniversary of the war, through 1915, the year in which Griffith's *The Birth of a Nation* appeared. The conventions of Civil War stage dramas and the issues raised by the theatrical and filmic representations of the causes of the war, the conduct of the war, and the postwar Reconstruction era are the subjects of the following chapter, but it should be noted that these films, as much as those previously discussed, also represent Griffith's continuing engagement with the

American theatre while at Biograph. It was only after leaving Biograph that Griffith was able to expend his full energy on this subject, but it was at Biograph that he was able to use his shorter Civil War films as developmental sketches for his subsequent major work.

The completion of *Judith of Bethulia* marks one of the peaks and—also—one of the transition points of Griffith's career. Now thirty-eight years old, he had directed 482 Biograph films, appeared in five as an actor, and supervised the making of additional films under the Klaw and Erlanger contract. Buoyed by the success of Griffith's films, Biograph had deserted its old studio on East Fourteenth Street and had built, to Griffith's specifications, a new studio in the Bronx. His *Judith of Bethulia*, if not the first American full-length film, was one of the most prestigious made by 1913. It proved again—as it had with *The Battle at Elderbush Gulch* and with some of his Civil War films (see the following chapter)—that Griffith achieved telling moments with spectacles of riot and combat. It proved that he could combine these epic scenes with moments of intimacy and tenderness. His credentials as a director were unequaled by any other American. He was also—by his own choice—unemployed. He wasn't stepping into a void but into a contract with colleagues and backers who were evasive and unreliable. But he was independent and followed by actors, cameramen, administrators, and technicians who wished to work with him and for him. *The Birth of a Nation* was two years in the future, but Griffith was free to begin preparing this project.

4 Dramas of Civil War, Ethnicity, and Race

The Birth of a Nation was the result of a lengthy learning process that, for Griffith, began in the Biograph studios and on exterior locations. His film was neither the first, nor even the first American film, to astonish audiences with its intricate expansive narrative, panoramic grasp of the national epic, blatant, if sectional, patriotism, and purported grasp of national history.[1] No one, however hostile to Griffith's aggressive racial and political stance, complained of the motion picture's quality. That was one of the film's problems: it was too effective. Audiences admired its scope, narrative complexity, and fine, detailed performances, even as many deplored and protested its racist content. Griffith, still largely unknown both to critics and to the general public in 1915, seemed to have become a master storyteller overnight. Rather, the opposite is true: his storytelling skills emerged film by film.

Even as he was developing his craft as a novice director at Biograph, Griffith, as early as 1909, had begun to explore the codes and conventions of American Civil War drama, revisiting dramas that he had previously encountered on the Louisville stage and on the road as a touring actor. While directing films that never exceeded two reels, he mastered the vocabularies of this genre and achieved the surehandedness necessary to move forward to a longer and more complex rendering of the national struggle. Eight years earlier, as a vaudeville actor and sketch writer, he had unknowingly served an apprenticeship learning to devise compact dramatic narratives. Then, as now, Griffith had stepped backward into a well-established theatrical form. Over the following five years, directing a dozen films on the subject of the Civil War and Reconstruction period (ca. 1860 to 1880) and drawing on plays recalled, he slowly gained the dexterity and dramaturgical strategies he was later to employ through 1914 and 1915 in realizing *The Birth of a Nation*. This film and its disturbing source, Thomas Dixon's *The*

Clansman, appear in the context of a substantial cluster of more than 120 Civil War stage plays,[2] and an even larger body, somewhere above 370,[3] of Civil War fiction-films. Griffith's Biograph Civil War films are but a fraction of this body.

The American Civil War has never been a stable field with an agreed-upon historical interpretation. Rather, it was—and is—an evolving, contested subject which is host to vehemence, disruption, and difference, a palimpsest upon which fresh questions about the past are inscribed. Through these 490-odd dramatic narratives, theatre and film jointly conducted and developed a debate which paralleled, and was entwined with, an extended period of national growth and postwar reconstruction. A broad constellation of stage melodramas and motion pictures not only maintained the debate before the American public for over five decades but also established the form, the vocabulary, and the frames of reference for that debate. Once in place, the conventions derived from this debate shaped audience expectations in determining plot trajectories, moral identities, and the spectator's empathetic alignment with, or antagonism to, dramatic characters. These conventions still remain in play today and characterize a dramatic genre which began in 1860s and which has never entirely vanished.

Critical examinations of Griffith's pre-1915 American Civil War films have followed one of three predictable, sometimes overlapping, pathways: (1) scholars discover in these early films narrative elements which would be elaborated when Griffith set his hand to *The Birth of a Nation*; (2) the films are scoured for details which relate to the Griffith family history and, in particular, its "Southern" or "Confederate" heritage; and (3) the films are viewed as discrete works, connected neither with a past or future place in the Griffith canon, and are explicated entirely within the visual means accessible to the viewer. All of these approaches are valid and, indeed, desirable, but they stop short of the further essential act of placing these Civil War films in the context of a significant national debate, a debate postulated, developed, and codified on the American stage almost from the very outbreak of the war itself in 1862, and in 1897 taken up by motion pictures and placed before new audiences.

Griffith's twelve Biograph films are not evidence of a teleological vision nor of a conscious decision to pursue this subject. Each was the result of the need to produce an unbroken succession of sellable films. The Civil War, only forty years in the past, still drew audiences. However, Robert Lang writes of these pre-1915 Biograph films as trial essays for *The Birth of a Nation*.[4] Although there is no evidence whatever to suggest that Griffith had this mammoth project in mind at such an early date, the one- and two-reel Civil War films offer convincing proof that Griffith and his contributing scenarists became increasingly conversant with—*steeped in* may be the more appropriate phrase—the theatrical tropes and structures of Civil War melodramas. Griffith not only joined the debate but also acquired and skilfully developed the visual language and practical means of dramatization. Griffith found the means to dramatize ideological and social division, war, resolution, and, as he approached Reconstruction, complex depictions of unresolved hostilities, resentment, and subversion. Not one of the Civil War films which Griffith directed for Biograph between 1909 and 1912 is itself derived from a specific play. Nonetheless, each film may be understood as Griffith, on the one hand, attempting to master the forms and conventions of Civil War drama and, on othe other hand, struggling to find his own authorial voice as, some forty years after the event, he viewed this destructive conflict and came to understand its immediate and long-term costs.

Although the conventions of Civil War drama appear consistent from work to work, there is considerable room for ideological movement within the genre. Stage plays and films which have as their subjects episodes from the American Civil War and its aftermath, especially the aftermath as experienced in the defeated states of the Confederacy, are a part of an active continuum of perception, analysis, and interpretation. Collectively and individually, these dramas have attempted to identify, understand, and justify the causes, conduct, and results of the most traumatic event in American history. To this extent, Civil War dramatic narratives always reflect current and evolving American thought regarding national and sectional division, political dissent, economic oppression, rebellion, war, conquest, and—only in modern times—race.

However, and in contrast to allowing ideological realignment in their audiences in terms of contemporary perceptions of world and national change, the ongoing process of interrogation and analysis of the Civil War has always sought to shape from this still-contentious subject matter an agreed upon national mythology or consensus: that of a healing or recuperated United States. Intersectional conflicts are resolved. Racial issues, still unresolved and considered beyond immediate resolution, rarely intrude into these dramas and never distract from the objective of reunifying a white nation. The Civil War, it was tacitly agreed by dramatists and audiences alike, was fought between white men. The peace that followed was a peace between whites. These were white plays for white audiences. No African American issues or significant African American characters were permitted to compromise, or distract from, either the white war or the white peace. There were no loose ends to unravel in the harmonious postbellum world depicted on the stage and in the films that followed.

The structures and conventions of Civil War drama had emerged, first, on the amateur stage as early as 1862[5] and, by the mid-1870s, in the professional theatre. The American Civil War ended in 1865. Union armies met in Washington for a final grand parade, then comfortably dispersed to their home states to disband. Those Confederate troops who hadn't already deserted—disarmed, humiliated, and impoverished—straggled to their often damaged or neglected homes. Both sides told their stories. Both sides described their heroes, their villains, and constructed their diverging histories and their even more divergent myths. The sectional values which divided North and South hardened to underlie and inform the processes of revision.

As the armies dispersed, they formed veterans' associations. In 1866, the Grand Army of the Republic (GAR) was organized by former members of the Union Army. A year later chapters of the GAR existed in most major Northern and western cities. There was to be no corresponding Confederate veterans' association south of the Mason-Dixon Line, the political boundary between the Northern "free" states and the former slaveholding states of the Confederacy, for another dozen years (although the Ku Klux Klan had secretly formed in 1865). In 1869, the Southern Historical Society, founded by William Dunning, was created to propagate the South's etiology and narrative of the conflict. Those lectures on Southern history, which Griffith may have attended at Macauley's Theatre in Louisville, were products of this movement. It is from historians influenced or educated by Dunning and his Southern Historical Society colleagues, as much as the Klan, that Thomas Dixon and Griffith inherit the "Confederate myth" of an aristocratic—or cavalier—genteel South, intent on defending the rights of independent states, rights guaranteed by the American Constitution, brought low by a consortium of Northern abolitionists, Republican politicians, and childlike, "uppity," incompetent blacks who were perceived, in the words of a Southern weekly, as "an inferior race whose natural condition is slavery."[6]

Southern historians added to these charges a Northern urban population incapable of understanding Southern ways or the happy plantation life which benefited both white masters and African American slaves helpless to care for or govern themselves. Northerners, vilified as "carpetbaggers," and Southern collaborators, stigmatized as "scalawags," were accused of overturning those earlier customs which prioritized white dominion. Additionally, Southern manhood, declared a natural aristocracy of gentlemen and yeoman farmers, had been charged with the care and protection of its womenfolk. Northerners, they insisted, knew no such chivalry or offered such protection against lust-driven blacks.

Northern interpretations of the Civil War were expressed through the Union veterans' organization, GAR, and were as simplistic and partisan as those of the Confederate veterans. These local GAR chapters, supported by official government historians, maintained that the Civil War was fought to preserve the Union from the devilish rebel secessionists. Liberation of African American slaves from oppressive masters was more an afterthought than a cause, but equally an essential and ethical act. There was little room for common ground between the two exhausted adversaries.

Conflicting views of the war were thereafter maintained and elaborated through veterans' organizations formed to foster comradeship among the many local militias and state regiments. Once established and seeking social events which might keep memories of their roles in the conflict alive, war veterans turned to amateur theatricals. Dramatized representations of the late war began within months of the cessation of fighting. According to Jeffrey Mason,[7] these plays were the work of nonprofessional performers, Northern veterans' organizations, and members of state and county militias, who, in GAR halls and hired local theatres, reenacted skirmishes in which their units had figured. Soon after, as early as 1868, still written by amateurs to be performed by amateurs, clumsy melodramas cast the wartime activities of these local units within a dramatic framework in which the unit was patriotically responding to calls to preserve the Union and "the old flag." GAR melodramas were boastful and crude, largely focusing on Northern successes and enacting struggles to chastise rebellious armies and treasonous individuals and to draw errant rebels back into the Union.

The damaged infrastructure of the South and its large, rural population necessarily meant that there were fewer Southern plays, and these few were of indifferent quality. Southern melodramas highlighted the hypocritical wickedness of the abolitionists and the ways in which Northern forces pillaged from Southern homes and insulted the local civilians.

These amateur Civil War melodramas always began with political alienation and estrangement, thereby giving rise to a convention that would transfer intact to professional melodrama and which would later be exploited by both Dixon and Griffith: a love affair across the Mason-Dixon Line, the political boundary between the Southern slaveholding states and the Northern "free" states. This intersectional love affair, in some dramas a pair of love affairs, was enacted by a man from the secessionist South and a woman from the North or, conversely, a Northern man and a Southern woman or sometimes, as in The Birth of a Nation, a pair of couples both deeply in love but opposed and mutually repelled by their lovers' political and social ideology. In some dramas, exposure to the horrors of war and to the dishonorable intentions of the soldiers on her own side converted the heroine to the cause of the Union or Confederacy.

The same emotional and patriotic divisions in loyalty and sympathies were seen to affect former friendships, military comradeships, domestic partnerships, and frequently to produce rancorous contention between siblings. In some dramas, couples met and fell in love before the war, and the couple were then separated by conflict until military operations inadvertently brought them together, in many instances the Yankee soldier finding himself billeted near the Southern woman's home or spying on Southern troops, or in circumstances which tested the couple's feeling for each other. Former comrades similarly met in adverse circumstances. Thus, many of these dramas took place in two time periods: the antebellum years, when courtship and friendships were feasible, and the wartime years, when military victory decided issues. Simple, boastful, inelegant in their plotting, and limited in character development, such melodramas were the chief means of revising and revisiting the Civil War until, in 1885, the twentieth anniversary of that war had passed.

The earliest of these amateur melodramas from the 1860s were crude narratives of daring and combat victories which vilified the enemy and celebrated the heroism and undiluted regional loyalties or national patriotism of the militias drawn from the local district. These amateur pieces were replaced from the 1880s with professional melodramas, many emanating from New York, but many more developed and performed on national and regional touring circuits. Professional melodramas offered dramatic narratives enacted with more exacting theatrical standards, with incisive characterization, and with deliberately scripted attempts to acknowledge personal hardships inflicted on both Union and Confederate adversaries and on civilians, both North and South, whose unprotected homes lay in the paths of military forces. These numerous professional pieces brought enactments in which, the threat of the Confederate secession overcome, parties on both sides of the conflict could resume their lives. Differences acknowledged and set aside, the characters achieved mutual and personal closure.

As professional dramatists began to invade amateur territory from the mid-1870s and attempted to express a national concern for a cessation to sectional conflict, a further necessary step was taken. What distinguished many of these professional Civil War melodramas from their amateur predecessors were the strategies, which soon become established conventions, employed to avoid partisan gloating and to effect a climate of reconciliation. There was, overall, recognition that the Civil War demanded huge sacrifices and entailed truly calamitous loss on both sides. There was little jubilation in military victory. What mattered was that the cessation of war had enabled individuals—formerly combatants or lovers, forced by the circumstances of sectional conflict into becoming adversaries—to bury their differences and to acknowledge the strength of their affections. It was a function of these professional plays to entertain, to acknowledge both personal and national sacrifice and individual heroism, and to depict villainy identified, shamed, and expelled from a traumatized world, thus restoring amity and tranquility, and, in the main, to suggest that some sort of closure and reconciliation had been achieved.

In consequence, rather than end their melodramas with a victory for one military unit and a defeat for its foes, professional dramatists extended the drama into the postbellum period and looked for means of resolution and reconciliation. Such a realignment of concern usually obliged a final act set in the war's aftermath and brought together couples estranged through misunderstandings or, as frequently and as plausibly, through sectional and ideological difference. In transsectional weddings and in restored amity between estranged partners, lovers, siblings, and parents and children, and, with a further final exposure of a villain's role in fomenting discord (often with the expulsion of the villain from the recovering world inhabited by the drama's other characters), the action of these plays dramatized the healing and reintegration of wounded and seriously fragmented families, regions, and ultimately, the [white] nation itself.

Reinforcing ideas of division, mutual loss, and ultimate, if painful, reconciliation was achieved through a deliberate symmetry of characterization which enacted discord, death, or injury in battle—sometimes of brothers, cousins, or boyhood friends. The same principle of symmetry divided and reunited lovers. It is significant to both the work of Dixon and the subsequent filmmaking of Griffith that professional Civil War stage plays employing these conventions were still popular, attracting audiences in metropolitan theatres, village halls, and rural tent fit-up theatres well into the 1930s.

Another convention to be reshaped for the professional stage was the villain. In contrast to the amateur melodrama, the villain was rarely a soldier. Rather—and this is important to the processes of reconciliation and creating a harmonious equilibrium—the villain was, chiefly, a civilian. His clothing—unless he illicitly or suspiciously wore a uniform—betrayed no allegiance. He thus belonged to neither side and was identifiably a compound of both sides: a spy, a double agent serving both North and South, furthering his own financial and romantic interests rather than a cause, a "copperhead," or Northerner, sympathetic to the Confederacy, to secession, and to slavery. In Southern plays the villain was identifiable because he was an abolitionist and sympathized with the Yankees, or, visibly an amalgam of genetic traits, he was a mulatto whose political leanings and sexual urges respected no loyalties or boundaries. In Dixon's and Griffith's hands the villain was to become Senator Austin Stoneman and

Silas Lynch, respectively. When we consider these several theatrical strategies of intersectional love affairs and the possibilities of villainy and then measure them against the two distinct halves of *The Birth of a Nation*, we might observe that what is also original to Griffith is that he brings together in one film the Northern and the Southern play.

In her exceptional study of *Uncle Tom's Cabin* and related depictions of race, Linda Williams explores the family home, especially the lost family home, as a "space of innocence."[8] Williams's recognition of the home thus encapsulates much of the action of melodrama, as heroes and heroines struggle to return to the Edenic life from which they have been driven by the machinations of the villain. In professional Civil War plays, the "lost home" is central. Because both the Union and Confederacy carried the war into hostile territory, the settings chosen for these melodramas were often family homes, now occupied and used as command posts by enemy troops. Melodrama's villains threatened these homes and their civilian—especially their female and child—occupants. Fights raged around these homes, and cavalries pastured in their gardens. The homes were searched for wounded soldiers, spies, and enemy couriers, and damaged by shellfire, but they were also the sites for timely rescues and lovers' reunions. The home was under constant threat of loss, but ultimately regained and restored.

Melodrama, of course, permits—indeed, encourages—these tropes of villainy, sectional discord, and the threatened loss of home while, at the same time, stimulating partisan sentiments seemingly at odds with empathic identification with dramatic characters. One of the pleasures of melodrama is that it indulges logical inconsistencies, allowing spectators to experience and to hold in suspension moral, emotional, and ideological irreconcilables. The swift action and rapidity of incident of most melodramas distract the spectator from the awareness that she or he may hold conflicting opinions and further, may tolerate, or even enjoy and support, repellent characters. As stage dramatists and as Griffith recognized, North and South, Union and Confederacy, abolition and slavery, Klan membership and Klan abhorrence were such irreconcilables. Describing the circumstances in which Shakespeare created *Hamlet* and *Julius Caesar*, James Shapiro writes of "tragedies constructed on the fault line of irresolvable ethical conflict,"[9] and Griffith's Civil War films traverse the same fault line. However, Griffith's films are not tragedies—which exact fatal penalties for calamitous choices—but melodramas. Melodrama does not force hard choices but, rather, allows its audiences all options and does not penalize them for failure to choose. Civil War dramas permitted audiences to be sympathetic to both sides of the conflict and to respect and admire individuals—the "Little

Colonel" Ben Cameron, for example—who, were we to meet them in real life, would be repugnant.[10]

When, between 1897 and 1916, film took up the North–South debate, it was not—apart from reaching a still-wider audience—breaking new ground. Rather, continuing with familiar dramatic narratives, employing structural similarities, and deploying similar conventions of character and incident, film extended discussion, now sharing discourse with professional stage plays still performed in regional companies and, still later, by amateurs. Griffith, to some degree familiar with the theatrical conventions of Civil War and Reconstruction plays but inexperienced in applying them, led Biograph's efforts to produce commercially viable films on this popular subject. He was to prove remarkably successful. Beginning in 1908 with *The Guerrilla* (1908), Griffith moved successively to *In Old Kentucky*, *The Honor of His Family* (1909), *In the Border States*, *The Fugitive*, *The House with Closed Shutters* (1910), *The Rose of Kentucky*, *His Trust*, *His Trust Fulfilled*,[11] *Swords and Hearts*, *The Battle* (1911), and *The Informer* (1912). He was then to turn away from the convulsions of that war for three years before embarking on his adaptation of *The Clansman*. Meanwhile, rival directors—Thomas Ince, Keanan Buel, Mack Sennett, Joseph Smiley—and studios—Kalem, Keystone, Klaw and Erlanger, Selig, Vitagraph, Domino—continued with films set against this national conflict.

The 370 Civil War films produced by the various studios between 1897 and 1915 were neither random nor coincidental. Rather, they may be understood as evidence of the film industry joining a debate which, if not of the industry's making, occupied American dramatists and drew large audiences for nearly fifty years. Although decades in the past, the American Civil War remained then, as it remains to this day, a contentious, unstable subject still capable of inducing acrimonious partisan debate. However, with time passing and with memories of the war and of the equally contentious Reconstruction period losing some of their sharpness, the climates in which plays and films were viewed and the emotional, social, and political resolutions of personal conflicts slowly moderated to appeal to still-broader audiences. The Civil War, with its narratives of campaigns, skirmishes, political strategies, and grave social and domestic disruptions, had become and was to remain the American epic and the American tragedy. Thus, these new films, as much as the stage melodramas before them, can be understood as contributing to an ongoing process of reexamining, reevaluating, and understanding the causes and effects of that conflict.

In July 1908, Griffith shot *The Guerrilla*, his first Civil War film. What is immediately apparent from this and subsequent Biograph films is that Griffith, despite his obvious sympathies with the Confederacy and his inherited distaste for the achievements of Reconstruction, was impartial in his depictions of those affected by the war. His impartiality may have been, to some degree, the consequence of his employment by Biograph, a New York company that sold films to a national market, and that would have resisted films which demonized or openly favored either side. However, there also appears recognition on Griffith's part that suffering and loss were widespread and mutual. If there is a Southern accent to these Biograph films, it can be detected in Griffith's insistence on honor both as an abstraction and as an active force to be observed by the war's participants. Honor dictates behavior, and honor, although linked to courage before the enemy and loyalty to a cause, extends into domestic relations.[12] The loss of honor is ruinous and infamous. And Griffith, who could be heavily ironic, was not ironic on this subject. There is never a Griffith Falstaff to catechize or undermine honor and declare it a mere scutcheon. Griffith's Southern patriarchs and matrons who are seen to insist on family honor and to decry its loss, and those hot-blooded younger women and men who link personal honor with sectional loyalties, and, finally, those (blacked-up) ancient family retainers who see the intrusion of unmannered Yankees into their masters' homes are all a part of a complex system of chivalric honor which defines character and immediately stigmatizes those who lack this essential virtue. The military needs of the Union troops are acknowledged, and females loyal to the Union or to Union officers are defended, but Union detachments and their officers and non-coms are portrayed as boorish and destructive. A few are decent; fewer are honorable.

Given the matter of partisanship in the depiction of those sympathetic to the Union or the Confederacy, questions respecting the authorship of the scenarios for these twelve films inevitably arise. Insofar as can be ascertained,[13] Griffith devised the scenarios for the first three Biograph Civil War films: The Guerrilla, In Old Kentucky, and The Honor of His Family. A further three, Swords and Hearts and the two His Trust films, are credited to Emmett Campbell Hall, The Informer is assigned to George Hennessy, The Fugitive to John McDonagh, and In the Border States to Stanner E. V. Taylor. Hennessy was a part-time actor in Biograph films. Taylor was married to Marion Leonard, a leading actress in Griffith's first Biograph company. Thus, both Hennessy and Taylor had some knowledge of Griffith's tastes in dramatic subjects. Hall, Hennessy, and Taylor freelanced scenarios to Biograph, Lubin, and Selig between 1908 and 1916. McDonagh is known only through his single film. Each scenarist appears to have been adept at scavenging plots from other popular narrative sources and, in some instances, passing them off as his own.[14] Each was familiar with the conventions of Civil War stage plays and collaborated with Griffith to exploit subjects which previous authors had explored and effectively developed. However, irrespective of who brought the material to Griffith, Griffith was the dominant partner in shaping the scenario for the camera.

For the first of his Civil War films, The Guerrilla, Griffith concocted a ride-to-the-rescue plot in which a Northern soldier bids good-bye to his sweetheart and rides off to rejoin his unit. Then, alerted to her danger by a loyal black servant, he returns at the head of his company to rescue the young woman from a band of marauding outlaws disguised as Confederate soldiers. Biograph publicists chose to see this twelve-minute film, not as a drama of the late war, but as a stirring exhibition of horsemanship and swordplay, as the Northern officer must duel with his adversaries to liberate his sweetheart.[15] In Griffith's 1911 The Rose of Kentucky, the besiegers threatening a Kentucky farm in the postbellum period are "night riders," forerunners of the Ku Klux Klan heroes of The Birth of a Nation. Here Griffith depicts the night riders as malevolent and dangerous, driven off only by the bravery of a farmer and his adoring ward. The farmer's courage in protecting his ward, contrasting with the cowardice of a younger man who has been courting the girl, establishes the older man's right to propose marriage.[16]

The depiction of marauding irregulars or night riders invading a Southern or border state home provokes questions addressing an element of Griffith family history (or mythology), with Griffith insisting:

> Down in Kentucky was the house of my [grand]father, Colonel Jacob Wark Griffith, a Confederate cavalry officer. . . . Once there had been quite a pretentious[17] place—more or less like the popular conception of Kentucky mansions. . . . Guerrillas, disguised as Union raiders, burned the house in the first year of the war.[18]

Griffith apparently believed enough in this family legend for it to provide episodes in The Guerrilla, again in His Trust, and once again in The Rose of Kentucky, where plantation homes are looted and torched—or unsuccessfully menaced—by bands of irregulars whose motive is plunder and intimidation rather than patriotism or tactical policy. A later variant is also found in The Birth of a Nation where the Camerons' Piedmont home is looted and vandalized by Yankee troops. Griffith's repeated use of this distressing scenario may owe as much to his knowledge of audience expectation as it does to his personal history or to spontaneous plot making. The besieged home, a convention of Civil War stage plays and films as well as numerous frontier dramas, was echoed in other Griffith theatrical sources and would subsequently appear in his later, non–Civil War, films.

This early effort notwithstanding, the ready-made, hand-me-down conventions of Civil War stage drama were there for the manipulating. Griffith was able to deploy in In Old Kentucky, a fifteen-minute film, situations previously spread over a four-act play. Griffith's second film enacts the dilemma of a family divided by war. Brothers, in their Kentucky home as war is declared, pledge their loyalty to opposite sides, their father praising the younger son loyal to the Union and turning his back on the elder who professes sympathy with the Confederacy. Later, the elder son, now a Confederate officer carrying important documents through the Union lines, shelters in the family home. When his brother leads a search party of Union soldiers to intercept the papers, the Confederate son is hidden in his mother's bed. The boys' mother, pistol in hand, forestalls further pursuit, threatening to kill herself if her elder son is discovered. At the war's end, the brothers return, the younger to a hero's welcome, the elder, ragged and worn, uncertain of the welcome he will receive. Encouraged by a blacked-up Negro servant, the brothers embrace.[19] Griffith here does not query or contest Reconstruction. Rather, he opts for the trope of reconciliation: of brothers, family, and a nation reunited and forgiving. A further film from the same year, The Honor of His Family, enacts the pain and pride of a Southern gentleman, whose concern for the Confederate cause and still greater concern for the honor of his family, leads him to shoot his son who has fled—a coward—from the field of battle, then, with the aid of a black servant, to falsify the circumstances of his son's death by placing his body on the battlefield facing the enemy.[20] Here, in both films, are issues which are at once politically, morally, and emotionally difficult. Patriotism, sectionalism, and loyalty to the Union or to the Confederacy are divisive issues and can be resolved only by pain and sacrifice and by risking humiliation and exposure.

Even as Griffith was resorting to the strategies of the Civil War play to enact what he perceived as the calamities of the war and Reconstruction, he was becoming more adroit as a dramatist. Observing the conventions he was incorporating into these films, his films increasingly assumed theatrical form. In his films In Old Kentucky and The House with Closed Shutters, again in the two His Trust films (had they been released, as intended, as a single film),[21] and later in Swords and Hearts, the rhythms and climaxes of Griffith's films echo the four-act structure of the Civil War plays. It may have been, partly, that the fractionally longer film, fifteen minutes rather than ten minutes, invited punctuation and changes of pace, partly because, as several scholars note,[22] Griffith increased the number of shots per film. But it may also have been that, in taking motifs and conventions of characterization and action from stage dramas, Griffith was finding climactic episodes to end scenes and discovering that he could realize plots which would not have to be compressed to fit Biograph's short-film marketing policies. In accepting the antebellum, wartime, and postbellum structures of

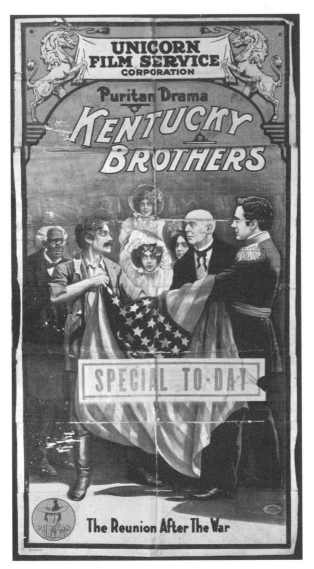

Poster for Griffith's *In Old Kentucky* (1909) reissued under a new title in 1915 to take advantage of the attention focused on *The Birth of a Nation*. A blurred photograph of this group appears in *Biograph Bulletin* 276, and the actors are identifiable as Henry B. Walthall (the "Little Colonel" in *The Birth of a Nation*), Owen Moore as the Union officer, Verner Clarges as the elderly father, Kate Bruce as the mother, Mary Pickford and Gertrude Robinson as sisters or sweethearts, and John R. Cumpson, blacked up as the Negro Servant. The scene pictured perfectly represents the image of a family—here a particular Kentucky family, emblematic of the national family—fractured by opposing loyalties but reconciled and reunited at the Civil War's end. Standing on the margin is a loyal African American slave/servant whose emancipation and fate are excluded from the narrative.

Civil War stage plays, he was, without necessarily being aware that he was doing so, imposing a guiding, disciplining structure onto his own work. The more he accepted a preagreed formula and allowed it to determine the structure of his films, the greater creative freedom Griffith allowed himself, and the defter his handling of incident and explorations of his characters' social circumstances became. Thus Griffith, by 1910, was developing an overall shape to his films which increasingly reflected the theatre rather than the vaudeville dramatic sketch.

Griffith's own early plays conspicuously suffered from logorrhea. His characters talked excessively. His acts and scenes dragged on past plausible endings. His characters were functions rather than dimensional beings. The legacy of vaudeville's dramatic sketch, which so assisted Griffith's early work at Biograph, curtailed or held in check his early tendency to ramble on, but the sketch, to its disadvantage, also encouraged Griffith to create abbreviated characters who were only marginally realized. That same limit to creating believable characters with individual emotional lives—still apparent in these Biograph Civil War films where, with the exceptions of Swords and Hearts and The Informer, his civilian characters merely represent attitudes toward the conflict and depict levels of suffering and privation—would last until 1918 with his films True Heart Susie and Broken Blossoms.

In the first of his five 1910 Civil War films, In the Border States, Griffith cast Gladys Egan, one of a pair of Biograph child actresses, as his heroine. The child assists a lone Confederate soldier who later returns with a search party to hunt a Union dispatch rider, coincidentally her father, who now shelters in the house. The Confederate soldier, recognizing the child who befriended him, calls off his troops.[23] Only weeks later, Griffith, using a scenario in part devised by Stanner Taylor, directed the first of two films which drew directly on his 1904 tour in Edward McWade's production of Winchester. Griffith chose for his central action the episode in which his heroine disguises herself in a Confederate uniform, concealing her hair under a soldier's hat, and misleads Union pursuers. In The House with Closed Shutters, this device enables the heroine to save the reputation of her brother, a Southerner carrying important dispatches, who runs from gunfire and hides at home. Wearing her brother's uniform and riding his horse at a gallop to outrace Union pursuers, she delivers the dispatches, then, going beyond the Winchester stage-and-film episode, engages bravely in combat against the Yankees until she is killed. To conceal her brother's infamy, their mother reports her brother killed, locks her coward son in the shuttered family home, reports him dead, and tells the heroine's rival suitors, who return from the war to continue their courtship, that she has gone mad with grief. Not until the brother—dying—throws open the shutters, is the truth revealed.[24] A similar depiction of waste and loss, joined to a macabre and sad celebration of honor, is visible in The Fugitive.[25] Two soldier sons, one Union, one Confederate, concurrently leave for war. The Union soldier kills the Confederate, then is obliged to take refuge in the Confederate mother's home. Her son's body is returned, but the Confederate mother, unaware of his role in her son's death, continues to shelter the Union soldier and later assists his escape. With the war's end, the Union soldier returns to his mother and sweetheart. The Confederate mother can only decorate her son's tunic with flowers. The binary pairs, which have been an enduring convention of the Civil War play and film, are in The Fugitive destabilized and rendered asymmetrical to telling effect.

Griffith's His Trust films[26] initially appear as the odd films out in this cluster of 1910 Civil War dramas because they feature the loyalty and devotion of a blacked-up Wilfred Lucas as George, an African American slave to a Southern family whose home is ruined and whose lives are jeopardized by the war which engulfs them. However, as much as the action speaks to black devotion to white families, it is also a further disquisition on honor: honor symbolized by a cavalry saber which passes from master to widow to emancipated servant. The span of action begins as the master, Colonel Frazier, puts on his sword belt and departs for battle at the head of his Confederate troops. Black field hands exuberantly cheer him on his way. Word is brought of the colonel's death in combat, the messenger indicating his death by handing to the widow her late husband's saber. The sword is hung above the family fireplace until a troop of invading Union soldiers torch the mansion. All that is rescued from the embers is the saber, transferred to George's cabin where he abandons his bed to the widow and her daughter and lies, protectively, across the threshold. Four years pass between His Trust and His Trust Fulfilled. Still occupying the slave cabin under George's protection, the widow sickens and dies, leaving the saber, now hanging above the crude fireplace, and her daughter's wardship to George's care. Formally emancipated, George may leave the plantation, but he stays to see the child grown to womanhood and married to her English cousin. The saber remains in his possession, an emblem of his trust fulfilled. In its depiction of close and enduring—entirely sexless—domestic relationships between white females and a black male, Griffith's films predict the kind of loyalty of black servants that will be used in The Birth of a Nation to contrast with the self-serving, malicious behavior of liberated slaves, black politicians, and black militias. The His Trust films also clearly demonstrate Griffith's belief in honor as a tangible and transferable quality rising above differences in race and station to shape noble behavior. Later, under Dixon's influence, Griffith would use, appropriately, the horse as a badge of chivalry, but here, in a smaller film, he effectively used the sword to the same purpose.

Griffith's final three Civil War films are, differently, his most ambitious and his most confidently handled. *Swords and Hearts*[27] remains his most complex work, despite relying, once again, on the twice previously used episode in which the film's heroine dons a Confederate uniform and rides to mislead and outwit Union cavalrymen pursuing the man whom she secretly loves. What is distinct and unique to any pre-1915 Civil War film is how Griffith and Emmett Campbell Hall harnessed the conventions of stage melodrama to depict and interrogate Southern class division, economic difference, and impoverishment brought by Reconstruction. In terms of depicting the vectors of class and inherited wealth as these impinge on poor whites, it is Griffith's most subtle study of pre- and postwar Southern life. *The Battle*, as its title informs, succeeds because, moving beyond skirmishes and raids, it depicts large-scale, full-on conflict and, in miniature, previews the camera strategies which Griffith would employ in battle scenes four years later. *The Informer*, Griffith's last in this group, makes a stab at psychological characterization. All borrow from the conventions of Civil War stage melodrama, but only in the battle episodes and in scenes of postwar Reconstruction-era poverty is there an action to foreshadow *The Birth of a Nation*.

In *Swords and Hearts*, Griffith and Hall began with the familiar symmetries: two households, the wealthy Fraziers and the poor Bakers, and two rival suitors—Confederate colonel Hugh Frazier and an unnamed Union officer—for the coquettish Irene Lambert's hand. There are two female rivals—the calculating Irene Lambert and the adoring Jennie Baker—for Frazier, and the film ends with two final pairings of couples, Irene Lambert and the Union officer and Jennie Baker and Hugh Frazier. Comedy is added by two seriocomic black servants—one dutiful and loyal and one lazy and selfish. In keeping with the convention of identifying the war as a dispute between whites, the two servants, as well as George from the *His Trust* films, are Griffith's sole African American characters—apart from walk-on blacks—to appear in his Biograph Civil War dramas. In the pattern of the professional pieces, *Swords and Hearts'* villain, Baker, is neither Yankee nor Confederate, but a member of the envious underclass, who fires on the Northern cavalry pursuing Colonel Frazier and then returns, disguised as a bushwhacker, to burn and loot the Frazier mansion and to kill its aristocratic owner. And the film ends, typically, with honor and love satisfied on all sides, with missing property restored by the dutiful black servant, and with the personal cost of the conflict—death and despoliation—swept aside by warm feelings of affection, regard, and reconciliation.

At first glance, *Swords and Hearts* is a romantic melodrama set in three now-conventional time periods: prewar, wartime, and a more complex Reconstruction era. Its protagonist, Jennie, is the active heroine who—having shown restraint and self-denial when the man she has secretly loved departs for war—finds the object of her love threatened with capture, dons the man's outer clothing, and, mounting a horse and riding skillfully, misleads his pursuers. Later, Jennie is forced to reveal her devotion when the fickle Irene breaks her engagement and pledges herself to the Union officer, a conqueror, not a vanquished soldier returning to a burned-out mansion and finding no slaves to replant abandoned fields.

As with *His Trust* and *His Trust Fulfilled*, Hall and Griffith broke with earlier, shorter Civil War films and followed the pattern set by both the Northern and Southern professional melodrama in taking the action beyond the cessation of the Civil War into the postwar South and noting the dire effects of Reconstruction: agricultural and domestic property destroyed, desolation, impoverishment, social opportunism. But this theatrically familiar solution, the union of Jennie Baker and Hugh Frazier, is sentimental and romantic, not yet savage and political. There is little in *Swords and Hearts* to foreshadow the anger, bitterness, and racial contempt which characterize the latter half of *The Birth of a Nation*.

However much *Swords and Hearts* owes to earlier dramatic narratives, Griffith went beyond the formal requirements of the Civil War film and brought this drama in line with some of his earlier Biograph pieces, such as *A Corner in Wheat* (1909) and *The Iconoclast* (1910), which depict and analyze the home life of the working poor. Griffith showed sympathy toward and understanding of these underclass characters, endowing them with a hitherto unseen psychological inner life. In this film it is the lower-class Baker family, headed by a father forced to subsist on the sale of produce from his small garden and resentfully envious of the upper-class Fraziers' wealth, which, in contrast, is derived from farming the big cash crop, tobacco. Biograph intertitles repeatedly call attention to the social and economic gulf between the upper-class Fraziers and the poor, white trash Bakers. The Bakers are identified in intertitles as "The Poor White Class . . ." and Jennie as "The 'Poor Class' girl in love with the handsome soldier." We observe Baker resentfully watching as "the father [Frazier] sells his tobacco," and Jennie's rival, Irene Lambert, presented on the veranda of her own elegant home, is described as "The Southern Belle." By contrast, Jennie hoes row crops, and the ex-colonel Hugh Frazier is obliged to undertake the same labor before the loyal ex-slave Old Ben returns the hidden family treasures for the deserving couple to share. Indeed, with the emblematic destruction of the rich plantation house—which Jennie, barred by her lowly class, never enters—a class barrier is removed and the New South permits a more egalitarian marriage.

Despite its impressive multiple-shot battle scenes containing an episode in which an ammunition convoy, carrying gunpowder to faltering Union forces, is menaced by Confederate bonfires which threaten to explode wagons, horses, and drivers, The Battle's[28] plot is depressingly familiar. Griffith allowed the well-used formula of cowardice before the enemy, panicked flight, and recovered courage and honor to take over, and the resulting film showed no gain in dramaturgical strategies. Leaving a prebattle ball, a young Union officer joins his regiment. As the battle grows in intensity, he flees to his sweetheart's home where, instead of succoring him, she reproaches him for his cowardice and persuades him to return to combat. He reports to headquarters and is assigned the task of bringing needed ammunition to his troops. He bravely fulfills his mission, is congratulated by his general, and regains his sweetheart's love.

Griffith was on better form with The Informer.[29] A narrative of jealousy, betrayal, and revenge, Griffith cast his two strong leading performers, Mary Pickford and Henry Walthall, in the crucial roles of a duped fiancée and a treacherous brother who persuades her, falsely, that her lover has been killed and who then attempts to insinuate himself in the place of the missing brother. When the Confederate soldier fiancé reappears to the girl, wounded and in flight and must be hidden from searching Yankee troops, the treacherous brother, ejected by the angry girl, reports his brother's hiding place to the Union patrol. In the gun battle that follows, the fiancée holds off the Yankees with her lover's pistol, and the betraying brother is killed by a stray shot. The Informer is distinguished by fine acting from Walthall, who invests his false-brother role with a withered hand—an effective metonym for his shriveled conscience (he tears his brother's letter with his teeth, "something not only perverse but perverted . . . biting his brother's words to bits"[30])—and whose subtle performance of jealousy and opportunism make the conventional plot plausible, especially when playing against Pickford's innocence, doubt, misgiving acquiescence to the false brother's courtship, and outraged virtue when his duplicity has become known. With The Informer shot and released, Griffith turned away from the Civil War. He gave no hint that he would return to this subject.

Griffith's twelve Civil War films expose the exercises that preceded and provided the vocabulary and structure for his epic The Birth of a Nation, but they provide no hint to the sources of that film's extraordinary racist content. Although The Birth of a Nation's immediate source was Thomas Dixon's The Clansman, and although Dixon's virulently racist play and novels were Griffith's principal sources, both Dixon's and Griffith's works need to be located and understood in the climate of early-twentieth-century preoccupations with race, ethnicity, and American identity. Here again, these concerns were expressed and fought out in the dramas of Broadway and the popular variety stage. Both the legitimate theatre and vaudeville, in their depictions of race, ethnicity, and national origins, described a distinct social hierarchy. Significantly, these various dramas—plays and films—upheld a predominantly white national culture which denigrated, marginalized, or altogether excluded alien arrivals. African Americans and other peoples of color had no allocated place—except at America's margins.

Such a racial and ethnic structure is schematically proclaimed in a 1907 Biograph film shot barely a year before Griffith began his film career. Billy Bitzer's *Fights of Nations*,[31] a six-minute comic film, is remarkable for two reasons: five of the brief combats staged for Bitzer's camera are abridged sketches from American vaudeville theatres, each sketch chosen because it was currently being performed in a local East Coast variety house and, with its own actors and scenery, consequently available to be restaged for Bitzer's camera. In *Fights of Nations*, we thus possess a snapshot of one of the kinds of entertainment currently on offer to vaudeville's patrons.

This compilation of variety sketches is further noteworthy for its casual, matter-of-fact racism and for its open and casual hostility to foreign immigration. Each sketch identifies a group whose presence in American society is distinctive, alien, anomalous, and disturbing. Together, the sketches imply that black Americans and foreigners, apart from white western Europeans, are disposed to brawl and instinctively fight savagely—or ludicrously—with whatever weapons come to hand. Each sketch within *Fights of Nations* denigrates a group perceived as alien or different from assimilated white Christian Americans. Those whose difference is distinctive—Spaniards, Mexicans, Jews, Irish, African Americans—are targeted for their allegedly quarrelsome natures, and as typical of those who cannot assimilate. Bitzer's film concludes with a congratulatory coda: Figures emblematic of white Europeans—French, German, and British—pay homage to Uncle Sam and to an entourage that includes American soldiers and a Native American female who kneels to her white "superiors."

Although more subtle and, unlike film, able to use speech to develop an argument, the American stage showed a similar preoccupation with race and Americanism. "Chimmie" comedies offer an immediate example. Chimmie (Jimmie) Fadden, an Irish American petty criminal reared in an Irish area of New York's Lower East Side, appeared as the creation of the journalist Edward Townsend in a cluster of short stories from 1895. Townsend's narratives projected America's immigrant urban poor as warmhearted rogues, termagants, and scamps, more sympathetic than dangerous but, significantly, more alien than assimilated. Through Townsend's stories, urban criminality had been made picaresque, if not endearing, while the unassimilated immigrant remained a troubling interloper who showed no signs of disappearing or humbly assuming his lowly place in American society. Further, the Irish Catholic Chimmie Fadden was seen in dangerous proximity to patrician, Protestant American females. Criminality, cross-class and cross-religion transgression, slum tourism, and xenophobia were brought together in a potentially explosive mix. The following year, Townsend and Augustus Thomas separately adapted Chimmie Fadden for the stage. By 1902 there were several one-reel "Chimmie" (with different surnames) films produced for American nickelodeons, and by 1915, the year in which The Birth of a Nation was released, Cecil B. DeMille realized Chimmie Fadden in a full-length film.

Dramas involving race testified to fears that Reconstruction, although formerly ended and some thirty years in the past, had left the South with social and political dilemmas unresolved and subject to corruption. Provocatively, George Hoey's The Law of the Land (1896) linked duplicitous alien ethnicity with antebellum Southern criminality in a drama in which a Jewish money lender swindles a plantation owner, an African American child (with mixed blood) passes as white, and a white child is nearly sold into slavery. Edward Sheldon's The Nigger (1909) dramatized the plight of a white governor of a Southern state who becomes the victim of intended blackmail when it transpires that he is the descendent of a liaison between his grandfather and a mulatto mistress. Acknowledging his mixed blood, the governor resigns and breaks his engagement to his white fiancée.

Numerous plays of this era articulated anxieties about racial and ethnic intermarriage. Four decades before 1900, amid the American Civil War, the term miscegenation was coined. Miscegenation—and all the negative connotations that this neologism implied—had entered American vocabularies in a political hoax intended to discredit Lincoln's Emancipation Proclamation.[32] Although the prefix misce was taken from the Latin miscere (to mix) and genation from genus (race), mis also seemed to refer to error or crime, as in mistake or misappropriate. Once miscegenation entered common usage, the concepts and practices of marital and sexual relationships between races and ethnic groups now had the language and well-publicized views of politicians, journalists, and class and race leaders to shape and maintain an endless national debate.

The resultant stage plays which broached this subject of anxiety and concern offered a cacophony of voices (some noble, others venal) and were optimistically resolved with dramatic solutions which frequently failed to match—or openly evaded—the high-minded rhetoric of assimilation offered by leading characters. Issues of intermarriage between races and different immigrant communities appeared in such dramas as David Belasco's *Madame Butterfly* (1900), Israel Zangwill's *Children of the Ghetto* (1899) and *The Melting Pot* (1909), William C. de Mille's *Strongheart* (1905), and Edward Milton Royle's *The Squaw Man* (1905). Despite Belasco's apparent sympathy for Cho-Cho-San in *Madame Butterfly*, the Japanese heroine's concubinage with an American naval officer must result in her suicide when the arrival of a white bride challenges her status as "wife" and mother to the couple's son. The same fate awaits Nat-u-rich, the Native American heroine of Royle's *The Squaw Man*, when a white fiancée appears from England to claim her husband. William C. de Mille's *Strongheart* ends in a stalemate when Sonagataha ("Strongheart"), a Native American scholar who, despite lofty arguments in which he asserts his American identity and claims his right to court his classmate's sister, is refused permission. Despite Sonagataha's moral triumph over white prejudice, he is defeated by the dramatist's timid solution: Sonagataha is called back to the reservation to lead his people through a crisis of famine, disease, and poverty. Thus, de Mille conveniently denies his Native American a white wife.

Similarly, in Zangwill's *The Melting Pot*, harsh disappointment and compromise override rhetoric describing the triumph of American assimilation. The often-quoted imaginative dialogue between the musician protagonist and the settlement worker, with whom he has fallen in love, has been used to describe the triumph of American assimilation:

> VERA: So your music finds inspiration in America?
> DAVID: Yes, in the seething of the Crucible.
> VERA: The Crucible? I don't understand!
> DAVID: Not understand! You, the spirit of the Settlement! Not
> understanding that America is God's Crucible, the great Melting-Pot
> where all the races of Europe are melting and re-forming! Here you
> stand, good folks, think I, when I see them at Ellis Island, here you
> stand in your fifty groups with your fifty languages and histories, and
> your fifty blood hatreds and rivalries. But you won't be long like that,
> brothers, for these are the fires of God you've come to. . . . A fig for
> your feuds and vendettas! Germans and Frenchmen, Irishmen and
> Englishmen, Jews and Russians—into the Crucible with you all! God is
> making the American.[33]

The reality the couple face is altogether different from these eloquent hopes. She is also being pursued by a wealthy Protestant aristocrat, and her parents are

Russian nobility who deplore and oppose her alliance with a Jew. Obstacles are thrown in the couple's way so that, although they eventually can marry, theirs is a bruised union, cursed by the recognition that the pure, American amalgam of David's vision has yet to be cast from the crucible and that old feuds and hatreds are carried intact and undiminished into the New World.

Thomas Dixon Jr.'s *The Clansman* is an immediate contemporary of these plays and films. However, unlike Sheldon, Belasco, de Mille, Royle, and Zangwill, Dixon showed neither regret nor anxiety about racial discrimination. African Americans are, in Dixon's lexicon, unambiguously inferior to white Americans, potentially dangerous to them, and best held at a distance from white society. Griffith, elaborating on Dixon's opinions, was to show the same uncompromising view in his depiction of those who threatened racial mixing.

More than a year would pass before Griffith would begin work on *The Birth of a Nation*. He had resigned from Biograph and had left its conservative management behind in New York. He was notionally free, but he had formed a commercial alliance which offered immediate work. When, in 1913, he joined Harry Aitken and the Reliance studios in Los Angeles, Griffith was faced with the immediate responsibility of directing four feature-length films. One of these films, *The Escape* (1913–1914), derived from a Zola-esque melodrama of the same title by Paul Armstrong[34] on the subject of eugenics and the biological and social consequences of heedless random breeding. The film no longer survives.

A year later, work began on *The Clansman*, the original title of *The Birth of a Nation*. Griffith had matured. He was now forty. He had made a full-length *Judith of Bethulia*, and its success had brought financial backers. He had left Biograph, taking with him Biograph's better actors, its best cameramen, assorted technicians, and financial advisors. He possessed undeniable skills and confidence. He was ready for this next challenge.

5 The *Clansman* and *The Birth of a Nation*

Of all his films, and Griffith's most ambitious to date, *The Birth of a Nation* (1915) drew most directly upon the theatre. Its plot and characters were taken from Thomas Dixon's play *The Clansman*, and the film's overall structure and strategies—tactics to prepare, confound, and disrupt audience expectations—drew upon the ingrained conventions of Civil War and Reconstruction stage plays, not least those exploited by Dixon. To a lesser degree, *The Birth of a Nation* also echoed the theatre's role in debating ethnicity, race, and American identity.

Griffith's inheritance from the theatre was, seemingly, untroubled. There had been nothing in nineteenth-century Civil War and Reconstruction-era plays to unsettle audiences, nor had early-twentieth-century dramas of American identity elicited more than a mild sense of discomfort from their predominantly white spectators. If anything, these dramas reassured their audiences of the continuity of a comfortable, unthreatening, white America. It was only when these two inherently stable theatrical genres were combined, first, by Thomas Dixon and more fully elaborated by Griffith that—rather like immersing magnesium in water—the violent hypergolic combustions that were *The Clansman* and *The Birth of a Nation* occurred.

It is difficult, if not virtually impossible, from our twenty-first-century perspective, to understand the artistic and financial risks Griffith faced as he undertook to bring Dixon's inflammatory and controversial play to the screen. It is equally difficult, given Griffith's reluctance to discuss his choice of subject in other than flippant and casual terms, to understand the pressures and anxieties he experienced as he progressed. *The Clansman* was to provide Griffith with a secure frame in which to begin filming, but it also imposed a confining structure from which he necessarily had to liberate himself in order to make a remarkable original work. What is apparent is that Griffith, in selecting *The Clansman* and in shooting *The Birth of a Nation*, once again retreated into the theatre he knew and understood in order to move forward with his epic film. Late in his life, Griffith, ending his unfinished autobiography, looked back on the emergence of *The Birth of a Nation* from *The Clansman* and joked that "*The Birth of a Nation* . . . might be said to have caused the shotgun wedding of the stage and the movies."[1]

"Shotgun wedding" calls to mind angry parents forcing marriage on an embarrassed bride and a reluctant groom. But here there was neither reluctance nor embarrassment. *The Clansman* was more a begetter than a reluctant victim, and *The Birth of a Nation* was *The Clansman*'s acknowledged offspring, neither illegitimate nor the product of a forced union. *The Birth of a Nation* was, however, a hybrid, the product of the stage and motion pictures. Further, Griffith, in expressing this union in negative terms, was forgetting his long prior involvement with the theatre, forgetting the plays he had adapted as Biograph films and, equally, ignoring the work of other film directors and artists who had adapted theatrical works with considerable success. He was nonetheless correct in observing that, in bringing a major film work from a contentious and disturbing stage play, he had once again yoked motion pictures to the stage. Beyond this, Griffith had yoked and elaborated a sequence of binary opposites (or near opposites): blackness and whiteness, male assertiveness and female passivity, female assertiveness and male passivity, chaste romance and lust, whole families and fractured families, the Union and Confederacy, loyalty and succession, political opportunism and good governance, nationalism and sectionalism, the rebirth of a convalescing, reunified nation and the birth of the Klu Klux Klan. Sometimes the action of this film allowed his audiences clear, unambiguous choices of values to uphold and characters to admire or deplore, but often these apparent binaries were compromised by, or diffused through, other issues and values.

The circumstances in which Griffith became acquainted with *The Clansman* are, like so many other incidents in his life, wrapped in his fabricated tales. In two accounts, the interview which he gave in 1916 to *Photoplay Magazine*[2] and again, in 1939, when he began work on his never-completed autobiography, Griffith claimed that he first knew of *The Clansman* when his colleague Frank Woods (occasional Biograph scenarist and critic for the *Spectator*) gave him a copy of Dixon's novel. According to Griffith,

> I skipped quickly through the book until I got to the part about the Klansmen, who according to no less than Woodrow Wilson, ran to the rescue of the downtrodden South after the Civil War. I could just see these Klansmen in a movie with their white robes flying. We had all sorts of runs-to-the-rescue in pictures

and horse operas. . . . It was always a hit. The pursuit and run-to-the-rescue seemed to be the most surefire gag in the business. . . . Now I could see a chance to do this ride-to-the-rescue on a grand scale. Instead of saving one poor little Nell of the Plains, this ride would be to save a nation. Here was a chance to make a moving picture that would rival the productions of the regular stage.[3]

Griffith's account of first encountering The Clansman through Dixon's novel is unlikely in several respects. Woodrow Wilson's endorsement of the Klan, although later cited by Griffith, is never mentioned by Dixon. Griffith would have known of Dixon, his novels and his play, and was certainly familiar with the disturbances that these works had generated well before 1913. Following the successful tour of Dixon's stage adaptation of his novel in 1905, three Clansman companies simultaneously toured American cities east of the Mississippi, each tour accompanied by protests from African American groups and endorsements from local whites, In 1906, Griffith and Linda Arvidson had been cast as the leads in a touring company of Dixon's The One Woman only to be informed that rehearsals had been indefinitely postponed. Moreover, building his second acting company for Biograph in 1909 and searching for stage-experienced actors, Griffith had recruited Claire McDowell and her husband, Charles Hill Mailes, both of whom had toured in one of Dixon's Clansman companies. Whether Griffith actually witnessed a performance of The Clansman is uncertain. In both the 1916 Photoplay interview and in his memoirs, Griffith was dismissive of The Clansman as a touring melodrama, implying, untruthfully, that the play failed to make money for Dixon and describing it as "a terrible frost."[4]

Yet, there may be some truth in Griffith's reiterated claim that Frank Woods interested Griffith in The Clansman as a film subject. In 1911, Dixon had entered into some sort of understanding over the performing rights to The Clansman with the Kinemacolor Corporation of America.[5] No money changed hands, and no agreement was signed, but Kinemacolor, optimistic that an agreement over price would be reached eventually, began work on a twenty-five-minute color version of the play.

Filming in the New Orleans area began under the supervision of George Brennan, The Clansman's original producer and Dixon's publicity manager for all national tours. Frank Woods had, by 1911, joined Kinemacolor and was probably involved in developing The Clansman's scenario from Dixon's play and Dixon's novel. Actors who had toured in The Clansman were allegedly hired to repeat their original roles, although no one has been able to identify who these actors were nor from which touring companies they had been recruited. Eventually, in fall 1912, *The Clansman* project was halted after Kinemacolor had spent $25,000 with little to show for their efforts, apart from some unedited reels of color negative. Dixon, still unpaid and now angry, withdrew whatever tentative permission he had given. For its part, Kinemacolor—because of this film and other episodes of fiscal mismanagement—was rapidly approaching financial liquidation.

Frank Woods was to leave Kinemacolor when the company foundered in 1913 and to join Griffith in 1914 as he shot *The Birth of a Nation.* Woods purportedly brought footage of Kinemacolor's *Clansman*—not Dixon's novel—to Griffith and urged Griffith to undertake his own version of the play. Whether Woods at this point presented Griffith with his own scenario for a film version or subsequently collaborated with Griffith on the final scenario for *The Birth of a Nation* is uncertain, but Woods shares screen credit with Griffith for this scenario. Irrespective of the sequence of these events, Griffith therefore had some early indication of how Dixon's stage drama might appear on film. Adding insult to injury, Griffith's Hollywood base, from 1913 to 1916, was the former Kinemacolor studio, abandoned when Kinemacolor went bankrupt. In summary, what is important to any discussion of Griffith's prior knowledge of *The Clansman* is that he was fully aware of the play as a money-earning property and, equally, as a drama which, on the two issues of presenting a true history of the Civil War and Reconstruction and depicting African Americans, would generate prolonged and acrimonious debate. When Griffith later expressed astonishment at the adverse responses *The Birth of a Nation* attracted, he was being disingenuous.

Eventually, Griffith obtained Dixon's consent and paid a deposit of $2,500 toward the full film rights.[6] The consequence of Dixon's relentless bargaining was that Griffith was obliged to sell shares in his film, a fund-raising device he was to employ on further occasions. He also continued to borrow money from various backers as *The Birth of a Nation* was shot. In all, *The Birth of a Nation* cost $110,000,[7] approximately $30 million in today's money.[8]

Once Griffith had acquired the performance rights, he began intensive research into the Civil War, reading accounts of campaigns and studying pictorial sources: paintings, engravings in journals, and battlefield photographs. Lillian Gish, recalling this period of research, also admitted that, although Griffith had reached such a level of creative proficiency that he might have devised his own film drama, he nonetheless relied upon Dixon's stage play as a narrative source and for psychological support. Gish was convinced that Griffith's confidence depended on adhering to a successful theatrical source:

[*The Clansman*] had done well as a book and even better as a play, touring the country for five years. . . . Mr. Griffith didn't need the Dixon book. His intention was to tell the story of the War between the States. But he evidently lacked the confidence to start the production of a twelve-reel film without an established book as the basis for the story.[9]

Lillian Gish's "book"—Griffith's narrative sources for *The Birth of a Nation*—were, to varying degrees, Dixon's three novels, *The Leopard's Spots* (1905), *The Clansman* (1905), and *The Traitor* (1907), and, crucially, a play also titled *The Clansman* (1905). *The Leopard's Spots*, while providing neither plot nor characters for Dixon's subsequent works, depicts a defeated, occupied South subject to intrusive white Northerners hostile to Southern tradition, and African American (or mulatto) characters who intermarry. It describes African Americans holding high office in state government, despite the established historical fact that only in Louisiana—and then only for a month—did an African American serve as lieutenant governor and that only in South Carolina was a black elected to that state's Supreme Court. In a single South Carolina county, blacks held the offices of sheriff, magistrate, school commissioner, and officer in the state militia.[10] Otherwise, "no African American held a major office during Reconstruction,"[11] but Dixon elected to circumvent fact and to substitute emotional polemic. The tone of *The Leopard's Spots* accords with that of Francis P. Blair, the Democrats' candidate for vice-president in the election of 1868, who described blacks as "a semi-barbarous race . . . who longed to subject the white women to their unbridled lust."[12] Permeated with this view and with misinformation which depicts a state under black rule and in political disarray, *The Leopard's Spots* ends with rescue from the purported iniquities of Reconstruction and deliverance from the threat of black dominance by the Ku Klux Klan.

Dixon's *The Clansman*, as both novel and stage melodrama, retains the author's earlier tone and introduces a new cast of characters. Both 1905 narratives begin with the postbellum reunion of Elsie Stoneman and Ben Cameron, moving on to depict the persecution and abuse of the Cameron family by newly liberated and enfranchised African Americans exhilarated by sudden empowerment. Both narratives deal with the founding of the South Carolina chapter of the Ku Klux Klan (under the leadership of the Confederate hero General Nathan Bedford Forrest) in a direct response to the rape of thirteen-year-old Flora Cameron, and both narratives depict the murder of the Negro perpetrator of Flora's rape by vengeful Klansmen. Again, both novel and play enact tensions between the Stoneman and Cameron families caused by the latter's refusal to submit to rule by African Americans (which Congressman Austin Stoneman perceives as "equality" and "uniting the Nation" and the Camerons as tyranny and racial contamination), leading to a denouement which depicts the abduction and threatened rape—or forced marriage—of Elsie Stoneman, menaced by a lust-driven Silas Lynch, Lynch's usurping of military authority, ordering the immediate execution of Ben Cameron, and a timely rescue of the endangered principals by masked Klansmen, led by Ben Cameron, who seize and imprison Lynch. In neither novel nor play is there any suggestion of reconciliation between North and South. Both end with the rescue of a white heroine, a humbled abolitionist, and a defeated and cowed African American populace. White men are unambiguously and firmly in control. There is nothing to suggest a future for either race beyond the immediate hour of rescue.

Rather than develop his screen adaptation from Dixon's novel, Griffith chose to work from and, subsequently, to modify the theatrical *Clansman* because Dixon, in adapting his novel for the stage, had already described a clear path through this work's discursive narrative. Following the success of the novel and aware of the value in transforming his work for the stage, Dixon had briefly studied playmaking with William Thompson Price, or, more likely—as Dixon was the wealthier and more successful of the two—he sought advice and, perhaps, actual practical assistance from Price. Price was the editor of a monthly magazine, *The American Playwright*, which dispensed advice to aspirant dramatists. He also served as house dramaturg to the producers Charles and Daniel Frohman and to Marc Klaw and Abe Erlanger. Additionally, Price worked directly—as a *play doctor* (the turn-of-the-century term for *dramaturg*)—with individual playwrights and taught a practical course in playwriting from his journal office. Price had articulated a system, called by Arthur Krows the "Price Formulation," which required the playwright to reduce his or her narrative material to a logical syllogism, or "proposition," under three headings: "conditions of the action; cause of the action; result of the action."[13] Applied to Dixon's novel, Price's proposition might have been expressed in these terms:

Conditions of the action: The Civil War has ended. Lincoln, who would have acted with restraint and compassion in dealing with the conquered South, has been assassinated. Negro militiamen and enfranchised slaves, urged on by black opportunist-politicians and Northern abolitionists, seek revenge against their former white masters and attempt to seize their property and their womenfolk. Defeated Southern soldiers straggle home to find chaos and insubordinate blacks threatening them.

Cause of the action: Southern manhood, aided by sympathetic women from South and North, move to protect their way of life and to oppose the unrestrained blacks.

Result of the action: The Ku Klux Klan is formed and, first, brutally punishes a black who has molested and killed a young white woman, the sister of the hero, and, second, rescues another young white woman, the heroine, from the clutches of a lascivious mulatto who has usurped political power.

Price's professional play-doctoring enabled Dixon to compact his novel into a well-constructed, four-act melodrama, clearly eliminating characters and simplifying actions. One of the Price-inspired changes is seen in the stage fate of the adolescent Cameron girl (in the novel named Miriam, in the play and Griffith's film, Flora): in the novel she is the victim of a gang rape when Gus and other blacks break into the Cameron home, knock her mother unconscious, assault the girl, and provoke a double suicide in which mother and child, unable to bear the shame of sexual contact with African Americans, die in joint leaps to their deaths. This emotive episode was changed for the stage with a simple abduction and, in a telling signal—a gunshot—that reports her implied rape and murder. Griffith, later, would restore Gus's pursuit and Flora's death leap but not the double suicide. Dixon then took his draft script[14] to an agent, Crosby Gaige, who in turn brought it to George Brennan, already an established—but minor—producer. With the producer and author investing an equal share of capital, Brennan and Dixon formed the Southern Amusement Company and began preparations for their first tour. One of their early preparatory acts was to secure advance bookings from the Klaw and Erlanger management, thereby assuring performances in theatres owned or controlled by the Theatrical Syndicate. After a month of casting and five weeks of rehearsal, The Clansman was ready for the road in the autumn of 1905.[15]

Dixon began The Clansman at a point where the fourth act of a Northern Civil War play normally begins and where—in Reconstruction-era dramas—economic, social, and romantic necessities, delayed and unfulfilled by the calamities of war, will set the agenda for three further acts. Unlike the models on which he built and whose expectations he recurrently invoked, Dixon's narrative ventures into darkness beyond reconciliation, or even impotent stalemate, and ends in entropy.

The Clansman is a four-act drama which begins in a defeated South on the day in 1867 when enfranchised freedmen, paying back their former masters for more than a century of slavery, use force, intimidation, fraudulent (repeat or multiple) voting, and premature poll closing to win places in the state legisla-

GEORGE H. BRENNAN

....PRESENTS....

"THE CLANSMAN"

AN AMERICAN DRAMA

By THOMAS DIXON, Jr.

Founded on His Two Famous Novels: "The Leopard's Spots" and "The Clansman."

The Greatest

Success

in the

Theatrical

History

of the

United States

Hundreds

Turned Away

at every

Performance

since the

Memorable

Opening in

Norfolk, Va.,

Sept. 22, 1905.

 COMING

Illustrated herald, ca. 1906, published by the Southern Amusement
Company for the tour of Thomas Dixon's *The Clansman*.

ture of South Carolina while preventing whites from voting. Through exposition, we learn that Ben Cameron, wounded on the battlefield and sent to a Washington hospital, has met and fallen in love with Elsie Stoneman. Cameron is now practicing law in his home state. It is in this first act that the audience becomes acquainted with a linked constellation of greater and lesser African American and mulatto villains: Alec, later sheriff, Gus, a sergeant, later commander of a company of an African American militia, and Silas Lynch. Crucially, there is also the white Austin Stoneman. Stoneman, at this point and for much of the action, is the architect of Southern humiliation. An abolitionist and the secret leader of "The Black League," he has arrived with a proclamation enforcing intermarriage between whites and African Americans. Unlike Griffith's Stoneman, whose intentions to foster race mixing are led by his own sexual slavery to the mulatto servant, Lydia, Dixon's Stoneman, true to his hateful abolitionist principles, is clear-sighted in his intent "to unite the Nation" through racial interbreeding. Only later, when he objects in the strongest possible racist terms to Lynch's proposed marriage to Elsie, is his hypocrisy exposed.

The second act plays on expectations generated by the nationwide popularity of such Reconstruction-era melodramas as Charles T. Dazey's In Old Kentucky (1893). In this drama a Kentucky farm, encumbered with liens and unpaid mortgages, is rescued from the predations of the play's villain, a self-styled "trader in niggers," by a racehorse's timely win of a purse large enough to clear all debts and to assure that the approved couples are united. Indeed, the farm threatened with foreclosure by a villain and his henchmen acting as a sheriff's bailiffs is so common as to be one of the parodied clichés of melodrama, but in Dixon's hands this cliché is still powerful in the anxiety it generates. Retaining the pattern of action but altering audience understanding of oppressed and oppressors, Dixon introduces the Cameron farm, now about to be auctioned to pay tax debts unfairly imposed by the new African American sheriff and soon to be claimed by Silas Lynch. Ignoring all chances to find the money to meet this arbitrary debt, the auctioneer, urged on by Lynch, rushes the bidding, only to be thwarted by Elsie Stoneman's capping bid, which restores the property to the Cameron family. The new African American masters nevertheless disarm white militia units and seize Ben Cameron. About to resist and fight back, Cameron is counseled by General Nathan Forrest, conveniently present in the Cameron home, that through the Klan "there is a better way."

Although Forrest, the Grand Wizard of the Klan, appears in one act only and has no direct role in the dramatic action, his person and presence are totemic. He is Dixon's *raisonneur*, the justifier for the Klan's formation. Arriving in the latter half of the second act and clearly extraneous to the business of saving the

ANSWERED AT LAST. 🍂

THOMAS DIXON, JR.,
AUTHOR OF
"THE CLANSMAN"

Specially Selected Metropolitan Cast of Forty Principals!

≪ ≪ ≪

Small Army of Supernumeraries and Horses!

≪ ≪ ≪

Carloads of Scenery, Mechanical and Lighting Effects!

≪ ≪ ≪

A Record Run at the Liberty Theatre, New York City!
Arrangements made for Lengthy Engagements in Chicago,
London and Australia!

Unqualified Endorsement of Governor Glenn of North Carolina.

" I unhesitatingly say that I wish every young man and woman to see this play.
Mr. Dixon's Drama rises far above his books.   I heartily approve of 'The Clansman.'
It will do good.   It will be gladly received by the better class of thinking people
in the North."

"I RAISE THE SYMBOL OF AN UNCONQUERED RACE OF MEN!"

Reverse page of herald for *The Clansman*.

Cameron farm from Lynch's clutches, Forrest speaks these lines in the act's closing moments immediately before Ben Cameron's arrest:

> I stood in the gallery of your legislature hall in Columbia yesterday, and looked down on your Black Parliament at work—watched them through fetid smoke, vapors of stale whiskey and the deafening roar of half drunken brutes, while they voted millions in taxes their leaders had already stolen, and I had a vision. I stood beside the open grave of the South! Beneath that minstrel farce I saw a tragedy as deep and dark as was ever woven of the blood and tears of a conquered people. I heard the death rattle in the throat of my race, barbarism strangling civilization by brute force. . . . Had we dreamed of this, we would have been fighting yet. . . . I have come to point the only way of peace—the secret Klan. . . . The next step downward and you enter the shadows of the unspoken terror—the grip of a black beast's claws on a white girl's throat.[16]

Even when he was not physically before the audience, Forrest remained an iconic presence in Dixon's play. Joseph and Percy Byron photographed the Northern Clansman company onstage before its New York opening. The Byrons' photographs show the interior of the Cameron home, the setting for two of the drama's four acts, decorated with chromolithographs of children, a visible sign of the family's domesticity and love for their young offspring. Significantly, pride of place—above the central doorway and high on the same wall—was allocated to enlarged photographs of Robert E. Lee and Forrest, a reminder to audiences that the Confederate cause had not been abandoned and that Forrest and the Klan were to continue the struggle against the North's dominion. Here again, like Griffith's claim to historical accuracy, Dixon's claim to enact the entire truth may be doubted. By 1868, the Confederate officers who had founded the Klan were deserting its ranks on the grounds of its violence and terrorist activities. Forrest, although one of the founders of the Klan in 1865, subsequently repudiated the organization and, by 1869, approximately a year after the episode dramatized by Dixon, called for the Klan's disbandment. With the passage of the Civil Rights Act of 1871, the Klan was declared illegal. Dixon never referred to these developments and led his readers and audiences to assume that the Klan remained an active—and popular—force.

The Clansman's third act begins with family and friends happily celebrating Flora Cameron's thirteenth birthday. A visitor, at first peering into the home and then, when the elder whites' backs are turned, intruding to bring Flora a box of chocolates—and to make it evident that he is strongly attracted to her— is Gus. Ben Cameron ejects Gus from the house, but moments later it is appar-

Interior of the Cameron home in act I of *The Clansman*, ca. 1906. The portraits on the wall
are of General Robert E. Lee, commander of Confederate forces, and General Nathan
Bedford Forrest, founder of the Ku Klux Klan. Photograph by Joseph Byron.

ent that Flora has been abducted. A search for the missing girl is immediately
organized. Anxiety about her whereabouts and safety prevails until a pre-
arranged signal, a single shot, informs all that she is dead. The act ends with
the formation of a posse to pursue and execute Gus. Later this scene was
extended to one in which masked and robed Klansmen, some on horseback,
interrogate Gus and, in a mimed entr'acte, fling his mangled body onto the
steps of the governor's home.

The final act is set in the home of Silas Lynch, now acting state governor.
Lynch exercises his authority to order the arrest of Ben Cameron and, should
he be apprehended, his immediate execution. Visited by the Stonemans, Lynch
proposes marriage to Elsie, but, when rebuffed, locks her in an adjoining
office. He instructs her guard to kill her immediately if gunshots are heard.
Lynch then attempts to blackmail Stoneman into forcing his daughter to marry
Lynch and is, for a second time, rebuffed as Stoneman reveals his personal
loathing of intermarriage and the disgrace and contamination that Elsie's marriage to Lynch would bring to her, himself, and his undiluted white aristocratic
lineage. Lynch is then prepared to violate Elsie to give her no option but to
marry, and Stoneman is prepared to shoot Lynch (and, with the sound of that
gunshot, to sacrifice his own daughter) when robed and hooded Klansmen, led
by Ben Cameron, rush in and liberate Stoneman and Elsie. United and reconciled to Ben's Klan leadership, Elsie and Ben receive assurance from Stoneman

Interior of the cave where Sam—in Griffith's film *Gus*—is tried for murder by hooded Klansmen and then executed. Photograph by Joseph Byron.

that the [presumably African American] army of occupation will be withdrawn from South Carolina and that, henceforth, "water be allowed to find its own level."

Typical for plays with a decided sectional interest, *The Clansman* was launched and premiered on tour. Although the company was eventually booked into major American cities—Newark, Brooklyn, Manhattan, Baltimore, Philadelphia, Washington, Omaha, Kansas City, and St. Louis—these performances followed from 1906 to 1908 only after *The Clansman* had proved successful on the road. Promoted under Brennan's banner, "*Uncle Tom's Cabin* Answered At Last,"[17] the company's itinerary began on September, 23, 1905, with two nights at Norfolk, Virginia, then played an additional two nights in the former capital of the Confederacy, Richmond, before heading south and playing one-night stands and split weeks through Virginia, North Carolina, South Carolina, Georgia, returning to Atlanta, then traveling westward to Chattanooga before swinging south through Alabama and Louisiana, playing Christmas week in New Orleans. Weekly receipts exceeded $9,000.

On the basis of this successful southern tour, a second company was rehearsed and, in January 1906, was sent on a westward circuit through Kentucky and Ohio before turning southward through Georgia, then returning to Norfolk to play through the duration of the Jamestown exposition which ended in March, 1907. A third troupe, the Northern Company, was formed in the autumn of 1906, playing a sequence of dates beginning in Delaware and continuing to Pennsylvania, Brooklyn, New York, Massachusetts, Connecticut, upstate New York, and eventually westward through Illinois and Missouri. The Western Company spent the season of 1906 on tour through Arkansas, North Carolina, Illinois, Indiana, Virginia, and Maryland. Once again, these companies had the backing of Klaw and Erlanger and the certainty of engagements in playhouses that were Syndicate-owned or -managed.

The Clansman's reception in many respects anticipates responses to The Birth of a Nation: rapturous audiences in the South, anger and dismay in the North. Reviews in the Southern press were largely enthusiastic, and Dixon was quick to republish these in his advance publicity, citing a New Yorker's account of a performance in Charleston, South Carolina:

Picture, if you will, a Southern playhouse crowded to the doors on a sultry night with whites. There are no negroes in the gallery, which is unusual. The audience is of the best and the worst. . . . There is the spirit of the mob. . . . It is as if they were awaiting the return of the jury, knowing already what the verdict will be. They know, but they must hear it again, and again. . . . The people have not come to be amused. . . . There is comedy, or what passes for comedy, in the play. True, there are laughs, but it is not hearty, wholesome laughter. There is an hysterical note in that laughter; and it hushes as if by common consent. Every reference to the maintenance of the power of the white race is greeted with a subdued roar. . . . Something like the tremendous wave of passion which [Uncle Tom's Cabin] wrought in the North, at a time when passion ran high, is being reproduced by The Clansman in the South at a time when passion sleeps, but sleeps restlessly. In Uncle Tom's Cabin the negro was shown at his best. In The Clansman the negro is shown at his worst. The glamour of his love of humor, his songs and pleasures, his faithfulness, is stripped from him. True, there is a "good nigger" in the play, but he evokes little interest.[18]

Nonetheless, there were strong dissenting voices, the Richmond News-Leader stating that The Clansman "was as elevating as a lynching" and the Chattanooga Times describing the play as "a riot breeder . . . designed to excite rage and race hatred."[19] Further north, Arthur Hornblow, editor of The Theatre, reported New York audiences' indifference to The Clansman's racist polemic but acknowledged that The Clansman had benefited from William Price's dramaturgy, describing the play as

excellent melodrama in that its interesting story is told with literary skill and with a fitting regard to the unities and the exactions of telling craftsmanship.

The suspense is cumulative, the action advances with dramatic vigor, and the humor, if somewhat conventional, meets with frequent responses. For three acts it is sterling drama. The last act with the members of the Ku Klux Klan in their full regalia is too suggestive of comic opera."[20]

The Clansman's Philadelphia opening brought the first protest. African Americans seated in the Walnut Street Theatre's segregated balcony[21] hurled eggs at the stage. No action was taken against these protestors. The same evening and the following day, large groups of African Americans demonstrated outside the theatre. Their leaders, unidentified Negro clergy, demanded a meeting with Mayor John Weaver at which both Dixon and Brennan were present. Weaver, more concerned with the threat of violence than injured African American feelings, insisted that the Walnut Street Theatre suspend further performances of The Clansman or lose its license for the remainder of the year. Dixon and Brennan countered, enlisting attorneys and bringing the case before Pennsylvania Judge Sulzberger. Dixon, as Griffith was later to do, answered his critics on the grounds of the drama's historical accuracy:

> My purpose in writing The Clansman was to focus the heart and brain of the nation on a great problem. I have put twenty years of research into this play. I have a standing offer of $1,000 reward for any man who can establish a single fundamental historical error.[22]

On the evidence that the play had not occasioned public disorder anywhere, Sulzberger ruled in favor of Dixon and Brennan. By the time of Judge Sulzberger's decision, the company's weeklong engagement had expired, but the company, encouraged by their court victory, returned in April for "an indefinite period" which, in the event, proved to be a month of good business. The critic of the Evening Bulletin[23] was scornful of the company's acting but praised the scenery and the staging of a third-act scene in the Klan's secret cave where Klansmen, using mesmerism as an interrogation tool, extract a confession from the captured Gus before lynching him.

The Northern Company encountered no more disturbances in 1906 or 1907. When re-formed in 1908 for a tour of the Far West, The Clansman's four-page herald announced,

> The Play You Have Been Eagerly Awaiting—Now on Its Fourth Record Breaking Tour—The Clansman by Thomas Dixon, Jr. From his two famous novels "The Clansman" and "The Leopard's Spots." Direction of George H. Brennan. Original New York Cast and Production Complete. 40 People on the Stage; A Carload of Stage Effects; A Troup of Spirited Cavalry Horses—Wit-

nessed and Cheered by more than 4,000,000 theatre-going people with unparalleled enthusiasm. Forty Weeks in New York City, Twenty-Six Weeks in Chicago.

The Clansman again attracted protests. In Los Angeles, African Americans petitioned Mayor Arthur C. Harper to ban performances. The petitioners noted that other western cities had banned the play.[24] As there is no record of the 1908 tour, it is not known where The Clansman played and where its performance was blocked. However, setting aside Brennan's exaggerated attendance figure of four million spectators (out of a national population of ninety-two million), The Clansman was a success on the road, hardly the financial or theatrical failure that Griffith was later to belittle as a "frost."

For the purposes of this book, Dixon's drama is invariably designated The Clansman and Griffith's film is referred to as The Birth of a Nation. Throughout negotiations with Dixon and in subsequent preparations and filming, Griffith proceeded with the certainty that he was adapting The Clansman and that his eventual film would also be titled The Clansman. It was his intent from the outset to adapt and to elaborate, but not fundamentally change, Dixon's play. Journalists who visited the sets and reported on Griffith's rehearsals described Griffith's work in progress as The Clansman.[25] There was no alternate title. Indeed, the film was first previewed in Riverside, California, on New Year's Day 1915, as The Clansman, and formally released in Los Angeles on February 8, 1915, again as The Clansman. Shown on the road in San Francisco on March 1, it was once more billed as The Clansman. But meanwhile, as Griffith sought U.S. copyright, the title had been changed to The Birth of a Nation. The first public change of title came when the film was premiered at the Liberty Theatre—the same Manhattan theatre in which The Clansman had been performed in 1906—on March 3, 1915.

Griffith's approach to the Civil War and the Reconstruction period and his use of his research reveal him at his most partisan and, it is accurate to say, his most dishonest. With the decision to adapt The Clansman for the screen and to follow Dixon's lead in locating the action in South Carolina—the first state to secede from the Union, the last to have Federal troops withdrawn, and the last to be readmitted to the restored Union—Griffith had already accepted a South in postwar turmoil and in the grips of what had become known among Southern mythmakers—although it never happened—as the "time of Negro rule."[26] His readings in history were thereafter limited to the writings by Southern historians of the "Dunning School," who denigrated or denied African American achievements—notably in effective roles as legislators in the South Carolina state legislature and as educators of emancipated blacks. Likewise, he sought pictorial inspiration in engraved illustrations and cartoons which demonized or ridiculed African Americans[27] and their efforts to rise above white-enforced illiteracy, economic hardship, and a voiceless role in American political processes. In some instances, these Dunning-led Southern historians recognized a dangerously violent element in the Ku Klux Klan but, skirting around these rogue members, were inclined to see the Klan as a harmless jape that soon evolved into a benign force. In Southern historians' accounts, the Klan thereafter restored social justice and intimidated—rarely harming—African Americans and whites working for the benefit of liberated slaves. Such historians credit the Klan with forestalling alterations to the Old South's social, economic, and political structures. In contrast, Eric Foner, a widely respected modern historian of Reconstruction, concludes that "the Klan during Reconstruction offers the most extreme example of homegrown terrorism in American history."[28]

Foner, among others, describes such rendering of the South's history by the emergent Southern historians as "dream history,"[29] quite distinct from "real" history. Dream history recounts events alleged or imagined to have happened against events and forces which actually occurred. Dream history is simple, straightforward, amenable to wishes and fantasies. It takes the shape the dream historians wish it to assume and ends at points compatible with their narratives. Real history is messy, complicated, incomplete, full of broken narratives, and far from straightforward. Although shaped by historians, real history struggles when it is shaped and confined. Dixon and Griffith create and maintain a Dream South unfenced by any controlling dates, names, or places, and unpatrolled by critical reality.

Woodrow Wilson provided the dream history for The Birth of a Nation. Wilson's dream history sees Reconstruction as a failure: intimidating and disenfranchising whites and giving African Americans unearned rights and powers, placing blacks in dangerous proximity to whites, allowing sexual misalliances (Lydia and Stoneman) and tolerating the possibilities of other interracial unions (Gus and Flora, Lynch and Elsie). Wilson's Reunion and Nationalization, the fifth volume of his A History of the American People, which appeared in 1902, coincides with the earliest of Dixon's novels. It was not a source that Dixon later cited, but Wilson's history of the South, with its condemnations of Reconstruction measures and justification of the Ku Klux Klan, served as Griffith's principal source and is quoted (and misquoted) in Griffith's intertitles.

Writing of the Northern abolitionists, Wilson wrote, "They would take counsel of moderation neither from northern men nor from southern. They were proof against both fact and reason in their determination to 'put the white South under the heel of the black South.'"[30] Griffith first put Wilson's generalized declaration of intent into the mouth of Stoneman, his Northern abolitionist villain. Then, directly quoting and citing Wilson as author, he further emphasized these words in an intertitle explaining the Republican Congress's behavior: "The policy of congressional leaders wrought . . . a veritable overthrow of civilization in the South . . . in their determination to '*put the white South under the heel of the black South*' WOODROW WILSON." This intertitle is instantly followed by a second intertitle again citing—and again misquoting—Wilson: "The white men were roused by a mere instinct of self-preservation . . . until at last there had sprung into existence a great Ku Klux Klan, a veritable empire of the South, to protect the Southern country. WOODROW WILSON."[31]

Wilson followed earlier Southern historians in designating the chief culprit of the South's ruin: Andrew Johnson, a villain ignored by both Dixon and Griffith. Johnson was the Kentucky Democrat who succeeded to the presidency following Lincoln's assassination. His temporizing responses to a hostile Republican Congress were perceived by the Southern historians to have allowed Reconstruction and to have paved the way for the three constitutional amendments which eroded white rule in the South. To these historians and to the dramatists who followed, conscious of the Lincoln legend and cautious in not impugning the motives and deeds of the martyred president, Reconstruction could be represented as the tragedy of a great man, weakened by alien—Yankee—abolitionists. (Griffith depicts such abolitionists forcing the Emancipation Proclamation on a weary, overburdened Lincoln.) Such Reconstruction histories continue with the sanctified Lincoln replaced by an invisible, incompetent, pliant, indecisive political cipher. It took only a small shift of dream history imagination to turn this national tragedy into a Manichean melodrama with Stoneman, a Republican villain supported by black and mulatto henchmen, opposed and vanquished by hero Klansmen.

The impact and originality of The Birth of a Nation lie partly in Griffith's decision to disguise his adaptation of The Clansman with a lengthy prologue—the First Part. This "prologue," in actuality, constitutes a full half of the total film. Audiences encountering the First Part of this film saw nothing to inform them that The Birth of a Nation was substantially different in method and attitude from the film's numerous theatrical predecessors. Nor, apart from duration, quality of filming, editing, performance, and remarkable battlefield episodes, is the First Part of The Birth of a Nation visibly different from Civil War films which Griffith had earlier made for Biograph nor, likewise, which fellow directors had filmed for Kalem, Vitagraph, Imp, Klaw and Erlanger, Keystone, and Domino.

From the moment in the First Part that the brothers Phil and Tod Stoneman declare their intent to visit the Cameron family, traveling from Pennsylvania to

South Carolina, audiences encountered classic binary pairs of North-South relationships. Griffith depicts Margaret Cameron and Phil Stoneman examining a cotton "blossom" in "Love Valley" and Duke Cameron and Tod Stoneman forming a juvenile alliance, described in the intertitle as "Chums—the Younger Sons—North and South." That some of these binaries lead to romance and others to death on Civil War battlefields falls within the givens of acknowledged conventions. The dreadful carnage of Petersburg underlines the symmetries of futile sacrifice and ideological obsession. Griffith exploited this convention of symmetry and destabilizing asymmetry in filming battlefield encounters between Ben Cameron and Phil Stoneman, in depicting the simultaneous deaths of Tod Stoneman and Duke Cameron, and in adding the further deliberate unbalancing death of Wade Cameron. This imbalance thereby reminds his audiences of greater Confederate losses and suffering.

The assassination of Lincoln was likely to have been the audience's first awareness that Griffith was departing from orthodox melodramatic dramaturgy, introducing an element which is present neither in American stage plays nor in previous Civil War films. The Lincoln assassination episode is a deliberate intrusion, a break in the narrative which signals a new direction in the plot and, significantly, a new direction for the nation. It confronted theatre and film audiences with an experience which they knew about but had never expected to witness and, thus disoriented, they could be easily led in a new direction.

Audiences were already familiar with Lincoln as a benign character because they had seen him, harassed by Stoneman and other abolitionist congressmen, reluctantly sign the Emancipation Proclamation. They had also observed him patiently hearing and granting Mrs. Cameron's plea for clemency for the "Little Colonel," Ben, now convalescing from his wound in a Washington hospital. Lincoln is thus depicted as a sympathetic friend to the South. Now, in Ford's Theatre, where Tom Taylor's *Our American Cousin* and Booth's strike at the president are witnessed by a shocked Phil and Elsie Stoneman, there is sudden disruption and a power vacuum. The assassination has cleared the way for the congressional abolitionists. There is no one to frustrate their plans. When the news of the assassination is brought to Stoneman, his mulatto mistress, Lydia, declares in an intertitle, "You are now the greatest power in America."

The assassination is followed, significantly, not by scenes of elegiac national mourning but, first, by a reel change, with a declared intermission, and, second, the start of the Second Part, in which news of the assassination reaches Stoneman's associates. Thus, it is in the opening moments of the Second Part that Griffith's overall strategy—to move his disoriented audience in a new direction—becomes apparent. Griffith has constructed one long film narrative from two discrete plays, cunningly employing the expectations generated by the typical Northern Civil War melodrama but then denying those expectations in a Southern Civil War *and* Reconstruction melodrama. In effect, Griffith had begun his adaptation of *The Clansman* by adding the first three acts of the standard Civil War melodrama, but he had then reinstalled Dixon's bleak, long "fourth act" set wholly in the Reconstruction period. There is an inherent conflict between these two melodramatic forms, but there is also a synergy gained by yoking together two deeply antagonistic and antithetical dramatic approaches to the same historic circumstances.

Thereafter, Griffith adhered to the plot, if not always to the finer details of the earlier stage work. His changes lay chiefly in motivations which propel the characters and in reweighting characters to add emphasis to different points, notably to valorize white characters and to villainize African Americans. Such alterations are apparent in the characters of the Cameron men. Where Dixon made Dr. Richard Cameron vigorous and active in his immediate scorn for and resistance to Stoneman's abolitionist views, Griffith aged the elder Cameron, making him vulnerable to harassment and less able to withstand persecution. Griffith's change foregrounds Henry Walthall's Ben Cameron, depicting him as a character transformed by war, love, and continual adversity into a leader who will change the South. Against our better judgment, we are compelled to sympathize with Walthall's Klan-leading "Little Colonel."

A further important alteration lay in Griffith's decision to eliminate the character of General Forrest, the Klan's founder, and the episode of Ben Cameron's arrest by black militiamen. This character and scene, so essential to Dixon's dramatic strategy, were replaced with a succession of scenes in which the Klan is conceived and formed: Ben Cameron observing white children dressed in bedsheets, who frighten two small black children—the concept of the Klan and its costume thus originating at this moment; horsemen in Klansmen dress frightening Negro "barn burners"; the making and hiding of Klan costumes; and a cluster of intertitles, one of which announces, "The result, The Ku Klux Klan, the organization that saved the South from the anarchy of black rule, but not without the shedding of more blood than at Gettysburg, according to Judge Tougee of the carpetbaggers."[32]

Dixon, through the agency of Forrest, had merely described black misgovernance. Griffith was to realize Forrest's description of the South Carolina "Black Parliament" governed by carousing, incompetent, newly freed slaves in a telling pictorial image which he claimed was reproduced from a photograph. Although Griffith normally used blacked-up white actors in episodes in which Negroes took more than background roles, here he cast African Americans and, re-creating Dixon's image of "fetid smoke [and] vapors of stale whiskey," put bottles into his actors' hands, cigars in their mouths, and placed their feet on the legislators' desks.

Well-crafted melodrama obliges us to side with those who are threatened and unjustly treated.[33] To this purpose, Griffith also reinflected Dixon's villains, reinterpreting them for audiences further from the postbellum South and less able to understand the South's readiness to lay the cause for the Civil War at the feet of the Northern abolitionists. Stoneman, the abolitionist, an unflattering portrait of the Republican politician Thaddeus Stevens, is a case in point. Dixon portrayed him as a hypocritical abolitionist and an advocate of racial intermarriage whose principles are compromised only when his daughter might become the mate of an African American. Griffith reconfigured Stoneman to be sexually vulnerable, susceptible to the lure of a scheming mulatto serving woman. This female character, absent in Dixon's drama and recovered from the novel by Griffith, is complicit in drawing Stoneman into contact with African Americans and in isolating him from his white allies.

Lydia, the mulatto is, by her very presence, an acknowledgment of miscegenation. In both Dixon's and Griffith's views, she is palpable evidence of racial impurity, and the fact that her body is appropriated by Stoneman (already weakened, Griffith implies, by an unspecified venereal infection) is a means of associating and implicating both females and blacks in a cycle of carnal corruption. In most melodramas, the "adventuress" can threaten personal or familial ruin. Lydia, herself diseased and infecting Stoneman, threatens the nation, encouraging Stoneman to promulgate Congress's "diseased" reforms, to tolerate miscegenation and racially mixed legislatures. She is the antithesis of Flora, who takes her own life rather than submit to a black man. Other females, white and black, in both Dixon's drama and Griffith's film, accept the established order of the Old South. Lydia, a freedwoman housed in the North and determining which political callers will have audiences with Stoneman, acts with the impertinent authority of a gatekeeper as well as a domestic consort. In this role, she enacts both the racist stereotype of innate black villainy and a bold female sexual trangressiveness.

Was it was in Griffith's mind to link seductresses and African Americans as subversive influences? It may well have been that as a repressed and inhibited Southern male, reared in a city where the theatre was itself a seduction and where both minstrel shows and female burlesque choruses offered their own forms of seduction and sexual pleasure, Griffith may have come to conflate, in some bizarre concatenation, blackness and female sexuality as a site for impurity and uncivilized passion.

Stoneman's early capitulation to Lydia reduces the importance of his villainy and renders this character less threatening—and less inherently evil—than Silas Lynch. Lynch was probably so named by Dixon to recall John R. Lynch, the first African American elected in 1873 to the U.S. Congress from Mississippi. Lynch, in Dixon's stage play scheming and self-serving, is credited by Griffith with intellect, guile, and ruthlessness which turn him into a formidable screen villain, one who threatens rape, political dictatorship, and the total extinction of Southern white culture. Griffith's Flora Cameron, played on-screen by Mae Marsh, is older than Dixon's thirteen-year-old Flora but as innocent and yet able to make a calculated choice between submitting to Gus's rape or accepting death rather than dishonor. In that choice, Flora makes a further statement about the repugnance of Griffith's African American villains.

As a novice playwright, Griffith had used the rape of his heroine in his unproduced *War* to focus on the hero's painful choice between aiding the woman he loves or furthering the Americans' campaign against the British: in short, personal considerations versus higher patriotic duty. He did not consider or empathize with the position of the female victim. In *The Birth of a Nation*, Griffith again—twice—uses the threat of rape as a construct to underline the brutality of African American oppressors, and he would again employ the actuality of implacable seduction (Lennox Sanderson's cruel, self-interested "mock marriage" to Anna Moore) in *Way Down East* and threatened rape in *America*. Griffith's recurrent resort to this trope may be a convenient dramatic device, a shorthand for male sexual selfishness, but it may also indicate his unacknowledged linking of violence and sex even as he criticized the perpetrators for their depravity.

Griffith took black depravity even further than Dixon by showing a progression of black acts against Southern whites which first threaten but which then break out into active acts of aggression and cruelty. In the early segments of the Second Part, the equivalent of act 1 of *The Clansman*, it is the Cameron home which is defiled by the presence of black invaders who confiscate property, claiming the home as their right, and who heedlessly wreck or carry off the Cameron's furniture and possessions. Griffith then shows the Cameron space of innocence progressively shrinking as Klan robes are made, hidden, and then discovered by prying blacks. But it is ultimately the white female body, Flora's and Elsie's, rather than the Cameron home, which is violated or threatened by blacks, first Gus, then Lynch, who cannot be restrained except by matching their violence with Klan "justice."

The question for the modern viewer, as much as for film audiences in 1915, is why Griffith exceeded Dixon in depicting the mythic "time of black rule" and why he thus exaggerated black villainy and celebrated the Klan's retributive violence? An answer, not *the answer*, may lie in Griffith's current circumstances. In his numerous enacted scenes, those episodes which reproduced or elaborated upon *The Clansman*, Griffith made no acknowledgment of present events.

On the occasions when he commented on and drew analogies to current crises, these editorial interjections, clothed in a cloying religiosity, appeared as intertitles or as intertitles accompanying allegorical, celestial, and biblical figures: "Dare we dream of a golden day when the bestial War shall rule no more? But instead—the gentle Prince of Peace in the Hall of Brotherly Love in the City of Peace."[34]

What is evident is that as much as he enacted a historic past and disguised present events, Griffith was deeply immersed in his own cultural moment: 1914 and 1915, when allied war propaganda described—and sometimes pictured—"Huns" bayoneting babies and raping Belgian nuns. Dixon imagined the atrocities attributed to the Reconstruction era but didn't show them; Griffith, bringing past and present together, magnified them, and the medium of film further enlarged the aberrant and grotesque.

Further, Griffith recognized in the Civil War—and less so in Reconstruction—the collision of deeply held principles embodied in characters who are destroyed or threatened with destruction when their high principles collide. This argument is weighted in favor of the Old South and the Confederacy, with only Lincoln, the great human arbiter, and the devious abolitionist Stoneman speaking for the Union. But Griffith, like other dramatists of the Civil War, also recognized the evil of slavery and, in keeping with the convention established by numerous earlier white dramatists, saw the desirability of a restored Union and a return to amity between former white opponents. However, unlike other dramatists, he then finessed the issue of black civil rights by making his African Americans ungovernable and without principles. In effect, Griffith implied, civil wars and military rule don't resolve conflict but provoke further bloodletting and chaos. If only this quarrel exclusively involved whites, such injustices would never have arisen.

Much as *The Clansman* had been praised and attacked, so *The Birth of a Nation* was met with enthusiastic endorsements and with dismay at the film's racism. A letter to the *New York Globe* criticizing Griffith for pettiness in depicting congressional leaders sexually enslaved to their mixed-race mistresses[35] prompted a reply from Dixon in which he asserted the truthfulness of his claim, but which also suggested that he retained rights over the film's distribution:

> The established facts are that [Thaddeus] Stevens, who lived and died a bachelor, separated a quadroon Negress from her husband of her youth and kept

her in his house for thirty-six years. For this woman he became a social out-
cast in Washington and at the last moment lost his place in Lincoln's cabinet, the appointment suddenly going to his rival, Simon Cameron. He left
this woman, Lydia Brown, with an annuity in his will and was buried in a
Negro cemetery in Lancaster, Pa, that he might sleep beside her in death. Do
you question these facts? If so, I will submit them to a jury of three historians
of established character, and if they decide against me, I will agree to withdraw *The Birth of the Nation* [sic] from the stage.[36]

As with *The Clansman*, praise and angry dissent reflected American demo-
graphics: high praise in the South, disgust, protest, and contempt in the
North.[37] These adverse comments stung Griffith. He was to reply in the press,
but his principal response was to come in *Intolerance*.

Eclecticism and Exploration

Hurt and perplexed by hostile responses to *The Birth of a Nation*, Griffith turned on his attackers. He answered calls for the film's banning from local and state movie houses and disparaging reviews with letters to newspapers, and in a defensive pamphlet[1] accused his critics of curtailing free speech and suppressing unpopular views. Concurrently, he was preparing *Intolerance* (1916), his ultimate riposte. To create this gigantic, sprawling film, Griffith devised his own narratives and an original structure which effectively interwove the historic and biblical past with a turbulent present. In this four-part film, he dramatized historic and modern instances when, because of religious or civil intolerance, individuals, societies, and doctrines clashed with devastating consequences: the ancient Babylonian civilization, subverted by a jealous priesthood, was laid open to invasion and destroyed; Jesus was tried and crucified by priests hostile to his preaching of a new creed; French Huguenots were massacred by their Catholic rulers intolerant of their Protestant faith; and an innocent American factory worker was dishonestly convicted of murder and threatened with execution, his wife persecuted, and their children taken from them by sanctimonious bigots arguing a higher civic morality.

These five discrete narratives, linked only by an amorphous concept of intolerance and by the recurrent image of a woman rocking a cradle, demanded a fresh approach from Griffith. The stage offered no model for this enterprise and had recently proved an unreliable source. Having previously put his trust in *The Clansman*, a stage play which had proved more controversial than he had initially recognized, Griffith stepped away from the theatre. He would make no attempt to convert stage plays into films between 1915 and 1919.

However, modern dance, a new, strikingly visual theatrical means, had caught Griffith's attention as early as 1912. Dance became a narrative and aesthetic element in his late Biograph films. From 1912 onward, he would increasingly incorporate dance into his films and, from 1916, into his live dramatic "prologues." Thus, although Griffith appeared to be in retreat from the theatre between 1916 and 1919, he nonetheless ventured into live performance and successfully introduced into his films episodes of modern dance, a dramatic art form which had emerged on American and European stages. In consequence, the years between 1913 and 1920, years in which Griffith produced some of his major films, was also a period of experimentation and eclecticism. Liberated from the confining timidity of Biograph, Griffith foresaw new options.

Griffith's decision to leave Biograph in 1913 had been taken for reasons which were both artistic and financial. He sought to make multireel narrative films which would realize his personal dramatic and aesthetic aspirations. He also sought what he hoped would be sufficient financial independence to underwrite his longer, more complex, films. In achieving his first aim, he was largely successful. Moviegoers and distributors were increasingly demanding and accepting films with running times between one and two-and-a-half hours. Yet such films were considerably more expensive than two-reelers. Thus, in reaching for his latter goal of financial independence, Griffith was less fortunate. Seeking capital investment and a ready supply of cash to meet large production expenses, he joined corporate ventures with other independent filmmakers and producers who had been at odds with the Motion Picture Patents Company. However, in forming such commercial alliances, in some respects beneficial, he found himself contractually indentured to complete a specified number of films each year. These contracts, first with Reliance-Majestic (1914) and, a year later, with Triangle-Fine Arts, did not specify that Griffith was compelled to direct the full quota of films assigned to him. Instead, he was allowed to meet his obligations by supervising and advising younger, less experienced directors brought into the orbit of the new independent film companies to whom these lesser films were then assigned. Movies released as Fine Arts films reassured exhibitors and audiences that Griffith was directly associated with the film's production. His supervision done, Griffith was then nominally free to pursue his own projects. As both Famous Players studio and Klaw and Erlanger were now commissioning motion picture adaptations of stage successes, it was expected that a portion of Griffith's annual quota would consist of films taken from popular stage plays. Fine Arts's most extravagant contract engaged the actor DeWolf Hopper, at a salary of $125,000, to film some seven of his comic opera successes. In all, "forty-two leading stars" were under contract to Fine Arts films.[2]

In this respect, Griffith did not disappoint. In 1915, he supervised George Nicholls, a former Biograph actor who had followed Griffith to California, as Nicholls directed an adaptation of Henrik Ibsen's *Ghosts* (1881) (variously released as *The Curse* and *The Wreck*).[3] In the same year, Griffith also supervised Raoul Walsh's filmed version of Ibsen's *The Pillars of Society* (1877).[4] A year later, under the nom de plume of "Granville Warwick," Griffith freely plagiarized Arthur Wing Pinero's 1898 comedy *Trelawny of the Wells* to produce a screenplay for *Diane of the Follies*,[5] directed by Christy Cabanne (another Griffith actor and Griffith's assistant director on *The Birth of a Nation*). *Diane* (sometimes listed as *Diana*) *of the Follies* provided Lillian Gish with one of her favorite roles, that of a vicious, sexually predatory gold digger, far removed from her usual angelic ingénues. Finally, early in January 1916, Griffith assumed supervisory responsibility for a production of Shakespeare's *Macbeth*, starring Sir Herbert Beerbohm Tree and Constance Collier.[6] That film, now lost, was directed by John Emerson. Each of these adaptations, although only distantly associated with Griffith, is notable for what it reveals of the processes of adapting stage dramas for the screen.

The reasons for Griffith's apparent distance from these films are apparent enough. In 1915 he was editing, previewing, reshooting, releasing, and defending from its critics *The Birth of a Nation*. Additionally, perhaps as early as 1914, he had begun work on the "Modern" narrative, which is interwoven with the "Babylonian," "Huguenot," "Judean," and "Eternal" stories of the giant film that was to become *Intolerance*. This "Modern" narrative, separately released in 1919 as *The Mother and the Law*, draws one of its more sensational episodes from a popular melodrama imported from London, while much of the theatricality of the "Babylonian" story is directly due to Griffith's lingering interest in, and recurrent explorations of, modern dance. As with *The Mother and the Law*, Griffith's "Babylonian" narrative was augmented with additional sequences, retitled *The Fall of Babylon*, and released as a stand-alone film in 1919.

In these same years, 1913 to 1919, Griffith increasingly promoted and made feature-length movies with admission prices reaching, and even exceeding, two dollars. Such increased prices, in effect raising admission prices by 2,000% from the previous ten-cent ticket, reflected the cost of longer films but also signaled the rising importance of well-crafted films, and served to establish motion pictures on a par with theatre.

Led, in part, by his interest in dance, but also drawing on his earlier experiences of theatre production, Griffith undertook intermedial events: live dramatic "prologues" and dramatic and musical interludes which deliberately introduced or interrupted screenings with theatrical and dance displays to orchestral accompaniment. These live prologues and interludes, thematically linked to the subject matter of his films, may be described as attempts to bring live performance and film into immediate contact. To this extent, but to this extent only, Griffith was making his "return" to live theatre that he threatened in his 1916 interview with *Photoplay Magazine*. In other respects, Griffith remained a filmmaker, following *Intolerance* with *Hearts of the World* (1917), *A Romance of Happy Valley* (1918), *Broken Blossoms* (1919), and *True Heart Susie* (1919). None of these important films is derived from a theatrical source. Not until 1919, when he began work on *Way Down East*, would Griffith adapt a major theatrical drama.

Griffith's arm's-length supervision of Ibsen's two dramas, *Ghosts* and *The Pillars of Society*, offers reasons why he chose to evade the modern repertoire and, rather, to adapt narratives from the established commercial theatrical repertoire, preferably from the nineteenth-century popular stage. The compact form of the well-made play, so popular with European dramatists, Ibsen especially, was not suited to Griffith's style of filmmaking. Both *Ghosts* and *The Pillars of Society* are "resolvent" dramas: their plots depend heavily on events which happened long in the past but which now cruelly impinge on the present. In Ibsen's theatre, that past is dealt with by gradual exposition which slowly enlightens the audience. In films, silent films especially, the past often is enacted and effectively dramatized through the means of flashbacks. Griffith, skilled at dramatizing concurrent—parallel and overlapping—actions, used the flashback technique infrequently and then only in single shots. His narratives unfolded in a forward direction and were set in "the present." Griffith's few occasional flashbacks were deliberate repetitions of earlier shots, usually a single pictorial image that might be stored in a character's memory, rather than multiple-shot episodes which narrated and explicated past events.

Pinero's 1898 comedy *Trelawny of the Wells* proved more amenable to adaptation.[7] Griffith's screenplay reimagined Rose Trelawny, a young actress performing in London theatres in the 1850s who marries into the gentry and scandalizes her new husband's family. In Pinero's version, marital discord is averted when the husband himself turns actor, and his staid aristocratic family is happily reconciled to vital new blood in the family. Griffith transformed Rose into Diane, a Follies dancer easily luring into marriage the wealthy, studious, and naive Phillips Christy. Christy, who fails to recognize that Diane is a "vamp," believes that marriage and living in comfort will have a settling effect, dampening her feverish energy and reconciling her to a life in respectable society. But Diane, once wed, pines for her former life of excitement. Even the birth of a child fails to still her restlessness. She invites her theatrical friends to their home, and their bohemian presence provokes a break with her husband. Diane returns to her former life, and even the death of her child is not enough to end her fecklessness. The film, now lost, was said to end unhappily for Diane.

Even as Lillian Gish was completing the small, but key, role of The Woman Who Rocks the Cradle in *Intolerance* in the summer of 1916, she was also filming *Diane of the Follies*. Diane was a role she enjoyed and it gave her the opportunity to perform something other than her previous "'ga-ga baby,' a term we gave to sweet little girl roles, which were actually difficult to do"[8] in a film which has, unfortunately, disappeared.

The circumstances in which *Macbeth* was produced were altogether different from those which impelled Triangle-Fine Arts's Ibsen and Pinero adaptations. The suggestion to film *Macbeth* appears to have come from the impresario Daniel Frohman. Frohman, always on the watch for London successes that he might bring to New York, was aware that Sir Herbert Beerbohm Tree's 1915 season at His Majesty's Theatre had experienced two expensive consecutive failures. Conscious that Tree was in need of money to recapitalize his London ventures, Frohman approached Griffith's Fine Arts partner, Harry Aitken, and negotiated a contract agreeing that Tree would repeat his 1911 production of *Macbeth* under Griffith's direction. As reported by Russell Merritt:

> [Such] high-priced projects were initiated entirely by Aitken, over Griffith's heated objections. They were of course part of the lingering vogue for Broadway celebrities in eminent dramas. Aitken insisted upon their inclusion the better to diversify Triangle's product line and the better to compete with the Famous Players-Lasky and, later, the Goldwyn blue ribbon series. . . . For Griffith, the Broadway specials struck a raw nerve: he saw in them a direct threat to his own method of producing films, built on cultivating unknowns in original stories. The guest celebrities, he argued, could seldom adapt their styles to the requirements of the screen, and the expensive budgets diluted the studio's resources. Most galling, the publicity lavished on the Great Ones threatened to overshadow Griffith's own discoveries.[9]

Griffith, wholly absorbed in filming *Intolerance*, declined to become involved in this production. He therefore arranged that *Macbeth* should be directed by John Emerson—under his supervision.[10] Erich von Stroheim, an assistant director on *The Birth of a Nation*, was engaged as Emerson's assistant director. Griffith further assured strong performances by casting two of his experienced actors, Wilfred Lucas and Mary Alden, as Macduff and Lady Macduff. Emerson, Griffith's elder by a year, had experience as a Broadway actor and director and had also directed films in California. A year before, Emerson had married Anita Loos, already a successfully established author of film scenarios and, crucially, for Macbeth, writer of literate and pertinent intertitles. Concurrent with her work on Macbeth, Loos was writing intertitles and portions of the screenplay for Intolerance. The Emerson-Loos combination proved essential to the success of Macbeth.

Tree and Constance Collier, his leading actress who took the role of Lady Macbeth, arrived in Hollywood in January 1916. Apart from personal clothing, Tree and Collier brought with them trunks containing their entire stage wardrobe and stage properties which they assumed would be required for their film. Tree, whose previous experience of films had been short extracts from King John (British Mutoscope and Biograph Co., 1899) and a truncated Trilby (London Films, 1914), assumed that he was to restage, in its entirety, his 1911 His Majesty's Theatre performance of Macbeth for the camera. Lillian Gish recalled her amazement on discovering that Tree expected to declaim his lines:

> When their first rehearsal was scheduled, all us young players gathered on the sidelines, sitting on the floor to watch them. Now, I thought, we'll learn how to act! At that time we had no ears. Words were used, but we scarcely heard them, as we were trained only to see with the eyes of the camera. We were startled to see two figures standing in one spot while only their mouths moved. The next few minutes were excruciating. Sir Herbert and Constance Collier were aware that films were silent, but that was the extent of their knowledge. They stood before us speaking Shakespeare's words—a cardinal sin, as it was hardly Mr. Griffith's plan to put the entire film in one long subtitle. Their exaggerated gestures and grimaces, though quite appropriate for the stage, were painfully overdone for the intimacy of the camera. Mr. Griffith had too much respect for Sir Herbert to cause him embarrassment. He decided that it would be better for the actor to see for himself the difference between theater and films. Once they had seen their first rushes, the English actors realized their failure. . . . Like a schoolboy, Sir Herbert sat through the rehearsal of another film, watching us and trying to be articulate without words. He remained in Hollywood and gradually learned the technique of acting for silent films.[11]

Tree's intent to simply record the entire play on film was frustrated by Emerson who, with Loos, determined that the film would reflect the "American technique" (Emerson's term)[12] of incident and action, as opposed to entire scenes complete with lengthy passages of dialogue and a static stage production. Tree, determined to include full dialogue in the scenes in which Macbeth appeared, was filmed—and tricked—with three cameras apparently operating simultaneously. Two cameras recorded action, and the third, a dummy without film, turned as Tree spoke his lines.[13]

In letters to the London *Times*, Tree offered his own gloss on the differences between stage and film acting:

Acting to the lens requires a peculiar temperament, and demands much more "natural" method than that of the stage; the great requisite in the actor is the power of momentary self-excitation. A mere resort to the technique of the theatre would not "register" satisfactorily on film—a relentless detective. To the new-comer it is somewhat disconcerting to act a scene of carousel immediately after your death scene. In the great studios one will often see as many as ten different plays proceeding on adjacent stages, a farce being acted in close proximity to a scene of tragedy. . . . I confess I have not outlived my preference for the spoken drama.[14]

Reviewers commended Tree for the vitality of his performance: fighting with a broadsword and shield, leaping into the saddle and riding swift horses, and for his interpretation of a usurping king, terrified of apparitions but ruthless and energetic in defending his crown.[15] Constance Collier was also praised for a Lady Macbeth outwardly ambitious and resolute but inwardly disintegrating. However, most critical praise fell to Emerson for confounding the public's expectation of a labored "Shakespearean" production and, instead, offering pageantry, vigorous out-of-door action, witches flying about their cave, and the spectacle of Birnam Wood on the move. Loos's intertitles were praised for the judicious editing of Shakespeare's text while eschewing a modernized vocabulary. Shakespeare's shortest play, *Macbeth*, was first released in eight reels (approximately eighty minutes), then reduced to five reels (approximately fifty minutes). Although dialogue was abridged, there appears to have been no elisions of meaning or reduction in characters or incidents. Griffith's name was not mentioned in reviews. Tree later complained of his treatment in Hollywood and declined to make further films.[16]

Thus, Griffith's function in this production remains ambiguous. It is clear that he played a role in assisting Emerson, Loos, and Stroheim to cast and organize filming, but he then appears to have stepped aside. He and Lillian Gish attended rehearsals and entertained Tree and Collier, but there is no record of him visiting the *Macbeth* set during filming. Tree and Collier, on the other hand, appeared in cameos in the "Babylonian" story of *Intolerance*.

In the "Modern" story of *Intolerance*, Griffith resorted to a convention of "sensation melodrama" familiar to theatre and film audiences from as early as 1906: a race between a car and a train. An attempt by occupants of an auto to outrace a train was staged in Lincoln J. Carter's melodrama *Bedford's Hope* (1906), where the excitement of a "forty-foot race across the stage between an automobile and a train of property steam cars" caused a frightened female spectator to drop her opera glasses from the balcony of the Fourteenth Street Theatre onto the head of another spectator seated in the orchestra below.[17] Edison restaged the race on film in *A Race for Millions* (1907), and the 101 Bison film company adapted Carter's drama for the screen in 1913. In that same year, Al Jolson and Gaby Deslys appeared in the Shuberts' musical *The Honeymoon Express*, where once again the denouement depended upon the outcome of a race to overtake a speeding train. Griffith had attempted this device in 1912 in *A Beast at Bay* with only qualified success, but the enduring popularity of the race and ensuing train wreck in *The Whip*[18]—a London melodrama, introduced to New York in 1910, held over, and, in 1915, its film rights purchased by the Shubert Organization,[19] and filmed in 1916 by Maurice Tourneur for the Shuberts[20]—may have acted as an incentive for Griffith to try again.

Resorting to the locomotive-automobile chase in *Intolerance*, but never acknowledging his numerous theatrical sources, Griffith made pursuit desperate and suspenseful, the sensation-climax to the "Modern" story: The blue-collar hero of this strand, identified only as "The Boy," has been framed and convicted of murder by a jealous, misguided woman. He is within hours of death at a penitentiary miles from the city in which his wife, identified as "The Dear One," resides. As his hour of execution draws nearer, his accuser repents and blurts out the truth that will exonerate and free him.

The State Governor, the only person with the power to halt the execution and release The Boy, is on a fast train heading for a weekend's rest. The Dear One, The Boy's repentant accuser, and The Dear One's friend manage to commandeer a roadster and, racing alongside the speeding train, eventually, and only after several mischances, overtake the train and reach the Governor in time to appraise him of the truth. The prison is called, and, as The Boy is being given his final comfort by a priest, the execution is countermanded. Griffith's work in this sequence with the train, the souped-up roadster, and the telephone—all appurtenances of modern life—skillfully completed one strand of *Intolerance*. Although a successful hair's breadth rescue, this ride-to-the-rescue ironically played against other, more significant, rescues which—historically—failed: the "Babylonian" story (where the Babylonians are tricked into complacency and then slaughtered); the "Judean" story (where there could be no last-minute rescue for Jesus); and the "Huguenot" story (where, again, rescuers arrive too late to save French Protestants from the vengeful Medicis).

The years in which the young Griffith served his theatrical apprenticeship as a touring actor coincided with important international developments in dance, and Griffith, now an established film director, was on hand to take full advantage of these changes. Led by a handful of female performers, the rigidly formal ballet of the opera houses had been challenged by advocates of expressive free movement in which the dancer's body became an instrument of narrative and medium for emotion, unencumbered by codified gesture and prescribed steps. In part, the justification for emotive and seemingly unstructured dance was both anthropological and cultural. Late-Victorian and early twentieth-century discoveries and writings by the so-called Cambridge [University] classicists and anthropologists[21] had drawn attention to ancient Greek, "oriental," and Near Eastern dance-as-ritual. Dances depicted on vases, statuary, and murals encouraged experimentation in achieving noncodified, spontaneous movements.[22] Associated with these experiments and with vivid public performances which astonished and disturbed late-Victorian and Edwardian audiences were, severally, Isadora Duncan, Ruth St. Denis,[23] Gertrude Hoffman, Maud Allan, and Löie Fuller. Each was to offer her own take on the ancient Dionysian dance; each, between 1904 and 1909, was to perform—in Paris, Vienna, Berlin, London, Athens, or in vaudeville houses in various American cities—a Salomé dance in which a seductive orientalized female contrived the decapitation of St. John. Indeed, Griffith himself briefly figured in a Salomé dance when, in San Francisco in 1904, he appeared as John the Baptist, repelled by Salomé's dance before King Herod, in Clarence Bennett's passion drama *The Holy City*.[24] Thus, the academic findings of the classicists and anthropologists, along with sexual titillation and biblical narrative,[25] were bigamously wedded to high art and sensationalized show business.

On a distinctly inartistic, but vastly popular, level were a cluster of world's fairs where, in imagined or reconstructed "native villages," non-Western, non-European cultures performed their own theatricals and dances for the amusement and titillation (and infrequent edification) of Western spectators. Unfortunately, apart from the known films of Löie Fuller and Annabel Whitford's brief mutoscope dances, there appear to be few surviving films of early experimental dances by the artists named above (or perhaps there were none or few made), but Kemp Niver's catalog of paper print films lists numerous examples of exposition and fair dancers performing for Western cameras.[26]

In November 1912, Griffith shot *Oil and Water*, the first film in which he introduced "modern" dance. He had shown dancers performing onstage in earlier Biograph films, notably *Behind the Scenes* (1908) and *The Dancing Girl of Butte* (1910), but to depict dancers in what were clearly intended to be understood by his audiences as vaudeville "leg-shows" was also intended to comment on the desperate, unwholesome nature of the female dancers' lives: trapped in an ugly, morally dubious profession which disqualified them as respectable wives and mothers. In *Oil and Water*,[27] the terms of reference had shifted. Griffith's leading actress, Blanche Sweet, appeared in what was an allegorical, aesthetically pleasing, and original ballet. The dancers, male and female, were crucially shoeless and minimally costumed "in the logical wrappings of reeds and skins,"[28] their near nakedness an accepted element of this dance *genre*. Vachel Lindsay described this dance and speculated as to its origin:

> Blanche Sweet is the leader of the play within a play which occupies the first reel. Here the Olympians and the Muses, with a grace that we fancy was Greek, lead a dance that traces the story of the spring, summer, and autumn of life. Finally the supple dancers turn gray and old and die, but not before they have given us a vision from the Ionian islands. The play might have been inspired from reading Keats' *Lamia*, but it is probably derived from the work of Isadora Duncan.[29]

Sweet's unnamed character, a dancer to her restless core, was still found unsuited to marriage and motherhood. After giving birth to a daughter she cannot effectively care for, she, the actress-dancer, and her "idealist" husband part.

Sweet, a voluptuous sixteen-year-old, had come into Griffith's company as an experienced dancer. From perhaps as early as her thirteenth year, she had been a "Hoffman girl," a member of Gertrude Hoffman's dance troupe in which Hoffman had toured vaudeville circuits performing "oriental" and Salomé ballets. It may have been Sweet's unique pulchritude, so different from the slight, etiolated actresses—the Gish sisters, Mary Pickford, Mae Marsh, Gertrude Bambrick, Dorothy Bernard, Carol Dempster, and Claire McDowell—whom Griffith customarily preferred, that led Griffith to explore modern dance, but that surmise is unlikely. Rather, as the American dance historian Ann Daly explains in reference to Isadora Duncan, the female dancer's visible, uncorseted, lightly clothed body served a different aesthetic end—less erotic and more social and political.

> Duncan served as a hopeful link to a liberated, post-Victorian future. For it was in the image of the female nude that modern artists, prominent among her spectators, were eliding "Culture" and "Nature" in order to justify the former within the discourse of the latter. . . . Why was the *female* body so important to this milieu? First, because it was the point of intersection between "Nature," which was already aligned with "Woman," and "Culture," which was newly aligned with women. For by the turn of the century, "Culture"—musical concerts, art museums, pageants, and the little theater movement—had been cultivated largely by women, as either artists or

patrons . . . a "Natural" body so much like Duncan's, functioned as a means of making the experimentalists' radical brand of "Culture" more acceptable, with its apparent association with "Nature." But, more important, the female body was marked and marginalized by its supposed tendency toward expression (e.g., the "hysteric"), and it was *expression* that modern artists, as well as the political reformers and iconoclasts, saw as the radical means of exploding oppressive, outmoded traditions. In this manner, the female body functioned as a strategy of cultural subversion. Duncan's female body, so full of movement, so full of expression, so full of kinesthetic drama, thus was read as the harbinger of a new America. . . . To the reformers and radicals, both political and artistic, she enacted the overthrow of the old order.[30]

Nude bodies were infrequently shown on-screen and were usually absent from Griffith's films. However, the "Natural body," which Daly explains as the emotionally expressive, but trained and disciplined, white female body—in contrast to the black or Asian (and allegedly undisciplined) female body—became a staple of Hollywood films, partly as a signifier of alien sensuality, so un-American and so decadent, but concurrently a herald of change and liberation. Here whiteness was not accidental, but deliberate, an intentional alignment with Greece's Olympian goddesses whom Duncan depicted in her dances. As it had been with both Dixon and Griffith, whiteness was a necessary consideration to Duncan and to her contemporaries. Daly further elucidates: " 'Nature' was 'Nature' only when it opposed base primitivism."[31] "Primitivism" was personified in the black female body, already identified with Aida Overton Walker of the Black Patti Troubadours.[32] "Duncan's construction of a 'Natural' body did therefore imply a race and class hierarchy . . . the 'Natural' body is a 'civilized' body."[33] Consequently, no matter how "oriental" Holofernes's harem dancers of *Judith of Bethulia* or the Temple of the Sun dancers of *Intolerance* were costumed and made-up to appear, they were light-skinned: white women visibly masquerading as "the other."

When, toward the end of 1912, Griffith began work on his film version of *Judith of Bethulia*, one of the crucial obligations inherited from Nance O'Neil's 1904 production was to find dances which matched or exceeded the oriental extravagance of the stage version. Whether it had been at the instigation of McKee Rankin or was Thomas Bailey Aldrich's original intent to intensify the oriental luxury and loucheness of the Assyrian invaders' entourage, Judith's presence in Holofernes's tent became the pretext to elaborate a small dance, specified in Giacometti's script, into a prolonged sequence of singing and "oriental" dancing with Arzaele leading a chorus of dancing "slaves." New orchestral music was commissioned from William McKinley.

The results were disappointing. In 1904, American theatre-goers knew of what passed as "oriental" from diverse sources: the hootchie-kootchie, or belly dance of "Little Egypt,"[34] as first seen at the Midway Plaisance at the World's Columbian Exposition of 1893 in Chicago, and from the eroticism of the various Salomé dances interpreted by the first modern dancers. American critics had clearly expected the undulations of Little Egypt and were visibly dismayed that O'Neil's dancer Ricca Allan, promoted to the role of Arzaele over other cast members and leading a chorus of newly engaged dancers, performed a piece which was declared "pretty dancing by pretty girls"[35] but merely "suggesting, rather than presenting, lascivious oriental movements."[36] New York critics were even less impressed, describing Holofernes's slaves as "the poorest apology for dancing girls."[37] When O'Neil's production reached San Francisco in January 1906, Ashton Stevens complained in the *San Francisco Examiner*, "The whole thing might be read at a ladies' club to the accompaniment of moving-pictures. It is vivid only in a moving-picture way; even in the tent scene . . . where, oh where, is the drama, the illusion?"[38] Griffith, a member of the San Francisco company, would have known of this flaccid attempt at staging oriental dancing and, six years later, would have realized—from his recent encounters with dance—the possibilities for improving upon it.

In this context, the 1912 arrival of Gertrude Bambrick at Biograph's New York studio is significant. Griffith had seen her dance in Gertrude Hoffman's *Ballets Russes Spectacle*, Hoffman's adaptation of Serge Diaghilev's Paris recitals. A year previously, Hoffman had witnessed Diaghilev's company in Paris and, recognizing the importance of the new dance vocabulary, had immediately studied Russian ballet before assembling a company of one hundred French and Russian dancers, re-creating Fokine's choreography, and initiating a season at Manhattan's Winter Garden Theatre.[39] Precisely the terms on which Griffith persuaded this fifteen-year-old girl to leave Hoffman and join Biograph are unknown, but Bambrick was soon teaching Griffith and Biograph's actors to dance between takes.[40] In November 1912, Bambrick was successively cast in *The Burglar's Dilemma*; *The God Within*, where she played a dancer in a frontier saloon; *The New York Hat*; and *Oil and Water*, where she appeared with Blanche Sweet as a dancer in Griffith's first essay into modern dance.

Griffith then engaged Bambrick as his choreographer and also cast her as lead Assyrian dancer in *Judith of Bethulia*. Resettled in California, Bambrick staged Judith's oriental harem "dance of the fishes" and a second dance to entertain the drunken Holofernes. However, Bambrick's principal function may have been to coach actors playing roles of Assyrian invaders in the stances, gestures, and moves of the *ballets russes*, thereby achieving in these actors a physical

The choreographer and pioneer of modern dance Ruth St. Denis as Salomé.
Photograph by Nickolas Muray, ca. 1926. George Eastman House.

dimension which distinguished them from the besieged Bethulians. According to the dance historian Elizabeth Kendall,

All the acting was a collage of current attitudes: some theatrical gestures, plus Salomé-dancing, Delsarte-posing, *ballets russes* impersonations, along with the latest fashionable mannerisms. The mixture made it American. Judith [Sweet] . . . prays to her Hebrew god or anoints herself with ashes in the grand manner of Sarah Bernhardt or Mrs. Leslie Carter, yet she is so young the gestures look softened and not so serious—playful. . . . All the characters are playing with more serious and "artistic" models. Opposite, Henry Walthall plays a sensuous king on the *ballets russes* model, while his eunuch, an actor named Jiquel Lanoe, is madly miming the attitudes of a Russian Ballet slave, just like Mikhail Mordkin, Theodore or Aleixis Kosloff in *Schéherezade*. Lanoe's favorite pose, or Griffith's, is a decorative one of listening, with head cocked, foot pointed back, arms thrust down, and palms flexed. And in among the pantomime close-ups we see several ensemble scenes of Assyrian dancing led by Gertrude Bambrick—an orgy of Salomé-Radha[41] snake-charmer motions. The mime and the dancing blend rhythmically with the story's narrative sweep. . . . Dance and mime marked pauses in the narrative and provided just the "deliberation and repose" Griffith was after. Moreover, the dancing rituals thickened the atmosphere, and the dancelike clothing, Biblical drapes, and Persian finery commented perfectly on the new fluid manners and costumes that were a part of modern-day society.[42]

In 1915, a further development occurred which was to link Griffith still closer to modern dance. Ruth St. Denis and her partner, Ted Shawn, established a dance studio in Los Angeles, offering, through advertisements in movie-fan magazines and professional journals, instruction in "the science of the human body as an expressive instrument," and advising that they created dances "especially created to film well."[43] The effect of the "Denishawn" school was immediate. Griffith sent the Gish sisters, Gertrude Bambrick, Mary Alden, Blanche Sweet, Carmel Myers, and Mae Murray to twice-weekly classes. Carol Dempster, then a fourteen-year-old girl, was already a member of the Denishawn dance troupe. Actresses from other studios—Mabel Normand, Florence Vidor, Ina Claire, Louise Glaum, Bessie Eyton, Theda Bara, Louise Huff, and Enid Markey—also took instruction in dance and movement.

Concurrently, Griffith was developing the "Babylonian" story for *Intolerance*. Ruth St. Denis and her dancers became essential to his planning and realization of that strand's narrative. There were, in all, fifteen choreographed sequences within the "Babylonian" story, some brief fragments of dance seen in palace or temple rooms beyond archways, some ritualized hieratic episodes accompanying court ceremonies of prayer and supplication, and four major set-piece ballets. Each of these sequences was choreographed by St. Denis; some were led by Gertrude Bambrick. What is so particularly appealing is that Griffith required— and St. Denis devised—dance which made little effort to be narrative. Like film before 1928, dance was another silent language directly supported by music, both discrete forms, although there was sometimes a temptation for film and dance to imitate each other. In the "Babylonian" story, there is no imitation, even though both dance and acting—separately, but distinct from one another—"tell the story." They remain in their separate spheres abutting, touching, but not blurring. The "Babylonian" story in Intolerance is the moment that two new twentieth-century art forms meet and are separately true to themselves.

Thus, the trajectories of dancers and actors only occasionally intersected on the vast set of Belshazzar's Hall, the major set-piece dance in the "Babylonian" story. Described by Lillian Gish,

> Two major scenes highlighted the Babylonian episode—the feast of Belshazzar and the fall of the city to Cyrus. For the feast, more than 4,000 extras in costumes filled the immense court and its ramparts. Hundreds of dancers, led by Gertrude Bambrick, opened the great feast. Three bands, placed strategically about the quarter-mile set, played for the dancers. Among the Denishawn-trained dancers was Carol Dempster, who was later to appear in films as a Griffith heroine.[44]

This episode—filmed mostly in long shot to emphasize the magnitude of Belshazzar's court, with its ramparts, balconies, broad stairway, rampant elephant pilasters, and statue of Ishtar, and to underscore the magnificence of the Babylonians' victory celebrations—eventually moves in on close-ups of "oriental" dancers.

Before that most famous of all Griffith film sequences was the more intimate, briefly erotic, episode of the "Love Temple of Ishtar," which segued into the court harem, where the dancing continued and, seen from a distance, became more active and less sexual. Lillian Gish again describes both Griffith's intent and the result:

> In the Babylonian period young girls went into the Temple of Sacred Fire, and as their contribution to the love goddess Ishtar, each one gave herself to a man who came to the temple to worship. Mr. Griffith wanted to show these young virgins in costumes that would be seductive yet in no way offensive. All

the young girls . . . were dressed in floating chiffons and photographed in a fountain, not dancing, but moving rhythmically and sensually to music. Some of the scenes were shot through veiling or fountain sprays to add to the erotic, yet poetic effect.[45]

Here, despite Gish's denial of eroticism, Griffith was true to his hidden inner self, his camera sometimes lingering over the dancers' half-clad bodies, isolating and fetishizing limbs and torsos before returning to the dance.

The fourth and final set piece in the "Babylonian" story was the "Sacred Dance for Tammuz," on a smaller scale than the Victory Feast, but one which, in a sequence of takes rather than a sustained tracking shot, brought the Denishawn dancers into closer view. This episode offered a solo dance by a female dancer (reputed to be Ruth St. Denis but denied by her) and a pas de deux danced by Shawn and Bambrick. Although these dances by corps de ballet and soloists were formal in their alignment within the camera's framing and in the deployment of dancers within the dancing space, the dances were largely free of the worn clichés and rigid spines of nineteenth-century ballet, the dancers gesturing with arms raised, their palms upward in approximations of figures projecting from Babylonian reliefs, but also permitting abdomens to contract and spines to flex, their movements viscerally emotive rather than daintily pretty or austerely hieratic. What St. Denis and her dancers were thus able to add to the "Babylonian" narrative of a rich hedonistic culture obliterated by an invading semibarbarian horde was the value of emotion, of private, domestic—personal—feelings challenging Griffith's rhetoric of historical authenticity. At the center of the spectacle lay intense emotions—fear, exultation, religious frenzy and sexual ecstasy, despair and grief—commensurate with Babylon's overpowering monumentality and luxury.

Griffith's work with dance and dancers also became a contributing element to promotional efforts which had begun with The Birth of a Nation and which were characterized by introducing live dramatic "prologues" or by interrupting film programs to inject live-action events. In these efforts, Griffith was frequently associated with one of his principal investors, the Los Angeles theatre owner, William H. Clune. Film scholar Eileen Bowser identifies a period of "refinement" in the presentation of motion pictures, the result of exhibitors speculating in purpose-built theatres and, as a consequence of raising admission prices, replacing the "lecturer"—still present in some houses—with live acts and choruses.[46] Bowser identifies a further contemporary element: the arrival of feature film.[47] Moviegoing, increasingly an approved middle-class recreation, now enabled prospective audiences to select their entertainment at cinema theatres of their choice, their decisions in part made by the ambience of the theatre and the publicity accorded the feature film. Clune, more than many cinema owner-operators, sought his audiences' comfort and actively drew their attention to his theatre's offerings through events staged in the street or sidewalk at the entrance to his Auditorium Theatre.

Clune, briefly a filmmaker and originally a partisan distributor of Famous Players films, had become an investor in The Birth of a Nation in 1914. He was known to have the largest theatre orchestra on the West Coast.[48] For the premiere and first run of The Clansman, as it was then titled, Clune's forty-piece orchestra, who interpreted Carl Breil's score of "The Theatre Beautiful," was, according to Lillian Gish, augmented by a large vocal chorus.[49] Other theatre owners and managers, as Eileen Bowser demonstrates, went in for live-action promotional stunts to herald film openings.[50] For The Birth of a Nation's premiere in Atlanta, Georgia, a dozen or so horsemen in Ku Klux Klan robes paraded in the street outside the cinema. Similarly, The Birth of a Nation's premiere in Portland, Oregon, brought robed Klan riders into the streets, a publicity stunt which backfired when it induced protests from local African Americans and Union Army veterans. Their protests, however, were not sufficient to have the film and its Klan riders banned. A more pedestrian dispute over exhibition rights prematurely ended the film's run.[51]

Griffith's opening for Intolerance at the Liberty Theatre in New York in September 1916, was more circumspect but grandiose in its own way: Griffith's press releases informing the public that the film was accompanied by the orchestra from the Metropolitan Opera.[52] However, in 1919, for the New York showing of Broken Blossoms, Griffith devised a program mixing live dance with filmed performances, cutting between the two. Lillian Gish recalled a moment in developing this program when stage lighting added further to the total effect.

> For its New York opening, Mr. Griffith leased the George M. Cohan Theatre on Broadway and Forty-second Street. Before the opening, he decided to film, on the stage of the theater, a prologue of Carol Dempster dancing. One day he ran the film during the dance rehearsal. The stage lights that he had ordered for the dance prologue were on while the film was being shown, and the blue and gold lights were accidentally thrown onto the screen. The effect was startling, and Mr. Griffith incorporated the results into the final movie, by having sections of the film tinted in the laboratory.[53]

In the same year, Griffith released The Fall of Babylon. For its first run at Manhattan's Liberty Theatre, Griffith appears to have recognized few limits in taste or action appropriate to his narrative. As described by Variety's critic (who may have been writing with a touch of irony or who may, conversely, have wholly admired Griffith's embellishments to his film), Griffith's stage show appeared remarkable. What is also evident is that Griffith's idea of a prologue anticipated and built upon the display of female dancers' bodies in the "Babylonian" story:

Pin another medal on D. W. Griffith for a stroke of master showmanship. . . . There was no attempt to bunk the public for there was an acknowledgment in all of the ads that the picture was the Babylonian story of *Intolerance* amplified and presented with ensemble numbers and a musical number or two. In doing this, the producer took another Griffith step forward and he at least gave the screen production a decidedly different atmosphere than a straight pictorial presentation would have been.

Variety's critic then explained how Griffith had linked film and live performance and how, in the process, the erotic subtext—the display of the partly clothed female body—of "the Babylonian story" had been raised to the surface:

He splits his program 50–50 between the stage and the screen, opening with a tableau that is part stage and part screen, a special small screen to show New York, the modern Babylon, which, after a dissolve, brings the large screen and the opening scenes of the feature. After the first series of scenes there is a dance on the stage by Kyra that outdoes anything that Gertrude Hoffman or Annette Kellerman[54] ever tried, and if it had been presented at the Olympic or the Columbia the cops would have been right on the job. It is a shawl dance and the principal idea seems to be how far Kyra can keep the shawl away from her body, but still retain a hold on it. She manages to see that it doesn't block the vision of the audience at any time and Kyra shows about all that she can and keep "within the law." After another period of screen entertainment there is a duet entitled "Love, Love, Love." This could just as well have been discarded before the opening. . . . Then the final scene of the first part is the beginning of the battle before the walls of Babylon. . . . The second part opens with a scene in one of the halls of Babylon and here there are twelve slave girls and Margaret Fritts, a soprano. A number here, entitled, "The Mountain Maid," is very pretty and the orchestra manages to plug it along nicely. A dance by the girls also helps to fill the picture nicely. They were not given too much to do and as they were rather pleasing in appearance the scene was a fitting prelude to the revels that followed on the screen. . . . After the revels, Kyra was on again for a snake dance that brought a full measure of applause.

"Kyra" was Kyra McKenzie, the wife of Herbert McKenzie, one of Griffith's business managers. According to her publicity, she was trained by a Syrian dancer, and often appeared "topless"—between 1917 and 1925—in "oriental" specialty dances. *Variety*'s critic concluded,

> Finally, the fall of Babylon was accomplished and the love story the D. W. threaded through the big battle scenes was brought to a fitting close with the lovers in a fond embrace. . . . The question now remains, will the public go to see the one story that there was in *Intolerance*. . . . If it does go over it will be the screen rather than the stage end that does it. The stage presentation had the dances arranged by Allan K. Foster who gave the pit simple but effective numbers. . . . Once more to Griffith. He is a showman first, last and always.[55]

The choice of Allan Foster as Griffith's choreographer further underlines Griffith's determination to eroticize *The Fall of Babylon*. Foster was a director, choreographer, and musical arranger specializing in musical comedy and review. In 1919, in addition to Griffith's musical and dance numbers, Foster staged the Shuberts' *The Passing Show of 1919*. Like all *Passing Shows*, it was notable for its chorus of barely clad female dancers.[56]

Griffith's 1919 promotional prologue and dance-and-music interludes for *The Fall of Babylon* formed his penultimate venture into live performance, perhaps because the subjects of his later films did not lend themselves to dance and erotic display. He continued, however, to surround his screenings with the trappings of showmanship. For the launch of *Way Down East*, his most profitable film ever, he announced that exhibitions of his film would be treated as "road shows," that is, major productions appearing at first-class legitimate playhouses converted to moving picture theatres for the occasion. Further, each screening was to be accompanied by a substantial orchestra, and each carefully selected orchestra, technicians and projectionists, and musical instruments accorded their own separate private railroad carriage.[57] Initially, Griffith projected twenty such supporting trains, but later reduced the number to fourteen.[58] For some of these premieres Lillian Gish appeared onstage in especially written prologues, but her appearances were few in number, and the exact nature of these prologues went unreported.[59] In the event, Griffith no longer required live-display and catch-penny theatrics, as a critic from *Variety* made evident.

> Without the aid of any especially spectacular or stupendous mechanical effects such as were utilized in *Intolerance* or the employment of a large ensemble of mob scenes as in the same picture and *The Birth of a Nation*, *Judith*

of *Bethulia*, etc., with the gathering together of a relatively small cast and less than half a dozen stellar film artists, "D. W." has taken a simple, elemental, bucolic melodrama and "milked" it for twelve reels of absorbing entertainment. . . . When a film producer can offer something bigger and finer than anything yet seen on the screen without the use of "effects" of any kind, either in or surrounding the presentation, any detailed review or "criticism" is entirely superfluous.[60]

In one sense, Griffith had turned his back on the live stage. In quite another sense, significant adaptations from the popular stage—*Way Down East, Orphans of the Storm*, and *Sally of the Sawdust*— lay in the near future.

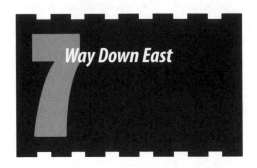

Way Down East

Mr. Griffith made a film version of a play . . . he bought a stage melodrama, 'Way Down East. The purchase price was over twice the entire cost of *The Birth of a Nation*. . . . We all thought privately that Mr. Griffith had lost his mind. 'Way Down East was a horse-and-buggy melodrama, familiar on the rural circuit for more than twenty years. We didn't believe it would ever succeed. As I [Lillian Gish] read the play I could hardly keep from laughing. I was to play the role of Anna Moore, a country girl who is tricked into a mock marriage by a city playboy and abandoned when she becomes pregnant. After bearing her child, who dies, Anna finds work on a farm. The farmer's son, played by Dick Barthelmess, falls in love with her. Unfortunately, the playboy owns the farm next door and, seeing Anna there, reveals her secret to the farmer.[1] True to tradition, the farmer raises his hand toward the door. Out Anna goes—straight into a blizzard. She stumbles through the snow to the river and out onto the ice floes, where she faints, unaware that the floes are breaking up as they head for a steep waterfall. At the last moment, the farmer's son comes after her. He leaps from floe to floe and scoops her to safety just as the ice teeters on the brink of the falls. Naturally they are married and everything ends happily.[2]

This "horse-and-buggy melodrama" in its several incarnations—a hugely successful stage play, a flimsy novelette, an intermediate-but-significant novel—jointly provided the subject matter and structural armature for Griffith's strongest film. The American stage play is Lottie Blair Parker's 1898 'Way Down East.[3] The novels are a cheap, catchpenny précis of the play and a second, longer, narrative which, expanding backward into the past, offers backstories of the principal characters' lives and, more significantly, provided Griffith with a workable structure for his film. The motion picture, produced some twenty-one years later, is Griffith's remarkable film bearing the same title.

Lillian Gish recalled a film in which she had made a notable success. In her mind was the finished film, and it is this text with its deception, seduction, sham marriage, child's death, and ice-choked waterfalls which she described. However, in the background of Lillian Gish's thought was the stage play which she disparaged as a lesser work but which, she also acknowledged, had been a hugely popular success for more than two decades. In her narrative, and, as she recalled the event from a vantage of forty-nine years later, a risible, inconsequential, inferior theatrical piece had been transmuted into something worthy and enduring. Art, D. W. Griffith's art, had been made, not merely from old stage dross, but from outdated, ludicrous dross. Her narrative is deceptively simple. Not only does it diminish the original play, it also diminishes her power to engage and move the viewer.

Way Down East (1920) was justly received as Griffith's most effective film to date and is still regarded among his very best. Unlike his *The Birth of a Nation*, *Intolerance*, and *Orphans of the Storm*, whose narratives bring numerous characters to the screen and sprawl over decades and numerous settings, *Way Down East* tightly focuses on a lone woman and a rural family sharing an intimate crisis. Griffith, retaining the principal characters of the stage drama, created additional scenes and episodes which enabled these characters, already well defined by Lottie Blair Parker, to acquire further depths and subtleties. His settings visit only a handful of New England locales and occupy a time span of little more than a year. His enlarging of the enacted action to depict Anna Moore's excruciatingly painful backstory and, similarly, widening the action to re-create the environments and circumstances in which Anna is seduced, betrayed, and abandoned, did not compromise the compactness of the original script. Rather, in creating what is, in effect, a lengthy enacted prologue, Griffith removed the need for clogging exposition and enabled his film narrative to move at an accelerating rate.

Gish's idea, albeit plausible, that a stage play could be picked up, dusted off, and readily transformed into a motion picture elides a complex history of the preparatory theatrical processes undertaken over at least two years by 'Way Down East's author, Lottie Blair Parker, and by her two principal co-adapters, the theatrical manager and impresario William A. Brady and the "play doctor," actor, and director Joseph R. Grismer. Lillian Gish similarly elides Griffith's own elaborate preproduction processes. Gish, who sometimes advised Griffith on his choice of plays which might be effectively adapted for the screen and who, of all Griffith's actors, had the best grasp of the technical crafts and equipment essential to filmmaking and who had actually played an important role in establishing

Griffith's studio in Mamaroneck, New York,[4] appears not to have been party to Griffith's thinking in the film's preparatory stages. She was apparently unaware how insistently Griffith, in fashioning his film, retraced Brady's, Grismer's and Parker's original steps. What Lillian Gish dismissed in a few words was the result of a lengthy and intricate developmental process which involved both trial and error and astute theatrical practice and which, when examined, illuminates much of the entwined relationship between the stage, novel, and silent film, between theatrical melodrama and its filmic counterpart. Griffith had previously made and was again to make complex adaptations from theatrical sources, but *Way Down East* stands out as his most nuanced film. Lillian Gish failed to acknowledge—or even to recognize—the quality and power of the the original stage drama, a power which Griffith acknowledged and utilized in this 1920 film.

As a stage drama, *'Way Down East* was a former mainstay of the American popular theatrical repertoire. What Gish stigmatized as a "horse-and-buggy melodrama"—a dismissive tone film historians have been quick to echo and amplify, most often without ever reading the playscript[5] and, consequently, unaware of its centrality and relevance to the development of Griffith's film— was actually a highly effective entertainment, knowingly crafted and manufactured by astute theatrical producers to meet the commercial and audience expectations of the late-nineteenth-century popular stage. It was a drama road tested and marketed with considerable forethought and skill. Under its own title and under aliases or locally invented titles,[6] *'Way Down East* continued as a successful theatrical piece for some years after Griffith's film had achieved popular success.[7] Although the connection between the stage play and motion picture has been acknowledged by a number of film historians, it has often been in their interest, whether that be underlining the creativity of Griffith or the acting of Gish, to reproduce Gish's stance and to dismiss the play as a primitive work transformed into greatness. Griffith's reputation, under attack because of racist polemic in *The Birth of a Nation*, has wanted repairing; Gish's playing of wronged innocence has been celebrated.[8]

These omitted acts of recognition and understanding are of concern in appraising both this stage play and Griffith's completed film. Equally, they are necessary and obligatory steps in describing and analyzing the lengthy intertextual process from stage play to silent film. *'Way Down East* is interesting in its own right as a theatrical event and as a still-playable theatre piece, but, importantly, it also serves as an invaluable map for Griffith's own complex journey. Parker's *'Way Down East* stands out, not merely because of its subtly inflected emotions, depth of characterization, and well-sustained balance of pathos and comedy, but also because close study of the play and its spin-offs offers evidence of Griffith's dramaturgical strategies as he turned an iconic, if sometimes derided, stage drama into a filmic masterpiece. Further, the pictorial record of this play, preserved in numerous photographs by Joseph Byron, became a visual reference which Griffith and his designers necessarily consulted.

Although the original play is chiefly credited to Lottie Blair Parker it is essential, in the light of Griffith's subsequent film, to underline the role of two theatrical collaborators, William A. Brady and Joseph R. Grismer. Their work was essential to the success of the play, and the impact of the changes they wrought as the play moved from early draft to its final version carried directly into Griffith's motion picture. Brady, already known to film historians for his role in promoting major boxing matches and for filming both the live fight and reconstructed facsimile matches, was first and foremost a theatrical impresario active from the 1880s through the 1920s. It was to Brady that Lottie Blair Parker's husband, Harry Doel Parker, brought the script of *Annie Laurie* in 1896. Brady later explained his enthusiasm for this play:

> I was definitely interested. At the end of the fourth [act] I began to figure it was something well worth while. At that particular moment the theatrical world was looking high and low for a play that could follow up the smashing success of *The Old Homestead* in what was known as the "by-gosh" drama. This was that play. There would be a lot of work to be done before its theatrical virtues were adequately brought out, but the fundamental stuff was there—straight, uncompromising heart-throbs with hayseed in its hair.[9]

Brady offered Parker $10,000 for the American rights to *Annie Laurie*[10] and, with these rights secured, then brought in a longtime associate, Joseph R. Grismer, a key figure in the development of the play and Griffith's film. As an apprentice actor on the California theatre circuit, Brady had worked for Grismer. Their fortunes currently reversed, and Brady now setting the parameters, Grismer was engaged, in the parlance of the day, as a "play doctor" to prepare this new drama for metropolitan audiences and for touring on America's rural circuits.

Grismer's significant role in reshaping Parker's *Annie Laurie* into *'Way Down East* was substantial enough for him to have negotiated inclusion in the authors' credits which acknowledge that, although the original play is by Lottie Blair Parker, it has been "elaborated by Joseph R. Grismer." He was credited by William A. Brady with mechanical as well as theatrical ingenuity: "the mechanical snowstorm used in the third act, which had no small part in making the play a memorable success, was specially invented by him for the production and then patented."[11] A glass-plate photograph by the theatrical photographer

Joseph Byron, cracked and therefore unusable as theatrical publicity, shows Grismer onstage in the role of the villain Sanderson and indicates that he was prepared to step into the role and to perform it while the play took its final form. Finally, Grismer's close association with the developing play brought a further privilege. He owned enough of the rights to be able to negotiate a contract to publish his own novelized version of 'Way Down East illustrated with eight Byron photographs of the stage production in 1900.[12] This novel and its plates gives insight into characterization and the actors' physicality and gestural vocabularies, but it nevertheless differs in critical particulars from the play and was instrumental in influencing D. W. Griffith's adaptation. Suffice it to say, Grismer continued to profit from his association with Lottie Blair Parker and William Brady.[13]

Although it had been Brady's original intent to launch Annie Laurie as a "b'gosh" drama as a successor to Denman Thompson's The Old Homestead (1885), Grismer and Brady began to develop Annie Laurie as a rival to the plays developed and popularized in the mid-1890s by Augustus Thomas. It was reasonable to assume such a ploy might work. Beginning in 1891 with Alabama, Thomas had written a series of notably successful money-spinning dramas which emphasized the diversity and unspoken sameness of rural America. Thomas's "plays of locality"[14] are peopled with characters who dress in the work and festive clothing of their region, observe the prejudices of their locales, and speak in regional dialect, but the dramas, whether in the Deep South, in the border state of "Mizzoura," under the hickories of Indiana, or the scrub oaks of Colorado, are not truly dependent on their environments. The surroundings in which Thomas's characters find themselves are unwelcoming, and they pose harsh questions of economic survival,[15] but these problems are secondary and linked to personal, especially romantic, relationships. The same plot and characters may be transposed to another sparsely settled state or territory without damage. Brady reasoned that he might make a similar transposition with Annie Laurie, and, apart from this change in regions from "down east" to rural Nebraska, make few other alterations.

Parker's play, first set in rural New England, had been briefly tried out before audiences in Newport, Rhode Island, and subsequently reappeared in Chicago in 1897 under various provisional titles with its locale transformed into the Nebraska prairie and its characters' names now shorn of New England associations. Grismer changed Parker's New England character names to ones less associated with the b'gosh genre. The heroine Annie Laurie became Ruth Walton, "More sinned against than sinning"; The old squire Amasa—an Old Testament name identified with righteousness[16]—became Martin Shaw, "Farmer

The musical entr'acte sleigh ride between acts 3 and 4 of *Way Down East*. In keeping with William Brady's decision to tour the play as a combination company, the Berry Pickers' octet of the first act reappears as a close-harmony group to sing current popular songs, while the set behind the forest backcloth is changed to the maple sugar-shed of act 4. Photograph by Joseph Byron, 1898. Harvard Theatre Collection.

and Justice of the Peace"; Lennox Robinson was replaced with Dwight Bradley, "A shadow of the past." Although each role was renamed, the cast remained no larger than in Parker's original text. These successive versions proved unsuccessful. Parker, meanwhile, on her own initiative and with the intent of protecting her property, sent her script to England where it was given a copyright performance in her own name in February 1897.[17] Griffith, in the course of his lenghty preparation process, recovered this script and extracted from it a memorably harrowing episode.

Faced with the failure of the Nebraska option, Grismer and Brady reinstated the original New England locale. They restored, with modest alterations, most of the names originally bestowed on Lottie Blair Parker's characters. The adapters also acknowledged the degree to which American melodrama had been restructured by the touring of combination companies, incorporating vaudeville, or variety, or "specialty" acts—frequently, but not invariably, musical ones—into otherwise serious productions. Mindful of melodramatic combinations and the appeal of integrated variety acts, they began enlarging the cast. Their first addition was a close-harmony sextet who were first styled "The Berry Pickers" and, later, "The Village Choir." These singers entertained at specified intervals with a medley of popular melodies and old-time favorites, changing their repertoire as musical fashions and regional audience taste dictated. As the adapters grew more confident of the appeal and effectiveness of their sextet, new scenes were added, most notably a sleigh-ride episode, a "carpenter's scene,"[18] in which the Choir travel from the Putnams' party through the forest toward the Bartlett farm, thereby creating a seamless musical bridge between the second and third acts. Griffith was to turn this episode into his sleigh-ride and barn-dance sequences, a joyous moment of rural revelry while Lillian Gish, as Anna, stands apart, ashamed of her past and unable to join the festivities.

At the same time, Grismer introduced new roles. Lottie Blair Parker's only comic countryman was the "Toby" character, Hi Holler. The Toby, with his red wig, abundant freckles, bucktooth, and collection of aphorisms, riddles, and corny jokes, was a staple of rural dramas irrespective of the locale in which these were set. Parker had humanized this role, making Hi Holler less grotesque and more sympathetic, while still retaining the Toby's comic irreverence and insubordination. Grismer supported Hi Holler by building up the comic scenes in which Professor Stirling appears and by adding Seth Holcomb, a "rube towner," who conceals his ever-handy supply of rye whiskey in a bottle deceptively labeled "medicinal bitters." The trio of rube comedians was complete when Grismer devised the role of Rube Whipple. As Brady recalled,

> One of his inspirations was laying hands on a vaudeville actor named [Charles V.] "Harry" Seamon, who had a small-time hick act, breaking his routine into three parts and running him into 'Way Down East. Old-timers will remember his first entrance: "Big doin's in town—pust-office bruk into and robbed last night—gret loss fer th' guv'mint—three dollars wuth o' stamps stole."[19]

With Seamon came a song—part nonsense, part narrative—of blighted courtship and marriage, "All bound 'round with a woollen string,"[20] which has no bearing on the content or action of 'Way Down East.

Although most of the dialogue and many of the situations which are found in Annie Laurie survive into the final version, Grismer made one essential excision. Seeking an almost-obligatory happy ending, but substantially "over-egging the pudding" by distributing rewards which the circumstances of the plot fail to justify, it was Parker's device to have Anna come into a substantial inheritance[21] from a hitherto unmentioned English relative just as she is confronted with a fourth-act choice between a chastened Sanderson and an ardent David. The arrival of money puts David at a disadvantage, but Anna is seen to make her choice from love rather than parity of wealth and to reject Sanderson in favor of David. Wisely, this inept plot thread was dropped in the earliest revision, although, in a sense, this weakens Anna, who remains poor, and makes her dependent upon David's protection.

Along with these revisions, Grismer rechristened this b'gosh drama 'Way Down East. B'gosh plays were so named from the expression by gosh. According to theatrical mythologies, country stage characters allegedly said "b'gosh" or, when severely provoked, "Gol durn."[22] The term b'gosh specifically referred to plays set in those parts of rural and village New England—apparently untouched by industrialization—which featured the lives of village and country folk linked to farmland and/or seacoast and far removed from the sophistications and perceived moral evasions and relativisms of city life. B'gosh dramas celebrate the distance between the innocent countryside and the corrupt and dangerous cities of Boston and New York now peopled by hostile strangers and foreigners.

The very title 'Way Down East was originally geographically specific: "down east" is that portion of Maine, "down" (i.e., south) and east of Canada. However, by the late 1890s "down east" had become generic for rural, northern New England: Maine, Vermont, New Hampshire, Connecticut, and northwestern Massachusetts. Although "down east" New England was rapidly industrializing and was already experiencing serious urban blight and racial and religious tensions by the 1880s, the b'gosh drama depicts an arcadia which is solidly Protestant and of Anglo-Saxon extraction. While South Boston and such manufacturing cities as Hartford, Bridgeport, and Lowell, expanding along the New England river valleys, harbored many thousands of immigrant families, not an Italian or Portuguese Catholic is to be seen in these plays. Irish Catholics and Jews are exceptions, but only as comic characters, and these are conspicuously out of place in rural settings. To some extent, b'gosh plays, with characters named Ruben and Josh, were a retreat to a sentimentalized past, a denial that the world was swiftly changing, that cities, and even country areas, were being settled by immigrants whose otherness was written in their non-Anglo-Saxon appearance, heard in their accents, and recalled in those faraway ports in eastern Europe. This ethnic and racial purity of a fictional New England instinctively appealed to Griffith. His Way Down East characters, whether urban or rural, are white, presumably Protestant, and uniformly of extraction from English stock.

Such an arcadian world was depicted in 'Way Down East's publicity. Brady was a master publicist, imaginative and inventive in promoting the play as it toured. He was one of the early users of theatrical photography in his promotional campaigns and, even before photolithography was widely available and sufficiently cheap to encourage large print runs of illustrated material, Brady "papered" his route with souvenir 'Way Down East almanacs indicating not only planting seasons and phases of the moon and tides, but also reproducing photographs of key scenes and leading characters from this drama. There is evidence—widely spaced clusters of serial numbers on glass photographic plates—that Brady repeatedly engaged the New York photographers Joseph and Percy Byron, the earliest photographers to make full-stage photographs the mainstay of their practice.[23] Joseph Byron made at least four visits to photograph 'Way Down East as it developed on tour.[24] Byron photographs thereafter adorned theatre foyers and public sites and, when photolithography became affordable, appeared in printed promotional heralds, newspaper advertisements, souvenir programs, postcards, and the ever-popular almanacs. Griffith, using these photographs as aide-mémoire, later reproduced or emulated groupings from the Byrons' photographs.

The looming shadow of The Old Homestead is necessarily connected with the development and final form of 'Way Down East. The Old Homestead, Thompson's personal vehicle and model for the numerous subsequent b'gosh plays, was a comedy-temperance melodrama, originally a vaudeville sketch, in which "Uncle Josh" Whitcomb searches for his long-absent son in perilous New York and, finding him, restores the youth to sobriety, happiness, and the assurance of marriage to a good local girl on his down-east farm.

The Brady management had previously invested in The Old Homestead's promotion, and the subsequent creation and extensive and prolonged development of 'Way Down East was reputedly—but possibly only in retrospect—an effort to find or manufacture a commercially effective successor and to beat off rival plays. Blue Jeans (1890), a comedy drama cowritten by Joseph Arthur and Andrew Carpenter Wheeler,[25] had challenged The Old Homestead's domination of rural drama and, in contrast to Denman Thompson's depiction of the American hinterlands as a bucolic paradise, had persuasively argued that the countryside and small towns, as much as American cities, were places of scheming treachery and personal danger. Whereas Thompson's characters faced only moral peril, the hero of Blue Jeans was knocked unconscious, thrown upon the bench of a whirling circular saw, and nearly sliced in two by the play's villain. Blue Jeans also

THE OLD OAKEN BUCKET.

How sweet from the green mossy brim to receive it   Not a full gushing goblet could tempt me to leave it
As poised on the curb it inclined to my lips,   Though filled with the nectar that Jupiter sips.

Francis Flora Bond Palmer's *The Old Oaken Bucket*, a lithograph struck for Currier and Ives, ca. 1870. Cheaply produced and widely circulated, this image became the iconic representation of the serene and stable rural American home with its veranda, well, and shading oak tree.

offered rural Indiana electioneering, a barbecue, a comic village band, and romance. On tour, its road managers brought live farm animals and automobiles onstage. But *Blue Jeans'* weakness lay in devising impediments thrown in the path of its hero and heroine—blackmail and consanguinous marriage—which were then resolved offstage and their solutions made known only through inept exposition. Brady immediately recognized that, in contrast, *Annie Laurie* tackled issues head-on and didn't dodge morally fraught issues.

Annie Laurie, later *'Way Down East*, grew out of traditional theatrical and literary material already widely familiar to nineteenth-century spectators. Lottie Blair Parker, as a stock company touring actress, was entirely at home with the American stage repertoire and the conventions of the late-Victorian stage. Her play echoed moments from domestic melodrama such as *East Lynne*; it recalled drowning and ice-floe sensation scenes such as Dion Boucicault's *The Colleen*

Bawn, George R. Sims's *The Harbour Lights*, numerous stage versions of *Uncle Tom's Cabin*, and T. W. Robertson's *The Sea of Ice*. As well, *Annie Laurie* may have reminded audiences of numerous novels: *Ruth*, by Elizabeth Gaskell, George Moore's *Esther Waters*, Thomas Hardy's *Tess of the d'Urbervilles*, as well as drawing directly on the local color of contemporary New England b'gosh plays.[26] Moreover, these texts all share certain themes which were of interest to Griffith and which are recurring motifs in his early plays and Biograph films: the tension between the innocent country and the corrupt urban world, illegitimacy, mock marriage, cross-class relationships, transgressive women cast out of their homes—sometimes into a snowstorm—by real or surrogate fathers, as in Steele MacKaye's *Hazel Kirke* and G. H. MacDermott's *Driven from Home*.

Brady, drawing on wide theatrical experience, instigated further changes to Parker's drama. His financial success had been assured when he invested his capital in supporting and promoting the Irish American prizefighter James J. ("Gentleman Jim") Corbett in his contest for the World Heavyweight Championship against John L. Sullivan and subsequent unsuccessful title defense against Bob Fitzsimmons. Seeking to extract more money from Corbett's boxing skills, Brady, in 1895, commissioned from the author Charles Vincent, and subsequently produced, a combination company melodrama, *A Naval Cadet*, which would exploit this talent. Brady was thus one of the creators of the American "sporting melodrama," which allowed audiences—especially female spectators, their modesty preserved—to view fights and sweaty men, otherwise proscribed by troublesome local ordinances. One of Brady's certain interventions in developing *'Way Down East* began with the Nebraska-version rewrite. In *Annie Laurie*, the fourth-act fight between David Bartlett and the precursor of Lennox Sanderson begins as this character lashes at David with his riding whip. David snatches the whip from him and thrashes him before the two men briefly grapple, and the chastened seducer is compelled to withdraw the offending word *mistress*. Drawing on his experience with Jim Corbett and melodramas which featured boxing matches and fist-fights-to-the-death, Brady reshaped this angry encounter, enlarging it as the play developed: first, an attempt by Sanderson to shoot David, followed by a scuffle in which David disarms his would-be assailant. Then, over subsequent versions, the encounter evolved to a savage bare-knuckle fight recalling the fourth-act combat in *A Naval Cadet*.

This scene, a climactic and brutal episode in the Parker-Grismer drama, posed a major problem for Griffith. Griffith understood that this fight, however it was conducted, marginalized Anna and detracted from her flight onto the river and collapse onto the drifting, shattering ice. His solution gave the screen *Way Down East* its most thrilling episode. He retained the fight in the sugar-shed

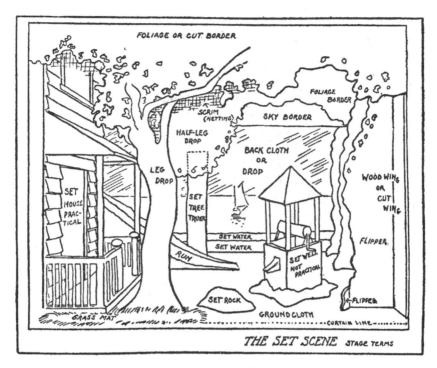

The labels in the figure read:

FOLIAGE OR CUT BORDER

FOLIAGE BORDER

SCRIM (NETTING)   SKY BORDER

HALF-LEG DROP

BACK CLOTH OR DROP

WOOD WING OR CUT WING

LEG DROP

SET HOUSE PRACTICAL

SET TREE TRUNK

FLIPPER

SET WATER
SET WATER

RUN

SET WELL NOT PRACTICAL

SET ROCK   GROUND CLOTH   FLIPPER

GRASS MAT   CURTAIN LINE

THE SET SCENE STAGE TERMS

Arthur Edwin Krows's 1916 representation of the typical farm setting, based on Currier and Ives's *The Old Oaken Bucket* and used successively in *The Old Homestead* in 1886, *'Way Down East* in 1899 and 1920, and, in more recent times, for *Oklahoma!* in 1943 and the film *State Fair* in 1945 and its stage play in 1996.

but reduced it to a brief flurry of blows, with neither David nor Sanderson the decisive winner, and with David leaving the shed, venturing again into the blizzard to track and follow Anna out onto the frozen river just as the ice breaks, sweeping her away with the spring thaw, carrying her to a deadly waterfall.

Restoring *'Way Down East* to its original New England setting enabled a return to the arcadian environment Parker had first imagined. Although not explicitly stated in the play's first-act directions, the farmyard stage and film set for this drama are integral to the action. Griffith was later to insist that the farm setting for his film version of *Way Down East* was derived from the appearance and layout of his family's former home in Oldham County, Kentucky, but this claim is another Griffith fiction.[27] While Griffith doubtless sought an image of rural serenity which inspired nostalgic longing in his audience and which also stirred his own memories of a boyhood home, his claim was implausible, partly because Charles Seesel's and Clifford Pember's film sets closely mimicked the

1899 stage setting, but more so because the design for the Parker-Grismer-Brady 'Way Down East was itself derived from a ubiquitous popular image of American rural life. The common source for both play and film—and for numerous other nineteenth- and twentieth-century-American b'gosh dramas—was a popular lithograph which had enjoyed a long life as an image of American domestic serenity and stability. This print, taking its imagery and title The Old Oaken Bucket from Samuel Woodworth's 1818 poem of the same name, was created by the artist Francis Flora Bond Palmer for the American lithographic firm Currier and Ives and first appeared in 1864.[28] In 1872, key elements of Palmer's print—the house, well, bucket, and tree—were reproduced on sheet-music covers sold by the music-publishing firm Oliver Ditson and Company to market Edward Kiallmark's musical setting of Samuel Woodworth's 1818 poem. With literally hundreds of thousands of prints and rip-off images of Palmer's lithograph in circulation, this vision of American rural life imprinted itself upon the national unconscious as the quintessential rendering of an unpretentious country dwelling. Grismer and Brady, as well as other contemporary theatrical producers, were able to exploit this expectation. Griffith and his designers, consciously or unconsciously, followed in their wake. The first view of the Bartlett farm, seen in a long shot, "realizes"[29] Palmer's print. Closer shots of the farm reprise details from that print and repeat the design of The Old Oaken Bucket and the standard stage setting for rural exteriors depicted in a leading contemporary guide to play production.[30]

Experienced in the business of mounting touring combinations, Brady was able to adapt this first-act farmyard setting to varied surroundings and to congratulate himself on the effect this had on city audiences. He later recalled that on its return to New York, 'Way Down East was booked into the cavernous Academy of Music but that its manager was dismayed because the production appeared too small for its vast stage. Accordingly,

> Grismer and I put our heads together and decided on a huge production, introducing horses, cattle, sheep, all varieties of farm conveyances, a monster sleigh drawn by four horses for a sleigh-ride . . . all in all, a veritable farm circus. It went over with a bang, and stayed in New York a full season, showing profits exceeding one hundred thousand dollars. After that, it was easy going. I launched a half-dozen touring companies. They all cleaned up.[31]

'Way Down East was enthusiastically received by the New York public, the trade press, and the metropolitain dailies, their critics remarking on full houses and commending text, staging, and performers. Subsequent press advertise-

1920 production still of Charles Seesel and Clifford Pember's set for Bartlett Farm in Griffith's film *Way Down East*. Museum of Modern Art Film Stills Archive.

ments, which indicate that prebooking was essential because many performances had sold out,[32] suggest that *Way Down East* was attracting numerous paying customers, if not meeting all of its overhead costs.

Within six months of its opening, the roles, dialogue, and stage business, especially Grismer's patented snowstorm, of *Way Down East* were well enough known to New York audiences to have been given the accolade of a parody sketch at New York's leading variety theatre. Joseph Weber and Lew Fields, who regularly burlesqued Broadway hits at their music hall, commissioned *Way Up East* from Charles Carton. Carton renamed the Bartlett family the Bartlett Pears; Lennox Sanderson was transformed into Lennox Lyceum;[33] Rube Whipple, the only country character retained, became Rube Whiffletree; and Anna was rechristened Ann Moore Besides. The one-scene sketch began as Ann[a] sat knitting, meanwhile gazing at her mirror and meditating on her postpartum pallor. As fistfuls of paper snow were cast through the windows, Ann[a] endured accusations from the Squire, and the sketch ended with Ann[a] rounding on her accusers:

> ANN: So you're on to me, eh? You've found out that I've been a mother. Why don't you go father? I believed myself to be an honorable wife, but the father of that child was a wretch who betrayed a poor soubrette into a mock turtle marriage. (*In a loud ranting style*) You've been hunting down a poor defenceless girl. There's a man (*looking at Lennox directly. Lennox is eating with a knife and slams it on the table with a bang. A searchlight directly on him*) An honored guest at your table——why don't you turn your searchlight on him? For he is the father of my child, that man there. (*Points to Rube instead of Lennox.*)[34]

Meanwhile, Brady, driven by the need to build future audiences to meet his touring productions, published eight-page booklets which offered illustrations from the play, Hi Holler's jokes, and poems, but also, more crucially, featured commendations from ministers who testified to the play's moral teaching. One such clergyman's endorsement insisted that "the tone of the play is pure and sweet, and shows how God-like is humanity when at its best. I should like every member of my congregation to see the play and learn its lesson."[35] Knowing that ministers were moved by the play and exhorted their parishoners to attend, Brady regularly prepared his company's way on tour by distributing, in advance, "ministers' tickets," that is, free tickets to clergymen and their families.

Brady had once been a member of the Theatrical Syndicate. Writing about the Syndicate years after the event, he referred to the "fatal damage" caused by its "stranglehold" and distanced himself from the worst excesses of its influence.[36] He was credited by other managers with being one of the "progressives"[37] who, in time, opposed and reformed this cabal. However, it is equally clear that Brady benefited from Syndicate membership. Brady's ability to gain entry to Syndicate theatres, to reside in these theatres while making adjustments to 'Way Down East, to travel circuits until the play had found an acceptable form, to then select a Broadway theatre to reintroduce the play to New York audiences, and to send it, thereafter, on a money-spinning tour on numerous provincial circuits were all to the play's advantage, and were all a likely consequence of playing ball with the Syndicate. It was through his specific association with Florenz Ziegfeld that Brady was able, in 1898, to co-lease the Manhattan Theatre, reducing the overhead of 'Way Down East until favorable reviews and good word of mouth assured capacity audiences.

Although 'Way Down East was now a New York hit, its great success lay on the touring circuits. When the New York *Dramatic Mirror* published a letter from a

Toronto critic to the effect that Canadian cities were not receiving the first-rate companies, Brady contested this complaint, insisting that his companies were of equal strength and arguing that box office returns confirmed their continuing popularity with the public. His letter of reply[38] provides information about 'Way Down East's on-tour earnings as well as the size of each company and quantity of equipment and effects necessary to sustain the tour and the number of employees whose wages were met by these earnings. This degree of success enabled Brady to send out annual tours through 1912. Thereafter, he mounted lesser tours at irregular intervals. Given the frequency of such tours and the near-ubiquity of 'Way Down East companies, it is unlikely that Griffith failed to witness the play in performance.

Annie Laurie is, of course, a melodrama, and, indeed, all subsequent theatrical revisions and filmic permutations of 'Way Down East are melodramas. Nevertheless, Parker's Annie Laurie and subsequent drafts of 'Way Down East offered innovations within the conventions of this genre which partly account for its value in challenging American mores and which speak to the duration of its appeal to American audiences. The most effective study of Griffith's 'Way Down East as melodrama is Linda Williams's incisive and eloquent Playing the Race Card, in which Williams acknowledges the power of melodrama and itemizes some of the larger characteristics of melodrama which this film shares with other dramas. Williams cites, in particular, the Bartlett farm as a "space of innocence" which, once enjoyed by Anna, must be reclaimed after her ordeal which is both arduously physical—undergoing trials by childbirth, poverty and exhaustion, snowstorm and freezing cold—and devastatingly emotional— deceived, seduced, and abandoned by her bogus husband, experiencing the death of her baby, rejected by would-be parents and a lover. It involves a process—painful, humiliating, and deeply unjust—of exposure and expulsion, which Williams calls a "dialectic of pathos and action," which Anna must endure and for which her detractors and persecutors must also suffer and repent.

Anna Moore's struggle throughout both play and film is to locate and to be accepted in a new, more secure home. Her first confession after arriving at the Bartlett farm is her disconsolate, "I have no home." Brady had emphasized this confession in posters for his touring play. Griffith highlights this line, both in an intertitle and, more significantly, by adding episodes which show Anna comfortable in her mother's home before being packed off to her rich Boston relatives, her unwelcome arrival in the house occupied by these strange, cold, and curiously jealous cousins, her elopement with Sanderson and the pretend home they briefly occupy, her expulsion from her barren room in the boardinghouse

Phoebe Davies, as Anna Moore, arrives at Bartlett Farm in the
opening moments of Act 1 in Lottie Blair Parker's 'Way Down East.
Photograph by Joseph Byron, 1898. Harvard Theatre Collection.

in Belden (scene of her baby's terrible death), and her cruel, self-righteous ejection from the Bartlett home.

To this extent, 'Way Down East shares common ground with The Old Homestead. The Old Homestead concerns an errant "prodigal" boy sought and reclaimed into the family and again embraced by his parents; 'Way Down East enacts the betrayal, tenuous reinstatement, rejection, expulsion, cleansing, and eventual reclamation of Anna, and she, too, is embraced by parents and accepted as a "daughter" and a wife fit for their son at the fourth-act curtain. But here similarities end. We know that Josiah Whitcomb's son is merely young and weak and that his vice, alcohol, although deeply troubling and injurious to his health, can be overcome and that, weak or not, he will be reincorporated into his fractured family. The moral climate into which Lottie Blair Parker ventured is not so forgiving. The chasm between inebriation and sexual transgression, especially if the transgressor is an unmarried female, was vast.

"You have been hunting down the defenseless girl who only asked to earn her bread in your house. There is a man, an honored guest at your table—why don't you find out what his life has been? For he is the father of my child—he is the man who betrayed me!" Anna (Phoebe Davies), on the point of expulsion from the Bartlett home, defiantly pointing out Lennox Sanderson (Frank Lander) as the father of her baby. Photograph by Joseph Byron, 1898. Harvard Theatre Collection.

The woman who had borne a child out of wedlock was a source of distur-bance and deep moral ambiguity frequently played out upon the nineteenth-century stage. By 1898, American melodrama, as much as the drama of Europe, had long traded in the errant and reclaimed female, both as heroine and as the "adventuress" or "woman with a past," and, as well, in her heartless or merely opportunistic seducer. At first glance, there is little to distinguish 'Way Down East from these other earlier and contemporary dramas where sexual transgres-sion and an offended society are opposed and, eventually, reconciled. Never-theless, all variants of 'Way Down East represent an important step in exploring and dramatizing this role. Moreover, each variant cannot be divorced from the ongoing issue of American female suffrage. In 1896, when Lottie Blair Parker wrote *Annie Laurie*, females were permitted to vote in local and state elections in some—but only a few—American states but were not legally permitted to vote in congressional or presidential elections. In 1919, just as Griffith was preparing his film version, American females were accorded full suffrage rights. The effects of these gradual changes on the developing 'Way Down Easts, on their various authors and interpreters, and, equally, on the play's and film's many audiences, were matters which colored each draft and every performance of this melodrama well into the twentieth century.

'Way Down East differs in a crucial particular from generic melodrama. Melodrama is invariably villain driven. Hero and heroine are destabilized and driven from their space of innocence by the behavior of a character, usually male, who is malign and wholly self-interested. Sanderson, lecherous and unscrupulous in using his unearned wealth to buy the good opinions of the Bartletts and access to their niece Kate, partly answers this description, but his villainy is revealed only in response to Anna's coincidental presence at the Bartlett farm. In the play, Sanderson's main acts of villainy lie in the past; within the play he is only reactive, threatening and blackmailing Anna into silence. Griffith, stepping back in time to underline Anna's vulnerability and to actually show Sanderson's cynical pursuit of Anna, changes the dynamic. That Sanderson is a villain is not in dispute, but he is not the only destabilizing character nor the only character who behaves badly.

The other villain—because she resents Anna's acceptance in the Bartlett household and connives and exults in her expulsion from this second home — is Martha Perkins. Martha Perkins, who is described in successive variants of the play as "Of the Village Sewing Society" and "Comedy Spinster," has two altogether discrete functions which Parker and Griffith both blend, not only with skill, but in such a manner as to reenergize the conventions of melodrama and invite reconsideration of the entire group of female characters. At first appearance, Martha is no different from other stock Victorian theatrical spinsters. Flirtatious, prudish, awkward, excessively curious and censorious, the theatrical spinster is a recurrent figure of derision and meant to be laughed at. Indeed, in the final versions of 'Way Down East, Martha does function as a comic counterpoint to Hi Holler, Rube, and Professor Stirling, and is eventually paired with Seth Holcombe.

However, to this ludicrous figure Parker has affixed a second melodramatic role, the under-villain. Lesser villains—henchmen and "adventuresses"—are common melodramatic troublemakers and are eventually disposed of or driven off in the final act. Here, Martha is the vindictive spreader of destructive gossip who rejoices at her capacity to sew discord and to cause Anna's expulsion without exposure or censure to herself. If Sanderson's villainy is physical and threat-

Anna Moore (Phoebe Davies) evicted from Bartlett Farm by Squire Bartlett
(Odell Williams). Joseph Byron must have taken the photograph as the play tried
out, because Lennox Sanderson, seated at stage left, is being played by Joseph R.
Grismer, William Brady's "play doctor" and, with Lottie Blair Parker,
codeveloper of 'Way Down East. Harvard Theatre Collection.

ening, Martha is malicious and hypocritical. She has little motive for her cruel
exposure of Anna, and Parker suggests that, although sexually inactive, she is
salacious and frustrated. She is, moreover, anxious to insinuate herself into the
Bartlett household. The stage direction which accompanies her revelation to
Amasa and Louisa states that she "sits in rocking chair . . . bus[iness] of hitch-
ing chair down between Squire and Mrs B[artlett]," thus physically intruding
between this long-married couple who are about to disagree about Anna's right-
ful place in their home. Afraid of strangers who taint and corrupt, the righteous
Amasa has uncritically welcomed the newcomer Lennox Sanderson into his
home—the hothouse flowers which he brings into the farmhouse in the dead
of winter are emblematic of the poison this villain carries—and now stands
ready to condemn and eject the good Anna. Griffith improves on this action,

depicting Vivia Ogden as Martha joyfully hugging herself and rocking orgasmically in her chair while pleasureably exclaiming, "Oh, it is awful!"

One of the ways to grasp the power of this role is to note how individual actors were perceived by the national press. As might be expected, most column inches were accorded to Phoebe Davies and to the other touring-company interpreters of Anna Moore. After Anna, and coequal in press attention, were the various Rube Whipples, commended for their singing, dancing, and rube comedy, and Marthas, recognized and criticized for their intrusive meddling. Corroborating these views is an article detailing how the actress Ella Hugh Wood, who played Martha in the original company until 1901 and who is described as "a pretty girl of quiet and sympathetic manner," transformed herself with makeup and wig from "a histrionic Jekyll" into an aged, wrinkled, stern-faced "Hyde . . . who resemble[s] the woman who comes to mind at the mention of New England spinsterhood."[39]

Martha, pure on the outside, a sanctimonious hypocrite within, forces reconsideration of how Parker—and perhaps Grismer and Brady—reshaped melodrama. Anna, impure to outsiders, pure within, is clearly in the protagonist's— the hero's—role, and David, although manfully dashing into the forest to rescue Anna, is a secondary character. Yet Anna was not presented to the audience as an audacious woman. That audacity was reserved for Kate Brewster, recognizable as the New Woman. Independent in spirit and material means, able to conduct her courtships, to come and go as she chooses, Kate masks the remarkable uniqueness of Anna. Parker introduced a notable modernity with Anna's role. Parker's obituaries reiterated that she was the first dramatist to use the word *baby*, not *infant* or *child*, on the American stage.[40] The latter two words distance the sexual act from its consequence. *Baby*, introduced in the second act and cast as an accusation of sin and contamination by Martha Perkins, foregrounds sex.

Unmarried in the eyes of church and state, Anna—because she admits to loving Sanderson until, abandoned, she understood his deceit and treachery—has had, and presumably enjoyed, sex with her seducer. Thus Anna appeared to theatre and film audiences as the traditional "girl who lost her character" and, normally hopeless for a female in her circumstances, someone obliged to cleanse her reputation and her status. Anna's audacity—her place as the melodrama's "hero"—was not to be the independent skeptical-of-marriage New Woman, but to fight to be a respectable, traditional woman, to be able to take her place in a family, to have the respect and love of a mother, and, eventually, to be a wife and mother herself. Moreover, because Anna arrives already suffering, the spectator's attention is focused on her. The greater and lesser villains threaten, but their behavior to her is reactive rather than—more normal for villains—instigative.

1920 production still of Squire Bartlett (Burr McIntosh) expelling Anna
(Lillian Gish) from Bartlett Farm. Museum of Modern Art Film Stills Archive.

Standing between the play and Griffith's film are two further narratives: a novelette and a full-length novel, both titled 'Way Down East. The novelette was a brief
work by Grace Miller White, an author whose literary output consisted chiefly of
prose précis of popular stage hits. It is not altogether clear whether White wrote
her novelettes as speculative ventures or whether these were invariably commissioned by theatrical producers who were concerned to generate promotional
materials and souvenir spin-offs, but White's 'Way Down East, somewhat less than
5,000 words in length, was published and distributed by the Brady Agency in
1899[41] as Brady's theatrical companies toured the American states.

The full-length novel is altogether a different matter. The significance of this
version of 'Way Down East (1900) lies in the fact that the novel and its author,
Joseph Grismer, played significant roles in 'Way Down East's progression from
the stage to film. Grismer's novel has extended the action of the Parker-Grismer-
Brady stage play to create a new narrative structure and to add embellishing
details which directly foreshadow Griffith's subsequent film adaptation.

Whereas the play begins midway through the entire narrative, with Anna's arrival at the Bartlett farm, her baby dead, her life in ruins, her unhappy past revealed only through the villain's threatening innuendo and local gossips' salacious tales, Grismer's novel begins with a still-innocent Anna's departure from her mother's home and continues with her arrival at the socialite Tremont home in Boston where her presence, as she watches Sanderson play football for Harvard, excites jealousy among her cousins. The novel thereafter narrates Anna's mock marriage, pregnancy, abandonment by the unctuous and predatory Lennox Sanderson, birth and death of her baby, and postpartum illness before bringing her to the point at which the play begins.

Grismer was anything but a major prose stylist. His writing was, by turns, effusive, lurid, and plain. Not surprisingly for someone who had worked for decades in the theatre, he thought visually, describing—in what might be his own supplementary stage directions to Parker's script and memories of performance—what occurred and how the characters moved and gestured. Where possible, the novel quotes dialogue from the play. Sensitive to the actors' need to find motivations for their behavior, he made attempts to explain his characters' psychologies and to account for motives behind actions.

Adhering to the structure of the novel conferred further advantages. Not only did Grismer's elongated enacted action "open out" Parker's narrative, roaming beyond the Barlett farm to show the city of Boston with its voluptuous social life and petty vanities, small Massachusetts hamlets and their gossipy sewing cliques, and rural festivities, but it also enabled Griffith to set up opposing dualities: urban America versus bucolic America and old ways versus heedless modernity. In the twenty-two years that had elapsed since 'Way Down East's New York opening, the nation, partly because of the First World War, had become more industrial and more urban, and women's lives, especially in the cities, had changed. The slow pace of farm life—churning butter, picking berries, and greasing harness—as described by Lottie Blair Parker, had given way to faster city life, to suburbs, flying, laboring in factories and shops, succumbing to pandemic disease, and divorce. Griffith could juxtapose the old values against the new and sometimes show the new values as shallow and wanting.

Brady had brought live farm animals onto the stage of New York's theatres to display a crude simulacrum of farm life. Now, with the dexterity afforded film, Griffith could show life in the rural hinterlands as well as cars and elegant party clothes and fraudulent parsons, thus offering a critique of urban modernity and its contrasting image of bucolic innocence. Over both of these juxtaposed environments, Griffith could impose the grandeur and occasional terror of a partly tamed landscape, benign with its seasonal apple blossoms and kitsch white doves and snoozing kittens, erupting into a blinding snowstorm and treacherous icy torrent hurtling toward deadly waterfalls. He used that freedom to transform New England from peaceable to terrible, to expand Anna's original suicide attempt into one of the most thunderous, suspense-filled last-minute rescues of his career. But David's pursuit of Anna onto the ice was more than the enactment of rescue. It was a recovery of wronged, abused innocence and the promise of a happier future. In these respects, Griffith shared an emotional intellect with Parker, both responding similarly to virtue and selfishness, both finding dramatic means in physical surroundings to convert action into powerful metaphor.

These links in the chain—play and novel—were in place by 1900, and both remained before the public beyond the period when Griffith began preparations for his film. Brady's management company, gradually merging with the major theatrical entrepreneurs, the Shuberts, continued to tour and to lease the rights to 'Way Down East. Indeed, such was the continuing appeal of the play that in 1920, Griffith signed agreements with J. J. Shubert promising to premiere his film in Shubert first-class theatres but also insisting upon his right to exhibit the film in theatres which were not owned by the Shubert family. In turn, Griffith agreed that the Shubert Organization might stage productions of 'Way Down East in any Shubert theatre not playing Griffith's film.[42] In 1912, Brady licensed Alice Guy-Blaché, America's first female motion picture director, to make the first film version of Way Down East for the Solax Company. Unfortunately, not a trace of this film remains. Meanwhile, Grismer's novel, originally illustrated with Joseph Byron's photographs and, from 1820, illustrated with stills from Griffith's film, remained in print through 1938.

Griffith's film acknowledged its predecessors but was not enslaved by them. Indeed, once having obtained the film rights to 'Way Down East, his first step was to commission the dramatist Anthony Paul Kelly to make a fresh adaptation of the drama which owed little to the stage version. Kelly's photoplay was subsequently discarded, nor has it survived. Griffith was later to claim that he had used only one episode from Kelly's version, the moment when Anna—while visiting her Boston cousins and imagining she will impress them and their footman (who holds her coat) with her sophisticated dress sense—stretches and releases the elastic-held mittens on her country-made "hug-me-tight." This device for disclosing Anna's susceptible naiveté was said by Griffith to be worth Kelly's $10,000 writer's fee.[43] The inclusion of this moment from the earliest photoplay also reveals that Kelly and Griffith had already determined to work from Grismer's novel, rather than the stage play alone, and to allow the spectator to meet a still-innocent Anna in her widowed mother's rural home. This was an important decision for Griffith, not merely because it lengthened the action of the drama and depicts in painful detail Anna's agonizing travels to the Bartlett farm gate, but also because it thus begins the film narrative with Anna leaving the care of a mother, her real mother, who lacks the resources and vitality to care for and protect her and concludes this narrative with Anna under the care and protection of her mother-in-law, a pleasing substitute in the circumstances. Anna's marriage to David is the completion and fulfilment of her sexual journey, but Louisa Bartlett's motherly kiss in the final sequence confirms Anna's rehabilitation and acceptance into a self-consciously respectable family. Not only is there closure, but there is an overall symmetry as the beginning and ending are joined.

Griffith's biographer, Richard Schickel, provides valuable evidence about the making of this film, most notably the extent to which Griffith was obliged to raise money for production by pledging his Mamaroneck studio assets, his personal property, and the negatives of his previous productions against a cluster of high-interest bank loans.[44] Schickel also cites the recollections of Griffith's crews and his stock company of performers that they were driven harder by Griffith while making Way Down East than on any previous or subsequent film.[45] The latter observation might indicate Griffith's desperation to recoup his investment, but it also reveals his confidence and certainty in approaching his material and confirms testimonies of his sure-handedness. That confidence and sure-handedness led to Griffith's comically ironic construction of the Boston environment which dazzles but which fails to corrupt Anna. Griffith achieves wry and wistful comedy from Anna's innocence, but laughs are intentionally muted as fearful certainty grows that the innocent fly is being drawn into the rapacious spider's web. Griffith's Boston is compounded of Anna's wealthy aunt, Emma Tremont, the film's representation of the urban New Woman, complete with lorgnette and "rational" dress, numerous Boston socialites—allegedly genuine members of Boston's elite—in current couture gowns, and Lennox Sanderson, the only man whom Anna meets before being gulled into a bogus marriage. It is the Tremont aunt who strips Anna of her excess of ruffles and transforms her frumpy ball gown into a dress which alerts Sanderson to Anna's sexual potential. As the torn fragments of her prudish dress are deftly rearranged into a sexy gown, Gish, too, subtly transforms. Traces of her "ga-ga baby" innocence remain, but slowly pushed to one side, yield to the expression of a woman who, though beguiled and disoriented, is enjoying romance and male attention.

Way Down East is a testimony to Lillian Gish's development as a film actor. Rare outtakes from Griffith's A Cry for Help (1912) show Gish, in the small supporting role of a maid, attempting to telephone for police aid. With the camera turning, Gish receives Griffith's off-camera instructions, responds to them as best she can, and then tries again, attempting to register dismay, confusion, and such overpowering fear that she faints. It is a far from convincing performance by the young Gish. Each successive take shows her to be entirely dependent on behind-the-camera instructions from Griffith. In many of her Biograph films and in The Birth of a Nation, she appears pictorially interesting, but her emotional moments come in bursts and rarely arise from a developing and sustained awareness of character. In Intolerance, she appears a mere cipher, a woman in long-shot rocking a cradle. Then, beginning with Hearts of the World (1918) and continuing through A Romance of Happy Valley (1919), Broken Blossoms (1919), and True Heart Susie (1919), Gish ceased to be the sometimes blank tablet Griffith wrote upon and became visible—and interesting—as characters with a rich, if sometimes troubled, inner life. She, as well as Griffith and her audiences, found that she could play roles which encouraged shadings of comedy, irony, and pathos. In Anna Moore, Gish's mental and emotional impulses—her own, not wholly Griffith's—were given free rein, with the result that her screen character was equal to the heavy dramatic load placed upon it.

Gish's mastery of Anna is evident in the courtship scenes, the sequence in which she is "married" by a friend of Sanderson's masquerading as a parson, and in the scenes in which she first "honeymoons" with Sanderson and then increasingly awaits his arrival until it is clear that she has been tricked and deserted. We see her fingering and kissing the wedding ring Sanderson has forbidden her to wear, writing variations of her married name, trying on a lacy peignoir, each sequence further revealing Anna's passage from adolescence to maturity and her heightened sexual awareness. Later, at Bartlett Farm, her anonymity compromised and fearful of Sanderson, she dutifully and lovingly serves the family, the bucolic life and domestic surroundings restoring and energizing, through Gish's performance, what modernity had destroyed. Gish, as Anna, also holds herself back from moments of joy and celebration. She performs the wounded outsider with delicate nuance.

Anna's life before reaching Bartlett Farm happens in interiors: her mother's home, her aunt's Boston mansion, Sanderson's dramatically elegant bachelor apartment, the country inn where the false marriage takes place, the hotel room where the "marriage" is consummated and Anna abandoned, and the grim lodging house in Belden in which Anna's baby dies. Griffith based this latter episode on an exterior scene from Annie Laurie that Brady or Grismer had cut from subsequent stage versions of 'Way Down East. Parker had written a third-act episode in which Annie, accused of giving birth to a bastard child by the

Squire, Amasa Wiggins, runs from the home-farm Christmas celebrations into a blizzard. David, pursuing her through the storm, tracks her to the edge of a lake and there watches as Anna, struggling in the deep drifts, finds a bird, trapped frozen and dying in the snow. Anna's grief as she cradles the bird resonates both into the distant past to recall and mourn her dead baby and into the immediate present with her expulsion into the blizzard, the bird serving as a double metonym for her baby and herself:

> Anna (*Enters, coming slowly down the run, as she gets about half way down the stage, which should be made to grow gradually lighter during the act, is made very light, and a sunlight effect is thrown upon the backing.*) The sun is up! I had not thought I should live to see it rise again! (*Comes slowly down the run: her hair is loosened and falling about her, her face pale, her eyes wild and staring as if blind with grief. She has neither hood nor wrap, and her dress is torn and soiled; she does not see David. He has retreated as if awed by her look of stony grief, and stands back of cut tree*[46] *L.U.E watching her and listening.*) This is the way to the lake—I couldn't find it last night—in the dark and in the storm. . . . (*Sinks down on the ground resting her arm and head on tree down R. After an instant her eyes fall upon something on the ground near the tree.*) What is that? (*picking up object*) Poor little bird—poor little snow bird, so cold, so cold.—(*Caresses it, seems to be trying to warm it in her hands and against her cheek.*) You've come to me for some company—we'll go to the lake together—the water will be dark and cold—but not so cold or dark as this world when all we love is lost—lost—(*Her manner and tone have become wild and incoherent—she laughs*). What was that you said? (*Talking to the bird*) You're cold? Then I'll build a fire to warm you—lie there now—you'll see! (*Puts the bird down and goes about humming. She breaks off a few twigs from the fallen tree and piles them in a little heap in the the centre of the stage; she smiling and singing; picks up the bird tenderly, sits down on the stage near fire and holds the bird toward the little bunch of twigs, rubs it and rubs her own hands as if it were alight and they both enjoyed the warmth.*) Isn't that nice? Isn't that warm? (*Sits smiling and crooning to the dead bird, rubbing it and rocking back and forth*) Not warm yet? And the fire out—Oh, I don't know—I don't know what to do! (*falls moaning and crying pitifully*) I don't know where to go. . . . Oh, yes, I remember now! (*Laughs.*) We were going to the lake—there's no one there to drive us away— We can stay there forever—and ever . . .[47]

Twenty years later Griffith brought the scene indoors to transmute it into the emotionally scarifying sequence of the baby's death.

Griffith's increasingly dismal interiors necessarily force the spectator's concentration on Anna and invite empathy as she becomes friendless and isolated in her grief and mortification. Lillian Gish registers pain with small gestures, slight inclinations of the head and eyes. Only as her dying baby's life ebbs is there significant movement: the placing of the baby on a chair, annointing it with baptismal water, rubbing its hands and vainly exhaling warm breath on them and its motionless face. This, Anna's "Gethsemane,"[48] was Griffith's rendering of Lottie Blair Parker's frost-killed-bird scene, but it is voiceless and the more harrowing for that silence. According to Gish's biographer, Griffith's direction and Gish's concentration on the baby were so intense as this sequence was filmed that the father whose baby was being used, was overcome by its heart-stopping realism. Filming while the baby slept, Gish recalled:

> We were over in a corner of the vast studio in as few lights as we could use. Not a sound could be heard except the camera turning and my whispered words. During the scene I heard a thud. Of course I couldn't look out to see what had happened. When it was over I saw a man's body stretched out on a bench. The father who had brought the baby was watching. The scene looked so real to him, he fainted. You can see the baby does look dead.[49]

After the baby's death and Anna's shamefaced eviction from the Belden boardinghouse, Griffith moves the action outdoors and to less-confining rooms. At Bartlett Farm, Anna and David Bartlett are identified with Nature's variety: water, cooling shade, doves, snow, the changes of seasons. The possibilities of new life mingle with recollections of her loss. Even when Anna is obliged to go on a winter's day to Belden and passes before the Sewing Circle's window to become grist to the gossips' mill, she stops to admire and briefly caress a young child on its sleigh. Here the wintry countryside is benign. Its cruelty—the "nor'easter" blizzard and the torrent of ice-floes—are the reverse, the hidden, dangerous side of arcadia.

Griffith's treatment of farm workers is a part of this eulogizing of rural life and at the same time, fulfills expectations of audiences still conditioned to the variety which came with touring theatrical combination companies. Gone is the Village Choir of farmhands who seemed to have few chores to do and, with their banishment, their mixed voices and their close-harmony melodies. In their place are the villagers and local farmers who arrive in the Bartlett parlor for an impromptu bout of square dancing, reels, grotesque duets, and solos before departing, only to repeat some of these dances in a neighboring barn. Charles Seamon's second-act solo dance is echoed by George Neville's shuffle, and Louis Silvers's score[50] briefly quotes his "All bound 'round with a woolen string."

Lillian Gish's characterization of *Way Down East* as "a horse-and-buggy melodrama, familiar on the rural circuit for more than twenty years" and her subsequent amazement at the film's success suggest that she assumed that

Griffith had transformed a creaky genre into something more modern. Nevertheless, whereas substantial changes have been introduced, Griffith's film version of Way Down East is still melodrama: melodrama, but with different inflections and with substantially different weighting to key characters. These differences are most evident in Griffith's treatment of Sanderson and, to a lesser extent, Martha Perkins. The Lennox Sanderson of the stage melodrama is abusive and threatening to Anna. He has the Squire's good opinion; he is a man; he has property; he has wealth with which to bribe Anna's silence. He is motivated by simple, if urgent, needs: to remove Anna from Bartlett Farm without blemishing his name and to court and win Kate Brewster. His visible sophistication consists of wearing riding clothes which are associated with leisure rather than work, owning a superior saddle horse, and bringing Kate roses—presumably obtained in distant Boston—in midwinter. Because the audience do not see him until the moment that Anna finds him on the Bartlett veranda, he has no prior history, and what is learned of him emerges from their dialogue—cryptic, wary, sotto voce. Yet, Sanderson immediately destabilizes Anna and is immediately recognizable as the one who might evict her from this refuge. In both play and film, he has the hubris to imagine that his word will be believed and that Anna can say nothing to protect her precarious position.

On film, partly because he is seen longer, partly because he is viewed in his own wealthy, urban environment, partly—and crucially—because he is observed manipulating Anna's responses and witnessed as he cheats and lies, Griffith's Sanderson is subtle and insinuating. His villainy is more intricate, springing from more complex urges: to impress Anna, to seduce her, to escape from her before she can detect she has been tricked, to cover his tracks. Only when they accidentally meet does his guard slip and then only briefly. On film, his villainy weighs less, and is less visible. Sanderson is explained in Grismer's novel as overindulged, morally unaware, irresponsible. His villainy arises more from youthful self-regard than the cruelty which the same role reveals in the stage version. Griffith chose the traits delineated by Grismer, but, in casting Lowell Sherman, already in his thirties and not the callow, spoiled undergraduate of Grismer's novel, and by showing Sanderson's immediate susceptibility to the female body—montage sequences underlining his continual awareness of women's legs and his arousal at the sight of Anna in a negligee—Griffith imbued his reworked villain with a pathological subtext of complacent self-indulgence and feckless promiscuity.

A further critical difference between play and film is the fight between David and Sanderson. Onstage it is a climactic moment because Anna—heading for an unknown destination, possibly the lake, deep in the forest—has been allowed to disappear from view and from the audience's immediate vision. The lake, unseen, is more interesting as a fearful destination than it is a site to re-create and animate. Griffith's major alteration, downgrading the sugar-shed fight, was to highlight Anna's desperate flight through the blizzard onto the icy river and to add David's dangerous and desperate rescue of the comatose hero-ine. The river is animate and unremittingly dangerous to Anna and to David. Their journeys, as the ice-floes head toward the lethal waterfall, recapitulate the plot: an accelerating race to near disaster averted by a timely rescue. Moreover, Anna, as if baptized by partial immersion in the icy water, is seen to experience a symbolic rebirth. These new moments of peril and recovery contribute directly to the plot and fully engage the spectator. Griffith still retains the fight, but, now virtually extraneous to the plot, it is merely a brief exchange of blows in a darkened sugar-shed, nothing decisive is achieved, and audience receive little satisfaction or sense of justice from the encounter.

With Martha Perkins, as with Lennox Sanderson, the play and film divide sharply. The stage Martha is jealous and vindictive; Vivia Ogden's film Martha is nosy and intrusive, but her métier is gossip, not vindictiveness. In stage ver-sions, Parker allows little reconciliation. Female duplicity and hypocrisy cannot be condoned. At best, Martha may be pushed into an upstage corner as act 3 reaches its emotional climax. She thereafter appears in the fourth-act sugar-shed to be berated by the Squire, then, for the sake of comic symmetry, paired off with a closet drunk. Griffith, who was understandably concerned for his audiences to witness and admire Anna's capacity to endure, appears to have been less aware of Martha's vindictive anger at being displaced from the Bartletts' close family circle and at her own reluctant chastity. He accordingly restored Martha more fully to the comic world; identifying chronic nosiness and unrestrained gossip as comic traits, he gave her two rival rube suitors and a place at the three-couple wedding which ends the film.

Diminishing the power of the greater and lesser villains necessarily changed the melodramatic character of Griffith's *Way Down East*. These differences led to an Anna whose arduous and fraught life was painfully familiar, but who—in the spectators' eyes, if not in the opinion of the Bartlett family—retained her virtue and moral integrity. Moreover, the villains, neither of them capable of long-term plans or self-aggrandizing schemes, appeared petty and selfish, merely feeding appetites for fleeting gratification. Thus, Griffith's *Way Down East*, contrary to much melodrama, including the Parker-Grismer-Brady ver-sion, where Sanderson's first-act arrival threatened to displace Anna only moments after she had made her entrance at Bartlett Farm, was not villain-instigated. Rather, Griffith, extending the duration of Anna's journey, had devised a heroine-centered melodrama of remarkable force. Strongly abetted by Lillian Gish's performance as Anna and by a strong supporting cast, *Way Down East* is a remarkable film which, neither bettering nor dimishing Lottie Blair Parker's 1898 "horse-and-buggy melodrama," stands alongside it. Both play and film endure as American classics.

8 Twilight Revels

In *Way Down East*, Griffith had created his most emotionally compelling work. His adaptation of Lottie Blair Parker's drama had again confirmed his mastery of filmmaking, of adapting and reshaping established stage classics, and perhaps more critical to his immediate future, his capacity to convert what critics and colleagues had judged as unpromising material into profitable movies. *Way Down East* was received by the critics with few demurs. The film's success left its initial doubters wondering at his skill in making such a drama of intimate domestic sensibility from what they had formerly perceived to be a banal stage melodrama.[1] Griffith's payments for screen rights and a scenario which he then failed to use had cost him $192,000, and production costs had been excessive, but his film had gross earnings of $4,000,000[2] and continued to earn, if at a diminishing rate.

Yet, the final dozen years of Griffith's productive career were far from successful. Despite the undenied success of *Way Down East*, Griffith's life was increasingly in turmoil, assuming—or providing—the pattern of Hollywood myth: a director's decline brought on by a combination of factors, some, industry related, beyond his understanding and control. His personal life was unstable: his relationships with women and with colleagues were erratic; he was drinking too much,[3] and his drinking led to imperious and arrogant behavior. He continued to live and dine alone.[4] Despite the profit made by *Way Down East*, Griffith remained financially encumbered. The overhead expenses of maintaining his Mamaroneck, New York, studio devoured his income faster than it was earned, and he was never to achieve the independence he sought without making embarrassing and debilitating compromises.

Moreover, his films were increasingly perceived as old-fashioned. Hollywood studios were now importing worldly directors from Europe, Germany and Hungary especially,[5] their more cynical views of human behavior shaped by four years of war and by postwar famines, epidemics, and economic inflation. Americans, too, were less optimistic. Mass deaths from the Spanish influenza pandemic and criminality linked to Prohibition brought their own cynicism. In this climate, Griffith's dramas of wronged innocence, of heroines threatened by abusive, predatory, and exploitative males, roles in which Lillian Gish had specialized, were being edged out of public favor by films featuring less ethereal and less fragile women, by dramas of emancipated women, with newcomer "WAMPAS Baby Stars"—as typified by Clara Bow, Mary Philbin, and Dolores Costello.[6] Although he had discovered more worldly actresses in Clairine Seymour (who died during the filming of Way Down East) and Carol Dempster to appear alongside the Gish sisters, Griffith, riding on the profit from Way Down East, was nevertheless prepared to manufacture the large-scale Orphans of the Storm for the Gishes alone. Orphans of the Storm brought critical approval and—too slowly—a small profit,[7] but the huge capital cost of making this film would eventually force Griffith to mortgage his personal property and become a public corporation issuing shares to unknown investors.[8]

Leaving Mutual and, in 1919, forming the United Artists Corporation with Mary Pickford, Douglas Fairbanks, and Charlie Chaplin, he was, once again, contractually obligated to produce and release a specified quota of films annually. Whereas Chaplin could satisfy exhibitors by releasing short films as well as features (and Chaplin's preference at that time was for short films), Griffith's personal aesthetic preferences and the commercial expectation of his exhibitors were only satisfied with longer, more expensive to produce, and more time-consuming films. Somehow, between 1919 and his final film, released in 1932, Griffith contrived to make twenty-eight films, some of these of poor and indifferent quality, some which lost money, exasperated colleagues and investors, and reduced the willingness of studio executives to finance further films. Of the final group of films, a quarter of these, his most praised and his more conspicuous failures during this period, were taken from stage plays.[9] However, the esteem formerly earned by these dramas did not assure Griffith's filmic adaptations of either artistic or financial success.

Even before he had completed Way Down East, Griffith's obligation to manufacture a quota film in order to free himself from his contract with Mutual resulted in the strangest of all his theatrical adaptations: an audacious, but unacknowledged, act of piracy in which he appears to have freely re-cast George Bernard Shaw's Mrs. Warren's Profession as a "western," disguising this bizarre rendering under the title of Scarlet Days (1919). Scarlet Days was followed by three nontheatrical films. These, in turn, were succeeded by Orphans of the Storm

(1922), notionally an adaptation of the N. Hart Jackson–Kate Claxton version of Eugene Corman's and Adolphe D'Ennery's 1874 *The Two Orphans*, but, in actuality, Griffith's most intricate use of multiple theatrical sources.

A year later, encouraged by Will Hays of the Motion Picture Producers and Distributors of America to make a moral, patriotic, and uplifting film,[10] and reluctantly backed by United Artists, Griffith borrowed from his 1901 vaudeville sketch *In Washington's Time* and, more liberally, from his 1907 unperformed play, *War*, to shoot a large-scale epic of the American Revolution titled *America*. Episodic and hampered by the same problems of limited characterization and iconic representations of figures from American history found in *War*, *America* stands as one of Griffith's costly failures.

In 1925, Griffith turned to the current theatre, on this occasion adapting a Broadway musical, Dorothy Donnelly's 1922 *Poppy*, into a "circus waif" comedy, *Sally of the Sawdust*, starring his lover Carol Dempster and, sadly, underusing the comic talents and juggling skills of W. C. Fields. Encountering his next theatrically related project, Griffith exercised only nominal supervision and attempted indifferent repairs when the venture was well beyond rescue and control. The film was *Topsy and Eva* (1927), a crude, supposedly comic variety sketch drawn from *Uncle Tom's Cabin*. This fiasco was followed by an attempt at a cynical, European-style drama, *Lady of the Pavements* (1928), the film's structure and concept taken from Edward Bulwer-Lytton's 1830s melodrama *The Lady of Lyons*, a play Griffith had encountered in his touring days. *Lady of the Pavements* provided Griffith with one of his few ventures with sound. Griffith's final film was *The Struggle* (1931), a temperance melodrama. Again, as with *America*, Griffith reverted to his earlier work, here adapting Charles Reade's *Drink* (1879) and his own Biograph adaptation of that play, *A Drunkard's Reformation* (1909). What had effectively chimed with social and medical understandings of alcohol addiction in 1909 seemed hopelessly inappropriate and outdated twenty-two years later. Prohibition and the nation's costly experiences with inebriation and alcoholism underlined Griffith's naive optimism. The theatre had offered Griffith his earliest subjects for films and was to do so to the very end of his career. The processes of adapting these seven theatrical works into films is the subject of this chapter.

The circumstance in which the subject matter of *Scarlet Days* was devised remains an unsolved puzzle. Eileen Bowser quotes a letter from Stanner E. V. Taylor stating that Griffith had mentioned devising a western but had specified neither plot nor characters.[11] However, Griffith had expressed interest in the Mexican patriot-bandit Joaquin Murrieta and, having auditioned actors and having rejected Rudolph Valentino as "too foreign-looking," cast Richard D.

Barthelmess ("David Bartlett" in *Way Down East*) as Alvarez, in what became a secondary role, important only in providing one of Griffith's trademark "rides-to-the-rescue."

Griffith's decision to focus attention on the role of "the wandering knight" Alvarez may have been a ploy to conceal the source for the main plot of Griffith's film. *Scarlet Days*—not by coincidence, but possibly by deliberate design—is an obvious reworking of Shaw's *Mrs. Warren's Profession*, the action and setting transposed from the London of 1894 to a California mining town during the 1849 gold rush. A step in this transposition in time and place was the deliberate coarsening of the drama's principal roles: Mrs. Warren was re-created as Rosy Nell, a working prostitute and dance-hall performer. Griffith underlined the earthiness of this role, played by Eugenie Besserer, a stocky, heavy-set actress regularly cast in character parts, by introducing her in a grotesque shuffling dance and, shortly after, depicting her in a fierce fight with "Spasm Sal," another unsavory dance-hall habitué, ending in Sal's death and Rosy Nell charged with murder. Vivie, played by Carol Dempster, became a self-reliant innocent educated in an Eastern boarding school. Sir George Crofts reappeared as Bagely, a proprietor of a dance-hall-cum-gambling-saloon and frontier bordello. Frank became a young prospector from Virginia, and the Reverend Samuel Gardner, an ineffectual sheriff. As Griffith's adaptation is presented in the guise of a "western," there is much gunplay as Bagely attempts to abduct "Vivie" (her character's name is never provided), to make her his mistress and to then turn her into another prostitute. "Vivie" learns of her mother's profession as they shelter in a root cellar during the final-reel shoot-out, and both are ultimately rescued by Alvarez who arrives in time to disperse Bagley and his henchmen. Griffith made a halfhearted attempt to allegorize the characters and to retain the aura of a chivalric romance even as his drama transposed the characters from the English lower middle class to the American frontier proletariat. Griffith's film has been justly described by the film scholar Scott Simmon as "Griffith's last and dullest western."[12]

Griffith and Taylor would have known of Shaw's play and its plot even if they hadn't attended a performance. *Mrs. Warren's Profession* was thrice offered in New York, first in October 1905, when the play was staged at the Garrick Theatre by Arnold Daly's repertory company for what proved to be a single performance. Vice-squad police arrested and tried Daly and another actor for giving a "lewd" performance; both were subsequently acquitted. *Mrs. Warren's Profession* was again performed for a three-week run at the Manhattan Theatre in March and April 1907, a period when Griffith was writing *A Fool and a Girl*, and there was a revival by the Washington Square Players in March and April 1918, when Griffith was again on the East Coast.

Griffith's decision to film The Two Orphans was strongly influenced by Lillian Gish. According to the film historian Kevin Brownlow, "Lillian . . . found the play of the The Two Orphans. 'I couldn't tell him what to do, I could only gently suggest. . . . Luckily, it was in an Italian theatre on 14th Street . . . and Dorothy and I took him to see it in Italian. Of course, he couldn't understand it, but he liked the story and decided to do it against the background of the French Revolution to make it more of a production.'"[13] This theatre visit was hardly Griffith's first encounter with The Two Orphans, a play he had known from his adolescence in Louisville. He had also taken small roles in The Two Orphans while in touring companies, and was aware that his mentor, McKee Rankin, had created the leading role of Jacques Frochard. As early as 1920, Griffith began research into the period of the French Revolution and the Reign of Terror of 1794 with the intent of creating a drama with Lillian Gish in an unspecified role and Monte Blue as Danton. In this year, he began to gather capital to finance a production which metamorphosed from an unnamed drama into The Two Orphans. Lillian Gish's crucial role had been to persuade Griffith of the viability of this project and to assure him that she would take a leading role in his film. She had become a "bankable" asset. Griffith anticipated few problems, and the completed Orphans of the Storm, filmed between June and October 1921, and released in January 1922, gives no hint of the financial problems which beset him, nor does it admit to the circuitous path he followed in wresting a screenplay from numerous theatrical sources.[14]

The title credits for Orphans of the Storm announce that Griffith's film is based on Eugene Corman's and Adolphe D'Ennery's The Two Orphans. Griffith's acknowledgment extends to include Kate Claxton, who created the role of the blind Louise and whose name was closely associated with the American adaptation of the play until her death in 1924. But these acknowledgments mislead the viewer and conceal the fact that Griffith was disingenuous in citing The Two Orphans as his only theatrical source. The Two Orphans was, unambiguously, the principal source for Orphans of the Storm and provided the backbone to the narrative of two "sisters" forcibly separated soon after their arrival in Paris and reunited only after each undergoes an arduous and terrifying adventure. However, Orphans of the Storm's screenplay was further indebted to at least four other dramas known to American audiences. Griffith was to make substantial alterations to the basic Two Orphans script, chiefly inflecting dramatic characterization and changing the overall balance between his characters.

Poster, ca. 1885, for the stage play of *The Two Orphans* showing the principal characters and settings which Griffith would later use in *Orphans of the Storm*. Harvard Theatre Collection.

Cabinet photo by Dana, New York, ca. 1880, of McKee Rankin
as the bully Jacques Frochard. Harvard Theatre Collection.

These changes, as well as the sources themselves, require scrutiny. *Orphans of the Storm*, far more than any other of Griffith's theatrical adaptations, drew extensively on his own theatrical past, both as spectator and actor. As much as this screen drama confirms Griffith's control over the vocabulary of filmmaking and his artistic vision, *Orphans of the Storm* also illuminates the degree to which his vision was shaped by his early participation in the late-Victorian theatre and his awareness, not only of the popular American repertoire, but, equally, of significant theatrical imports from abroad. Thus, what at first appears straightforward and free from complications was, rather, intricate and complex. The tangled pedigree of *Orphans of the Storm*—the most complicated of all Griffith adaptations—is worth the unraveling because it explains Griffith's working processes.

The Two Orphans' trajectory—rival translations, competing actresses, an enduring place in the popular repertoire—is in some respects typical of favored stage pieces. The drama first appeared as *Les Deux Orphelines* at Paris's Théâtre Porte St. Martin in January 1874 and, receiving favorable notices and drawing large audiences, was soon pirated by anonymous translators who hawked their English-language versions to foreign managers, who then rushed these illicit translations into production before injunctions halted their transgressions. Simultaneously, but more circumspect in commissioning playable scripts, London and New York managers negotiated agreed adaptations by John Oxenford (London) and N. Hart Jackson (New York), the latter for A. M. (Harry) Palmer, manager of Manhattan's Union Square Theatre. Meanwhile, unauthorized versions, in some respects more faithful to the original French text than adaptations reshaped to meet London and New York tastes, were suppressed by prosecutions but never wholly eradicated from the repertoire. These rogue translations periodically surfaced on American rural circuits and were later to compromise Griffith's rights to the Jackson-Claxton American version of the play. Unlicensed texts also provided Griffith with alterations to the drama's plot as he searched for a suspenseful filmic climax.

N. Hart Jackson's licensed version, premiered in December 1874, cast the twenty-six-year-old Kate Claxton as Louise. Kitty Blanchard, another popular young actress of the day, took the role of Henriette. Blanchard moved on to other parts, but Claxton became so identified with the role of the abused and exploited blind heroine that, soon after 1874, she purchased the U.S. copyright from Palmer and Jackson and, forming her own combination company, supplemented Jackson's melodrama script with variety turns and additional musical numbers. Claxton then toured the play though the American hinterlands for over thirty years, eventually staging a major New York revival in 1904. In 1921, Griffith leased from Claxton what he assumed were exclusive performance

Poster, ca. 1885, of Kate Claxton as Louise, singing
her begging song on the steps of St. Sulpice.

rights to this play, only to discover that Claxton's copyright had lapsed. He further found that, by virtue of William Fox's 1915 film version of the play, starring Theda Bara as Henriette and Jean Southern as Louise—which apparently drew on several versions, authorized and pirated, of the script—Fox now held U.S. copyright. Griffith was obliged to settle with Fox, paying a costly $85,000 above the $10,000 he had paid to Claxton for a valueless property.[15] Therefore, the phrase "through arrangement with Kate Claxton" on the main title to *Orphans of the Storm* conveniently obscured vexed issues of ownership which Griffith found it preferable to elide. It was at this point that Griffith, already aware that he was running over budget, issued stock shares in this production.

The Jackson-Claxton version of the play was set forth in seven scenes, initially arranged as a four-act drama but, by the 1890s, structured as a three-act. Anxious to copy as much as possible of the Paris production, Palmer dispatched his stage manager to the Théâtre Porte St. Martin to obtain the designers' costume sketches and renderings and maquettes of stage settings viewed by Paris spectators. Four of these settings were again closely reproduced in Griffith's film: the Paris street where the two orphans arrive and are separated, the Frochards' underground lair, the west front of St. Sulpice, complete with the addition of Richard Marston's stage snowstorm effect, and in the opening shot of La Salpêtrière women's prison where Henriette, originally arrested and imprisoned by the Count de Linieres, was about to be dispatched to the penal colony of Cayenne. Images of these stage sets, popular and known to theatre audiences, were also reproduced on posters advertising the play and on sheet-music covers when songs and incidental music by Henry Tissington, the play's musical director and conductor of the orchestra at the Union Square Theatre, were published in simplified "reductions" for domestic pianos.

Both in the Paris and American versions of *The Two Orphans*, the action is set entirely in the year 1784. Nothing of the French Revolution, neither the initial uprisings of 1789 nor the Reign of Terror of 1794, intrudes. There is no Bastille to storm, no tribunal, no guillotine, no Committee of Public Safety, no Danton, no Robespierre, no orgiastic carmagnole dance. These elements were taken—almost unaltered—from other Victorian plays by other dramatists. The only note of social unrest and political protest in *The Two Orphans* is a reference to the long-delayed performance, to be attended by de Vaudrey, of Beaumarchais's *The Marriage of Figaro*. Neither is there a prologue in *The Two Orphans*, which enacts the assassination of the Countess de Linieres's first husband, the abduction of her infant daughter Louise, Louise's rescue from the cold church steps, and her arrival in the poor family where the infant Henriette also lives. Griffith found and took his models for a prologue from other dramas. Instead, the stage play

Sheet music derived from Henry Tissington's incidental music for *The Two Orphans*.
The cover features Kitty Blanchard as Henriette and Kate Claxton as Louise.
Surrounding the two actresses are vignettes of the stage settings which Griffith
would later use in *Orphans of the Storm*. Harvard Theatre Collection.

begins with the sisters' arrival in Paris, Henriette's kidnapping, and Louise's forced co-option into the Frochard family. Subsequently, Henriette meets de Vaudrey, an appalled and unwelcome spectator at the Marquis de Presles's orgy, and is rescued by him.

The developing romantic relationship between Henriette and de Vaudrey is realized more slowly in The Two Orphans than in Griffith's film, and much of the suspense and spectators' anxieties are focused, not on this love affair, but upon the plight of Louise. Sympathy for Louise was intensified by her plaintive begging song. Henry Tissington's melody was later remembered and recycled in the andante passages of Louis Gottschalk's and William Peters's 1921 film score. Jackson's stage adaptation called for a number of agonizing near-misses, the sisters just failing to meet, until a relieved audience was prepared to ascribe total plausibility to their eventual reunion.

One of Griffith's more conspicuous and astute alterations to The Two Orphans was to accord more weight to Lillian Gish's Henriette. This re-balancing of roles resulted in a more passive and helpless Louise, imprisoned and sexually intimidated by Jacques Frochard. This version of Louise played against Henriette's desperation and her almost futile search to recover her sister. Henriette's character was further enlarged by her unpremeditated sheltering of Danton, her consequent alienation from Robespierre, and her sacrifice of love and marriage until Louise might be found. Performing such confused and often simultaneous emotions—love, fear, bewilderment, denial—were Lillian Gish's known strengths.

Exploiting these abilities, Griffith visibly expanded Lillian Gish's part, and the circumstances in which she developed Henriette's role tell much about the creative, sometimes abrasive, relationship between actress and director. The events of filming reveal Griffith in the personas of autocratic controller, annoyed critic, and, later, as pupil and subordinate, attentive—and even submissive—to Gish's own fine-tuned actor's instinct and directorial knowledge. According to Kevin Brownlow,

> Griffith's effectiveness as a director was never more apparent than in the sequence at the end of Part One where Lillian hears the voice of her long-lost sister, begging in the street below. It was daring enough to base a scene in a silent film upon a voice which no one would hear, but to convey so important a voice demanded a great deal from Lillian Gish. Griffith spoke to her throughout the scene, and one can almost hear his voice as well as that of Dorothy [whose voice comes up to the room in which Henriette lives]. When they viewed the final cut, Lillian said she thought the climax had been drawn out too long. "He was quite peeved, and told me that I had forced him to do

Cabinet photograph by Dana, New York, ca. 1880, of Kate Claxton as Louise
in the clutches of Marie Wilkins as Mère Frochard. Harvard Theatre Collection.

so by acting too intensely at the climax of the first act. "You carried that climax too high. I can't top it."[16]

As they filmed the final reel in which Henriette and de Vaudrey are brought in tumbrels to their impending execution, Gish and Griffith again clashed:

> In the final reunion of the Gish sisters, at the base of the guillotine, Griffith sensed Lillian's dissatisfaction. "He could tell by looking at me if I liked something," she remembered. "He said, 'I see Miss Geesh,' as he called me, 'isn't pleased with this scene.' And I said, "It isn't that, Mr. Griffith, it's just that it's like other scenes of the films I've seen, and I think they expect more than this of you." He said, 'If you're so smart, you get up there and show me how it should be done.' Well, there were all the extras around; there must have been a hundred people there hearing this. So I came down the steps again, and I played the meeting with my sister as I felt would be the reaction of a girl that thought she'd be dead instead of walking down the steps. He didn't say anything when it was over. He got down on both knees in front of me, took my two hands and kissed them, and turned round and said, 'Well, you've got to say, she does know.'"[17]

Griffith's other significant alteration to character balance lay in his rendering of the relationship between the Frochard brothers. In the original Corman-D'Ennery drama, and in both British and American sanctioned adaptations, the Frochard bothers are as necessary to the plot as Louise and Henriette. The blood brothers' dissonant moral characters, their jealousy, rivalry, loathing, and propensities to sudden violence, contrast starkly with the two girls whose sisterly concern and affection for each other is so continually evident. This inverse mirroring of pseudo-sisters with real brothers assured that Victorian productions of The Two Orphans be cast with the chief female roles falling to the theatre company's leading actresses, while the company's two most able and better-known actors assumed the roles of the Frochard brothers. Of the two Frochards, Pierre's was the favored male role as it called, first, for whimpering and cringing before Jacques's bluster, casting covert glances of adoration and sympathy toward the helpless Louise, then finding a sudden reversal in courage and agility when required to challenge his brother and abet Louise's escape. Diminishing the brothers' roles in the interest of an altogether different ending, Griffith elected to ignore this practice, casting his stronger male actors in the roles of de Vaudrey, Robespierre, Danton, and Jacques-Forget-Not.

Stage versions of The Two Orphans stress the degree to which the stronger Jacques dominates and bullies Pierre. Indeed, Pierre's deformities are attributed to cruel beatings from his elder sibling. In the American stage version Pierre, overcome with despair at the treatment Louise receives from his mother and by his awareness that Jacques intends to rape the blind girl, finally helps Louise to escape, to find Henriette, and, moments later, to guide de Vaudrey into the Frochards' lair where the Chevalier captures the thief at the point of his sword. However, in the original Paris version and in the unauthorized English-language versions to which Griffith reverted, Pierre, tormented by Jacques and aware of his brother's intentions toward Louise, turns on Jacques and in a brutal knife fight kills him. Thus, in *Orphans of the Storm*, Griffith has intentionally departed from the Jackson-Claxton text to remove Jacques from the final race-against-the-Terror's-guillotine episode and to focus instead on the more engaging villainies of Jacques-Forget-Not and Robespierre. Griffith also effectively excised minor or lesser characters from his text in order to keep focus on the main dramatic action. Most notably, he eliminated Jacques Frochard's unhappy and penitent mistress, whose hardened heart is softened, first by Louise, then by Henriette, and who, in turn, assists Henriette's escape from La Force prison.

The above are substantial changes from the stage version, but even these seem modest when measured against borrowings from four other Victorian and Edwardian stage plays. The four plays, so influential and listed here in chronological order—Charles Reade's *The Courier of Lyons* (1854), later revised and retitled *The Lyons Mail* (1878), Watts Phillips's *The Dead Heart* (1859), Freeman Wills's and Frederick Langbridge's *The Only Way* (1898–1899), and Victorien Sardou's *Robespierre* (1899)—share a common response to the French Revolution. This response is expressed as denial of a nation liberated from arbitrary royal tyranny and, in its place, emphasis on the excesses of the Reign of Terror. The Terror in these dramas is characterized in the indiscriminate vengeance of mob rule—a mob easily swayed by demagogic oratory to condemn—and the unstoppable procession of virtuous—guiltless—people to the scaffold. These four dramas share a horrified appraisal of the Paris mob and the self-serving ambitions of some of the Revolution's leaders, most notably Robespierre. Such consistent disparagement of the French Revolution renders the events between 1789 and 1796 a pliable metaphor which accords with Griffith's 1920s views of bolshevism and the Russian Revolution and the political turmoil, moral laxity, and social disruption both revolutions were alleged to promulgate.

All four plays dealt directly with the limitations of French justice; all stressed the cruelty of public executions and the grim relentlessness of the guillotine. Two of the dramas were adaptations of French plays by established Parisian dramatists, which later entered the American stage as plays reworked by British dramatists and commissioned for the British stage. Two were by British dramatists.

Repeated performances of all four plays in the period between 1889 and 1910 sharply reflected British skepticism toward French celebrations of the French Revolution's centenary and international dismay at French hypocrisy on public view in the courts-martial, imprisonment, repatriation, and retrial of Alfred Dreyfus, a miscarriage of justice and display of deceit and hypocrisy on which Western attention was fixed between 1894 and 1906. Significant to the later fashioning of *Orphans of the Storm*, all four plays separately found their way into the American theatrical repertoire and were individually well known to American audiences who saw the plays performed and toured by American actors and visiting British stars.

Because three of these plays were directly associated with the English actor-manager Sir Henry Irving, and because the fourth play was the theatrical property of another English actor-manager, Sir John Martin Harvey, Griffith would have known these plays by reputation, if not as a spectator, although it seems unlikely that he wouldn't have seen all or most of them. These pieces, filling the stage with numerous minor characters and many dozens of supernumeraries, would have stimulated Griffith's interest in crowd and battle scenes with representations, more theatrically vivid than the actual event, of the French Revolution's fêtes and large-scale civil skirmishes, including the taking of the Bastille, liberating its prisoners, show trials, public orgies, and public beheadings. The published souvenir program to *Orphans of the Storm* boasts that the production was "supported by a cast of twelve thousand." The deft handling of smaller stage crowds, but crowds nonetheless, was apparent as these four dramas toured the American continent. Griffith's borrowings from these plays reveal awareness of their staging strategies, their structures, and the effectiveness of their coups de théâtre.

The Courier of Lyons was introduced to American spectators in 1878 upon word that Irving had successfully revised Charles Reade's drama as *The Lyons Mail* for London's Lyceum Theatre. Irving was to bring the Lyceum company to America and to tour *The Lyons Mail* from New York, along the eastern seaboard to the South and Midwest in 1883, 1884, 1888, 1893, 1895, and 1901. Both plays, under these titles and thinly disguised variants, were to be performed along provincial circuits well into the twentieth century. In 1906, Irving's son, H. B. "Harry" Irving, brought a "replica" production of his father's property on a North American tour, and, in 1914, at the instigation of Charles Samuelson, of Samuelson's Films, the younger Irving made a full-length version of *The Lyons Mail*, mixing indoor settings and outdoor locations. H. B. Irving's film was exhibited in the United States, but it is not known whether Griffith saw it.[18]

It was from *The Lyons Mail* that Griffith took an essential plot element: the unjust conviction of an innocent person and that person's last-minute rescue from the guillotine despite opposition and interference so nearly fatal to the innocent party. *The Courier of Lyons* and *The Lyons Mail* were both based on an actual criminal case which occurred in 1795. A mail coach, traveling between Paris and Lyons, was held up and robbed, and the coach's driver, resisting, was fatally shot. Before the crime, the murderer and thief had noted his physical resemblance to a respectable citizen and had contrived to have this innocent man, a Joseph Lesurques, observed by persons who would later associate him with the crime scene. Searching for the culprit, the police arrested Lesurques, who understandably protested his complete innocence. Witnesses, however, confirmed police suspicions, and Lesurques was tried, found guilty, guillotined, and his property, assumed to be profit from his crimes, confiscated. It was not until he was arrested for another crime that the true murderer, Dubosc, was identified as the actual criminal. Dubosc was subsequently guillotined and Lesurques posthumously pardoned and his property restored to his heirs. Nearly fifty years later, these events were dramatized by Emil Moreau, Paul Siraudin, and A. C. Delacour as *Le Courier de Lyons*, performed at the Théâtre de la Gaîté with Lacressionière in the double role of Lesurques and Dubosc. Soon thereafter, *The Courier of Lyons*, adapted for London audiences by Charles Reade, was offered by Charles Kean at the Princess's Theatre. As with the original Paris version, Reade's text specified the roles of both Dubosc and Lesurques to be performed by the same actor, double roles especially relished by Irving who specialized in enacting characters with split or multiple identities. The French version offered variant endings: on alternate nights Lesurques, true to historical sources, was condemned and guillotined, but on the following night, surrendering to melodramatic convention, Dubosc's criminality was discovered just in time for him to be seized and carried to the scaffold in Lesurques's place. English audiences, in the main, preferred the melodramatic ending in which Lesurques is rescued; it was that dramatic rescue which was carried in both English-language versions to America. Given Griffith's marked predilection for final-curtain rescues, it is not difficult to imagine which ending appealed to him.

The Dead Heart provided one of Griffith's inspirations for a dramatic prologue, for a Bastille-storming scene, and for a last-minute device to cheat the executioner of his victim. First performed in London by Ben Webster in 1859 and entering the American repertoire in 1871, *The Dead Heart* was seen in further Manhattan productions in 1879 and again in 1884. Later, chosen by Irving as a vehicle to note—not celebrate—the French Revolution centenary, a revised and refurbished *Dead Heart* reached America in 1889 and was included on several of Irving's North American tours.

Yuri Tsivian cites the influence of Charles Dickens's *A Tale of Two Cities* (1859) on *Orphans of the Storm*,[19] but this influence was only indirect. Griffith was, of course, aware of Dickens's novel, but his immediate source was the Wills-Langbridge dramatization of this novel, *The Only Way*, which was commissioned in 1898 by John Martin Harvey and, as *The Jackal*, toured in the provinces for a year prior to its London opening. Once reworked, retitled, and performed for audiences in the capital city, *The Only Way* was a sensational success, and Harvey was recognized as a claimant to Irving's preeminence. Success brought immediate demands from Harvey's backers and creditors to restage *The Only Way* in New York, but commitments to British tour dates kept Harvey in the United Kingdom. Unable to secure John Martin Harvey's presence in the leading role, Daniel Frohman, in 1900, forced Harvey to lease the American rights to his play and to permit Frohman to cast Henry Miller in the part of Sidney Carton. Harvey was obliged to wait until 1902 to bring his own production on an American tour, and this venture proved so successful that *The Only Way* was frequently toured through the United States and Canada, remaining in Harvey's repertoire until his death in 1943. In 1926, Harvey appeared in a film version of *The Only Way*, directed by Herbert Wilcox for London Films.

What particularly links *The Only Way* to *Orphans of the Storm* are the dramatic prologue, the menacing character of Jacques-Forget-Not, the lengthy tribunal episode in the Conciergerie, and the play's final moments as Carton and Mimi, "the little seamstress," together step from a tumbrel and mount the steps of the guillotine. Griffith's prologue to *Orphans of the Storm* probably owes more to this drama than to *The Dead Heart* as *The Only Way* enacts an aristocratic crime and its long chain of consequences: the summoning of Dr. Manette to treat Defarge's sister, raped and fatally injured by a Darnay relative, Manette's lengthy imprisonment to assure his silence, and Defarge's commitment of the event to memory. Jacques-Forget-Not is recognizably Griffith's unsubtle reprise of Defarge with his long memory of aristocratic crime and his personal vendetta against one family which links de Vaudrey and Henriette in one confused recollection. The tribunal scene in *The Only Way* is the play's most elaborate, an opportunity for Harvey to shed the illusion of a drunken Englishman and to reach heights of persuasive oratory, employing rhetoric so powerful and so logically and emotively structured as to turn a hostile Paris mob against a court determined on a guilty verdict and almost immediate execution. On film, where Harvey displays the brilliance of this transformation, we may still witness what Griffith had in mind in the episode where Georges Danton speaks in defense of Henriette and de Vaudrey. As in *Orphans of the Storm*, where an ancient wrong recollected by Jacques-Forget-Not forestalls freedom for Henriette and de Vaudrey, a technicality found by Defarge prevents this freedom, and Carton must use the ruse of substituting himself for Darnay to save his client from the guillotine.

Finally, there is the legacy of Victorien Sardou's *Robespierre*, commissioned in 1898 by Irving for performance in Britain and America in 1899–1900. In Irving's most lengthy and elaborate tour, organized by the Theatrical Syndicate and reaching cities and even tank towns on the East Coast, the South, the Midwest, the north Midwest, and Canada, *Robespierre* was performed to sold-out houses. Given Griffith's developing interest in theatre, it is plausible to suppose that he saw *Robespierre* performed when, on February 2, 1900, it was given at Macauley's Theatre in Louisville, or that he witnessed a performance when his touring and Irving's intersected.

Griffith's borrowings from this drama were on a lesser scale but nevertheless made a significant addition to *Orphans of the Storm*. Typical of Irving's repertoire, Robespierre is both a villain and a hero, calculatingly manipulative and bloody to his adversaries, but, because this *Robespierre* is more fiction than fact, he was written with a tender, paternal, sexually vulnerable side. What Griffith extracted from this character, however, was Robespierre's narcissistic dandyism, emphasized with preening, lace-collar twitching and self-approving glances into the mirror. Until Sardou's play appeared, Robespierre had been characterized as cold, invulnerable to charm and flattery, driven solely by ideology and his perception of the nation's interest. From *Robespierre*, Griffith also took Robespierre's tampering with justice to satisfy his personal whims. The main antagonist to Henriette's freedom is Robespierre, and his covert courtroom signals, exchanged with Jacques-Forget-Not, leave no doubt that he wants dead a woman who rejected him and appeared to favor his rival Danton. Political rivalry is transformed into sexual jealousy. Above all, Griffith had found in *Robespierre* a huge play: huge in scope, huge in the size of cast and scenic effects demanded. A Joseph Byron photograph of this play reveals seventy-nine actors and supers onstage in the final tribunal scene.[20] Irving allegedly used a total of 235 supernumeraries, choristers, and dancers, the latter for a revolutionary fête which degenerated into a rowdy procession and riotous, discordant carmagnole dance.[21] Griffith's sure-handedness with crowds, his ability to use large movements and visible countercurrents, to place subtlety and gross action in the same sweeping episode, may have derived from *Robespierre* and other stage dramas which he not only knew as an actor, but also studied as a would-be dramatist, and admired as spectator.

America (1924)[22] required the same level of directorial imagination and skill as *Orphans* but faltered as a drama because too much was demanded of its subject. It could not, without loss to one element or the other, be both an episodic sweeping history and an intimate drama, although both national history and personal romance were attempted. *America* is distinctive in the Griffith canon because, although he was increasingly desperate for financing and for achievable projects, this film did not arise from his own initiative and preplanning. Will Hayes had noted the anti-bolshevism stance of *Orphans of the Storm* and, with the implied support of the Daughters of the American Revolution,[23] encouraged Griffith to undertake an epic film which would celebrate the American Revolution and the commonality of the "English" on both sides of the Atlantic. Griffith may have been initially pressed for an approach that would lend itself to wide-ranging subject matter that such a drama would require. His first impulse was to adapt Clyde Fitch's 1899 stage drama *Nathan Hale*, and he went so far as to investigate the film rights to Fitch's play and to contract Ivor Novello to play the title role. He later abandoned this plan and, in consequence, was obliged to pay Novello a substantial fee.[24] The *Nathan Hale* project shelved, he sought the services of the popular novelist Robert Chambers for a historical narrative that he might dramatize.[25] In the event, and despite Chambers's suggested screenplay, Griffith fell back on theatrical strategies—structures, characters, narrative conventions, realizations and tableaux—which he had used, first as a vaudeville sketch writer, revisiting his own *In Washington's Time* (1901), then as the author of his unperformed drama of the American Revolution titled *War* (1907), and later—and frequently—as the deviser-director of American Civil War dramas (1909–1912) which concluded with *The Birth of a Nation* (1915). *America*, thus, is a work largely dependent on earlier theatrical sources, but these sources are Griffith's own, and he adapted from familiar, if hackneyed, material. In some instances *America* fared better than the original Griffith stage dramas; at other times, notably his reworking of Civil War films and *The Birth of a Nation*, Griffith's work appears tired, repetitive, and skimpy.

Although intricate and convoluted in its application, the narrative scheme of *America* should appear familiar to those already acquainted with these theatrical sources. Griffith's film depicts the progress of the American Revolution, beginning with early instances of English injustice and oppression through to the outbreak of the war, to some significant skirmishes and battles, to attempts to bring in Native Americans against the rebelling colonists, and ends with a final pitched battle as experienced through the vicissitudes of a young couple (he a dispatch rider for Boston's Committee of Public Safety, she an English aristocrat uncertain whether her loyalties lie with the colonists and independence or with her Tory [Loyalist] English family). Between them—and like *Zelig* and *Forrest Gump* before there was either a *Zelig* or a *Forrest Gump*—they manage to be present at most of the significant and iconic events of the conflict. This narrative scheme is that of Griffith's *War*,[26] with the exception that the hero is not a bondsman but Griffith's dispatch rider, Paul Lawrence, now renamed Nathan

Holden, from In Washington's Time. As in War, there is an orgy, the second of two, in which the British officer, named and modeled on the historic figure of Walter Butler (played by Lionel Barrymore), attempts to rape the heroine (Carol Dempster). Rape, however, is averted at the last moment when one of the Native American tribal leaders insists on an immediate raid, and the offending officer dumps his swooning prey halfway up a hard, wooden staircase. Further, as this rape threatens, the pair of lovers are threatened with the same moral choice as the corresponding pair in War: rescue one beloved person or allow many to perish and a crucial mission to fail. As an intertitle explains, "Nathan [Neil Hamilton] must sacrifice either his country or his loved one."

Griffith's other dramatic source was a collective one: four-and-a-half decades of Civil War stage plays and his own Civil War films account for the movie's characterizations. As in these earlier dramas, loyalties to opposing causes divide formerly closely knit families. An intertitle, appearing as the rebellion begins, underlines the "parting of old friends." In America, these divisions fall within the heroine's family, her father loyal to the King, her brother joining with the rebels and dying in the fighting at Bunker Hill. Thus, this rupture between two related "English" cultures is represented by repeated intertitles and on-screen action, as a family quarrel which can be patched up and smoothed over. As in the pattern of Civil War plays, the heroine's allegiances swing with the conflict but tend to be focused more on personal and moral positions rather than political divisions. Captain Walter Butler, reprising the character of the Civil War play's standard villain, is depicted as loyal to neither Crown nor patriot causes but to his own vision of an American empire which he will dominate as "viceroy." Self-interest, sadistic leanings, and carnal appetites dictate his role.

In significant ways, America echoes The Clansman and The Birth of a Nation. Native Americans, freed by the British forces from their treaties, behave as Griffith's vengeful emancipated African Americans, attacking and looting white settlements. When the war ends with an "armistice," not the defeat of the British, there is, typically, an amnesty and reconciliation among the white population. Native Americans, much as African Americans in Civil War plays, are excluded from this narrative of national and international healing. The heroine's father, a reprise of The Birth of a Nation's Austin Stoneman, sides with the Crown and promises his daughter to the film's villain. Only when the villain's true character has emerged and he can be recognized as both disloyal and morally corrupt, is the father converted to the American cause. Finally, there is a last-reel Klan-like ride-to-the-rescue, as the hero leads a mounted detachment of Morgan's Rifles to relieve a besieged fort, where the heroine and her injured father face the villain's and the Native Americans' savage vengeance.

In one further way, *America* followed the pattern Griffith set in *War*. Whereas in *War*, Griffith had "realized" the paintings of Emanuel Gottlieb and Archibald Williams, in *America* he deliberately realized painted visions of American history. These images were widely known through cheap lithographs, most notably *Patrick Henry's Speech to the Virginia Legislature*, *The Signing of the Declaration of Independence*, *Cornwallis' Surrender at Yorktown*, and *George Washington Resigning His Commission*, all painted by John Trumbull between 1785 and 1787. Additionally, Griffith realized Henry Bruecker's kitsch icon, *The Prayer at Valley Forge* (1866), depicting George Washington kneeling in the snow.

Critics, writing disparagingly of *Sally of the Sawdust*, have cited, as the film's several obvious flaws, Griffith's unease with the *métier* of comedy, the quickly discernable limits of Carol Dempster as the ingénue Sally, and the unfortunately thwarted talent of Alfred Lunt as her romantic support.[27] These critics and Griffith biographers located the principal theatrical source of *Sally of the Sawdust* in the 1923 stage play *Poppy*, but none questioned the stage play's considerable weaknesses: an entertainment long on music, song, and dancing but altogether deficient in originality. *Poppy* lacks the kind of plot and characterization which would readily translate into a compelling film. Further, and typically, Griffith visited more than a single dramatic source for his material, electing to go back to the "circus waif" plays of the 1890s for mise-en-scène and characterization. *Poppy*, itself, was distinctly secondhand: an attempt to resurrect, and to render an American version of, a once-viable artifact from an earlier decade of musical comedy. In that respect—and also to the degree that it offered Griffith a subject for a modern comedy—it was a questionable choice.

In justification, Dorothy Donnelly, in 1923, and Griffith, two years later in 1925, may have been moved by the ethos of the "Twenties." Europe and America were recovering from postwar economic depression, high unemployment, a dearth of males of marriageable age (many having died in the First World War), and, more recently and more devastatingly, the great worldwide Spanish influenza pandemic of 1918–1919 which, through fear of contagion, had necessarily restricted theatregoing and other forms of public sociability. Re-creating *Poppy* from earlier material and following it with *Sally of the Sawdust* were, severally, gestures in refashioning a more opulent, more joyous, more innocent, and more democratic world than many had experienced for somewhat above a decade.

Poppy's immediate source, and the shadow behind *Sally of the Sawdust*, was the 1896 Gaiety Theatre (London) production of *The Circus Girl*, a musical play in two acts by James Tanner and Walter Palings, with music by Ivan Caryll and Lionel Monkton, and song lyrics by Adrian Ross and Harry Greenbank. Running for 494 performances in London, a second company reached Manhattan in 1897, where it gave 197 performances. *The Circus Girl* was, in many respects, typical of the Gaiety Theatre musical. It had *Girl* in its title (e.g., *A Gaiety Girl*, *The Shop Girl*, *The Runaway Girl*, *A Country Girl*, *The Earl and the Girl*, etc.) which focused attention on its fashionably attired female chorus and leading actresses. Gaiety musicals were also notable for the elaborateness and pictorial accuracy of their mise-en-scènes. Typically, *The Circus Girl*'s subject matter involved an ingénue—in this drama, an English tourist stranded in Paris and, coincidentally, a singer and dancer—who is initially despised and condescended to by other performers. A romance with another English performer further jeopardizes her status until it is discovered that he is a wealthy, titled aristocrat. However, before such discovery can be made, the girl and her suitor have fallen out—over misunderstandings of sincerity, the barrier of class, and strategies of coping with, or eliding, social disapproval—but are eventually reconciled. In Gaiety dramas, intermarriages between social classes were permissible and even desirable when money was a part of the adhesive. Gaiety musicals stopped briefly after 1903, when the theatre was demolished, but emerged in a second Gaiety and continued on a reduced scale, regularly arranging North American tours until 1939. Griffith certainly would have known Gaiety musicals through their New York engagements and their survival in regional light opera company and amateur repertoires.

Poppy was performed at the Apollo Theatre in Manhattan from early September in 1923 and would have come directly to Griffith's notice. At that date a resident in nearby Mamaroneck, Griffith, in every likelihood, attended more than one performance, viewing enough to have realized that its insubstantial "book" required substantial alteration to translate it into a film. As a stage musical, *Poppy*, a three-act drama by Owen King and Dorothy Donnelly (and not exclusively by Donnelly, as Griffith's opening title announces), with music by Stephen Jones and Arthur Samuels, enacts the reintegration of the orphaned Poppy (Sally's predecessor) into the polite society of Green Meadow through the unlikely agency of her foster father, "Professor" Eustace McGargle. McGargle, in this pre-Griffith version, is a former actor, now reduced to petty theft, forgery, and illegal gambling on street corners and at fêtes and fairs. Poppy wins the love and respect of the local rich juvenile. Marriage will follow. Poppy finds, if not a mother, then a grandmother and a relationship with McGargle, which still acknowledges his parental role. She puts her questionable past behind her. She wins respect and approval from the local community. Although *Poppy* is a comedy, it shares many similarities with Griffith's more serious efforts. To the degree that *Poppy* enacted the rehabilitation and social reintegration of its lowly heroine, it followed a path which had already appealed to Griffith. Donnelly's play may be described, without too much exaggeration, as *'Way Down East* in motley.

If *Poppy* presented Griffith with a degree of singing and dancing which were simply beyond reproduction in silent film and which, in any event, lay beyond the deplorably finite talents of Carol Dempster,[28] the stage production handed to Griffith, by way of compensation, W. C. Fields in the role of Professor McGargle. Fields, whose variety bill–matter identified him as "The Eccentric Tramp Juggler," had appeared in seven successive annual productions of the Broadway revue-spectacle *Follies* from 1915 through 1921. As a variety artist, he had taken part in comedy sketches, but, until *Poppy*, had not sustained a full-length dramatic role. Fields was most notable for his intentional juggling "accidents," "unintentionally" dropping a ball or a hat or a balancing stick, then abruptly recovering the errant prop, the hat kicked from the floor onto his head, the ball slammed to the floor only to flip into a coat pocket or back into the rotating circle of juggled objects, the fallen stick to rise and balance on his instep or elbow. Fields likewise juggled cigar boxes and, keeping three or more in the air, switched outer boxes from left to right or high to low, always maintaining a center box hovering directly in front of him. Fields would then throw all boxes into the air and, drawing tight an unseen elastic string, cause them all to land in a neat stack. Fragments of these beloved routines appear in two film episodes where Sally and McGargle appear onstage together, but Griffith subverted these moments, pushing Fields into the soft-focus background and foregrounding Dempster. Fortunately, video and the replay button allow savoring these brief traces of Fields's glory. *Poppy*'s script was loosely structured, giving Fields the character of a mendacious, cowardly, self-aggrandizing, and only occasionally principled rascal, but also providing narrative gaps into which Fields might insert these practiced juggling routines or moments of improvised comedy. When *Poppy* was performed elsewhere than Broadway, the role of McGargle was allocated to other variety artists, often those who played implausible homemade musical instruments. Fields's xylophone-playing in *Sally* is an echo of such alternative casting.

Although misusing Fields, Griffith made amends by altering the setting of *Poppy*—originally not so much a carnival (although it is called that) as a genteel fête patronized by the gentry, nouveau riche, and middle class of a village in Connecticut's commuter belt—to a more robust and demotic environment. Griffith, perhaps recalling that the Gaiety *Circus Girl* was praised for the gritty-yet-glittery realism of an entire act in the ring and for the variety and skill of the acts presented there, shifted *Sally* to a working circus—a one-ring "mud-show"—tank-towning through western Pennsylvania (i.e., the coal fields of West Virginia) with parades, caged lions, obedient elephants, tired voltige acts, and a sleazy midway where such grifters as McGargle and his gambling cohorts and adversaries congregate and prey upon each other. Only belatedly did Griffith revert to the local fête, but then used this setting to underline the shallowness and vast wealth of the community in which Sally is to settle. Griffith knew that these two worlds were set far apart.

Griffith also made substantial and improving alterations to Sally's plot: whereas Poppy's identity and her position as the local heiress were revealed by McGargle to the inhabitants of Green Meadow at the end of the first act, Griffith shifted his disclosure of Sally's identity to the latter moments of his film with a twofold effect. Suspense as to whether Sally will be reunited with her family is maintained, but, more importantly, the character of McGargle remains ambiguous. His paternal concern for Sally is undiminished, but his uncertainty whether or not to restore her to her family and his protracted willingness to use Sally as a means to escape those he has bilked encourage the audience to believe that the pair will depart Green Meadow with Sally none the wiser and her fortune unclaimed.

There remains a further clue to Griffith's attitude to his principal theatrical source in the film's incidental music. Some of Poppy's vocal numbers by Stephen Jones and Arthur Samuels were published in dance-band arrangements and piano reductions for domestic consumption. These arrangements enjoyed some popularity apart from the musical throughout the early 1920s, yet, in contrast to his usual practice of incorporating music from his theatrical sources, none of these tunes found their way into the finished film.[29] Griffith, perhaps more than slightly embarrassed by his choice of Poppy, chose to put some distance between his source and his finished film, changing title, names of characters, locales, and even plot. Poppy was consigned to history.

The bizarre Topsy and Eva (1927) marked Griffith's return to Hollywood. Since the filming of Scarlet Days (1919), out of tune with West Coast studios and indifferent to West Coast locales, he had worked in his own Mamaroneck studio, in the Famous Players-Lasky Paramount Studio on Long Island, in Florida, and, briefly, filmed in Europe. The need for work drove him west. Topsy and Eva[30] was his first commission.

Topsy and Eva arose from a theatrical template common to other film sources, a twenty-five-minute vaudeville sketch enlarged into a full-length stage play, and thence, and only latterly, into a motion picture. It was built around the byplay of two sisters, Vivian and Rosetta Duncan, who appeared in 1923 in a musical entertainment in which Vivian took the role of a sweet, innocent white child, and Rosetta, blacked-up, played an irrepressible African American hoyden. The act, dependent on audience preknowledge of stage versions of Uncle Tom's Cabin, depicted actions in which the two children, tormented by the slave master Simon Legree, finally bested him.[31] In 1924, their sketch was enlarged by Catherine Chisholm Cushing and opened in Chicago in January 1924, as a three-act play with a cast of twenty-two actors in speaking roles, a "Plantation Quartet," sixteen white female dancers, and seven "Pickaninnies"[32] performing twenty-eight musical and dance numbers.[33]

The impulse to make a film from this unpromising, unwieldy source may have arisen from the ignoble wishes of executives at United Artists and First National Pictures to create an inexpensive "spoiler" to take audiences from Universal's lavish *Uncle Tom's Cabin* (1928) currently being filmed under Harry Pollard's direction, with George Siegmann (Silas Lynch in *The Birth of a Nation*) as Legree.[34] Because there had been so little preplanning of *Topsy and Eva*, with several changes of scenario writers, the director Del Lord's ability to direct sight gags but incompetence in fashioning a coherent narrative, and production costs mounting to an unacceptable level,[35] Griffith was called in to rescue the project. He was claimed to have "shot quite a few additional scenes and recut the greater part of it . . . and improved it a rare degree,"[36] but the evidence of the finished film contradicts this optimistic assessment.

Griffith's improvements, which may have enhanced the overall coherence of the narrative, did little to make the film enjoyable or sufficiently brief so that audiences were left wanting more. He did nothing to mitigate the musical's innate racism. Despite excising Cushing's musical numbers, the finished film ran for a long eighty minutes. What remained of this botched effort was described by *Variety*'s critic "Ung":

> "Topsy and Eva" on the screen is nothing but a lot of burlesque gags and situations on the "Uncle Tom" story with a bit of drama and pathos here and there. What drama is in the picture that has any effect on a patron might be credited to D. W. Griffith, who was called in about 10 days before the picture got its initial showing to straighten things out. He no doubt did his best, but is probably not bragging about it.[37]

Griffith certainly did not brag about his role in *Topsy and Eva*. Indeed, even his biographers seem unaware that he was connected with the project, and he left no recorded thoughts about a venture which would, inevitably, raise questions of lingering or unabated racism.

"Ung" continued, now describing Del Lord's painful comedy:

> The story opens with miniature shots being shown on the screen of the stork racing the doctor to the home of the St. Clares and winning out in delivering Eva ahead of him. Two months later a black stork raises havoc by going through rain and lightning and after being driven away from the homes of colored folks, drops Topsy into a barrel. Then the incidents which

lead to the slave market where Uncle Tom and Topsy are sold to the St. Clare family. In the situation surrounding the sale Topsy has great opportunities for comedy . . . though in many instances the effects are a bit crude and grotesque . . . it is nothing pleasant to witness on the screen.

Much of the ensuing action was knockabout:

After the sale everything goes well at the St. Clare home until Legree comes to foreclose on Christmas eve. . . . Topsy . . . raises cain with Legree and makes a getaway. Shelby and Legree start to mix it, with the result that it is a great battle, with Topsy slugging the slaves, trying to help Legree. . . . Topsy makes one of those comedy getaways, grabs a saddle from his horse, throws it on a fence, riding down hill, chute-the-chute fashion, on it for long distance . . . with Legree and his bloodhounds on the trail. . . . They catch up with her after a time. . . . Eva is, of course, on her death bed, but when Topsy comes on the scene, comes to life. . . . Topsy gets alongside of Eva on the bed and every one then knows the story of "Topsy and Eva" as the Duncan girls tell it, which in no way should have any effect on the next "Uncle Tom" picture, which Universal will release.[38]

Hardly Griffith's finest hour.

For nearly twenty years, from 1908 until 1927, Griffith had thought in visual terms, composing and unfolding pictorial narratives. Motion pictures had demonstrated a powerful primacy to the visual image over the spoken or written word. Films, although mute, were given the means to convey explicit and complex and expressive meanings,[39] and words, when needed, were confined to intertitles which either contextualized episodes or supplied terse passages of dialogue. For all the absence of spoken dialogue, "silents" discoursed eloquently. There was no perceived deficit. That was to change abruptly. Already there had been experiments to add sound to the "silents." The Warners' *The Jazz Singer* was released in 1927 to the few theatres which could afford to invest in the successful, but expensive, Vitaphone sound system. Seeking means of sound film more immediately affordable to exhibitors, United Artists was trying out its own Movietone sound-on-film system. Thus, Griffith's next—and penultimate—theatrical film, *Lady of the Pavements* (1928), gave him a rickety bridge into sound motion pictures.

Such early sound films were not yet the films known to modern audiences. Dialogue was difficult to record without confining actors' movements to the immediate environment of a hidden microphone. Music, songs especially, could be recorded separately and synchronized with the performers' movements. Griffith's instructions, accordingly, were to make these musical interludes plausible and entertaining. His functions were consequently technical as well as dramatic, and he had to squeeze dramatic action into what would otherwise be a static conversation. He had a reputation as an artist to uphold, but he was now employed as a facilitator putting pictures to words and framing musical episodes.

Lady of the Pavements was intended by United Artists' producer Joseph Schenck to serve as a showcase for the singing and dancing talents of Lupe Velez, the "Mexican Spitfire." To that end, and with the further purpose of generating spin-off products—phonograph records and sheet music—Irving Berlin was commissioned to create musical numbers. Berlin's "Where Is the Song of Songs for Me?" is a memento of Schenck's wish. In addition to the scenario by Sam Taylor and Gerrit Lloyd, a "dialogue" author, George Scarborough, provided Griffith and his actors with a vocal script.[40] Griffith was newly compelled to think in words and sounds. Now the verbal text was about to assert its own claim to importance, if not yet to primacy.

Although its narrative was taken, allegedly, from a short story by Karl Gustav Vollmöller,[41] the plot was actually an inversion of a drama, Edward Bulwer-Lytton's *The Lady of Lyons* (1838), which Griffith had encountered numerous times as a spectator and touring actor. On three occasions during the period in which Griffith frequented Louisville's theatres, Otis Skinner had brought *The Lady of Lyons* to Macauley's. Although this play was subsequently dropped from Skinner's touring repertoire after 1896, to be replaced by another Bulwer-Lytton play, *Richelieu*, *The Lady of Lyons* remained popular with amateurs and lesser companies who took advantage of its potential to be performed by a small cast.

The Lady of Lyons; or, Love and Pride enacts the consequences of a pair of marriage proposals made to the socially aspiring Lyons beauty, Pauline Deschapelles, and scornfully rejected by her. Pauline snubs two wealthy suitors of her own bourgeois merchant class and insists that she will marry above her social rank. Humiliated by her haughty disdain and plotting an appropriate revenge, her suitors persuade a penurious young man, Claude Melnotte, to impersonate a gentleman of wealth and title. With the suitors' coaching and financial backing, Claude is to court and marry her before the hoax is exposed and she, in turn, is brought to despair. All goes to plan, but, contrary to expectations, Pauline and Claude fall in love. Rather than cause her to become the object of malicious jeers, Claude leaves to join Napoleon's army, expecting to be killed in battle. Instead, rather than dying, he returns triumphantly to Pauline a decorated general with wealth, titles, and estates.

Griffith and his writers modified Bulwer-Lytton's plot, reversing the genders of his protagonists so as to make Velez's the dominant role. Karl Arnim, an officer in the French army,[42] enters the apartment of his noble fiancée, the countess Diane des Granges, to find her in the arms of another man. Over her protests, Arnim breaks their engagement, declaring that he would "rather marry a lady of the streets"[43] than Diane. Stung and humiliated, Diane and the court chancellor seek revenge, bribing a louche cabaret singer, Madame Ninon (Velez), to impersonate a virginal, convent-educated innocent. After training Ninon—an intertitle describes it as "putting a little wild bird in a golden cage"[44]—Arnim and Ninon are introduced, and soon the pair are married. When the hoax is revealed, they separate but are soon reconciled.

Directing, but, with little latitude to improvise, Griffith moved the action swiftly, less concerned with character development than maintaining a coherent narrative. His handling of actors resembled the clear and necessarily perfunctory style he had brought, decades earlier, to Biograph costume dramas, where he had depicted cultures, distant in time and locale, that he had tacitly accepted but never interrogated or interpreted. Griffith was at his best when drawing on his experiences of combination melodrama, setting up the cabaret episodes so that Velez's songs and dances were effectively integrated and appeared, less the distinctive variety turns that they clearly were, than essential extensions of Ninon's world and character. His handling of the new medium of sound was effective. United Artists could offer its exhibitors the option of a *Lady of the Pavements* "Available Silent or with Sound Effects and Musical Synchronization."[45]

Had the D. W. Griffith Company not belatedly received a substantial tax refund in 1929, *The Struggle* would not have been shot, and Griffith would have been spared the painful embarrassment of having his final picture mocked by its audiences. According to Eileen Bowser,[46] Griffith's overpayment on the earnings of his 1920s films was used to underwrite what is a deliberate updating and modernizing of Charles Reade's *Drink*, the temperance melodrama that Griffith had partly restaged in his 1909 *A Drunkard's Reformation*.[47] Zola's *L'Assommoir* and Reade's *Drink* were taken seriously in 1879 and still had power to move audiences and to argue for sobriety in 1909, but, by 1929, these dramas were recognized as simplistic and naive. Addiction was not cured so easily or abruptly or permanently.

In choosing the drama of a sober, puritanical, working man who is led into drink and to a foolish criminal investment by an "adventuress" and who then, through continued drinking, jeopardizes both marriage and family, Griffith had seriously misread the zeitgeist of the late 1920s. The Volstead Act and Eighteenth Amendment, which had led to national Prohibition, were being defied and ignored.[48] Griffith himself was drinking continually and had no personal reasons to place faith in the redemptive powers of temperance melodrama.

What is even more unfathomable is that Griffith supposedly developed his screenplay with the collaboration of John Emerson and Anita Loos, both moderate drinkers themselves, and both sophisticated and attuned to contemporary problems. However, the Emersons had only recently separated. They no longer worked together.[49] Emerson may have discussed the film's structure with Griffith. Loos, admired for her sharp and pertinent dialogue, "contributed little to it except some polishing of someone else's [Griffith's?] dialogue."[50] When The Struggle was released, audiences expressed their disbelief in the narrative with inappropriate sniggers at the film's intimate moments. Distributed by United Artists, The Struggle was rereleased as a "laugh movie" under the title of another temperance melodrama, William Pratt's 1858 Ten Nights in a Barroom,[51] a play which had long been clumsily burlesqued as a "meller-dramer."

Griffith made no further films. He gave few interviews and made no promises to resume filmmaking or to work in the theatre. He was briefly married to his last leading actress, Evelyn Baldwin (Nan Wilson in The Struggle), but his heavy drinking placed limits on this relationship as it had on his directorial career. In 1935, the Motion Picture Academy of Arts and Sciences invited him to present an Academy Award for best acting and the following year awarded him an Oscar for his life's work, rather than for a designated film. He was recognized with an honorary lifetime membership in 1938 by the Directors Guild, and in 1953, its annual award for directorial excellence was named for him.[52] In 1935, Iris Barry, who joined the staff of the recently formed Museum of Modern Art, had the foresight to recognize the extent of Griffith's role in creating the dominant art of the twentieth century. In 1938, she began collecting his papers and, in 1940, organized the first Griffith retrospective with screenings of his films and Barry's own monograph celebrating Griffith's achievements.[53] Thus, Griffith became known for his films, but these astounding works have, until recently, been shorn of their connection with the theatre and have stood alone, as if there were neither antecedent nor contemporary sources worth exploring.

Griffith never turned his back on the theatre. Anita Loos, recalling her collaboration with Griffith, observed to Kevin Brownlow that she regarded Griffith as a poet and "that there was only one person on the Triangle lot who was really dedicated to motion pictures—and that was not D. W. Griffith, but Lillian Gish."[54] Griffith, said Loos, "was always longing to go away and write plays."[55] Although not writing plays, he continued to keep one foot in his theatrical past. The papers Iris Barry gathered from Griffith, his coworkers, and his family and admirers confirm his enduring interest in, and passion for, the theatre.

In 1945, three years before his death, perhaps still contemplating a comeback, Griffith brought to the Screen Writers Guild a ninety-page screenplay which he may have hoped to direct. This screenplay unveils a coda to Griffith's work: its title, *The Twilight Revellers*, the name of Griffith's first touring theatre company. Set in 1845, fifty years before he trouped Ohio River Valley villages with the original Twilight Revellers, Griffith disclosed his overall intent:

> Our story begins about a hundred years ago and concerns a little group of barnstormers, strolling players, and their adventures and hardships which they take in their stride. From Chicago, then a great promising city of two thousand people—down through the slave states—New Orleans—and on to an extraordinary adventure with the fierce, marauding Comanche Indians in the wilds of Texas. As we take our little group on their adventure, we will try to paint also a part of this young America.[56]

More a comic celebration of the actors' lives and their romantic entanglements than a bleak narrative of survival, Griffith's band of actors head south, chasing the forlorn hope of paying audiences at their next engagement. On their journey they endure every form of bad transport that nineteenth-century touring had to offer, from river rafts to ox carts, and runaway stagecoaches pursued by Comanche horsemen. Finding that a village theatre into which the company had been booked had burned to the ground, they perform tragedy and variety turns in a shed from which pigs have only recently been evicted and who make a sudden, noisy, and unwelcome return in mid–clog dance. They assist fugitive slaves to escape and, when arrested and brought to trial by Southern slavers, are defended by no less an attorney than Abraham Lincoln. They are attacked by Indians who, having looted their belongings and now disconcertingly attired in costumes for *Richard III*, still pursue the fleeing actors. The desperate actors nearly starve and share a Christmas meal of bologna and stale bread. These are *The Twilight Revellers*' large set-piece incidents. But holding these events and hardships together is an understanding and love of the theatrical company as a warm, variegated family of talented misfits, a recognition, too, that the theatre brought culture and color to a dreary, barren frontier, and, further, that the life of a performer had recognizable merit and a redeeming social value. In dramatizing slavery and slave hunters, Griffith continued to venture into the territory of race and racial injustice. His black fugitive slaves, barely characterized, held little interest for him. What mattered was to depict the heartlessness of the slavers, the white actors' sympathy for the victims, and Lincoln's concern and compassion for the runaways. Had he survived to cast and shoot his screenplay, *The Twilight Revellers* might have revealed his affection for his own theatrical beginnings, but in other respects there would have been little change. It was a film for and about white actors, white historico-political figures, and white villains.

If Griffith's racial politics remained inflexible and stationary, much else in his life had changed. While he had first entered the theatre as a curious, uncritical adolescent spectator, his subsequent experiences of the various Louisville commerical stages determined Griffith to be an actor—or, he had imagined, a playwright. He served an actor's apprenticeship in a series of small, insignificant, but active, profit-share theatre companies touring in widening orbits through the Ohio River basin. He learned about America's mobile theatrical business as he graduated to supporting roles in touring combination companies, venturing farther from home. He witnessed, in Louisville and on tour, large-scale productions with famous actor-managers on stages crowded with numerous supernumeraries artfully arranged and deployed about the stage and from them drew his first lessons in handling large casts and massive movement. He traveled widely and endured weeks of unemployment, sleeping rough, and hard manual labor, which tested his resolve to continue in the theatrical profession. By temperament sentimental, if not occasionally mawkish, and, with a sense of justice derived from literature and a taste for last-minute rescues derived from "ten-twent-thirt" melodramas, Griffith absorbed the mode, tropes, and conventions of melodrama. He acquired melodrama's dramatic strategies. It ran in his blood. Comedy gained barely a foothold.

Although he afterward spoke loftily about the rights of the working man and dramatized workers' unjust exploitation, their strikes, and battles with overweening and indifferent bosses, Griffith was remarkably fortunate (and forever silent) that opportunity came for him to enter vaudeville as a strikebreaker. Once in vaudeville, Griffith served as an actor and, latterly, an author of a successful dramatic sketch. He did not know his luck. Sketch writing taught him the craft of devising brief narratives.

He married and moved to New York to look for work. There, his career took another tack when he sold a play to James K. Hackett. Its subsequent rapid closure during its Washington tryout failed to dissuade him from a further attempt. Verbose and sprawling, *War* never found a producer, but it served as a quarry for later films. Two failures as a dramatist and the lack of acting work forced a desperate shift. He would have to try acting in films until something better came along.

Acting in Biograph films, Griffith was no more successful than he had been acting on the stage, but his arrival at Biograph helped him realize that narrative films were the way forward. Within weeks, Griffith discovered that his experience of the vaudeville dramatic sketch enabled him to devise short, lucid narrative films. From devising screenplays, he moved to directing. Even more than before, he learned to tell stories through action and to use the camera as a stage on which to inscribe movement. Within a year, he was the studio's leading artist, able to build his own corps of performers in the image of a theatrical repertory company, to hire professionally skilled actors, to take his actors on summer locations and to be among the first performers who discovered winter work in Hollywood. He led a stable team of artist-craftsmen who, under his guidance, developed and enlarged their skills—and the vocabularies of film-making. When he left Biograph for California, his team followed him across the continent.

Hampered by Biograph's conservative management and thwarted in his ambitions to devise longer films, Griffith struck out on his own, forming alliances and partnerships that allowed him to work on lesser films until he began work on *The Birth of a Nation*. Working from Thomas Dixon's *The Clansman* was a serious error in judgment, but it resulted in the largest and most provoca-tive film American audiences had experienced to date. From this point, Grif-fith, whether he worked in partnership from a shared studio or devised or adapted films on his own, was a known figure, setting an example of prodigious productivity to other directors and studios. As one of an international constel-lation of directors, Griffith joined the ranks of filmmakers who increasingly had the skills and confidence to take their subjects from the stage and to rival the stage in the excellence of their productions. Motion pictures began to attain a status equal to film in artistry and to emerge as a major American industry.

Griffith left behind a legacy of more than five hundred films. Some four hun-dred of these are brief one- and two-reelers shot for Biograph between 1908 and 1913. Some were derived from theatre—from plays Griffith knew or knew about. His numerous feature-length films, some of which—*Judith of Bethulia*, *The Birth of a Nation*, *Intolerance*, *Hearts of the World*, *Broken Blossoms*, *Way Down East*, *Orphans of the Storm*, and *Sally of the Sawdust*— are acknowledged screen classics, still screened today, still shown on television, still successfully marketed on video and DVD. Of these eight films, only three, *Intolerance*, *Hearts of the World*, and *Broken Blossoms* were devised without recourse to specific theatrical sources. His tastes in plays suitable for adaptation were conservative. The New Drama of Europe was not for him, and his preference remained for dramas—stage melo-dramas—which had been the mainstays of America's turn-of-the-century repertoire. *Intolerance*, not derived from a play, owes much of its spectacle to Griffith's discovery of modern stage dance and his determination to employ America's leading modern choreographer to reveal a new vocabulary of move-ment in his film.

Faced with critical rebuffs and public outcry over the overt racism of *The Birth of a Nation* and, a year later, encountering critical indifference for what was per-ceived as the vast and impressive, but emotionally cold, *Intolerance*, Griffith had threatened to leave filmmaking and to "return" to the theatre. The question arises: had Griffith ever left theatre or had theatre ever left him?

The evidence of *The Twilight Revellers*, or indeed, of any other of the numerous Griffith films taking their subjects or their techniques from the live stage, does not insist that Griffith was altogether dependent on the theatre. Nor does it in any way diminish his unique talent in shaping early motion pictures. It doesn't imply that the theatre should be assigned the full credit for the successes of Griffith's films. Indeed, issues of credit are irrelevant. Had he not come from the theatre, other factors might have contributed to Griffith's remarkable stature as an artist. He might have found another path to a similar destination. But that speculation seems unlikely. However, the evidence, such as it is, makes clear the profound role that the American theatre played in the development of this filmmaker. It makes evident that he stayed intricately and inextricably bound to the theatre all through his professional life, irrespective of the upward or downward arc of his career's trajectory.

And that evidence is beyond doubt. Griffith, at heart a man of the theatre— an actor, a vaudevillian, a dramatist before he became a filmmaker—used the resources of theatre to great purpose and to great ends. What had begun as an active and specific engagement with the stage, continued as a resource on which he drew. Experiences of the live theatre and its vast repertoire inevitably—constantly—seeped into his filmmaking. The theatre gave him subject matter and a broad range of character types. It introduced him to music and dance. It provided form and structure and techniques that readily translated from the live stage into film. Theatre gave him the start of his career and it fueled his numerous masterpieces and, finally, accompanied him into a sad terminal decline in self-imposed exile.

It was not altogether a one-way transaction. If theatre gave these elements to Griffith's films, Griffith, in return, gave back to the theatre. He recovered and revivified stage works which had drifted into obsolescence and neglect. Through Griffith's films, we can glimpse and admire and—crucially—enjoy a vital fin de siècle theatrical culture in which he had participated and, with few reservations, admired. It is through Griffith's films that we again engage with the vitality of the American stage of the nineteenth and early twentieth centuries. He is our lens onto that stage, even as his films require little justification for their artistic pedigrees and stand apart as wondrous, if sometimes disturbing, dramas.

Notes

INTRODUCTION

1. Henry Stephen Gordon, "The Real Story of *Intolerance*," p. 40.

2. Lillian Gish, *The Movies, Mr. Griffith, and Me*, p. 75.

3. Griffith's tendency to demonstrate how to perform is apparent in outtakes which, among other gestures and grimaces, show "his long face assum[ing] a kind of Grünewaldian twist of horror." Joyce Jesionowski, "*Judith of Bethulia* (Outtakes)," p. 129. Lillian Gish, among others, also mentions Griffith's instructing actors in gesture and facial expressions; see Gish, *The Movies, Mr. Griffith, and Me*, p. 99.

4. Gish, ibid., p. 92.

5. Lawrence Reamer, *New York Herald*, Sunday, September 11, 1921.

6. Vachel Lindsay, *The Art of the Moving Picture*, pp. 47–48.

7. From William A. Dunning (1857–1922), who, as Professor of History at Columbia University, wrote *Essays on the Civil War and Reconstruction* (1898) and *Reconstruction, Political and Economic, 1865–1877* (1907). These works influenced further American historians (John W. Burgess, E. Merton Coulter, James McPherson, and James F. Rhodes) predisposed to regarding Reconstruction as a political and social disaster and viewing African Americans as intellectually and socially inferior to white Americans.

8. Woodrow Wilson, *A History of the American People*.

9. Such as Bruce Catton, Alan Nevins, Shelby Foote.

10. These conflicts are fully described in J. Anthony Lukas, *Big Trouble*.

11. D. W. Griffith, *A Fool and a Girl*. See David Mayer, "A Fool and a Girl," pp. 1–70.

12. The U.S. Census Bureau's notional figure of slaves emancipated in former slaveholding states in 1865 is put between 395,000 and 400,000. An additional 50,000 free African Americans were estimated to live in Northern states.

13. Such a cast is present in Scott Marble's *The Great Train Robbery* (1896). More about this play and the film derived from it can be found in chap. 1.

14. "The color line must be drawn through the tenements to give the picture its proper shading. The landlord does the drawing, does it with an absence of pretense, a frankness of despotism that is nothing if not brutal. . . . Ever since the [Civil] war New York has been receiving the overflow of colored populations from the southern cities." Jacob A. Riis, *How the Other Half Lives*, p. 115.

15. The Chinese Exclusion Act, 1882, the first of several U.S. laws to exclude immigrants by nationality.

16. The Western Federation of Miners was organized in 1894 on an anti-Negro, antiforeigner platform. These caveats were later removed when, in 1897, the miners' union was brought into the American Federation of Labor. See Lukas, *Big Trouble*.

17. The Ku Klux Klan was formed in 1865, and by 1900, had formally disbanded. However, a second Klan was formed in Atlanta in 1915 and spread northward. Detractors of *The Birth of a Nation* claimed that the film spurred recruitment. Some Klan members made similar claims, but there is no quantitative evidence to support either claim. Paul Johnson, *A History of the American People*, pp. 551–553. In private correspondence, J. B. Kaufman refers to letters written to Griffith by the Ohio Klan offering the Klan's influence in bypassing that state's Censor Board's ban of *The Birth of a Nation*.

18. This phrase is not found in Justice Henry Billings Brown's majority decision, but its implication was soon read into interpretations of the court's ruling, and "separate but equal" public amenities (e.g., drinking fountains, swimming pools, etc.) and public transport (e.g., separate coaches or seating at the front and rear of buses) became an ugly norm of Southern life.

19. Geoffrey C. Ward, *Unforgiveable Blackness*. Jack Johnson, the Negro boxer, whose courage and perceived temerity to pursue and win the world heavyweight title, was hounded—with death threats—and prosecuted because of his sexual liaisons with white women, eventually spending three years in a federal prison, convicted of violating the Mann Act, although his partners were all of legal age and willing accomplices.

20. Small, private museums in American cities and in the public rooms of numerous saloons had regularly displayed the garments and artifacts of other cultures. From the Philadelphia Centennial Exposition (1876) to the World's Columbian Exposition (1893) in Chicago to the Louisiana Purchase Exposition (1904) in St. Louis, "native dwellings," regalia, and actual members of "exotic" cultures were on display in popular zones designated as the "foreign quarter." Buffalo Bill's Wild West and Congress of Rough Riders of the World, styled *The Drama of Civilization*, encouraged its patrons to visit "encampments" and to mingle with Native American and alien peoples engaged as "rough riders." See in particular, Rosemarie K. Bank, *Theatre Culture in America*; see also Bernth Lindfors, *Africans on Stage*.

21. David Mayer, "*Why Girls Leave Home*," pp. 575–593.

22. Richard Schickel, *D. W. Griffith and the Birth of Film*, pp. 55–60.

23. Ibid., pp. 55–60.

24. Kim Marra, *Strange Duets*, p. 38.

25. James S. Moy, *Marginal Sights*, pp. 23–47.

26. Arthur Edwin Krows, *Playwriting for Profit*, pp. 76–79. See chap. 5.

27. Roberta Pearson, *Eloquent Gestures*, pp. 18–51.

28. Ben Brewster and Lea Jacobs, *Theatre to Cinema*, pp. 18–56.

29. As late as 1925, Lillian Gish, appearing in Victor Sjöstrom's *The Scarlet Letter*, utilizes large, unnaturalistic gesture. There are numerous examples of screen actors, frequently commended for their restrained playing, who resort to the sort of histrionic gesticulations that Pearson, Brewster, and Jacobs have declared extinct.

30. Hedda Gabler's offstage piano playing, music indicated by Ibsen as an index to her character and mental states, provides an example of such diegetic music. In such

circumstances, incidental music became a distraction, and there was no call for further music from the pit.

31. Schickel, *D. W. Griffith and the Birth of Film*, p. 193.

32. Lillian Gish, describing the filming of her baby's death in *Way Down East* (1920), writes of the total silence accompanying that scene. Gish, *The Movies, Mr. Griffith, and Me*, p. 231. See chap. 7.

33. Sidney Sutherland, "Lillian Gish," p. 73.

34. David Mayer, "Learning to See in the Dark," pp. 92–114.

35. Such harmonies of performance are evident in Griffith's *A Romance of Happy Valley* (1918), a film which draws on such improbably paired theatrical sources as *The Old Homestead* and *The Bells*. Cf. Ben Brewster, "A Romance of Happy Valley," pp. 176–191.

36. Desirée J. Garcia, "Subversive Sounds," pp. 213–227.

37. These several linked developments are described at length in Charles Musser, *The Emergence of Cinema*, and Eileen Bowser, *The Transformation of Cinema*.

38. Fred Silva has gathered these opposing voices in *Focus on "The Birth of a Nation,"* pp. 22–103.

39. Denis Gifford, *Books and Plays in Films*.

40. A. Nicholas Vardac, *Stage to Screen*.

41. Ernest Bradlee Watson, *Sheridan to Robertson*; Ernest Reynolds, *Early Victorian Drama*; Allardyce Nicoll, *A History of English Drama* and *English Drama*.

42. George Rowell, *The Victorian Theatre*.

43. One of the ways to encounter—and counter—this skewed understanding and the subsequent politics of the naturalism/realism debate is to consult Thomas Postlewait, "From Melodrama to Realism," pp. 39–60.

44. William Archer, *The Old Drama and the New*.

THE MOBILE THEATRE

1. Gregory A. Waller, *Main Street Amusements*, pp. 3–95.

2. Cf. Alfred L. Bernheim, *The Business of the Theatre*.

3. There is no direct evidence which proves that Griffith saw *The Great Train Robbery* during its Louisville engagement, but a second-act coup de théâtre, exclusive to the play and omitted in the film—in which the hero's sister, Louise, arrives at the Never Shut Saloon in a packing case shipped from Kansas City—was later used by Griffith in his 1910 *The Banker's Daughters* as a means for a burglar to enter a banker's home, delivered in a trunk by Confederates posing as expressmen. This device did not originate with Marble and differently echoes previous hostile and sexually charged precedents (e.g., the Trojan horse, Iachimo in Shakespeare's *Cymbeline*, the tales of Boccaccio, Painter, and Scheherezade).

4. *New York Clipper*, undated cutting, probably from September, 1897, Harvard Theatre Collection.

5. This film was made by the theatrical producer William Brady, who was concurrently developing Lottie Blair Parker's *'Way Down East* on road trials. This fight was one

of the models for the final-act "fight in the sugar-shed" between David Bartlett and the villain, Lennox Sanderson. See chap. 7 on *Way Down East*.

6. Rosemarie K. Bank, "A Reconsideration," pp. 61–75.

7. *New York Clipper*, June 16, 1873. See also Peter A. Davis, "From Stock to Combination," pp. 1–9.

8. Frank Rahill, *The World of Melodrama*, p. 179.

9. Joseph Jefferson's *Rip Van Winkle* toured as this kind of combination. The *New York Clipper* uses the term from the late 1860s.

10. Three separate scripts of *The Great Train Robbery* survive, none of these in print. Two are held by the New York Public Library, both identified as the property of Davis and Keogh. One of these is a typescript, and the second, a mixture of manuscript and typescript headed by the notation "Cincinnati, 1897," is in all likelihood the tour manager's copy. This version includes floor plans, actors' designated onstage positions, and, on an attached handbill, substitutions to the second-act variety program as *The Great Train Robbery* company toured Ohio. A third text, designated "Working Copy," is the [earlier?] copyright text. Identical texts are held by the Library of Congress and New York Public Library. Numerous reviews of *The Great Train Robbery* are held by the Harvard Theatre Collection.

11. David Mayer and Helen Day-Mayer, "A Secondary Action," pp. 220–231. Numerous reviews of *The Great Train Robbery* are held by the Harvard Theatre Collection.

12. The wrestling bear, quite possibly, at times, an actor in a bearskin costume but at major engagements a genuine bear, is an obligatory element.

13. *The Great Train Robbery* proved so popular that it was frequently reissued. Some versions appeared—and survive—without any intertitles.

14. Although the identity of this "Tom" company remains unknown, Cooper Graham, a scholar formerly employed by the Library of Congress, has traced the company's sets to a scene-painter's studio in Battlecreek, Michigan. Private conversation, 1987.

15. For a full account of this film, see Musser, *The Emergence of Cinema*, pp. 242–245.

16. Relics of the combination continue into the sound era. A sound version of Charles T. Dazey's *In Old Kentucky*, a popular combination "sporting," (i.e., horse racing), melodrama from 1893 released by Twentieth Century Fox in 1935, replaces the original African American eccentric marching band, the "Woodlawn Whangdoodles," with monologues and bits of rope spinning from Will Rogers, and equally gratuitous interludes of tap dancing—one of these while setting a dining table—by Bill "Bojangles" Robinson.

17. Julius Cahn, *Julius Cahn's Official Theatrical Guide*.

18. Based on listings in the *Dramatic Mirror* and republished in *Theatre Magazine*, May 1903, p. iii.

19. Thomas L. Riis, *Just Before Jazz*, pp. 1–47.

20. Griffith's memory of Marlowe's performance of the virtuous, heroic, and defiant Parthenia may have inspired his decision to restage *Ingomar* for the Biograph camera (1908) and to cast his then-strongest actress, Florence Lawrence, in this role.

21. M. B. Leavitt, *Fifty Years in Theatrical Management*, p. 464.

22. Gertrude Lamson ("Nance O'Neil"), in whose company Griffith was to act between December 1904 and May 1906, was barred from Syndicate theatres until 1908, by which time the Syndicate was beginning to lose control of its hegemonic domination over American circuits and individual theatres.

23. In addition to Klaw and Erlanger, and the Frohman brothers, the Syndicate was headed by Alfred Hayman, who owned theatres in the Far West, J. Fred Zimmerman, who controlled theatres in the Philadelphia area, and Samuel Nixon.

24. Steven M. Archer, "E Pluribus Unum," p. 161.

25. Linda Williams, *Playing the Race Card*, pp. 77–87.

26. Young's adaptation of Lew Wallace's novel, mounted and toured by Klaw and Erlanger, was clandestinely pirated by the Kalem Company. Klaw and Erlanger brought a suit in the U.S. Federal District Court to the effect that this unauthorized adaptation debased the original product. The court's decision upheld Klaw and Erlanger's complaint, fined Kalem, and ordered all prints destroyed (fortunately, they were not). This decision remains the basis for U.S. intellectual property law. See my *Playing Out the Empire*.

27. Stephen Johnson, "Evaluating Early Film," pp. 101–122.

28. My mother, born in 1903, was reared in a family which considered vaudeville "low." On her twelfth birthday, she and a small party of friends were taken to Kansas City's Orpheum Theatre to see Sarah Bernhardt in a "sketch" which consisted of extracts from longer dramas in which she had previously toured.

29. Variants of these rural characters migrated to summer tent shows and circuit Chautauqua entertainments. Charlotte Canning (*The Most American Thing in America*, pp. 201–202) identifies "skits"—playlets—featuring a "Toby" and his girlfriend Suzy performed to middle-class families seeking wholesome diversions in temporary pastoral environment. These skits and the various monologues which appeared on the Chautauqua platforms were essentially verbal, in contrast to the less verbal, more active vaudeville sketch, and are unlikely to have influenced the shape or content of early films.

30. Brett Page, *Writing for Vaudeville*, pp. 4–6.

31. Henry Jenkins, *What Made Pistachio Nuts?*, pp. 59–95.

32. Robert C. Allen, "A Decided Sensation," pp. 77–79.

ACTOR AND PLAYWRIGHT

1. This common practice was described to me in 1958 by B. Iden Payne, who had spent his early years as an actor in touring melodrama companies.

2. Merritt's findings served Richard Schickel in his biography of Griffith. I, too, follow the Merritt chronology except when further information is available. See Russell Merritt, "Rescued from a Perilous Nest," pp. 2–30.

3. D. W. Griffith, *The Man Who Invented Hollywood*, p. 42.

4. Henry Stephen Gordon, "The Story of David Wark Griffith," p. 162. That Griffith's first-ever experience of American professional theatre should be a minstrel show in a southern theatre in which many of the participants were similarly blacked-up

necessarily invites further questions about how he perceived theatrical blackness and the degree to which he found it normal practice. How, in the light of Griffith's subsequent twelve films on the subject of the Civil War and the Reconstruction period, did stage traditions regarding racial stereotypes guide Griffith's hand? A partial answer is to be found both in Thomas Dixon's dialogue for *The Clansman* and in Griffith's intertitles in *The Birth of a Nation*. In both dramas, stage-Negro dialect is attached to characters of low station. Newly enfranchised African Americans (e.g., Gus) and old retainers who cling to their antebellum subservience converse with a white's clichéd rendering of stage "darky" speech, whereas a villainous mulatto lieutenant governor speaks with the same unaccented voice as the white characters. Thus dialect was, to some degree, a function and signifier of class and, to a further degree, a legacy from English-language stage melodrama in which characters of the lower orders spoke dialect and those at the drama's center spoke unaccented English.

5. The Grand Theatre, admission prices ten cents, twenty cents, and thirty cents.

6. Ellipsis is Griffith's.

7. Griffith, *The Man Who Invented Hollywood*, p. 43.

8. Restaged and filmed by Griffith at Biograph in March 1909.

9. William A. Brady, *Showman*, pp. 77–184. Brady describes how Corbett was versatile in both boxing and baseball. Brady managed to present Corbett in both sports.

10. Schickel, *D. W. Griffith and the Birth of Film*, pp. 47–48.

11. Cahn, *Julius Cahn's Official Theatrical Guide*, vol. 7, 1902–1903, p. 209.

12. Probably H. P. Grattan's *Faust, or, The Demon of Drachenfels* (1842).

13. Griffith, *The Man Who Invented Hollywood*,

14. Alan Dale was a pseudonym for Alfred J. Cohen, a popular critic who reviewed for Hearst's *New York Journal*. Tice L. Miller, "Alan Dale: The Hearst Critic," pp. 69–80. There is no evidence that "Dale," who wrote chiefly about the "legitimate theatre," reviewed vaudeville sketches. Griffith's claim for this review may be one of his fictions.

15. Gordon, "The Story of David Wark Griffith," p. 162.

16. Merritt, "Rescued from a Perilous Nest," pp. 2–30.

17. Dwight Tilton, *Miss Petticoats*.

18. I deduce Griffith's strikebreaking action from the circumstances of his opportune entry through Dodson's company. There was no other way for him to have come into Keith's main-circuit vaudeville except as someone who defied White Rat pickets. Russell Merritt, with whom I discussed this discovery, concurred with my judgment. Griffith's lifelong silence on this matter further confirms that he wished to keep the circumstances hidden.

19. *New York Dramatic Mirror*, November 10, 1900, p. 18.

20. Not the preferred, number 3, slot described by Brett Page.

21. *New York Dramatic Mirror*, August 10, 1901, p. 16.

22. Osterman is an interesting but shadowy figure in terms of the links between the legitimate theatre, vaudeville stage, and early film. Little is known of her career before 1902, apart from the fact that she toured in vaudeville with a one-woman sketch. In 1900

this act was filmed by Biograph as *The Art of Making Up*, but not released until 1902. Between 1901 and 1904, Osterman made an additional thirteen Biograph films all viewable as paper prints. She appeared in the title role in a three-part narrative, possibly an adapted vaudeville dramatic sketch, *The Unfaithful Wife*, shot at Biograph in July 1903, only weeks before she formed her *Miss Petticoats* company. Remarkably, Kathryn Osterman's appearances in film did not bring the stigma generally attached to legitimate and variety performers who—even briefly—left the live stage for film work. In 1904 Osterman returned to the legitimate stage, appearing in Broadway comedies and musicals. Still later, she appeared in films.

23. New York *Dramatic Mirror*, undated cutting (ca. January 1903) in the Harvard Theatre Collection.

24. New York *Dramatic Mirror*, December 13, 1902. See also Paul C. Spehr, *The Civil War in Motion Pictures*, no. 312, p. 40. For a full description of this film starring the actress Margaret May, see also Charles Musser, *Edison Motion Pictures*, pp. 302–304. Edison's vitascope, fifty feet long and running for just over a minute, was released in 1897 as *The Little Reb*.

25. Gwendolyn Waltz, "Embracing Technology," pp. 543–560.

26. Griffith, *The Man Who Invented Hollywood*, pp. 58–65.

27. Ibid., p. 59.

28. Ibid., p. 59.

29. "He began his career with Alexander Salvini and took leading parts in the stock company of James K. Hackett. He was leading man with J. E. Dodson, the English actor in Dodson's *Richelieu's Stratagem* in the Fifth Avenue Theatre in New York. Last spring he played the leading part of Kephren, the slave, at the Columbus Theatre, in which Miss Crawley of the Ben Greet Company, played Cleopatra." *Los Angeles Times*, February 26, 1905.

30. Ibid.

31. David Beasley, *McKee Rankin and the Heyday of the American Theater*, pp. 347–400.

32. Griffith remembered the title as *The Fool and the Girl* and on several occasions refers to it by this title. It was, however, produced as *A Fool and a Girl*, and the surviving typescript also bears this title.

33. Griffith, *The Man Who Invented Hollywood*, p. 69.

34. Griffith was to earn seventy-five dollars per week, Arvidson thirty-five dollars. Linda Arvidson, *When the Movies Were Young*, pp. 21–23.

35. Described in Griffith's first-act stage direction, "ALBERT enters. He is a very young unsophisticated youth, pale face, slender, very well dressed though a little old-fashioned, wears a soft hat. His hair, which should be parted on one side, and is very much longer than is fashionable at the present day, is full over the ears and at the back. He speaks with a very slight Southern accent, or none at all, merely a little softness in the voice very slight slurring of r's, 'Mysef,' instead of 'Myself,' a certain old-fashioned precision of speech, marking him different from that of the ordinary fairly educated man of the streets." D. W. Griffith, *A Fool and a Girl*, typescript, p. 3.

36. Arvidson, *When the Movies Were Young*, p. 21.

37. Schickel, *D. W. Griffith and the Birth of Film*, p. 70.

38. Ibid.

39. Ibid.

40. *New York Dramatic Mirror*, October 12, 1907.

41. David Mayer, "War," pp. 71–136.

42. The question, of course, is why such roles and such trajectories appealed to Griffith. A partial explanation may be found in the late-Victorian theatrical repertoire, where errant or damaged heroines, rejected by their families, reappeared cleansed and ready to enter marriage (if not already married offstage, between the acts). This pattern undeniably attracted Griffith and satisfied some inner need. However, there likely was a lesion in Griffith's psyche that led to his periodic restaging of this pattern of abuse, condemnation, expulsion, and reintegration. Nothing in his known early life offers a ready explanation.

GRIFFITH AT BIOGRAPH

1. Brian Coe, *The History of Movie Photography*, p. 89.

2. Sutherland, "Lillian Gish," p. 53.

3. Billy Bitzer, *Billy Bitzer: His Story*, p. 90. Steven Higgins identifies the film as Griffith's *The Cord of Life*, released on January 28, 1909.

4. Arvidson, *When the Movies Were Young*, p. 56.

5. Ibid., p. 94.

6. Bitzer, *Billy Bitzer: His Story*, pp. 63–64.

7. Ibid., p. 64.

8. Arvidson, *When the Movies Were Young*, p. 75.

9. Robert M. Henderson, *D. W. Griffith: His Life and Work*, p. 8.

10. Schickel, *D. W. Griffith and the Birth of Film*, p. 106.

11. Ibid., p. 63.

12. Gish, *The Movies, Mr. Griffith, and Me*, pp. 76–78.

13. Schickel, *D. W. Griffith and the Birth of Film*, p. 154.

14. The most vicious of attacks is to be found in *The Matinee Idol*, directed for Columbia Pictures in 1928 by Frank Capra. Here Belasco, played by Lionel Belmore and rechristened "Col. J. J. Bolivar," is characterized as an inept, cliché-ridden, befuddled director of a "ten-twent-thirt" repertory company performing for uncritical yokels in rural New Jersey. A good representation of this kind of theatre, *The Matinee Idol*, offers an excellent parody of Civil War melodrama—a hilarious pastiche of Bronson Howard's *Shenandoah* (1888), William Gillette's *Secret Service* (1897), and Augustus Thomas's *The Copperhead* (1918)—and most specifically caricatures Belasco's *The Heart of Maryland* (1895), long popular on rural circuits. Available on DVD.

15. Gish, *The Movies, Mr. Griffith, and Me*, p. 77.

16. Florence Lawrence, who had prior experience as a stage dancer, and Marion Leonard and Linda Arvidson, both of whom had stage experience as actors before coming to Biograph.

17. Arvidson, *When the Movies Were Young*, pp. 71–72.

18. The presence and work of the narrator or explicator or *bonimenteur* in early film theatres remains a matter of debate. Smaller nickelodeons might not have been able to afford a full-time narrator. In theatres catering to polyglot immigrant audiences, the English-speaking narrator might have been redundant, except for claims that immigrants learned the language of the host country by attending films and having them interpreted by the narrator. The best evidence for the use of the narrator is found in illustrations of men at lecterns speaking as film is projected.

19. Most notably in "True Americanism," *Forum Magazine*, April 1894; *American Ideals*, New York, 1897; *True Americanism* (pamphlet), New York (Ariel Booklets), 1903; and an address to the Knights of Columbus in New York City, October 12, 1915.

20. Steven Higgins, "A Fool's Revenge," pp. 36–38.

21. *Daily News*, June 4, 1879.

22. In 1891, 1895–1896, and 1903–1904.

23. Henry Byron Charles Stuart Lickfold, the actor known as H. B. Warner, who beginning as a stage actor, was to make 104 films—from silent to sound movies. H. B. starred as Jesus Christ in Cecil B. DeMille's *King of Kings*. He is seen occasionally in rescreenings of *Lost Horizon* and, every Christmas, as Mr. Gower, the druggist, in Frank Capra's *It's a Wonderful Life*.

24. *A Drunkard's Reformation* survives as a Paper Print (FLA 5347), deposited at the Library of Congress without connecting intertitles. Fortunately, the acting effectively conveys the full narrative.

25. *Biograph Bulletin*, no. 227, 1909.

26. Other examples of American and English temperance pieces drawn from Zola's *L'Assommoir* are described in John W. Frick, *Theatre, Culture and Temperance Reform*.

27. Amateur actors were shown various examples of how actors applied makeup. Charles Harrison, *Theatricals and Tableaux Vivants*, p. 26.

28. B'*gosh*, a contraction of "by gosh," was supposed to be a typical expression of rural New Englanders; *rubes*, a term taken from typical stage New Englanders' Old Testament names, e.g., Ruben, Seth, Josh, etc.

29. Bitzer, *Billy Bitzer: His Story*, p. 68.

30. Kelly R. Brown, *Florence Lawrence*, p. 36.

31. See my *Playing Out the Empire*, pp. 298–299. Kalen's *Ben-Hur* was not destroyed. The chariot race survives as a Paper Print (FLA 4991) in the Library of Congress, and the full film circulates in murky videos. The ownership of the film print is unknown.

32. *New York Evening World*, August 16, 1911.

33. Unnumbered *Biograph Bulletin*, May 23, 1910.

34. Yuri Tsivian, "Ramona," pp. 78–79.

35. Kemp R. Niver, *D. W. Griffith: His Biograph Films in Perspective*, pp. 130–131.

36. Charles Townsend, *The Golden Gulch, an original drama in three acts*. First performed at Tony Pastors, August 5, 1899, published New York, 1893.

37. Unnumbered *Biograph Bulletin*, October 10, 1910.

38. For Griffith's relationship with Hall and other Biograph scenarists, see chap. 4.

39. James McCloskey, *My Partner*, p. 63.

40. See Jacqueline Romeo, "Charles T. Parsloe"; James S. Moy, *Marginal Sights*; and Matthew Bernstein and Gaylyn Studlar, *Visions of the East*.

41. Schickel, *D. W. Griffith and the Birth of Film*, pp. 196–201.

42. For discussion of these Civil War dramas, see chap. 4.

43. J. B. Kaufman and David Mayer, "Judith of Bethulia," p. 135.

44. Ibid.

45. Schickel, *D. W. Griffith and the Birth of Film*, p. 188.

46. For a more thorough account of Griffith's brief tenure in the O'Neil-Rankin Company, see chap. 2.

47. J. B. Kaufman, "Judith of Bethulia: Producing the Little Epic," pp. 176–191.

48. This version (sold in the theatres as an interlinear translation, the text appearing in parallel columns in Italian and English) was identified as *Giacometti's Tragedy of Judith— a Scriptural Drama: As Represented by Madame Ristori and Her Dramatic Company.*

49. Hedda Gabler, Sudermann's Magda, the younger Dumas's Marguerite "Camille" Gautier, Giacometti's termagant Queen Elizabeth, Medea, and Lady Macbeth.

50. With her earnings, Nance O'Neil purchased a country estate at Tyngsboro, Massachusetts, but the title soon came into dispute. In 1910, while the case was still sub judice, O'Neil was obliged to sell this collection to meet legal costs. Later she won her suit, but Ristori's effects were not recoverable.

51. Griffith was with the O'Neil-Rankin Company in San Francisco in 1905 when they were touring *Judith of Bethulia*. According to Rankin's biographer (Beasley, *McKee Rankin and the Heyday of the American Theater*, pp. 384–385), Griffith understudied Rankin's character roles and appeared in them when Rankin was absent on company business. Nevertheless, Rankin did not appear in either production of *Judith*, and, although it is highly likely that Griffith acted small, unnamed roles in *Judith of Bethulia*, there is no direct evidence to support such speculation. However, Griffith did appear in Giacometti's *Queen Elizabeth* in O'Neil's company. Griffith, *The Man Who Invented Hollywood*, p. 62. Lionel Barrymore, married to McKee Rankin's daughter, Doris, was with O'Neil in 1903, when he appeared in a production of Maria Lovell's *Ingomar the Barbarian* in which O'Neil performed the role of Parthenia. Scott Simmon and David Mayer, "The Barbarian Ingomar," pp. 117–121. It was Rankin who, in 1910, brought the unemployed Barrymore to Biograph and introduced him to Griffith.

52. Normand's *Bondage* is held in the Royal Museum, Truro, Cornwall, and has been exhibited and cataloged in recent exhibitions of the British nude and the influence of the East on British painting. The theatrical technique of "realizing" paintings was not new to Griffith. His play *War* called for the realization of Emanuel Gottlieb Leutze's *Washington Crossing the Delaware* and Archibald Williams's *The Spirit of 1776*. He had realized two of Sir Luke Fildes's paintings, *The Doctor* and *Applicants to a Casual Ward*, in his Biograph films *Behind the Scenes* and *A Corner in Wheat*. He realized an illustrated sheet-music cover for the song "All Quiet on the Potomac" in the opening shot of *In Old Kentucky* (1909), and

he would go on to realize further iconic images for the duration of his career as an independent filmmaker.

53. Jesionowski, "Judith of Bethulia (Outtakes)," pp. 129–130.

54. Griffith's decision to cast Bambrick in this role will be discussed in chapter 6.

55. Boston *Globe*, March 25, 1904.

DRAMAS OF CIVIL WAR, ETHNICITY, AND RACE

1. One film to achieve this acclaim was Thomas Ince's five-reel *The Battle of Gettysburg* for the New York Motion Picture Company (1913). The film is now lost. For a synopsis and critical responses, see Frank Thompson, *Lost Films*, pp. 19–26.

2. This figure is based on advertisements and reviews in the *New York Clipper*, the *New York Dramatic Mirror*, and plays republished in modern anthologies.

3. Spehr, *The Civil War in Motion Pictures*. Spehr identifies 868 motion pictures on the subject of the Civil War. Of this total, 370 are fictional narratives of the war produced between 1897 and 1915.

4. Robert Lang, *The Birth of a Nation*, p. 29.

5. Rosemary L. Cullen, *The Civil War in American Drama*, pp. 17–24.

6. *The Mercury*, Saturday, November 12, 1864.

7. Jeffrey D. Mason, "*Shenandoah* (1899) and the Civil War," in *Melodrama and the Myth of America*, pp. 155–186. I am indebted to this chapter for its description of the veterans' amateur melodramas.

8. Williams, *Playing the Race Card*, pp. 26–29, 188–189, 225–226.

9. James Shapiro, *1599: A Year in the Life of William Shakespeare*, p. 336.

10. For a development of this point, see Michael Hammond, "'A Soul Stirring Appeal to Every Briton'," pp. 353–370.

11. It is generally held by Griffith scholars that Griffith intended that *His Trust* and *His Trust Fulfilled* were to be released as one complete film. Certainly, their filming over two days in November 1910, and the overall sequence of antebellum, wartime, and postbellum episodes performed by the same cast suggest a single dramatic work. However, their combined running times of thirty minutes is thought to have alarmed Biograph's executives who were fearful that films longer than a reel would not be purchased by exhibitors. Accordingly, the two *His Trust* films—publicized by two discrete *Biograph Bulletins*, the second describing *His Trust Fulfilled* as "a sequel to *His Trust*"—were released two days apart in January 1911.

12. Scott Simmon, "Mr. Griffith's Civil War, *The Birth of a Nation* and Family Honor," in *The Films of D. W. Griffith*, pp. 111–112.

13. Cooper C. Graham, Steven Higgins, Elaine Mancini, and João Luiz Vieira, *D. W. Griffith and the Biograph Company*. This reference lists Griffith's films and all personnel connected with Biograph films during Griffith's tenure.

14. Hall claimed credit—and may have received payment—for Griffith's 1910 *That Chink at Golden Gulch*, although the play from which it was drawn was the known work of

Charles Townsend. See chap. 3. Taylor, still freelancing scenarios, worked with Griffith into the 1920s.

15. *Biograph Bulletin* 187, quoted in Scott Simmon, "The Guerrilla," pp. 148–149.

16. Tom Gunning, "The Rose of Kentucky," pp. 105–108.

17. Griffith used the word in its then-positive connotation, the equivalent of "splendid" or "elegant."

18. Griffith, *The Man Who Invented Hollywood*, p. 19.

19. Ben Brewster, "In Old Kentucky," pp. 36–38.

20. Scott Simmon, "The Honor of His Family," pp. 167–170.

21. Kristin Thompson, "His Trust" and "His Trust Fulfilled," pp. 246–251.

22. In particular, Scott Simmon and Tom Gunning.

23. Steven Higgins, "In the Border States," pp. 94–96.

24. Tom Gunning, "The House with Closed Shutters," pp. 141–146.

25. Lee Grieveson, "The Fugitive," pp. 211–214.

26. Thompson, "His Trust," and "His Trust Fulfilled," pp. 246–251.

27. David Mayer, "Swords and Hearts," pp. 110–119.

28. Steven Higgins, "The Battle," pp. 139–141.

29. Joyce Jesionowski, "The Informer," pp. 180–186.

30. Ibid., p. 183.

31. *Fights of Nations*, Paper Print (FRA 5382) at Library of Congress. Kemp R. Niver, *Early Motion Pictures*, p. 103.

32. An anonymous pamphlet, *Miscegenation: The Theory of the Blending of the Races, Applied to the American White Man and Negro*, appeared in December 1863, approximately eleven months after Lincoln had signed the Emancipation Proclamation. It was erroneously presumed by many—politicians, journalists, and the public at large—that this widely circulated pamphlet, thought to be the work of abolitionists, supported Lincoln and the Republican Party's advocacy of black freedom and integration. It was later revealed that the pamphlet was a hoax, a dirty-trick stratagem, by Democrats opposed to emancipation. The authors were subsequently identified as George Wakeman and David Crowley.

33. Israel Zangwill, *The Melting Pot*, pp. 36–37.

34. Paul Spehr, "The Escape," pp. 12–17.

THE CLANSMAN AND THE BIRTH OF A NATION

1. Griffith, *The Man Who Invented Hollywood*, p. 97.

2. Gordon, "The Story of David Wark Griffith," p. 90.

3. Griffith, *The Man Who Invented Hollywood*, pp. 88–89.

4. Ibid., p. 89.

5. Information in this paragraph has been provided by film historian Luke McKernan, who has undertaken substantial research on the Kinemacolor enterprise and its American founder, Charles Urban. Private correspondence, February 2007.

6. As with so many details of Griffith's life, the terms under which he acquired film rights to *The Clansman* are unclear. The consensus is best expressed by Bowser ("The Birth

of a Nation," p. 60), who states that Dixon was paid $10,000. But Gish (*The Movies, Mr. Griffith, and Me*, p. 132) claimed that Dixon also received ten percent of the film's net earnings.

7. Gish, *The Movies, Mr. Griffith, and Me*, p. 132.

8. American Institute for Economic Research index.

9. Gish, *The Movies, Mr. Griffith, and Me*, p. 132.

10. Eric Foner, *Forever Free*, p. 168.

11. Ibid., p. 161.

12. Ibid., p. 147.

13. Krows, *Playwriting for Profit*, pp. 76–79. According to Krows, the "Price Formulation" was developed in Price's writings: an 1892 book titled *The Technique of the Drama*; in an undated bound pamphlet, *The Analysis of Play Construction and Dramatic Principle*; and a third, unfinished, work, *The Philosophy of Dramatic Principle and Method*, circulated in mimeographed installments.

14. No standard text for *The Clansman* exists because scripts were modified with use by each combination company as it played different regional venues. The Library of Congress holds a copyright script, the Harvard Theatre Collection holds a touring script and actors' "sides," the New York Public Library holds a single printed script (no others are known to exist), and the British Library holds another, but variant, copyright script for a performance which was never given in the United Kingdom.

15. Anthony Slide, *American Racist*, p. 53.

16. Thomas Dixon, *The Clansman*, act 2.

17. Four-page promotional flyer for *The Clansman*, n.d. The designation of *The Clansman* as a riposte to *Uncle Tom's Cabin* corresponds to the telegraphed urgings of Howard Herrick to his advance-publicity staff to promote *The Clansman* with this phrase. The Southern Amusement Company's loose-bound press book, stuffed with Herrick's telegraphed correspondence, is held at the Harry Ransom Humanities Research Center, Austin, Texas.

18. Thomas Dixon, "Why I Wrote *The Clansman*," *Theatre*, vol. 6, no. 59, January 1906, pp. 20–22.

19. Quoted in Slide, *American Racist*, p. 60.

20. Arthur Hornblow, editor's introduction to Dixon's essay, "Why I Wrote *The Clansman*," p. 20.

21. The term *nigger heaven* for segregated balconies was still in use in some American communities in the last decades of the twentieth century. Testimony of egg throwing, given by witnesses subpoenaed to attend the Walnut Street Theatre hearing, was reported in the Philadelphia press. See *Evening Bulletin*, May 8, 1906.

22. "Dixon Blames Politics," *Evening Bulletin*, Friday, October 26, 1906.

23. *Evening Bulletin*, May 8, 1906.

24. "Negroes Want 'Clansman' Barred from Stage," *Los Angeles Herald*, October 16, 1908.

25. Selwyn A. Stanhope, "The World's Master Picture Producer" in Fred Silva, *Focus on "The Birth of a Nation*," p. 60.

26. Foner, *Forever Free*, p. 160.

27. The episode in which the black-dominated South Carolina legislature, feet on desks and drinking from pocket flasks, is depicted by Griffith was almost certainly taken from the lithograph *Practical Illustration of the Virginia Constitution (so-called)*, reproduced in Foner, *Forever Free*, p. 153.

28. Ibid., p. 171.

29. Ibid., pp. 176–178.

30. Wilson, *A History of the American People*, p. 50.

31. This passage is an elaborate paraphrasing of Wilson, *History of the American People*, pp. 58–63.

32. Robert Lang, *The Birth of a Nation*, pp. 114–118.

33. Ibid., pp. 14–24.

34. Ibid., p. 155.

35. Silva, *Focus on The Birth of a Nation*, p. 74.

36. Ibid., p. 76.

37. A good selection of these press reviews and private statements have been gathered by Lang, *The Birth of a Nation*, pp. 159–189; and Silva, *Focus on "The Birth of a Nation,"* pp. 41–103.

ECLECTICISM AND EXPLORATION

1. D. W. Griffith, "The Rise and Fall of Free Speech in America," 1916.

2. *Motion Picture World*, September 11, 1915.

3. Tom Gunning, "Ghosts," pp. 116 117.

4. David Mayer, "Pillars of Society," pp. 118–120.

5. David Mayer, "Diane of the Follies," pp. 130–131.

6. David Mayer, "Macbeth," pp. 29–30.

7. *Variety*, October 6, 1916.

8. Gish, *The Movies, Mr. Griffith, and Me*, p. 167. By "ga-ga," Gish refers to baby talk and, by implication, to infantilized heroines, not to dementia. Gish had recently filmed *True Heart Susie* in which, as Susie, she had played an innocent country girl, in behavior much younger than her twenty-six years. She had previously made *Broken Blossoms* in which she played another innocent, but here an adolescent severely brutalized and finally murdered by her savage father. The young Anna Moore of *Way Down East* is another such heroine, but one who matures rapidly and painfully. Susie and the younger Anna might be justly labeled as "ga-ga," but Lucy, although naive and guileless, was one of Gish's major roles of which she was justly proud.

9. Russell Merritt, "The Griffith Third," p. 256.

10. Anita Loos, *Kiss Hollywood Good-bye*, p. 46.

11. Gish, *The Movies, Mr. Griffith, and Me*, p. 173.

12. *New York Times Film Reviews*, June 3, 1916.

13. Gary Carey, *Anita Loos*, p. 34.

14. Ibid., p. 285.

15. *New York Times Film Reviews*, June 3, 1916; *New York Times*, June 5, 1916.

16. Hesketh Pearson, *Beerbohm Tree*, pp. 224–225.

17. "Scared by Race on Stage," *New York Times*, January 28, 1906.

18. Cecil Raleigh and Henry Hamilton, *The Whip*.

19. Correspondence in the Shubert Archive, New York.

20. The sensation-episode culminates in an authentic train wreck. According to publicity noted by the American Film Institute, the wreck sequence was shot in Maryland at a cost exceeding $25,000.

21. Notably Gilbert Murray, Jane Harrison, F. M. Cornford, and Sir James Frazer.

22. Maurice Emmanuel, *The Antique Greek Dance*, 1916.

23. Ruth St. Denis, who was to figure so prominently in the making of *Intolerance*, made her public debut in a "Hindu temple" dance in New York in January 1906. Before that date, she had performed "oriental" dances at private recitals. "A Hindu Temple Dance," *New York Times*, January 28, 1906.

24. Unfortunately, no account of this dance survives.

25. Mark 6:21–29.

26. Niver, *Early Motion Pictures*, lists, among many others, Crissle Sheridan, Ameta, Arab Jewish dance, Annabel's flag dance, Little Lillian, Pompey's honey girl, Geisha dance, French acrobatic dance, Moki snake dance by Wolpi Indians, and Ella Lola Turkish dance, p. 420.

27. J. B. Kaufman, "Oil and Water," pp. 220–223.

28. Lindsay, *The Art of the Moving Picture*, p. 67.

29. Ibid.

30. Ann Daly, *Done into Dance*, pp. 172–174.

31. Ibid., p. 174.

32. Riis, *Just Before Jazz*, pp. 139–149.

33. Daly, *Done into Dance*, p. 112.

34. There are several claimants to this title. The most plausible was the Syrian dancer Farida Mazar Spyropoulos (c. 1871–?) who, under the stage name of "Fatima," performed on the Midway Plaisance's "A Street of Cairo" in 1893.

35. *Boston Transcript*, October 14, 1904.

36. *Boston Herald*, October 14, 1904.

37. Undated cutting, probably from the *New York Clipper*, refering to the production which had opened at Daly's Theatre on December 5, 1904. Harvard Theatre Collection.

38. Undated cutting, *San Francisco Examiner*, Harvard Theatre Collection.

39. Kendall, *Where She Danced*, p. 84.

40. Ibid., p. 139.

41. Ruth St. Denis's best-known solo "oriental" dance role.

42. Kendall, *Where She Danced*, p. 140.

43. Ibid., p. 142.

44. Gish, *The Movies, Mr. Griffith, and Me*, pp. 174–175.

45. Ibid., p. 170–171.

46. Bowser, *The Transformation of Cinema*, pp. 121–147.

47. Ibid., pp. 191–215.

48. Obituary in *Variety*, October 26, 1927.

49. Gish, *The Movies, Mr. Griffith, and Me*, p. 153.

50. J. B. Kaufman, "Distribution and Reception: *The Birth of a Nation*," vol. 8, p. 95.

51. *Moving Picture World*, October 9, 1915.

52. Gish, *The Movies, Mr. Griffith, and Me*, p. 179.

53. Ibid., p. 221. The accuracy of Gish's recollection may be questioned. By 1919, the use of tinted film stock was common. However, Griffith may have added tinting to a section of his prologue.

54. Annette Kellerman, a swimmer from New Zealand, achieved fame in 1905 when she thrice attempted to swim the English Channel. Although she failed, she began a career in vaudeville and motion pictures and appeared fully nude in the film *The Daughter of the Gods* (1916).

55. "Fred," *Variety*, July 25, 1919.

56. Steven M. Vallillo, "Broadway Reviews in the Teens and Twenties," pp. 25–34.

57. *Moving Picture World*, October 23, 1920.

58. *Moving Picture World*, October 30, 1920.

59. American Film Institute Catalog, *Way Down East*, 2002.

60. "Jolo," *Variety*, September 10, 1920.

WAY DOWN EAST

1. Gish misremembers. The villain Sanderson merely threatens to reveal her secret. The secret comes out when the village gossip, hearing about Anna's unwed motherhood at a sewing circle, carries the tale back to the Bartlett farm and informs the Squire.

2. Gish, *The Movies, Mr. Griffith, and Me*, pp. 229–230.

3. The title '*Way Down East*, spelled with an apostrophe, which, in New England dialect, replaced an elided A (Away), was used for the stage version and was again used for Joseph Grismer's 1900 novel on which Griffith drew for the film's structure. Griffith and his publicists were less consistent, sometimes dropping the apostrophe because the title was given—or reviewed—in quotation marks. Griffith's film was registered employing an apostrophe, but the apostrophe is missing from the main titles. For the sake of clarity, I have used the apostrophe for the play title, the absent apostrophe for the film.

4. Kevin Brownlow, "Griffith and the Gish Sisters," p. 18. Gish recognized the filmic value of the soft-focus lens technique employed by the portrait photographer "Sartov" (Henrik Sartov, 1885–1970) when she sat for him in 1918. She then introduced him to Griffith as they filmed *Broken Blossoms* (1918). Sartov made the close-up shots of Gish in that film, in *Hearts of the World* (1918), and again in *Way Down East*. Sartov later became a principal photographer for Greta Garbo and Marlene Dietrich. For Gish's collaboration with Griffith on the choice of plays, see chap. 8.

5. To some extent their failure to consult the script arises from the difficulty of finding copies. See n. 8, this chapter.

6. False titles were frequently devised to enable theatrical managers to advertise and perform unlicensed scripts and thus avoid paying royalties to the copyright holders. Although authors and legitimate managers were quick to sue if their properties were performed without license, abuse of copyright was not uncommon at the beginning of the twentieth century. W. L. Slout, *Theatre in a Tent*, p. 31, cites a 1901 touring production of 'Way Down East offered to circuit managers as *Pike County People*.

7. Harlowe R. Hoyt, *Town Hall Tonight*, p. 91. Slout, *Theatre in a Tent*, p. 74.

8. Although the play is occasionally mentioned by historians of the American stage, no one has studied 'Way Down East as a major drama of the American popular theatre. Tied up in copyright litigation after the release of a sound remake of *Way Down East* (1935), a satisfactory script has never been published. Once film versions of *Way Down East* were released, publication of the playscript was refused because ownership was in dispute. In 1944, Bennett Cerf and Van Cartmell attempted an anthology of outstanding American stage hits. Their intention to include Lottie Blair Parker's play was frustrated: "Some of the old scripts were harder to come by than we had anticipated. One play, 'Way Down East, which certainly merited inclusion, we were forced by legal complications to omit." Bennett Cerf and Van Cartmell, S.R.O., p. vii. The final version of four surviving variant texts exists chiefly in American and British copyright archives and in the Billy Rose Collection of the New York Public Library.

9. Brady, *Showman*, pp. 186–187.

10. In view of the eventual success of 'Way Down East, the Parkers' willingness to sell their share of this property so cheaply—which was alleged to have made millions for Brady and Grismer—appears naive or, at best, premature. However, in 1896, $10,000 was not an inconsequential sum and vastly exceeded what many professional dramatists earned for writing a touring hit. It was only in retrospect, when Lottie Blair Parker apparently derived no further benefit from the sale of the dramatic rights to Griffith and, later, to Fox Pictures, that their business sense was questioned. According to her obituary in the *New York Times* (January 6, 1937), Lottie Blair Parker told an unidentified interviewer in 1935 that she had received no further money for 'Way Down East, but Lillian Gish's biographer, Charles Affron, states that, above the purchase price paid by Griffith to Brady in 1919, Mrs. Parker was paid an additional $7,000 for non-English language rights (Charles Affron, *Lillian Gish*, p. 140). Knowing Lottie Blair Parker's worth as a dramatist encouraged the Parkers to strike out on their own. Harry Parker left Brady's theatrical agency to set up his own dramatic agency and, in 1901 successfully produced Lottie Blair Parker's *Under Southern Skies*, which, nine years after its New York premiere, had been toured by three theatrical companies giving a total of 5,171 performances, had been pirated by rural companies, had played 613 consecutive weeks in Pittsburgh, and had been seen by over four million people. Lottie Blair Parker subsequently wrote a successful novel, *Homespun*, based on rural New England life. In 1910, she adapted it for the stage. Although announced for the 1911 season, it was never produced.

11. Grismer's snowstorm device, Patent No. 635,043, granted October 17, 1899, was described in his application: "The object of the invention is to provide means for

producing a realistic snow-storm, in which the snow appears to be driven past the windows and doors by gusts of wind, as in heavy snow-gales, and is caused to drift and bank against the door-jamb, window-frames, and other places, thus simulating in the highest degree a violent snow-storm. To get this effect, I employ flakes of paper and combine them with pulverized or granular substances, preferably of greater specific gravity than the paper flakes—such, for instance, as salt, meal, or white sand." Grismer also sought a British patent, and a drawing of his device appears in Rees and Wilmore, British Theatrical Patents, p. 149. Twenty-one years later, Griffith, dissatisfied with the mild snowfall at his Mamaroneck, New York, studio, used a battery of Grismer's snow machines to create the nor'easter blizzard through which Anna and David travel to the icebound river.

12. Joseph R. Grismer, 'Way Down East, novelized version, 1900.

13. Having safely launched 'Way Down East, Grismer turned to other theatrical ventures, still occasionally working as an actor, but chiefly functioning as a play doctor and dramatist. Phoebe Davies died in 1912, and he subsequently remarried. Still involved in theatrical activities at the age of seventy-three, he was killed when struck by a New York streetcar. New York Times, March 4, 1922.

14. Arthur Hobson Quinn, A History of the American Drama, p. 245.

15. Daniel C. Gerould, American Melodrama, pp. 27–28.

16. 1 Kings 2:5 and 2:32.

17. Dramatic copyright in the United Kingdom was granted when a play was performed—either as a full performance or as a public reading—on a public stage before a paying audience. Parker's Annie Laurie, on application from the Aquarium Theatre, Great Yarmouth, Suffolk, England, was licensed on January 9, 1897 (Lord Chamberlain's Collection, add. mss. 53622c) and, according to The Stage, January 21, 1897, was given a full performance on January 15, 1897.

18. A "carpenter's" or "front-cloth" scene was played downstage, often before a painted backdrop, while a setting for the next act or scene was prepared upstage. As the setting sometimes required hammering or other noisy activity, carpenter's scenes used singing and orchestral sound to mask this unwanted clamor.

19. Brady, Showman, p. 188.

20. This is one of numerous versions of the popular American folk song "The prettiest gal I ever saw was sippin' cider through a straw." Griffith retained this song for the score of his film and introduces the refrain in an intertitle as Rube dances in the barn-dance sequence.

21. The sum of this inheritance is $8,000, enough for Anna to be described as a "rich" woman. This figure throws light on the $10,000 which Parker was paid by Brady for the rights to 'Way Down East.

22. Readers seeking a more contemporary counterpart may look to television's The Waltons or The Beverly Hillbillies.

23. Joseph Byron's technique is described in "Taking Scene Pictures: The Difficult Art of Getting Them by Flashlight," New York Tribune Illustrated Supplement, Sunday, October 25, 1903, pp. 7–8.

24. Byron's photographs, made at variously spaced intervals between 1896 and 1899, are useful evidence of how 'Way Down East developed on tour.

25. Joseph Arthur and Andrew Carpenter Wheeler ("Nym Crinkle"), Blue Jeans.

26. William Brady, "Drama in Homespun," credits the term b'gosh to the "raconteur" James L. Ford, who allegedly coined it to describe 'Way Down East, but the label was current before 1898.

27. Kevin Brownlow and David Gill, D. W. Griffith, Father of Film. Thames Television, 1993. This claim, no source identified, is also made by Affron, Lillian Gish, p. 140.

28. David Mayer and Helen Day-Mayer, "D. W. Griffith's Old Kentucky Home," pp. 21–35.

29. To realize—that is to make "real" reproducing a known image on stage—was common practice in the Victorian theatre. Mayer and Day-Mayer, ibid., p. 21.

30. Arthur Edwin Krows, Play Production in America, p. 127.

31. Brady, "Drama in Homespun," p. 100.

32. As Brady has placed these advertisements, it may well be that they are intended to paint a false picture of 'Way Down East's success and to induce further ticket sales from anxious patrons.

33. Named after a wooden theatre in New York City where, in 1890, the tachyscope, an early attempt at motion pictures, was demonstrated and subsequently used for masquerades and fraternal lodge conventions.

34. Charles N. Carton, 'Way Up East.

35. The Rev. L. M. Clement, quoted in an eight-page leaflet ca. 1898–1899. No denomination, church, or locale is provided.

36. Brady, Showman, p. 149.

37. Leavitt, Fifty Years in Theatrical Management, pp. 292–293.

38. Brady defended himself in the New York Dramatic Mirror: "Your Toronto correspondent is under a distinct misapprehension when he states that the company recently seen in his city 'does not play anywhere in places outside the category of one-night stands.' It played the Academy of Music, Baltimore, to $6,100 on the week last season while the piece was enjoying its phenomenal run at the New York Academy of Music. It played Paterson, N. J., in March last to $3,300 in three nights and a matinee, the third engagement of this same company in that city within one year. It played Lowell one week to $5,800, Portland [Maine], one week, to $5,500; Hartford, two nights and a matinee, to $3,000. Bridgeport yielded $3,250 for three nights and a matinee, and the company— the one recently in Toronto, mind you—returned inside of thirty days and played a Wednesday matinee and night—not a holiday—to $1,580. The Brockton and New Bedford receipts were $5,900, three nights in each town. Rochester gave this organization $5,000 on the week, and Albany and Troy $5,370 in a divided week. It is to return for a week in each city at the earnest request of the local managers.

"Another of the 'Way Down East companies—the one seen at the Academy of Music, New York—played Worcester two nights and a matinee last November to over $2,000.

Five weeks later the company criticised by your Toronto correspondent went there and played to $5,800 in a week.

"The profit last season of the company that played Toronto was over $40,000. Its expenses in round figures are $2,000 a week. It carries two carloads of scenery and properties, asking nothing of the local theatre but a clear stage from wall to wall. Its equipment includes six electric calciums, all the original snow storm effects, rustic furnishings, and amplified farm yard accessories. Its working staff includes three stage carpenters, two property men, and two electricians. Altogether there are twenty-nine people in the organization." New York Dramatic Mirror, November 24, 1900.

39. Unidentified cutting, dating between 1898 and 1901, in the Harvard Theatre Collection.

40. The New York Herald Tribune, January 7, 1937, places this information in a subhead. The entire headline reads "Mrs Parker, Author of 'Way Down East, Dies / Once an Actress, Her Drama Was One of Great Hits at Close of Last Century / Considered Daring Play / First to Have Character Say 'Baby' in Plain Language."

41. Grace Miller White, 'Way Down East, 1899. No publisher listed. A six-page summary of the play.

42. Two letters in the Shubert Collection from Griffith to Sam Shubert, June 9 and September 28, 1920, acknowledge Shubert's rights. Griffith's first letter books the Shuberts' Forty-fourth Street Theatre in Manhattan from August 16, 1920, for film exhibition. Shubert acknowledges, in turn, that he has no financial expectations, apart from theatre rental, from Griffith's film. This agreement obviously satisfied both parties because the fee Griffith paid on this occasion was a token one dollar.

43. Gish, The Movies, Mr. Griffith, and Me, p. 231.

44. Schickel, D. W. Griffith and the Birth of Film, pp. 436–438.

45. Ibid., pp. 429–433.

46. A two-dimensional tree shaped by a jigsaw.

47. Lottie Blair Parker, Annie Laurie, act 4, scene 2.

48. Robert Lang points to a narrative, developed through the intertitles in the Belden segment of this film, which underlines Anna's martyrdom and passion, and identifies her journey from Belden to Bartlett Farm as a Via Dolorosa along which Anna bears her cross of shame. Robert Lang, American Film Melodrama, pp. 70–71.

49. Gish, The Movies, Mr. Griffith, and Me, p. 231.

50. Performed by pit orchestras when the film was first shown, then recorded and added as a sound track in 1928.

TWILIGHT REVELS

1. Typically, Alexander Wolcott (unsigned) in the New York Times, September 4, 1920. Schickel, D. W. Griffith and the Birth of Film, pp. 440–441.

2. Russell Merritt, "Roadshows Put On the Ritz," pp. 93–95.

3. Schickel, D. W. Griffith and the Birth of Film, p. 480.

4. Ibid., p. 465.

5. Ibid., p. 475.

6. WAMPAS Baby Stars were groups of "modern" actresses selected annually by the Western Association of Motion Picture Advertisers. The acronym WAMPAS intentionally linked the actresses with the mythical predatory Wampus cat—half woman, half mountain lion—believed to inhabit America's southern states.

7. Schickel, *D. W. Griffith and the Birth of Film*, p. 461.

8. Ibid., p. 468.

9. I have exempted from this study Griffith's *The Sorrows of Satan*, shot in 1926 for Famous Players-Lasky. Although Marie Corelli's 1895 novel was adapted for the stage on at least four occasions in both Britain and America, Griffith appears to have worked entirely from the novel and to have avoided theatrical versions. Kristen Thompson, "The Sorrows of Satan," pp. 193–200.

10. Schickel, *D. W. Griffith and the Birth of Film*, p. 486.

11. Eileen Bowser, "Scarlet Days," pp. 50–53.

12. Simmon, *The Films of D. W. Griffith*, p. 12.

13. Brownlow, "Griffith and the Gish Sisters," p. 18.

14. Yuri Tsivian and David Mayer, "Orphans of the Storm," pp. 116–137.

15. Schickel, *D. W. Griffith and the Birth of Film*, p. 455.

16. Brownlow, "Griffith and the Gish Sisters," p. 18.

17. Ibid.

18. Unfortunately, only the first quarter of this film survives, held in the Library of Congress.

19. Tsivian and Mayer, "Orphans of the Storm," p. 136.

20. Laurence Irving, *Henry Irving: The Actor and His World*. The photograph appears opposite p. 641.

21. Alan Hughes, "The Lyceum Staff," p. 12.

22. Eileen Bowser, "America," pp. 162–165.

23. Schickel, *D. W. Griffith and the Birth of Film*, p. 486.

24. Ibid.

25. Ibid.

26. David Mayer, "War," pp. 71–136.

27. Schickel, *D. W. Griffith and the Birth of Film*, pp. 511–513.

28. Carol Dempster danced well, moved gracefully, and managed scenes where she was to be cheerfully coy, flattered, and poised on the verge of falling in love. Apart from her most successful Griffith film, *Isn't Life Wonderful*, where she took the dour role of a woman attempting to rebuild life in postwar Germany (1924), there was little emotional or intellectual depth visible in her characters.

29. Dr. Philip Carli, who reconstructed and recorded the piano sound track for the Kino video of *Sally of the Sawdust*, reports that not a trace of the Jones-Samuels score was used either by Louis Silver, who regularly scored for Griffith, or by James C. Bradford, who provided the more than ninety musical cues from Silver's orchestral score. Private letter to the author, 2005.

30. J. B. Kaufman, "Topsy and Eva," pp. 204–206.

31. John Sullivan, "Topsy and Eva Play Vaudeville."

32. It is unclear whether these were African American performers or blacked-up whites.

33. Program for The Selwyn Theatre, Chicago, October 12, 1924.

34. Kaufman, "Topsy and Eva," p. 205.

35. $300,000 according to "Ung" (who found this figure modest rather than extravagant). *Variety*, June 22, 1927.

36. Letter from Raymond Klune quoted in Simmon, *The Films of D. W. Griffith*, p. 127.

37. *Variety*, June 22, 1927.

38. Ibid.

39. Joyce Jesionowski, *Thinking in Pictures*.

40. Steven Higgins, "Lady of the Pavements," pp. 216–220.

41. Vollmöller was the author of the Max Reinhardt stage production *The Miracle* and the screenplay for *The Blue Angel*. The short story alleged to have been the source for *Lady of the Pavements* has been named but not located.

42. Played by William Boyd, later to become the cowboy star Hopalong Cassidy.

43. Anonymous, *Joseph M. Schenck Presents D. W. Griffith's Lady of the Pavements*, p. 7.

44. Ibid., p. 17.

45. Ibid., p. 31.

46. Eileen Bowser, "The Struggle," pp. 239–243.

47. See chap. 3 in this book.

48. Bowser, "The Struggle," p. 242.

49. Gary Carey, *Anita Loos*, p. 141.

50. Ibid.

51. Bowser, "The Struggle," p. 239.

52. In 1999, the Directors Guild of America "retired" the Griffith Award on the grounds that "the time is right to create a new ultimate honor for film directors that better reflects the sensibilities of our society at this time in our national history. . . . There is no question that D. W. Griffith was a brilliant pioneer filmmaker whose innovations as a visionary film artist led the way for generations of directors. However, it is also true that he helped foster intolerable racial stereotypes." DGA press release, December 14, 1999.

53. Iris Barry, *D. W. Griffith: American Film Master*.

54. Kevin Brownlow, *The Parade's Gone By*, pp. 104–105.

55. Ibid. Loos, in an interview to Brownlow, March 1964.

56. D. W. Griffith, *The Twilight Revellers*.

Playlist

Plays are listed by title, followed by author(s), and date of first known performance and, when imported from abroad, first recorded American performance. Some of the productions, which Griffith may have witnessed, may never have been performed in major cities and existed as road companies only. The dates given in such circumstances are occasions when Griffith may have seen them on the road.

PLAYS AND ENTERTAINMENTS
WHICH GRIFFITH MAY HAVE SEEN,
1894–1907

Al G. Field Minstrels. Macauley's, 1894.

Alabama. Augustus Thomas, 1891.

The Banker's Daughter. Bronson Howard, 1878.

Ben-Hur. William Young, 1899.

Blue Jeans. Joseph Arthur, 1891.

The Carpetbagger. Opie Read and Frank Pixley, 1898.

Chris and Lena. Pete Baker, 1894.

The Clansman. Thomas Dixon Jr., 1906.

Claudian. W. G. Wills and Henry Herman. U.K., 1882; U.S., 1886. Source for The Slave.

The Danger Signal. Henry C. DeMille, 1896.

The Dead Heart. Watts Phillips, U.K., 1859; U.S., 1871. Source for Orphans of the Storm.

A Fair Rebel. Harry P. Mawson, 1891. Source for A Fair Rebel.

The Fast Mail. Lincoln J. Carter, 1890.

Forbidden Fruit. Dion Boucicault, 1876.

Gentleman Jack. Charles T. Vincent & William Brady, 1892.

The Great Train Robbery. Scott Marble, 1896. Source for The Great Train Robbery.

Honest Hearts and Willing Hands. Duncan Harrison, 1890.

Ingomar the Barbarian. Maria Lovell's adaptation, 1851, from Friedrich Halm's Der Sohn der Wildniss, 1842. Source for The Barbarian Ingomar.

In Mizzoura. Augustus Thomas, 1893.

A Kentucky Colonel. Opie Read, 1892.

The Lady of Lyons. Edward Bulwer-Lytton, 1838. Source for Lady of the Pavements.

The Lyons Mail. Charles Reade, U.K. (as The Courier of Lyons), 1854; U.S., 1878. Source for Orphans of the Storm.

The Middleman. Henry Arthur Jones, U.K., 1889; U.S., 1892.

A Midnight Alarm. A. Y. Pearson, 1892.

Miss Helyett. David Belasco, 1891.

A Naval Cadet. Charles Vincent, 1897.

The New South. Joseph R. Grismer and Clay M. Greene, 1893.

Old Homestead. Denman Thompson: initially Joshua Witcomb, a variety sketch, 1875; revised in 1876 under that title as a full-length play; again revised as The Old Homestead, 1885.

The Only Way. Freeman Wills and Frederick Langbridge, U.K., 1898–1899; U.S., 1899. Source for Orphans of the Storm.

Primrose and West's Minstrels. Macauley's, 1896.

Rip Van Winkle. Dion Boucicault, 1870. Source for Rip Van Winkle.

Romeo and Juliet. William Shakespeare. Griffith's first experience of professional theatre. In repertoire with Twelfth Night, As You Like It, Henry IV, Ingomar the Barbarian, The Hunchback, Pygmalion and Galatea. Julia Marlowe and Robert Taber, Macauley's, 1893(?).

Sam'l of Posen. George H. Jessop, 1881. Source for Old Isaacs the Pawnbroker and Romance of a Jewess.

Shenandoah. Bronson Howard, 1888.

A Southern Gentleman. Clay Clement, 1897.

The Stowaway. Tom Craven, U.K., 1884; U.S., 1888.

The Two Orphans. Adapted by N. Hart Jackson, 1874, from Les Deux Orphelines by Eugene Corman and Adolphe D'Ennery, 1874. Source for Orphans of the Storm.

Uncle Tom's Cabin. Numerous adaptations; the principal ones by George Aiken, 1859, 1869, and 1876. Source for Uncle Tom's Cabin and Topsy and Eva.

'Way Down East. Lottie Blair Parker (with Joseph R. Grismer), 1898. Source for Way Down East.

The Wicklow Postman. Mark Price, 1894.

PLAYS AND ENTERTAINMENTS IN WHICH GRIFFITH APPEARED AS AN ACTOR OR MAY HAVE SEEN WHILE TOURING, 1895–1907

DWG** indicates plays in which Griffith is known to have performed.

All the Comforts of Home. William Gillette, 1890. DWG**

The Arabian Nights. Sydney Grundy, U.K., 1887; U.S., 1888. DWG**

Bedford's Hope. Lincoln J. Carter, 1906.

Children of the Ghetto. Israel Zangwell, 1899.

Chimmie Fadden. Augustus Thomas, adapted from E. W. Townsend's short stories, 1896.

Cleopatra. Émile Moreau and Victorien Sardou, France and U.S., 1890.

Damon and Pythias. John Banim and Richard L. Sheil, U.K., 1821; U.S., ca. 1825. DWG**

East Lynne. John Oxenford, U.K., 1866; U.S., 1869. DWG**

Elizabeth, Queen of England. Paolo Giacometti, Italy, 1866; U.S. 1866, 1905. DWG**

Faust. An unidentified version, possibly Frank Burnand's burlesque Faust and Marguerite, U.K., 1864; U.S. ca. 1870. DWG**

Fedora. Victorien Sardou, France, 1882; U.S., 1883. DWG**

The Fires of St. John. Hermann Sudermann, Germany, 1900; U.S., 1904. DWG**

A Fool and a Girl. D. W. Griffith, 1906–1907. Griffith's only performed play.

Gismonda. Victorien Sardou, France, 1894; U.S., 1894.

Giudetta. Paolo Giacometti, Italy, 1863; U.S., 1866. Source for Judith of Bethulia (play and film). DWG**(?)

The Golden Gulch. Charles Townsend, 1889. Source for That Chink at Golden Gulch.

Hedda Gabler. Henrik Ibsen, Germany, 1890; U.S., 1892. DWG**

The Holy City. Thomas W. Broadhurst and Clarence Bennett, 1904. San Francisco passion play. DWG**

How London Lives/London Life. Martyn Field and Arthur Shirley, U.K., 1897; U.S., 1899. DWG**

In Old Kentucky. Charles T. Dazey, 1893.

In Washington's Time. D. W. Griffith, vaudeville sketch, 1901. Source for *War and America.* DWG★★

The Jewess. William Moncrieff, U.K., 1835; U.S., 1905, adapted by McKee Rankin. DWG★★

Jim the Penman. Sir Charles Young, U.K., 1886; U.S. 1886.

Judith of Bethulia. Paolo Giacometti and Thomas Bailey Aldrich, 1904. Source for *Judith of Bethulia.* DWG★★(?)

Lady Windermere's Fan. Oscar Wilde, U.K., 1892; U.S., 1893. DWG★★

The Lights o' London. George R. Sims, U.K., 1881; U.S., 1881. DWG★★

Little Lord Fauntleroy. E. V. Seebohm, adapted from Frances Hodgson Burnett, U.K., 1888; U.S., 1888. DWG★★

The Lost Paradise. Henry C. DeMille, 1891. Adapted from *Das Velorene Paradies* by Ludwig Fulda. DWG★★

Madame Butterfly. David Belasco, 1900.

Magda. Hermann Sudermann, Germany, 1895; U.S., 1904. DWG★★

The Melting Pot. Israel Zangwell, 1909.

Miss Petticoats. Dwight Tilton (pseudonym for George Tilton Richardson and Wilder Dwight Quint), 1903. Full-length play and vaudeville sketch. DWG★★

Monna Vanna. Maurice Maeterlinck, France, 1902; U.S., 1905. DWG★★

Moths. Henry Hamilton, adapted from Ouida [Marie Louise de la Ramée], U.K., 1882; U.S., 1883. DWG★★

Myrtle Ferns. Joseph Clifton, 1889. DWG★★

New York Day by Day. George R. Sims, 1889. Adapted from Sims's *London Day by Day.* DWG★★

The Nigger. Edward Sheldon, 1909.

Oliver Twist. Nance O'Neil, adapted from Charles Dickens's novel, ca. 1904. DWG★★

The One Woman. Thomas Dixon Jr., Griffith and Avidson cast, but then released, 1907.

Our American Cousin. Tom Taylor, U.S., 1858; U.K., 1861.

Pygmalion and Galatea. William S. Gilbert, U.K., 1871; U.S., 1872. DWG★★

Ramona. Johnstone Jones and Virginia Calhoun, adapted from Helen Hunt Jackson, 1905. DWG★★

The Red Cockade. Anonymous, ca. 1899. DWG★★

Richard III. William Shakespeare, 1898. DWG★★

Richelieu's Stratagem. J. E. Dodson, 1900–1901, adapted from Edward Rose, *Under the Red Robe,* U.K., 1896. DWG★★

Robespierre. Victorien Sardou, translated by Laurence Irving, 1899.

Rosmersholm. Henrik Ibsen, Germany, 1886; U.S., 1904. DWG★★

The Silver King. Henry Herman and Henry Arthur Jones, U.K., 1882; U.S., 1883. DWG★★

The Squaw Man. Edwin Milton Royle, 1905.

Strongheart. William C. de Mille, 1905.

Theodora. Victorien Sardou, France, 1882; U.S., 1892. DWG★★

La Tosca. Victorien Sardou, France, 1887; U.S., 1890. DWG★★

Trilby. Paul M. Potter, 1895. DWG★★

War. D. W. Griffith, unproduced play, 1907. Source for *America.*

The Wife. David Belasco and Henry C. DeMille, 1887. DWG★★

Winchester. Edward McWade, 1901. Source for *Swords and Hearts.* DWG★★

PLAYS AND ENTERTAINMENTS
WHICH GRIFFITH ADAPTED
WHILE EMPLOYED AT BIOGRAPH,
1908–1913

Each play's data is followed by the title of
the Griffith film for which the play
served as a source.

The Auctioneer. Lee Arthur, Charles Klein,
and covertly, David Belasco, 1901; and
an older play, George H. Jessop's
Sam'l of Posen, 1881. Sources for *Old
Isaacs the Pawnbroker* and *The Romance of
a Jewess.*

Claudian. See above.

Darkest Russia. H. Grattan Donnelly, 1894.
Source for *Professional Jealousy.*

Drink. Charles Reade, adapted from
Emile Zola's *L' Assommoir,* France,
1878; U.K., 1879; U.S., 1879. Source
for *A Drunkard's Reformation* and *The
Struggle.*

The Fool's Revenge. Tom Taylor, from Victor
Hugo's *Le Roi s'amuse,* France, 1832;
U.K., 1859; U.S., 1870. Source for *A
Fool's Revenge.*

Humanity. John Lawson, U.S., 1896; U.K.,
1897. Source for *Money Mad.*

Ingomar the Barbarian. See above.

Reform. Anonymous, n.d. Police court
burlesque sketch. Source for *Monday
Morning in a Coney Island Police Court.*

Sam'l of Posen. See above.

Winchester. See above.

PLAYS AND ENTERTAINMENTS
WHICH GRIFFITH ADAPTED AS AN
INDEPENDENT DIRECTOR-
PRODUCER

Where not previously indicated above,
each play's data is followed by the
title of the Griffith film for which the
play served as a source.

Annie Laurie. Lottie Blair Parker, 1897. The
first version of *'Way Down East.*

Dance events; especially Gertrude
Hoffman's re-creation of the *ballets
russes,* 1910. Sources for *Oil and Water,
Judith of Bethulia, Intolerance, Fall of
Babylon,* and intermedial "prologues."

The Dead Heart. See above.

Drink. See above.

The Escape. Paul Armstrong, 1913. Source
for *The Escape.*

Ghosts. Henrik Ibsen, Germany, 1881;
U.S., 1882 (in Norwegian); U.S., 1927
(in English). Source for *Ghosts.*

In Washington's Time. See above.

Lady of Lyons. See above.

The Lyons Mail (The Courier of Lyons). See
above.

Macbeth. William Shakespeare. Source for
Macbeth.

Mrs. Warren's Profession. George Bernard
Shaw, U.K., 1894; U.S., 1905. Source
for *Scarlet Days.*

The Only Way. See above.

The Pillars of Society. Henrik Ibsen,
Germany, 1877; U.S., 1904. Source for
The Pillars of Society.

Poppy. Owen King and Dorothy Donnelly,
1922. Source for *Sally of the Sawdust.*

Robespierre. See above.

Trelawny of the Wells. Arthur Wing Pinero,
U.K., 1898; U.S., 1898. Source for
Diane of the Follies.

The Two Orphans. See above.

Uncle Tom's Cabin. See above.

War. See above.

'Way Down East. See above.

The Whip. Arthur Collins and Cecil
Raleigh, U.K., 1909; U.S., 1910.
Source for *A Beast at Bay, The Mother
and the Law,* and *Intolerance.*

Filmography

Each film is listed by title, followed by director, author (if known), studio, release date (as opposed to production dates), duration (sometimes given in linear feet, sometimes in number of reels, sometimes in running time (at 16 fps), theatrical source, and video and/or DVD (when the film is available in these formats from commercial sources). Also listed, variously, are the names of actors (cited in brackets) who may have influenced Griffith and his films.

FILMS WHICH GRIFFITH MIGHT
HAVE SEEN, 1896–1915

"The American Biograph" depicting, in turn: *McKinley at Canton, Niagara Falls, Herald Square Fire Department,* Joseph Jefferson's *Rip Van Winkle, Trilby and Little Billee, Beach at Atlantic City, Stable on Fire, Niagara Upper Rapids, New York Boulevard,* and the *Empire State Express. Uncle Josh at the Moving-Picture Show.* Edison, Macauley's Theatre, Louisville, 1897, approximately 25 minutes.

The Art of Making Up. Billy Bitzer, director, [Kathryn Osterman], Biograph, 1900, 28 feet. No given source.

La Caduta di Troia (The Fall of Troy). Giovanni Pastrone, director, Oreste Mantasi, script, Itala Film, 1911, 33 minutes. No given source.

Elizabeth, Queen of England. Henri Desfontaines, director, [Sarah Bernhardt and Jean Mounet-Sully], Famous Players, 1912, 44 minutes.

Sources: Émile Moreau, *Elisabeth, Reine d'Angleterre.*

Fights of Nations. Billy Bitzer, director, Biograph, 1907, 308 feet. Source: vaudeville stage acts.

The Great Train Robbery. Edwin S. Porter, director, Edison Manufacturing Co., 1903, 302 feet. Source: Scott Marble, *The Great Train Robbery.* Video and DVD.

Quo Vadis? A Narrative in the Time of Nero. Enrico Guazzoni, director, Guazzoni, 1912, 9 reels (in U.S. version). Sources: *Quo Vadis?,* Henryk Sienkiewicz (novel), and Wilson Barrett (play).

Rip Van Winkle. Directors unknown, [Joseph Jefferson], Biograph, 1896, 1897, and 1903, 108 feet. Source: Dion Boucicault, *Rip Van Winkle.*

The Silver King. Sigmund Lubin, director, Lubin Films, 1908, 655 feet. Source: Henry Arthur Jones and Henry Herman, *The Silver King.*

Uncle Tom's Cabin, Edwin S. Porter, director, Edison Manufacturing Co., 1903, 507 feet. Source: *Uncle Tom's Cabin* by George Aiken, 1876, with additions from anonymous combination companies. Video and DVD.

The Unfaithful Wife. Billy Bitzer, director, [Kathryn Osterman], Biograph, 1903, Part 1, *The Lover,* 19 feet; Part 2, *The Fight,* 25 feet; Part 3, *Murder and Suicide,* 20 feet. No given source.

Veriscope—portraying the contest between James J. Corbett and Robert Fitzsimmons at Carson City, Nevada, March 17, 1897, Macauley's Theatre, Louisville, 1897, approximately 25 minutes.

GRIFFITH FILMS FROM IDENTIFIABLE THEATRICAL SOURCES AT BIOGRAPH, 1908–1913

Each film's data is followed by the title of the play or theatrical event which served as a source. Unless otherwise noted, Griffith directed.

The Barbarian Ingomar. 1908, 806 feet. Sources: Friedrich Halm, *Der Sohn der Wildniss*, and Maria Lovell, *Ingomar the Barbarian*.

The Battle. 1911, 1 reel. Source: conventions of Civil War stage melodrama.

A Beast at Bay. 1912, 998 feet. Source: Cecil Raleigh and Henry Hamilton, *The Whip*.

A Drunkard's Reformation. 1909, 983 feet. Source: Charles Reade, *Drink*.

A Fair Rebel. David Miles, director, Griffith supervised, made by Biograph for Klaw and Erlanger, 1914, 1,228 feet/3 reels. Source: Henry Mawson, *A Fair Rebel*.

A Fool's Revenge. 1908, 1,000 feet. Sources: Victor Hugo, *Le roi s'amuse*, and Tom Taylor, *The Fool's Revenge*.

The Fugitive. 1910, 996 feet. Source: conventions of Civil War stage melodrama.

The Guerrilla. 1908, 898 feet. Source: conventions of Civil War stage melodrama.

His Trust. 1911, 996 feet. Source: conventions of Civil War stage melodrama.

His Trust Fulfilled. 1911, 999 feet. Source: conventions of Civil War stage melodrama.

The Honor of His Family. 1909, 998 feet. Source: conventions of Civil War stage melodrama.

The House with Closed Shutters. 1910, 998 feet. Source: conventions of Civil War stage melodrama.

In Old Kentucky. 1909, reissued 1915 by Unicorn Film Service as *Kentucky Brothers*, 983 feet. Source: conventions of Civil War stage melodrama.

In the Border States. 1910, 990 feet. Source: conventions of Civil War stage melodrama.

The Informer. 1912, 1,080 feet. Source: conventions of Civil War stage melodrama.

Judith of Bethulia. 1913, 4 reels. Sources: Paolo Giacometti, *Giuditta*, and Thomas Bailey Aldrich, *Judith of Bethulia*. 1908, 757 feet. Video and DVD.

The Kentuckian. Wallace McCutcheon Sr., director, Griffith an actor, 1908, 757 feet. Source: Edwin Milton Royle, *The Squaw Man*.

Monday Morning in a Coney Island Police Court. 1908, 414 feet. Source: American burlesque sketch.

Money Mad. 1908, 684 feet. Source: John Lawson, *Humanity*, vaudeville and music hall sketch.

Oil and Water. 1912, 1,513 feet. Source: developments in modern dance.

Old Isaacs the Pawnbroker. Wallace McCutcheon Sr., director, scenario by Griffith, 1908, 969 feet. Sources:

Charles Klein, Lee Arthur, and David Belasco, *The Auctioneer*, and G. H. Jessop, *Sam'l of Posen*.

Ostler Joe. Wallace McCutcheon Sr., director, Griffith an actor, 1908. Source: George R. Sims, "Ostler Joe," narrative ballad (for parlor and platform recitation), 1879.

Professional Jealousy. Wallace McCutcheon Sr., director, Griffith an actor, 1908, 609 feet. Source: Grattan Donnelly, *Darkest Russia*.

Ramona. 1910, 995 feet: Sources: *Ramona*: (novel), Helen Hunt Jackson; (play), Johnstone Jones and Virginia Calhoun. DVD only.

The Romance of a Jewess. 1908, 964 feet. Sources: Charles Klein, Lee Arthur, David Belasco, *The Auctioneer*, and G. H. Jessop, *Sam'l of Posen*.

The Rose of Kentucky. 1911, 1 reel. Source: conventions of Civil War stage melodrama.

The Slave. 1909, 998 feet. Source: W. G. Wills and Henry Herman, *Claudian*.

Strongheart. James Kirkwood, director, Griffith supervised, made by Biograph for Klaw and Erlanger, 1914, 1,144 feet/3 reels. Source: William C. de Mille, *Strongheart*.

Swords and Hearts. 1911, 1,000 feet. Source: Edward McWade, *Winchester*, and conventions of Civil War stage melodrama.

That Chink at Golden Gulch. 1910, 998 feet. Source: Charles Townsend, *The Golden Gulch*.

GRIFFITH-DIRECTED FILMS FROM IDENTIFIABLE THEATRICAL SOURCES, POST-BIOGRAPH, 1913–1934

Each film's data is followed by the title of the the the play which served either as the principal source or as a source for an episode. Unless otherwise specified, the film was directed by Griffith.

America. For D. W. Griffith, Inc., 1924, 14,700 feet/15 reels. Sources: D. W. Griffith, *In Washington's Time* (vaudeville sketch) and *War* (unpublished, unproduced play). Video & DVD.

The Birth of a Nation. For D. W. Griffith, Inc., 1915, 12 reels. Source: Thomas Dixon Jr., *The Clansman*. Video and DVD.

Diane of the Follies. William Christy Cabanne, director, scenario by D. W. Griffith (under nom de plume "Granville Warwick"), Griffith supervised for Fine Arts Film Corp., 1916, 5 reels. Source: Arthur Wing Pinero, *Trelawny of the Wells*.

The Escape. For Reliance-Majestic, 1914, 4 reels. Source: Paul Armstrong, *The Escape*.

The Fall of Babylon. For D. W. Griffith Inc., from *Intolerance* (issued, with additional footage, as a discrete film), 1919, 7 reels. Source: developments in modern dance.

Ghosts. George Nicholls, director, Griffith supervised for Triangle Film Corp., 1915, 5 reels. Source: Henrik Ibsen, *Ghosts*.

Intolerance. For D. W Griffith, Wark Producing Corp., 1916, 11,663 feet/ 14 reels. Sources: developments in modern dance and Cecil Raleigh and

Henry Hamilton, *The Whip*. Video and DVD.

Lady of the Pavements. For Art Cinema Corp., 1929, 8,329 feet/9 reels. Source: Edward Bulwer Lytton, *The Lady of Lyons*.

Macbeth. John Emerson, director, Griffith supervised for Triangle-Fine Arts Film Corp., 1916, 8 reels. Source: William Shakespeare, *Macbeth*.

The Mother and the Law. For D. W. Griffith, from *Intolerance* (issued as a discrete film), 1919, 7 reels. Source: Cecil Raleigh and Henry Hamilton, *The Whip*.

Orphans of the Storm. For D. W. Griffith, Inc., 1922, 12,000 feet/12 reels. Sources: Eugene Corman and Adolphe D'Ennery, *Les Deux Orphelines*, N. Hart Jackson, *The Two Orphans*, Charles Reade, *The Lyons Mail*, Watts Phillips, *The Dead Heart*, Freeman Wills and Frederick Langbridge, *The Only Way*, and Victorien Sardou, *Robespierre*. Video and DVD.

Pillars of Society. Raoul Walsh and George Nicholls, directors, Griffith supervised for Triangle Film Corp., 1915, 4 reels. Source: Henrik Ibsen, *The Pillars of Society*.

Sally of the Sawdust. For Famous Players-Lasky, 1925, 9,500 feet/10 reels. Source: Owen King and Dorothy Donnelly, *Poppy*. Video and DVD.

Scarlet Days. For D. W Griffith-Paramount-Artcraft, 1919, 6,916 feet/7 reels. Source: George Bernard Shaw, *Mrs. Warren's Profession*.

The Struggle. For D. W. Griffith, Inc., 1931, 9 reels. Sources: Charles Reade, *Drink*, and Emile Zola, *L'Assommoir*. Video only.

Topsy and Eva. For Features Production Corp., Del Lord and D. W. Griffith, directors, 1927, 7,456 feet/8 reels. Sources: Catherine Chisholm Cushing, *Topsy and Eva* (vaudeville sketch), and *Uncle Tom's Cabin* (anonymous combination company versions).

Way Down East. For D. W. Griffith, Inc., 1921, 13 reels. Sources: Lottie Blair Parker, *Annie Laurie*, the earliest version of the play '*Way Down East* by Lottie Blair Parker and Joseph R. Grismer. Further source: '*Way Down East* (novel) by Joseph R. Grismer. Video and DVD.

Bibliography

BOOKS, ARTICLES, AND WEB SITES

Affron, Charles. *Lillian Gish: Her Legend, Her Life.* New York and London: Scribner, 2001.

Allen, Robert C. "A Decided Sensation: Cinema, Vaudeville, and Burlesque." In Patricia McDonnell, ed. *On the Edge of Your Seat: Popular Theater and Film in Early Twentieth Century American Art.* New Haven and London: Yale University Press, 2002, pp. 61–90.

———. "Vaudeville and Film, 1895–1915: A Study in Media Interaction." Doctoral dissertation, University of Iowa, 1977.

American Film Institute online catalog.

Anonymous. *The Film Preservation Guide: The Basics for Archives, Libraries, and Museums.* San Francisco: National Film Preservation Foundation, 2004.

———. *Joseph M. Schenck presents D. W. Griffith's "Lady of the Pavements."* United Artists' thirty-two-page promotional booklet, with photographs, narrative, intertitles, and dialogue. New York: Longacre, 1931.

Archer, Stephen M. "E Pluribus Unum: Bernhardt's 1905–1906 Farewell Tour." In Ron Engle and Tice L. Miller, eds. *The American Stage: Social and Economic Issues from the Colonial Period to the Present.* Cambridge: Cambridge University Press, 1993, pp. 159–162.

Archer, William. *The Old Drama and the New: An Essay in Revaluation,* London: William Heinemann, 1923.

Arthur, Joseph, and Andrew Carpenter Wheeler ("Nym Crinkle"). *Blue Jeans: A Comedy Drama in Four Acts.* New York: Samuel French, 1890.

Arvidson, Linda [Mrs. D. W. Griffith]. *When the Movies Were Young.* New York: Arno Press, 1977.

Bank, Rosemarie K. "A Reconsideration of the Death of Nineteenth-Century American Repertories and the Rise of the Combination." *Essays in Theatre,* vol. 5, no. 1, November 1986, pp. 61–75.

———. *Theatre Culture in America, 1825–1860.* Cambridge and New York: Cambridge University Press, 1997.

Barry, Iris. *D. W. Griffith: American Film Master.* Museum of Modern Art Series 1. New York: Museum of Modern Art, 1940.

Beasley, David. *McKee Rankin and the Heyday of the American Theater.* Waterloo, ON: Wilfred Laurier University Press, 2002.

Bernheim, Alfred L. *The Business of the Theatre.* New York: Actors' Equity Association, 1932.

Bernstein, Matthew, and Gaylyn Studlar. *Visions of the East: Orientalism in Film.* New Brunswick, NJ: Rutgers University Press, 1997.

Bitzer, Billy. *Billy Bitzer: His Story—The Autobiography of D. W. Griffith's Master Cameraman.* New York: Farrar, Straus and Giroux, 1973.

Bordman, Gerald. *American Theatre: A Chronicle of Comedy and Drama, 1869–*

1914. New York and Oxford: Oxford University Press, 1994.

Bouchier, Chili. *Shooting Star: The Last of the Silent Film Stars.* London: Atlantis, 1996.

Bowser, Eileen, ed. *Biograph Bulletins, 1908–1912.* New York: Octagon Books, 1973.

———. *The Transformation of Cinema, 1907–1915.* Vol. 2, History of the American Cinema. Berkeley: University of California Press, 1990.

Brady, William A. "Drama in Homespun." *The Stage,* no. 14, January 1937, p. 99.

———. *The Fighting Man.* Indianapolis: Bobbs-Merrill, 1916.

———. *Showman.* New York: E. P. Dutton, 1937.

Brewster, Ben, and Lea Jacobs. *Theatre to Cinema.* Oxford: Oxford University Press, 1997.

Brown, Karl. *Adventures with D. W. Griffith,* ed. Kevin Brownlow. London: Faber and Faber, 1973.

Brown, Kelly R. *Florence Lawrence, the Biograph Girl: America's First Movie Star.* Jefferson, NC, and London: McFarland, 1999.

Brownlow, Kevin. "Griffith and the Gish Sisters." *Catologo Le Giornate del Cinema Muto/26th Pordenone Silent Film Festival, XXVI edition.* Pordenone: Giornate del Cinema Muto, 2007, pp. 17–18.

———. *The Parade's Gone By.* London: Secker and Warburg, 1968.

Byron, Joseph. "Taking Scene Pictures: The Difficult Art of Getting Them by Flashlight." *New York Tribune Illustrated Supplement,* Sunday, October 25, 1903, pp. 7–8.

Cahn, Julius. *Julius Cahn's Official Theatrical Guide: Authentic Information of the Theatres and Attractions in the United States, Canada, Mexico and Cuba.* New York: Publication Office, vols. 1–18, 1896–1913; vols. 19–20, 1912–1913, as *Cahn–Leighton Official Theatrical Guide;* vols. 21–27, 1914–1921, as *The Julius Cahn–Gus Hill Theatrical Guide and Moving Picture Directory.*

Canning, Charlotte M. *The Most American Thing in America: Circuit Chautauqua as Performance.* Iowa City: University of Iowa Press, 2005.

Carey, Gary. *Anita Loos: A Biography.* New York: Alfred Knopf, 1988.

Carton, Charles N. *'Way Up East,* Weber and Fields Music Hall, 1898, from manuscript "sides" in the Harvard Theatre Collection.

Castle, Dennis. *Sensation Smith of Drury Lane.* Edinburgh: Charles Skilton, 1984.

Cerf, Bennett, and Cartmell, Van. *S.R.O.: The Most Successful Plays in the History of the American Stage.* Garden City, NY: Doubleday, Doran, 1945.

Cherchi-Usai, Paolo. *Burning Passions: An Introduction to the Study of Silent Cinema.* London: British Film Institute, 1991.

Clinton, Craig. *Mrs. Leslie Carter: A Biography of the Early Twentieth Century Stage Star.* Jefferson, NC: McFarland, 2006.

Cockrell, Dale. *Demons of Disorder: Early Blackface Minstrels and Their World.* Cambridge: Cambridge University Press, 1997.

Coe, Brian. *The History of Movie Photography.* Westfield, NJ: Eastview Editions, 1981.

Cohen, Paula Marantz. *Silent Film and the Triumph of the American Myth*. Oxford and New York: Oxford University Press, 2001.

Cullen, Rosemary L. *The Civil War in American Drama Before 1900: Catalog of an Exhibition, November 1982*. Providence, RI: Brown University Library, 1982.

Daly, Ann. *Done into Dance: Isadora Duncan in America*. Bloomington and Indianapolis: Indiana University Press, 1995.

Davis, Peter A. "From Stock to Combination: The Panic of 1873 and Its Effect on the American Theatre Industry." *Theatre History Studies*, vol. 8, 1988, pp. 1–9.

de Mille, William C. *Strongheart: An American Comedy Drama in Four Acts*. New York: Samuel French, 1909.

Dixon, Thomas, Jr. "Why I Wrote *The Clansman*." *Theatre*, vol. 6, no. 59, January 1906, pp. 20–22.

Drew, William M. *D. W. Griffith's Intolerance: Its Genesis and Its Vision*. Jefferson, NC: McFarland, 1986.

Dunning, William A. *Essays on the Civil War and Reconstruction*. New York: Harper, 1898.

————. *Reconstruction, Political and Economic, 1865–1877*. New York: Harper, 1907.

Eaton, Walter Prichard. *Plays and Players: Leaves from a Critic's Scrapbook*. Cincinnati: Stewart and Kidd, 1916.

Eckhardt, Joseph P. *The King of the Movies: Film Pioneer Siegmund Lubin*. Madison and Teaneck, NJ: Fairleigh Dickinson University Press, 1997.

Emmanuel, Maurice. *The Antique Greek Dance*. Translated by Harriet Jean Beauley. New York: J. J. Little and Ives, 1916.

Foner, Eric. *Forever Free: The Story of Emancipation and Reconstruction*. Illustrated and Edited, with commentary, by Joshua Brown. New York: Alfred A. Knopf, 2005.

Frick, John W. *Theatre, Culture and Temperance Reform in Nineteenth-Century America*. Cambridge and New York: Cambridge University Press, 2003.

Fyles, Franklin. *The Theatre and Its People*. New York: Doubleday Page, 1900.

Garcia, Desirée J. "Subversive Sounds: Ethnic Spectatorship and Boston's Nickelodeon Theatres, 1907–1914." *Film History*, vol. 19, no. 3, 2007, pp. 213–227.

Garelick, Rhonda K. *Electric Salome: Löie Fuller's Performance of Modernism*. Princeton and Oxford: Princeton University Press, 2007.

Gerould, Daniel C. *American Melodrama*. New York: Performing Arts Journal Publications, 1983.

Giacometti, Paolo. *Giacometti's Tragedy of Judith: As Represented by Madame Ristori and Her Dramatic Company Under the Management of J. Grau: The English Translation by Isaac C. Pray*. New York: John A. Gray and Green, 1866.

Gifford, Denis. *Books and Plays in Films, 1896–1915: Literary, Theatrical and Artistic Sources of the First Twenty Years of Motion Pictures*. London and New York: McFarland and Mansell, 1991.

Gillespie, Michael K., and Randall Hall. *Thomas Dixon and the Birth of Modern America*. Baton Rouge: Louisiana State University Press, 2006.

Gish, Lillian. *The Movies, Mr. Griffith, and Me*. London: Columbus Books, 1969.

Gordon, Henry Stephen. "The Real Story of *Intolerance*," *Photoplay Magazine*. July–November, 1916.

———. "The Story of David Wark Griffith: His Early Years, His Struggles, His Ambitions and Their Achievement." *Photoplay Magazine*, vol. 10, no. 5, October 1916, p. 90.

Graham, Cooper C., Steven Higgins, Elaine Mancini, and João Luiz Vieira. *D. W. Griffith and the Biograph Company.* Metuchen, NJ, and London: Scarecrow Press, 1985.

Griffith, D. W. *A Fool and a Girl.* 1906. Also titled *A Fool and the Girl.* Typescript, D. W. Griffith Papers. New York: Museum of Modern Art.

———. *The Man Who Invented Hollywood: The Autobiography of D. W. Griffith,* ed. James Hart. Louisville, KY: Touchstone Press, 1972.

———. *The Twilight Revellers.* Unpublished manuscript, Registered with the Screen Writers Guild, 1945. Reel 35, Series 5, the Killian-Sterling Collection, D. W. Griffith Papers. New York: Museum of Modern Art.

———. *War.* 1907. Typescript, D. W. Griffith Papers. New York: Museum of Modern Art.

Grismer, Joseph R. *'Way Down East: A Romance of New England Life. Founded on the Phenomenally Successful Play by the Same Title by Lottie Blair Parker.* New York: J. S. Ogilvie, 1900.

Gunning, Tom. *D. W. Griffith and the Origins of American Narrative Film.* Urbana and Chicago: University of Illinois Press, 1991.

Hall, Roger A. *Performing the American Frontier, 1870–1906.* Cambridge: Cambridge University Press, 2001.

Hammond, Michael. "'A Soul Stirring Appeal to Every Briton': The Reception of *The Birth of a Nation* in Britain (1915–1916)." *Film History,* vol. 11, no. 3, 1999, pp. 353–370.

Hapgood, Norman. *The Stage in America, 1897–1900.* London: Macmillan, 1901.

Harrison, Charles. *Theatricals and Tableaux Vivants for Amateurs.* London: ca. 1885.

Henderson, Robert M. *D. W. Griffith: His Life and Work.* New York: Oxford University Press, 1972.

———. *D. W. Griffith: The Years at Biograph.* New York: Farrar, Straus, and Giroux, 1970.

Hoyt, Harlowe R. *Town Hall Tonight.* Englewood Cliffs, NJ: Prentice Hall, 1955.

Hughes, Alan. "The Lyceum Staff: A Victorian Theatrical Organization." *Theatre Notebook,* vol. 28, no. 1, 1974, pp. 11–17.

Irving, Laurence. *Henry Irving: The Actor and His World.* London: Faber and Faber, 1951.

Jenkins, Henry. *What Made Pistachio Nuts? Early Sound Comedy and the Vaudeville Aesthetic.* New York and Oxford: Columbia University Press, 1992.

Johnson, Paul. *A History of the American People.* London: Weidenfeld and Nicholson, 1997.

Johnson, Stephen. "Evaluating Early Film as a Document of Theatre History: The 1896 Footage of Joseph Jefferson's *Rip Van Winkle.*" *Nineteenth Century Theatre,* vol. 2, no. 2, 1992, pp. 101–22.

Kaufman, J. B. "*Judith of Bethulia:* Producing the Little Epic." *Griffithiana,* May 1994, pp. 176–191.

Kendall, Elizabeth. *Where She Danced: The Birth of American Art-Dance.* Berkeley: University of California Press, 1979.

Koszarski, Richard. *An Evening's Entertainment: The Age of the Silent Feature Picture, 1915–1928.* Vol. 3, History of the American Cinema. Berkeley: University of California Press, 1994.

Krows, Arthur Edwin. *Play Production in America.* New York: Henry Holt, 1916.

———. *Playwriting for Profit.* New York, London, and Toronto: Longmans, Green, 1928.

Lang, Robert. *American Film Melodrama: Griffith, Vidor, Minnelli.* Princeton, NJ: Princeton University Press, 1989.

———. *The Birth of a Nation: D. W. Griffith, Director.* New Brunswick, NJ: Rutgers University Press, 1994.

Lasky, Jesse L. *I Blow My Own Horn.* London: Victor Gollancz, 1957.

Laurie, Joe, Jr. *Vaudeville: From the Honky-Tonks to the Palace.* New York: Henry Holt, 1953.

———, and Abel Green. *Show Biz: From Vaude to Video.* New York: Henry Holt, 1951.

Leavitt, M. B. *Fifty Years in Theatrical Management, 1859–1909.* New York: Broadway Publishing, 1912.

Lindfors, Bernth. *Africans on Stage: Studies in Ethnological Show Business.* Bloomington and Indianapolis: Indiana University Press, 1999.

Lindsay, Vachel. *The Art of the Moving Picture.* Edited by Martin Scorsese. Original edition 1915. New York: Modern Library (reprint), 2000.

Loos, Anita. *Kiss Hollywood Good-bye.* London: W. H. Allen, 1974.

Lukas, J. Anthony. *Big Trouble: A Murder in a Small Western Town Sets Off a Struggle for the Soul of America.* New York: Simon and Schuster, 1997.

Magnuson, Landis K. *Circle Stock Theater: Touring American Small Towns, 1900–1960.* Jefferson, NC: McFarland, 1995.

Marra, Kim. *Strange Duets: Impresarios and Actresses in American Theatre, 1865–1914.* Iowa City: University of Iowa Press, 2006.

Mason, Jeffrey D. *Melodrama and the Myth of America.* Bloomington and Indianapolis: Indiana University Press, 1993.

Mayer, David. "Acting in Silent Film: Which Legacy of the Theatre?" In Alan Lovell and Peter Kramer, eds. *Screen Acting.* London and New York: Routledge, 1999, pp. 10–30.

———. "Changing Horses in Mid-Ocean: *The Whip* in Britain and America." In Michael Booth and Joel Kaplan, eds. *Edwardian Theatre: Essays on Performance and the Stage.* Cambridge: Cambridge University Press, 1996, pp. 220–235.

———. "Learning to See in the Dark." *Nineteenth Century Theatre,* vol. 25, no. 2. Winter 1997, pp. 92–114.

———. *Playing Out the Empire: "Ben-Hur" and Other Toga Plays and Films, 1883–1908.* Oxford: Oxford University Press, 1994.

———. "*Why Girls Leave Home:* Victorian and Edwardian "Bad-Girl" Melodrama Parodied on Early Film." *Theatre Journal,* vol. 58, no. 4, December 2006, pp. 575–593.

———, and Helen Day-Mayer. "D. W. Griffith's Old Kentucky Home and

Other Mythic Dwellings." *Living Pictures*, vol. 1, no. 2. 2001, pp. 21–35.

———, and Helen-Day-Mayer. "'A Secondary Action' or a Musical Highlight? Melodic Interludes in Early Film Melodrama Reconsidered." In Richard Abel and Rick Altman, eds. *The Sounds of Early Cinema*. Bloomington: University of Indiana Press, 2001, pp. 220–231.

McArthur, Benjamin. *Actors and American Culture, 1880–1920*. Iowa City: University of Iowa Press, 2000.

McCloskey, James. *My Partner*. In Napier Wilt, ed. *The White Slave and Other Plays, America's Lost Plays*, vol. 19. Bloomington: Indiana University Press, 1940.

Meer, Sarah. *Uncle Tom Mania: Slavery, Minstrels, and Transatlantic Culture in the 1850s*. Athens: University of Georgia Press, 2005.

Meisel, Martin. *Realizations: Narrative, Pictorial, and Theatrical Arts in Nineteenth-Century England*. Princeton, NJ: Princeton University Press, 1983.

Merritt, Russell. "The Griffith Third: D. W. Griffith at Triangle." In Paolo Cherchi-Usai and Lorenzo Codelli, eds. *Sulla via di Hollywood, 1911–1920*. Pordenone: Le Giornate del Cinema Muto, 1988, p. 256.

———. "Rescued from a Perilous Nest: D. W. Griffith's Escape from Theatre into Film." *Cinema Journal*, vol. 21, no. 1, 1981, pp. 2–30.

Miller, Tice L. "Alan Dale: The Hearst Critic." *Educational Theatre Journal*. vol. 26, no. 1, March 1974, pp. 69–80.

Moy, James S. *Marginal Sights: Staging the Chinese in America*. Iowa City: University of Iowa Press, 1993.

Musser, Charles. *Before the Nickelodeon: Edwin S. Porter and the Edison Manufacturing Company*. Berkeley: University of California Press, 1991.

———. *Edison Motion Pictures, 1890–1900: An Annotated Filmography*. Washington, DC: Smithsonian Institution Press, and Pordenone: Le Giornate del Cinema Muto, 1997.

———. *The Emergence of Cinema: The American Screen to 1907*. Vol. 1, *History of the American Cinema*. Berkeley: University of California Press, 1994.

Nicoll, Allardyce. *English Drama, 1900–1930: The Beginnings of the Modern Period*. Cambridge: Cambridge University Press, 1973.

———. *A History of English Drama, 1660–1900*, vol. 4, *Early Nineteenth Century Drama, 1800–1850*. Cambridge: Cambridge University Press, 1955; vol. 5, *Late Nineteenth Century Drama, 1850–1900*, 1959.

Niver, Kemp R. *Biograph Bulletins, 1896–1908*. Los Angeles: Locare Research Group, 1971.

———. *D. W. Griffith: His Biograph Films in Perspective*. Los Angeles: John D. Roche, 1974.

———. *Early Motion Pictures: The Paper Print Collection in the Library of Congress*, ed. Bebe Bergsten. Washington, DC: Library of Congress, 1985.

———. *Klaw and Erlanger Present Famous Plays in Pictures*, ed. Bebe Bergstren. Los Angeles: Locare Research Group, 1976.

Page, Brett. *Writing for Vaudeville*. Boston: Home Correspondence School, 1915.

Pearson, Hesketh. *Beerbohm Tree: His Life and Laughter*. London: Methuen, 1956.

Pearson, Roberta. *Eloquent Gestures: The Transformation of Performance Style in the Griffith Biograph Films*. Berkeley: University of California Press, 1992.

Pitou, Augustus. *Masters of the Show As Seen in Retrospection By One Who Has Been Associated with the American Stage for Nearly Fifty Years*. New York: Neale, 1914.

Postlewait, Thomas. "From Melodrama to Realism: The Suspect History of American Drama." In Michael Hays and Anastasia Nikolopoulou, eds. *Melodrama: The Cultural Emergence of a Genre*. New York: St. Martin's Press, 1996.

Quinn, Arthur Hobson. *A History of American Drama from the Civil War to the Present Day*. London: Sir Isaac Pitman, 1937.

Rahill, Frank. *The World of Melodrama*. University Park: Pennsylvania State University Press, 1967.

Raleigh, Cecil, and Henry Hamilton. *The Whip*, Lord Chamberlain's Collection, Lic. no. 103, licensed 13. 9. 1909. Never published. Other variant copies, dating from 1910 to 1911, are held by the Shubert Archive.

Rees, Terence, and David Wilmore, eds. *British Theatrical Patents, 1801–1900*. London: Society for Theatre Research, 1996.

Reynolds, Ernest. *Early Victorian Drama*. Cambridge, UK: W. Heffer, 1936.

Riis, Jacob. *How the Other Half Lives*. New York: Charles Scribners and Sons, 1890.

Riis, Thomas L. *Just Before Jazz: Black Musical Theatre in New York, 1890–1915*. Washington: Smithsonian Institution Press, 1989.

———, ed. *Uncle Tom's Cabin*, Nineteenth-Century Musical Theater, vol. 5. New York: Garland Press, 1996.

Romeo, Jacqueline. "Charles T. Parsloe and the Popularization of the Comic Coolie in Nineteenth-Century Frontier Melodrama." Doctoral dissertation, Tufts University, 2007.

Roosevelt, Theodore. Address to the Knights of Columbus. New York City, October 12, 1915.

———. "American Ideals," in *True Americanism*. New York: Ariel Booklets, 1903.

———. "True Americanism." *Forum Magazine*, April 1894.

Rowell, George. *The Victorian Theatre: A Survey*. Oxford: Oxford University Press, 1956.

Rydell, Robert W., and Robert Kroes. *Buffalo Bill in Bologna: The Americanization of the World, 1869–1922*. Chicago and London: University of Chicago Press, 2005.

Schickel, Richard. *D. W. Griffith and the Birth of Film*. London: Pavilion Books, 1984.

Shapiro, James. *1599: A Year in the Life of William Shakespeare*. London: Faber and Faber, 2005.

Sheldon, Edward. *The Nigger*. New York: Macmillan, 1910.

Silva, Fred, ed. *Focus on "The Birth of a Nation."* Englewood Cliffs, NJ: Prentice-Hall, 1971.

Simmon, Scott. *The Films of D.W. Griffith*. Cambridge: Cambridge University Press, 1993.

———. *The Invention of the Western Film: A Cultural History of the Genre's First Half-*

Century. Cambridge: Cambridge University Press, 2003.

Slide, Anthony. *American Racist: The Life and Films of Thomas Dixon.* Lexington: University Press of Kentucky, 2004.

Slout, W. L. *Theatre in a Tent: The Development of a Provincial Entertainment.* Bowling Green, OH: Bowling Green University Popular Press, 1972.

Spehr, Paul C. *The Civil War in Motion Pictures: A Bibliography of Films Produced in the United States since 1897.* Washington, DC: Library of Congress, 1961.

Stanhope, Selwyn A. "The World's Master Picture Producer." In Fred Silva, *Focus on "The Birth of a Nation."* Englewood Cliffs, NJ: Prentice-Hall, 1971.

Storms, A. D. *The Players' Blue Book.* Worcester, MA: Sutherland and Storms, 1901.

Sullivan, John. "Topsy and Eva Play Vaudeville." In *Uncle Tom's Cabin and American Culture,* ed. Stephen Railton. Online exhibit and interpretation mounted by the University of Virginia, 2003. http://www.iath.virginia.edu/utc/interpret/exhibits/sullivan/sullivanf.html

Sutherland, Sidney. "Lillian Gish—the Incomparable: Being the True Story of a Great Tragedienne." *Liberty Magazine,* September 3, 1927.

Thompson, Frank. *Lost Films: Important Movies That Disappeared.* New York: Citadel Press, 1996.

Tilton, Dwight [George Tilton Richardson and Wilder Dwight Quint]. *Miss Petticoats.* Boston: C. M. Clark, 1902.

Toll, Robert C. *Blacking Up: The Minstrel Show in Nineteenth-Century America.* New York: Oxford University Press, 1974.

Vallillo, Steven M. "Broadway Reviews in the Teens and Twenties: Smut and Slime?" *The Drama Review,* 1981, pp. 25–34.

Vardac, A. Nicholas. *Stage to Screen: Theatrical Method from Garrick to Griffith.* Cambridge, MA: Harvard University Press, 1949.

Waldman, Harry. *Maurice Tourneur: The Life and Films.* Jefferson, NC: McFarland, 2001.

Waller, Gregory A. *Main Street Amusements: Movies and Commercial Entertainment in a Southern City, 1896–1930.* Washington and London: Smithsonian Institution Press, 1995.

Waltz, Gwendolyn. "Embracing Technology: A Primer of Early Multi-Media Performance." In Leonard Quaresima and Laura Vichi, eds. *La Decima Musa: Il Cinema E Le Altre Arte— The Tenth Muse: Cinema and Other Art.* Udine: Forum, 2001, pp. 543–560.

———. "Filmed Scenery on the Live Stage." *Theatre Journal,* vol. 58, no. 4, December 2006, pp. 547–573.

———. "Projection and Performance: Early Multi-Media in the American Theatre." Doctoral dissertation, Tufts University, 1991.

Ward, Geoffrey C. *Unforgiveable Blackness: The Rise and Fall of Jack Johnson.* New York: Knopf, 2004.

Waters, Hazel. *Racism on the Victorian Stage: Representations of Slavery and the Black Character.* Cambridge: Cambridge University Press, 2007.

Watson, Ernest Bradlee. *Sheridan to Robertson: A Study of the Nineteenth-Century London Stage.* Cambridge, MA: Harvard University Press, 1926.

Weisert, John Jacob. *Last Night at Macauley's: A Checklist, 1873–1925.* Louisville, KY: University of Kentucky Press, 1950.

Williams, Linda. *Playing the Race Card: Melodramas of Black and White from Uncle Tom to O. J. Simpson.* Princeton, NJ: Princeton University Press, 2001.

Wilson, Woodrow. *A History of the American People.* Vol. 5, *Reunion and Nationalization.* Honolulu: University Press of the Pacific, 1902 (reprint).

Zangwell, Israel. *The Melting Pot.* New York: Macmillan, 1913.

ESSAYS FROM
THE GRIFFITH PROJECT VOLUMES
The number which appears after the essay title indicates the order in which each film or item associated with Griffith was made, irrespective of whether Griffith was the director, scenarist, actor, author, supervisor, or, in some few instances, the subject of a film.

Bowser, Eileen. "America." No. 609, Paolo Cherchi-Usai, ed. *The Griffith Project.* Volume 10, *Films Produced in 1919–1946.* London: British Film Institute, and Pordenone: Le Giornate del Cinema Muto, 2006, pp. 162–165.

———. "Old Isaacs the Pawnbroker." No. 11, Paolo Cherchi-Usai, ed. *The Griffith Project.* Volume 1, *Films Produced in 1907–1908.* London: British Film Institute, and Pordenone: Le Giornate del Cinema Muto, 1999, pp. 21–22.

———. "Professional Jealousy." No. 1, Paolo Cherchi-Usai, ed. *The Griffith Project.* Volume 1, *Films Produced in 1907–1908.* London: British Film Institute, and Pordenone: Le Giornate del Cinema Muto, 1999, pp. 1–2.

———. "The Struggle." No. 627, Paolo Cherchi-Usai, ed. *The Griffith Project.* Volume 10, *Films Produced in 1919–1946.* London: British Film Institute, and Pordenone: Le Giornate del Cinema Muto, 2006, pp. 239–243.

———, and David Mayer. "A Drunkard's Reformation." No. 118, Paolo Cherchi-Usai, ed. *The Griffith Project.* Volume 2, *Films Produced January–June 1909.* London: British Film Institute, and Pordenone: Le Giornate del Cinema Muto, 1999, pp. 57–60.

Brewster, Ben. "A Beast at Bay." No. 409, Paolo Cherchi-Usai, ed. *The Griffith Project.* Volume 6, *Films Produced in 1912.* London: British Film Institute, and Pordenone: Le Giornate del Cinema Muto, 2002, pp. 57–60.

———. "In Old Kentucky." No. 183, Paolo Cherchi-Usai, ed. *The Griffith Project.* Volume 3, *Films Produced in July–December 1909.* London: British Film Institute, and Pordenone: Le Giornate del Cinema Muto, 1999, pp. 36–38.

Cherchi-Usai, Paolo, ed. *The Griffith Project*, 12 vols., *Films Produced in 1907–1906.* London: British Film Institute, and Pordenone: Le Giornate del Cinema Muto, 1997–2008.

Grieveson, Lee. "The Fugitive." No. 298, Paolo Cherchi-Usai, ed. *The Griffith Project.* Volume 4, *Films Produced in 1910.* London: British Film Institute, and Pordenone: Le Giornate del Cinema Muto, 2000, pp. 211–214.

Griffith, D. W. "The Rise and Fall of Free Speech." New York: Privately printed, 1916. Reproduced, with an introduction by Tom Gunning in Paolo Cherchi-Usai, ed. *The Griffith Project*, Volume 11, *Selected Writings of D. W. Griffith*. London: British Film Institute, and Pordenone: Le Giornate del Cinema Muto, 2007, pp. 137–169.

Gunning, Tom. "Ghosts." No. 515, Paolo Cherchi-Usai, ed. *The Griffith Project*. Volume 8, *Films Produced in 1914–1915*. London: British Film Institute, and Pordenone: Le Giornate del Cinema Muto, 2004, pp. 116–117.

———. "The House with Closed Shutters." No. 277, Paolo Cherchi-Usai, ed. *The Griffith Project*. Volume 4, *Films Produced in 1910*. London: British Film Institute, and Pordenone: Le Giornate del Cinema Muto, 2000, pp. 141–146.

———. "Monday Morning in a Coney Island Police Court." No. 42, Paolo Cherchi-Usai, ed. *The Griffith Project*. Volume 1, *Films Produced in 1907–1908*. London: British Film Institute, and Pordenone: Le Giornate del Cinema Muto, 1999, pp. 91–92.

———. "The Rose of Kentucky." No. 356, Paolo Cherchi-Usai, ed. *The Griffith Project*. Volume 5, *Films Produced in 1911*. London: British Film Institute, and Pordenone: Le Giornate del Cinema Muto, 2001, pp. 105–108.

———. "Strongheart." No. 495, Paolo Cherchi-Usai, ed. *The Griffith Project*. Volume 7, *Films Produced in 1913*. London: British Film Institute, and Pordenone: Le Giornate del Cinema Muto, 2003, pp. 153–155.

Higgins, Steven. "The Battle." No. 370, Paolo Cherchi-Usai, ed. *The Griffith Project*. Volume 5, *Films Produced in 1911*. London: British Film Institute, and Pordenone: Le Giornate del Cinema Muto, 2001, pp. 139–141.

———. "The Dancing Girl of Butte." No. 224, Paolo Cherchi-Usai, ed. *The Griffith Project*. Volume 3, *Films Produced July–December 1909*. London: British Film Institute, and Pordenone: Le Giornate del Cinema Muto, 1999, pp. 157–158.

———. "A Fool's Revenge." No. 108, Paolo Cherchi-Usai, ed. *The Griffith Project*. Volume 2, *Films Produced January–June 1909*. London: British Film Institute, and Pordenone: Le Giornate del Cinema Muto, 1999, pp. 36–38.

———. "In the Border States." No. 262, Paolo Cherchi-Usai, ed. *The Griffith Project*. Volume 4, *Films Produced in 1910*. London: British Film Institute, and Pordenone: Le Giornate del Cinema Muto, 2000, pp. 94–96.

———. "True Heart Susie." No. 538, Paolo Cherchi-Usai, ed. *The Griffith Project*. Volume 10, *Films Produced in 1919–1946*. London: British Film Institute, and Pordenone: Le Giornate del Cinema Muto, 2006, pp. 18–27.

Jacobs, Lea, and David Mayer. "Way Down East." No. 598, Paolo Cherchi-Usai, ed. *The Griffith Project*. Volume 10, *Films Produced 1919–1946*. London: British Film Institute, and Pordenone: Le Giornate del Cinema Muto, 2006, pp. 80–103.

Jesionowski, Joyce. "The Informer." No. 438, Paolo Cherchi-Usai, ed. *The Griffith Project*. Volume 6, *Films Produced* in 1912. London: British Film Institute, and Pordenone: Le Giornate del Cinema Muto, 2002, pp. 180–186.

———. "Judith of Bethulia (Outtakes)." No. 491, No. 438, Paolo Cherchi-Usai, ed. *The Griffith Project*. Volume 7, *Films Produced in 1913*. London: British Film Institute, and Pordenone: Le Giornate del Cinema Muto, 2003, pp. 129–130.

———, and David Mayer. "Sally of the Sawdust." No. 611, Paolo Cherchi-Usai, ed. *The Griffith Project*. Volume 10, *Films Produced in 1919–1946*. London: British Film Institute, and Pordenone: Le Giornate del Cinema Muto, 2006, pp. 177–186.

Kaufman, J. B. "Oil and Water." No. 448, Paolo Cherchi-Usai, ed. *The Griffith Project*. Volume 6, *Films Produced in 1912*. London: British Film Institute, and Pordenone: Le Giornate del Cinema Muto, 2002, pp. 220–223.

———, and David Mayer. "Judith of Bethulia." No. 492, Paolo Cherchi-Usai, ed. *The Griffith Project*. Volume 7, *Films Produced in 1913*. London: British Film Institute, and Pordenone: Le Giornate del Cinema Muto, 2003, pp. 131–142.

———, and David Mayer. "Ostler Joe." No. 19, Paolo Cherchi-Usai, ed. *The Griffith Project*. Volume 1, *Films Produced in 1907–1908*. London: British Film Institute, and Pordenone: Le Giornate del Cinema Muto, 1999, pp. 39–43.

Loughney, Patrick. "The Kentuckian." No. 25, Paolo Cherchi-Usai, ed. *The Griffith Project*. Volume 1, *Films Produced in 1907–1908*. London: British Film Institute, and Pordenone: Le Giornate del Cinema Muto, 1999, pp. 53–54.

Mayer, David. "Diane of the Follies." No. 555, Paolo Cherchi-Usai, ed. *The Griffith Project*. Volume 9, *Films Produced in 1916–1918*. London: British Film Institute, and Pordenone: Le Giornate del Cinema Muto, 2005, pp. 130–131.

———. "A Fool and a Girl." Paolo Cherchi-Usai, ed. *The Griffith Project*. Volume 11, *Selected Writings by D. W. Griffith*. London: British Film Institute, and Pordenone: Le Giornate del Cinema Muto, 2007, pp. 1–70.

———. "Macbeth." No. 542, Paolo Cherchi-Usai, ed. *The Griffith Project*. Volume 9, *Films Produced in 1916–1918*. London: British Film Institute, and Pordenone: Le Giornate del Cinema Muto, 2005, pp. 29–30.

———. "Pillars of Society." No. 516, Paolo Cherchi-Usai, ed. *The Griffith Project*. Volume 8, *Films Produced in 1914–1915*. London: British Film Institute, and Pordenone: Le Giornate del Cinema Muto, 2004, pp. 118–120.

———. "Swords and Hearts." No. 358, Paolo Cherchi-Usai, ed. *The Griffith Project*. Volume 5, *Films Produced in 1911*. London: British Film Institute, and Pordenone: Le Giornate del Cinema Muto, 2001, pp. 110–119.

———. "That Chink at Golden Gulch." No. 291, Paolo Cherchi-Usai, ed. *The Griffith Project*. Volume 4, *Films Produced in 1910*. London: British Film Institute, and Pordenone: Le Giornate del Cinema Muto, 2000, pp. 187–190.

———. "War." Paolo Cherchi-Usai, ed. *The Griffith Project*. Volume 11, *Selected Writings by D. W. Griffith*. London: British Film Institute, and Pordenone: Le Giornate del Cinema Muto, 2007, pp. 71–136.

Merritt, Russell. "The Slave." No. 168, Paolo Cherchi-Usai, ed. *The Griffith Project*. Volume 2, *Films Produced January–June 1909*. London: British Film Institute, and Pordenone: Le Giornate del Cinema Muto, 1999, pp. 189–191.

———, et al. "Intolerance." No. 543, Paolo Cherchi-Usai, ed. *The Griffith Project*. Volume 9, *Films Produced in 1916–1918*. London: British Film Institute, and Pordenone: Le Giornate del Cinema Muto, 2005, pp. 31–99.

Simmon, Scott. "The Guerrilla." No. 64, Paolo Cherchi-Usai, ed. *The Griffith Project*. Volume 1, *Films Produced in 1907–1908*. London: British Film Institute, and Pordenone: Le Giornate del Cinema Muto, 1999, pp. 148–149.

———. "The Honor of His Family." No. 229, Paolo Cherchi-Usai, ed. *The Griffith Project*. Volume 3, *Films Produced in July–December 1909*. London: British Film Institute, and Pordenone: Le Giornate del Cinema Muto, 1999, pp. 167–170.

———. "The Mother and the Law." No. 575, Paolo Cherchi-Usai, ed. *The Griffith Project*. Volume 9, *Films Produced in 1916–1918*. London: British Film Institute, and Pordenone: Le Giornate del Cinema Muto, 2005, pp. 207–211.

———, and David Mayer. "The Barbarian Ingomar." No. 52, Paolo Cherchi-Usai, ed. *The Griffith Project*. Volume 1, *Films Produced in 1907–1908*. London: British Film Institute, and Pordenone: Le Giornate del Cinema Muto, 1999, pp. 117–121.

———, and David Mayer. "Romance of a Jewess." No. 57, Paolo Cherchi-Usai, ed. *The Griffith Project*. Volume 1, *Films Produced in 1907–1908*. London: British Film Institute, and Pordenone: Le Giornate del Cinema Muto, 1999, pp. 132–134.

Spehr, Paul. "The Escape." No. 505, Paolo Cherchi-Usai, ed. *The Griffith Project*. Volume 8, *Films Produced in 1914–1915*. London: British Film Institute, and Pordenone: Le Giornate del Cinema Muto, 2004, pp. 12–17.

Thompson, Kristin. "His Trust" No. 310 and "His Trust Fulfilled" No. 311, Paolo Cherchi-Usai, ed. *The Griffith Project*. Volume 4, *Films Produced in 1910*. London: British Film Institute, and Pordenone: Le Giornate del Cinema Muto, 2000, pp. 246–251.

———. "The Sorrows of Satan." No. 613, Paolo Cherchi-Usai, ed. *The Griffith Project*. Volume 10, *Films Produced in 1919–1946*. London: British Film Institute, and Pordenone: Le Giornate del Cinema Muto, 2006, pp. 193–200.

Tsivian, Yuri. "Ramona." No. 255, Paolo Cherchi-Usai, ed. *The Griffith Project*. Volume 4, *Films Produced in 1910*. London: British Film Institute, and Pordenone: Le Giornate del Cinema Muto, 2000, pp. 77–79.

———, and David Mayer. "Orphans of the Storm." No. 603, Paolo Cherchi-Usai, ed. *The Griffith Project*. Volume 10, *Films Produced in 1919–1946*. London: British Film Institute, and Pordenone: Le Giornate del Cinema Muto, 2006, pp. 116–137.

NEWSPAPERS

Boston Globe
Boston Herald
Boston Transcript
The Era
Los Angeles Herald
Los Angeles Times
The Mercury
Motion Picture
Motion Picture News
Moving Picture World
New York Clipper

New York Dramatic Mirror
New York Globe
New York Herald
New York Herald Tribune
New York Times
New York Times Film Reviews
Philadelphia Evening Bulletin
Photoplay Magazine
San Francisco Examiner
Theatre Magazine
Variety

Index

109; comic, 3, 14, 193; dramatic, 16, 121, 221; exotic, 8, 11, 17–18, 107, 113, 138; females, 15–17, 162, 204; foreigners, 11, 15, 17, 18–19, 107–109, 138; girl, 15, 19, 40, 80, 98, 136, 186; "girl who lost her character," 206; hobo/tramp, 67, 82, 94, 240; leading, 17, 104, 107, 140, 194; metonyms, 3, 137, 212; Mexicans, 219, 224; performers, 12, 38, 80; Native Americans, 11, 17, 75, 107; rube, 52; screen characters, 2, 211; Uncle Josh Whitcomb, 52, 103, 194

choreography, 4, 63, 98, 177, 179, 180, 184, 249

circuits, 45–47, 53, 200; American, 50; Black performers, 45; companies, 46, 51, 53, 69–70, 100; Jacobs and Procter Circuit, 46; Keith-Albee Circuit, 49, 69, 70, 100; locales, 32, 39, 46, 66, 74, 154, 189; McVickers-Miner Circuit, 46; Montana Circuit, 46; Ohio Circuit, 46; Orpheum Circuit, 69; Petroleum Circuit, 46; regional, 34, 46, 154, 185, 189, 200, 213, 224, 232; Silver Circuit, 46; types of, 46, 49, 51–53, 67, 95, 104, 114, 125, 175, 200

circus, 15, 198, 219, 238, 240

Civil War, 3, 20, 30, 84, 113, 118, 121–123, 128, 139; Confederacy, 10, 14, 18, 72; dramas, 120, 236; films, 121; melodramas, 62, 111, 122, 124–125, 161; veterans organizations, 20, 123–124

Claire, Ina, 179

Clark, Creston, 62

Clark, W. T., 70

class differences, 15, 25–26, 37, 50, 82, 136–137, 139, 181, 184, 195, 209, 220, 239–240, 244

Claxton, Kate, 219, 221, 224, 225, 226, 227, 229, 231

Clune, William H., 181–182

Cody, William F., 11

Cohen, Alfred J., 68

Collier, Constance, 168, 171–172

combination, 37–39, 45, 53, 56, 66, 117, 171, 198; business arrangement, 38; companies, 3, 31, 34, 37, 39, 42, 43, 46, 67, 80, 191, 192, 195, 213, 224, 248; dramas, 39, 42, 53, 192, 245; Davis and Keogh, 39; system, 37–39; "Tom combination," 42

comedies, 3, 11, 38, 53, 54, 55, 64, 93, 108–109, 135, 155, 168–169, 188, 210–211, 219, 238–239, 240, 242–243, 248; "Chimmie" comedies, 138–139; cup-and-saucer romantic comedies, 28; types, 23, 28, 32, 44, 54–55, 70–71, 194, 240; roles in, 11, 103, 108, 206

contracts, 47–49, 66, 111, 119, 167, 170, 181, 190, 218, 236

conventions and codes, 3, 21, 22, 37, 39, 64, 108, 118, 120–122, 124–126, 128–131, 134–135, 142, 160, 164, 172, 195, 201, 204, 233, 235–236, 248

Corbett, James J., 36, 63, 196

Corman, Eugene, 219, 230

Costello, Dolores, 218

costumes, 19, 40, 55, 90, 92, 97, 103, 109, 161, 175–176, 179–180, 210, 226, 245, 247

Cottrell, Harry D., 76

Craig, Edward Gordon, 28

credits, 1, 25, 110, 112, 129, 145, 158, 163, 189, 200, 221, 234, 242, 250

Cressy, Will M., 52, 53, 54

Crinkle, Nym. See Andrew Carpenter Wheeler

critics, 22, 28, 32, 75, 82, 91, 113–114, 116–117, 120, 143, 156, 166, 168, 177, 182–184, 198, 201, 217, 228, 238, 242

Cumpson, John R., 97, 132

Cushing, Catherine Chisholm, 241–242

entrepreneurs, 4, 34, 37, 44, 46, 69, 109, 110, 209
Erlanger, Abraham, 47–48, 50, 78, 147
ethnicity, 8, 11–12, 14, 15, 26, 107, 109, 193
Eyton, Bessie, 179

faces: of actors, 22, 25, 206; blackface, 61; expressions, 2, 115, 171
Fairbanks, Douglas, 27, 97, 179, 218
feature films, 181, 182; feature length, 5, 25, 27, 111–112, 141, 168, 249; longer films, 50, 109–111, 131, 168, 249
females, 15; character types, 8, 15–17, 19, 108, 115, 134, 138–139, 162–163, 174–176, 181, 183–184, 203–204, 214, 242; gender issues, 16, 143, 162, 206; motherhood, 79, 82, 85, 92–93, 131, 132, 133–134, 140, 148, 168, 175, 200–201, 206, 208–211, 220, 231, 239; professionals, 54, 109. *See also* women
Field, Martyn, 67
Field, Al G., 61
Fields, Lew, 199
Fields, W. C., 35, 219, 240
Fildes, S. Luke, 66
film, 65, 96, 118, 188–189, 201, 218, 224; film-stock, 56, 87, 88, 89, 182; historians, 20, 22, 24, 29, 31, 188–189; industry, 26, 30, 105, 110, 128; projection equipment, 16, 44, 49, 55; running times, 4, 50, 60, 167; projectionists, 184; scenarios, 2, 5, 9, 34, 60, 90–91, 93, 102, 104–105, 129–130, 133, 144–145, 171, 217, 242, 244; sequences, 29, 180; silent, 4, 22, 28–29, 169, 171, 188, 228, 240
film production companies: Ambrosio Film Company, 26–27; American Mutoscope and Biograph Company, 87; Biograph Studio, 1, 25, 67, 88, 89, 97, 120; British Mutoscope and Biograph, 171; Domino Brand, 128, 159; Edison Manufacturing Company/Edison studio, 88–89; Famous Players Film Company, 27, 109–110, 167, 170, 182, 241; Fine Arts Corporation, 167, 170; First National Pictures, 242; Independent Motion Picture Company, 27, 159; Kalem Company, 50, 105, 128, 159; Keystone, 128, 159; Kinemacolor Corporation of America, 144–145; London Films, 171, 234; Lubin Films, 129; Mamaroneck studio, 210, 241; Metro-Goldwyn-Mayer, 24; Movietone, 243; Mutual Film Corporation, 218; Paramount Studio, 110, 241; Pathé Films d'Arte, 27, 97, 105; Reliance studios/Reliance-Magestic, 141, 167; Selig Polyscope Company, 128–129; Solax Company, 209; Thanhauser Film Corporation, 27; Triangle Film Corporation, 167, 170, 246; Triangle-Fine Arts Corporation, 167, 170; United Artists Corporation, 218–219, 242–246; Universal Pictures, 242–243; Vitagraph Company of America, 128, 159; Vitaphone, 243; Warners, 243; William Fox, 226
filmmaking and filmmakers, 2, 4, 8, 14, 25, 26–27, 31, 35, 52, 67, 87, 92, 95, 105, 126, 167, 169, 182, 187, 217, 224, 246, 249–250; cinematic control, 19; cinematic language, 8; cinematic recreation, 6; close-up, 22, 25, 179–180; editing, 25, 159, 168; film intercutting, 29; flashback technique, 169; framed screen, 25; independent, 49, 110, 167; medium shot, 25; mobile camera-work, 25; outtakes, 112, 115, 210,; reshooting, 168; shooting, 88, 143, 168, 219, 247; sound-on-film system, 243

Frohman, Daniel, 47, 109, 147, 170, 234
frontier, 11, 13, 15, 247; dramas, 130;
    liminal frontier line, 13; proletariat,
    220; locales, 13, 14, 39–40, 107, 110,
    177, 220
Fuller, Ethel, 75
Fuller, Loïe, 174

Gaige, Crosby, 148
Gaskell, Elizabeth, 196
Giacometti, Paolo, 76, 109, 113–117, 176
Gifford, Dennis, 27
Gilbert, William S., 66
Gillette, William, 66
Gish, Dorothy, 16
Gish, Lillian, 16, 24, 85–86, 91–92, 98,
    114, 145–146, 168, 170–172, 180–182,
    184–216, 221, 228, 230, 246
Gish sisters, 175, 179, 218, 230
Glaum, Louise, 179
Gottschalk, Louis, 228
Granville-Barker, Harley, 28
Greenbank, Harry, 238
Griffith Award, 246
Griffith, D. W.: as apprentice/actor, 1, 3,
    35, 42, 56–90, 120, 173, 189, 248;
    autobiography, 80–82; family, 35, 58,
    121, 130, 246; biographers, 238;
    financial issues, 4, 26, 30, 69–70, 79,
    82, 84, 90, 105, 111, 126, 141–142, 145,
    167, 210, 218, 221; as Granville
    Warwick, 168; as Laurence/Lawrence
    Griffith, 57, 59, 66, 70, 75, 76;
    manuscript, 78–80; marriage, 75, 246;
    as playwright and sketch writer, 7, 30,
    49, 56–89, 120, 220, 236; as promoter,
    35, 181, 184, 194; psychological
    profile, 16; racial struggles of, 1, 8–12,
    18–22, 96, 107, 120, 162, 164, 188, 242,
    249; as sketch writer, 2–4, 30, 49, 248;
    as storyteller, 8, 63, 69, 72, 87, 110,
    120; strategies of, 21, 31, 35, 120, 127,
131, 135, 137, 142, 189, 232, 236, 239,
    248; as strikebreaker, 1, 69, 248; use of
    dance and multimedia, 3–4, 30, 80,
    98, 116, 118, 167–168, 173–177, 179–
    184; and vaudeville, 1, 3–4, 30, 49,
    67–72, 76, 106, 237; "The Wild Duck"
    (poem), 78
Griffith, Jacob Wark, 130
Griffith, Thomas, 66
Grismer, Joseph Rhode, 64, 186–216
Grover, Leonard, 53
Grundy, Sidney, 66
Guazzoni, Enrico, 111–112
Guy-Blaché, Alice, 209

Hackett, James K., 12, 23, 78–81, 248
Hall, Emmett Campbell, 107, 129, 135–
    136
Halm, Friedrich, 95–96
Harper, Arthur C., 157
Harris, Augustus, 28
Harrison, Charles, 101
Harrison, Duncan, 62
Harron, Bobby, 114
Harte, Bret, 17, 108
Hawkins, Anthony Hope, 78
Haworth, William, 67
Hays, Will, 219
Hennessy, George, 129
Herman, Henry, 50, 104
Herne, James A., 23
heroines, 3, 6, 16, 19, 40, 62, 71–72,
    74, 84–86, 106, 108, 117, 124, 127,
    133–136, 140, 147–148, 163, 180, 190,
    195, 203–204, 215–216, 218, 224, 237,
    239
Hoffman, Gertrude, 30, 98, 174–175,
    177, 183
Hopper, De Wolff, 167
Hornblow, Arthur, 155
Huff, Louise, 179
Hugo, Victor, 97

Ibsen, Henrik, 23, 28, 76, 168–170

immigrants and immigration, 4, 8, 12–15, 19, 26, 96–97, 108–109, 138–140, 193

Ince, Thomas, 128

Inslee, Charles, 97

International Workers of the World, 49

intertitles, 19, 50, 102, 136, 158, 161, 164, 168, 171–172, 231, 234, 237, 243. *See also* retitling

Irving, H. B. "Harry," 232

Irving, Henry, 48, 67, 232–235

Irving, Washington, 50

Italy and Italians, 27, 111–113, 193, 221

Jackson, Helen Hunt, 75–76, 106

Jackson, N. Hart, 219, 224, 226, 228, 231

Jacobs, Lea, 22

Jefferson, Joseph, 36, 50

Jenkins, Henry, 55

Jessop, J. H., 93

Jews, 8, 19, 93, 107, 115, 138–141, 193; Yiddish comedians, 71

Johnson, Arthur, 97, 102

Johnson, John Arthur "Jack," 14

Jolson, Al, 173

Jones, Henry Arthur, 50, 66

Jones, Johnstone, 75, 106

Jones, Stephen, 241

Julius Cahn's Official Theatrical Guide, 42, 44–45

Kaufman, J. B., 112

Kean, Charles, 233

Keith, B. F., 69

Kellerman, Annette, 183

Kelly, Anthony Paul, 209

Kendal, Madge, 94

Kendall, Elizabeth, 179

Kennedy, Jeremiah, 109, 111

Keogh, William T., 34, 39–40

Keystone Kops, 94

Kiallmark, Edward, 198

kinetoscope, 36

King, Owen, 239

Kirkwood, James, 98

Klaw, Marcus, 47–48, 50, 78, 147; Klaw and Erlanger Company, 27, 48, 79–81, 105, 111, 119, 128, 148, 155, 167

Klein, Charles, 93

Kleine, George, 112

Kosloff, Alexis, 179

Krows, Arthur Edwin, 147, 197

Ku Klux Klan, 10, 14, 19, 123, 127, 130, 143, 144, 146–147, 153, 154, 156, 159, 161

La Verne, Lucille, 9

labor, 8, 12, 15, 48–49, 56, 69, 72, 83, 110, 136, 208, 248; blacklisting, 48–49; strife, 2, 10, 12, 15, 17, 48–49, 56, 69, 72, 248; strikes, 1, 2, 48–49, 56, 69, 72, 248; unions, 49, 69, 158; Western Federation of Miners, 240; White Rats union, 49

Lamson, Gertrude, 52, 76, 77, 78, 90, 97, 112–114, 117, 176–177; company, 52, 76, 78

Langbridge, Frederick, 231, 234

Lanoe, Jiquel, 179

Lawrence, Florence, 16, 97, 103

Lawrence Griffith and Company, 76

Lawson, John, 95

Lee, Robert E., 152, 153

Lestina, Adolph, 97

Lesurques, Joseph, 233

Leutze, Emanuel Gottlieb, 84

liberation, 8, 13, 15, 124, 176, 179

lighting/illumination, 23, 87; styles, 87–88, 182, 213; technical systems, 23, 47, 55, 66, 87

Lincoln, Abraham, 18, 20

Lloyd, Gerrit, 244

Loos, Anita, 170–171, 246

motion picture studios (*continued*)
    Paramount, 109–110, 167, 241;
    Hollywood, 217; Independent, 110;
    Kalem, 128, 159; Keystone, 128, 159;
    Kinemacolor, 145; Klaw and Erlanger,
    128, 167; MPPC, 110; Mamaroneck,
    188, 210, 213, 217, 241; New York film
    studios, 86; Reliance studio, 141; Selig,
    128–129; studio system, 26; Vitagraph,
    128, 159; West Coast studios, 241
Mounet-Sulley, Jean, 109
Murray, Mae, 179
Murrieta, Joaquin, 219
music, 5, 12, 24, 38–39, 45, 88, 93, 140,
    173, 176, 180–181, 184, 191, 192, 194,
    198, 238–245; accompaniment, 24,
    80, 168–169, 192; African American
    musical and dramatic companies,
    45; comic music and opera, 156, 167,
    231; conductors/composers, 7, 226;
    cues, 40; and dancing, 12, 241;
    directors, 44, 51, 226; forms, 12, 61,
    80, 175, 183, 224, 242, 244; halls, 28,
    31, 51–52, 55, 94, 199; incidental, 22,
    24, 55, 226, 227, 241; instruments,
    24, 40, 88, 184, 226, 240, 241;
    musicians, 24, 38; orchestral, 24, 169,
    176; scores, 23, 182, 213, 228; sheet,
    198, 227, 244, 260; tempo, 24, 36. *See
    also* songs
musicals, 173, 191, 192, 194, 198, 238–
    242, 245; Broadway, 219
mutoscopes, 36, 174; "smokers," 90, 94
Myers, Carmel, 179

narrative, 6, 10, 17, 19, 23–24, 27, 29, 31,
    34, 39, 42, 43, 50–51, 53, 55–56, 63,
    72, 74, 93, 97–98, 102–104, 106, 110,
    112, 117, 120–121, 128–129, 132, 138,
    145–148, 158, 160, 166–169, 174, 179–
    182, 186–187, 192, 207–208, 210, 221,
    236–237, 240, 242–248; historic, 22,

236; sources, 19, 22, 24, 29, 34, 37,
    174; structure, 6, 14, 26, 29, 31–32, 34,
    37, 50–51, 55–56, 68–69, 94, 120–122,
    125, 128, 136–137, 160, 167, 187, 207,
    210, 248; styles, 7, 10, 22, 29, 51, 93,
    168, 236
National Association of Theatrical
    Producing Managers (NATPM), 105
Native Americans, 8, 12, 13, 17–18, 40,
    81, 86, 105, 107, 110–111, 138, 140,
    236–237, 247, 250
naturalism, 22–24, 27–28, 81. *See also*
    realism
nickelodeon, 25–26, 53, 92
Nicholls, George, 168
Nicoll, Allardyce, 27
Normand, Mabel, 179
North and Northerners, 9, 10, 19–21, 60,
    123–128, 146–148, 152, 155, 160, 162,
    165; "carpetbaggers," 10, 123, 161;
    "scalawags," 10, 123
North American tours, 67, 104, 232–233,
    239
Novello, Ivor, 236

Ogden, Vivia, 206, 215
Oliver Ditson and Company, 198
O'Neil, Nance. *See* Gertrude Lamson
orientalism, 17, 77, 107, 108–109, 174–
    177, 180, 184
O'Rourke, Eugene, 63
Osterman, Kathryn, 57, 58, 68, 70–72,
    73
O'Sullivan, Anthony, 109
otherness, 8, 11–12, 14–15, 18–19, 77, 81,
    96, 107, 176, 193
Ouida. *See* Marie Louise de la Ramée
Oxenford, John, 224

Page, Brett, 54
Palings, Walter, 238
Palmer, A. M. "Harry," 224, 226

actor-producers, 12; director-producers, 26, 111; film producers, 49, 110, 185; playwright-actor-producer, 74; producer-director-manager, 113; television, 23; theatrical, 82, 188, 198, 207

prohibition, 218–219, 245

prologues, 4, 18, 64, 104, 107, 159, 167–169, 181–184, 187, 226, 233–234

promotion and promoters, 1, 4, 34, 35, 73, 97, 181, 182, 184, 194, 207, 263

prostitution, 76, 82, 85, 94, 220

protests and protesters, 26, 45, 65, 120, 144, 156–157, 165, 182, 226, 233, 245

race and racism, 1, 3, 8, 9–12, 14, 17, 19–22, 26, 75, 96, 106, 107, 111, 119, 175, 188, 241–242, 247, 248, 249, 256; Griffith's racism, 8–11, 14, 18, 20; "separate but equal," 14; white exclusionary groups, 14

Ramée, Marie Louise de la, 66

Rankin, McKee, 52; and Griffith, 63–64; and Nance O'Neil, 76, 112–114, 221, 223

rape, 19, 83, 85, 96, 116, 146–148, 163, 179, 231, 234, 237

Reade, Charles, 98, 100, 101, 219, 231–233, 245

realism, 22–24, 27–28, 74, 81, 213, 240

Reconstruction, 3, 9, 10, 18, 20–22, 30, 64, 118, 120–121, 128–129, 131, 135–136, 139, 142, 145–146, 148, 150, 157–159, 161, 164

religion, 70, 139; Catholic, 13, 139, 167, 193; Christian, 13, 93, 138; Eastern Orthodox, 13; intolerance, 11; Protestant, 3, 13, 34, 83, 139–140, 166, 173, 193–194

Remy, Marcel, 118

repertoire, 7, 44–45, 61–62, 74; amateur, 239; American theatrical, 5–7, 95, 188, 195, 224, 232–233; American stage, 93; commercial theatrical, 169; Creston Clark's, 62; Martin Harvey's, 234; Henry Irving's, 235; MacDowell, 74; modern classical, 44; modern, 169; modern theatrical, 5; Nance O'Neil's, 76; Otis Skinner's, 244; popular, 61, 224; recitation, 94; seasonal, 44; touring, 93

repertory companies, 1–2, 16, 61, 76, 90, 249

rescues, 3, 19, 34, 35, 36, 74, 83, 89, 96, 109, 127, 130, 134, 143–144, 146–148, 150, 173, 206, 209, 215, 219–220, 226, 228, 232–233, 237, 242, 248

retitling, 21, 70, 168, 231, 234

Revolutionary War, 70

Reynolds, Ernest, 27

Richardson, George T., 57, 68, 71–72, 73

Ristori, Adelaide, 112–114, 117

Rivington Street, 83

Robert Haight's Company, 65

Robertson, T. W., 196

Robertson, Tom, 28

Roosevelt, Theodore, 96–97

Rose, Edward, 69

Ross, Adrian, 238

Rowell, George, 27

royalties, 49, 94

Royle, Edward Milton, 17, 140–141

rural life, 6, 198, 213; family, 187, 209; festivities, 192, 208; hinterlands, 32, 208; serenity, 197; population, 124

Ryan, Paddy, 63

St. Denis, Ruth, 4, 174, 178, 179–181

Sardou, Victorien, 74, 231, 235

Scarborough, George, 244

scenarios, 2, 5, 9, 34, 60, 90–91, 93, 102, 104–105, 129–130, 133, 144–145, 171, 217, 244; scenarists, 42, 68–69, 107, 121, 129, 143; scenarist-directors, 7

STUDIES IN THEATRE HISTORY & CULTURE